e-Business Readiness

A Customer-Focused Framework

James Craig

Dawn Jutla

Addison-Wesley

Boston • San Francisco • New York • Toronto • Montreal
London • Munich • Paris • Madrid
Capetown • Sydney • Tokyo • Singapore • Mexico City

The publisher offers discounts on this book when ordered in quantity for special sales. For more information, please contact:

Pearson Education Corporate Sales Division
One Lake Street
Upper Saddle River, NJ 07458
(800) 382-3419
corpsales@pearsontechgroup.com

Visit AW on the Web: www.awl.com/cseng/

Library of Congress Cataloging-in-Publication Data

Craig, James, 1967–
     e-Business readiness: a customer focused framework/James Craig,
Dawn Jutla.
          p.   cm.—(Addison-Wesley information technology series)
     Includes bibliographical references and index.
     ISBN 0-201-71006-4
     1. Electronic commerce   2. Customer relations   I. Jutla, Dawn
II. Title.   III. Series.

HF5548.32.C73 2000
658.8'12—dc21   00–048533

ISBN 0-201-71006-4
Text printed on recycled paper
1 2 3 4 5 6 7 8 9 10—MA—0403020100
First printing, December 2000

To our magic makers:

Cathy, Owen, and Emily
JC

Logan, Julia, and Peter
DJ

Contents

CHAPTER THREE   **YOUR REASON FOR BEING:
YOUR CUSTOMERS   61**

CHAPTER SIX — HAND-IN-HAND INTO THE FUTURE: STRATEGIC PARTNERING 185

CHAPTER SEVEN **eBIZ RULES!: GOVERNANCE** **231**

CHAPTER TEN   **STRATEGIC PLANNING: ATTACK AND DEFEND   361**

Foreword

E-business is the transformation of key business processes through the use of Internet technologies. People discuss convenient business, collaborative business, networked business, road warrior mobile users, actionable information, and new opportunities. These are what make e-business exciting. Perhaps, the most important aspect of daily e-business is how e-business itself is used within society, within business, within our lives, and not just as another new technology. When people can feel its importance and see its huge impact, they will realize immediately that they will have to participate in e-business to avoid getting left behind. Imagine how frequently businesses are being asked the following:

- What will it take to put your company on the cutting edge of offering electronic services?
- How can your company realize the most value from e-business initiatives?
- How can you create and promote value to the company's customers? To your company's partners?
- What rules does your company need to create if you have a Web channel?

As e-business evolves, many new and wonderful things will happen. "You ain't seen nothin' yet" springs to mind when thinking about the services we will be buying in the future—services that allow us to spend more time on things we really enjoy doing. We will "take care of business" more quickly than ever before, thanks to upcoming realities of ubiquitous access through low-cost, small-footprint routes to the Internet. Already, 24-hours-a-day/7-days-a-week Web banking, self-serve stock trading via voice-commerce, and online bill presentation are commonplace to many of us.

A colleague recently asked a credit card company for a copy of a three-month-old statement and was told it would take 10 to 21 days for to receive it. This exemplifies the major advantage of e-business—*reducing customer frustration,* or the need for better customer relationship management (CRM). The customer service representative told my colleague that she, too, thought the delay was too long, but unfortunately, the company does not generate the copy of the statement; it comes from somewhere else. Again, this restates how important the efficiency of our partners are to our businesses. We cannot create value in a vacuum; we must do it in collaboration, that is, networked collaboration for speed.

Let me reemphasize that through Internet and related technologies, e-businesses can create business value and realize the promise of far greater payoffs with streamlined processes, collaborative environments among business partners, better management of customer relationships, and efficient revenue and cost structures.

E-businesses are open and experimental. However, some people do wear rose-colored glasses when approaching e-business. Students across various disciplines fiercely defend the view that if they were to start Internet businesses, they would be guaranteed millionaires. Some may, but unrealistic expectations of many are what can harm the reputation of the e-business revolution. Separating hype from reality is where a framework is very useful. The e-Biz Readiness!™ framework presented in this book provides a structured approach to e-business. It breaks the complexity of e-business into "bite-size" chunks and shows how business stakeholders can collaborate to create value.

I highly recommend this book to anyone who wants to know the necessary components of effective e-business strategies and tactical plans and who really wants to be successful in the e-business world. Let's get e-business ready!

Weidong Kou, PhD

Weidong Kou was formerly a researcher at the IBM Center for Advanced Studies in Canada. In the last few years, he has led many workshops and conferences in the electronic commerce area under IBM's sponsorship. Kou holds various invention achievement and technical excellence awards from IBM, AT&T, and Siemens. He is a respected author in network security and standards, a member of the IEEE, and the New York Academy of Science. He is presently posted in Hong Kong at the e-Business Technology Institute, University of Hong Kong.

Ready, Set, Go: Setting the Stage

> *Readiness:* (n) a ready quality or state.
>
> *Ready:* (adj) prepared or equipped to act or be used immediately.

Why You Are Reading This Book

- You are from an established firm that is considering transitioning its current business models.
- You are part of a start-up that is challenging the status quo.
- You want to distinguish small-to-medium enterprise (SME) e-business capabilities from big business capabilities.
- You are part of a company that is commercializing e-business technologies to assist other businesses with achieving their vision.
- You are a consultant trying to determine how you can assist businesses with achieving their vision.
- You are an investor who wants to invest or is already investing in the e-business space and needs a way to look at the overall big picture of e-business.
- You are an individual who is simply expanding your horizons.

We all have a common mission—we want to achieve some form of success and we hope to glean some insight from others to make us more successful. Big and small enablers and purveyors of e-business are operating in the marketplace. Each has its own unique challenges and contexts that affect whether it will be successful. Your challenge is to apply their ideas to your situation, learn from other people's mistakes, get some service that enhances your business, and apply new ideas. Your situation is unique, and you are trying to separate the wheat from the chaff.

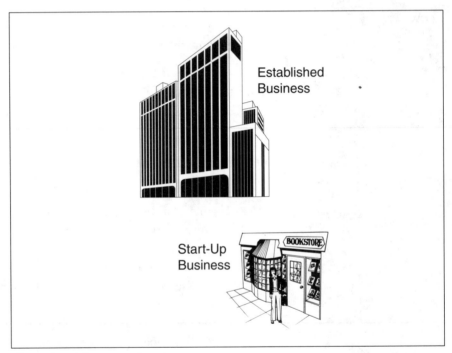

Established Business

Start-Up Business

Big and Small Companies

What This Book Is All About

This book is all about e-business readiness. What are the many implications of moving into e-business? We have this stateless environment that we call *the Internet*. Globalization is making our world seem smaller. We see Korean companies forming e-business portals with Commerce One. Vertical Net has opened up shop in Japan and localized its site in Kanji. In countries throughout the world, we notice the many initiatives that have been implemented to try to stimulate e-business adoption. E-business is a complex beast. To do it, you must understand it. We understand the traditional business "levers" to a great extent, but what makes e-business tick? We want to show you, actually build before your eyes, a framework—the eBiz Readiness! framework—that will make you e-business ready.

A framework is needed to give structure to complex situations. Our framework for e-business readiness supports modularity, reusability, and extensibility and also includes monitoring and feedback tools. Our eBiz Readiness!™ framework has successfully been used by a *midsize* enterprise to develop its e-business strategy and create tactical plans. In addition, we validated the framework through consultation with many business executives and "New Age" consultants throughout the globe as we were writing this book.

The questions you need to answer as you prepare to become e-business ready today are the following:

- *The Now:* What are you doing today to become e-business ready?
- *The Future:* What do you have to do to ensure that you will be competitive in the future?
- *The Feedback:* What are the gaps that you've identified, and how are you going to achieve your future vision?

The ultimate goal is to be e-business ready! The framework is targeted toward all businesses, ranging from SMEs to lines of business (LOBs) to Fortune

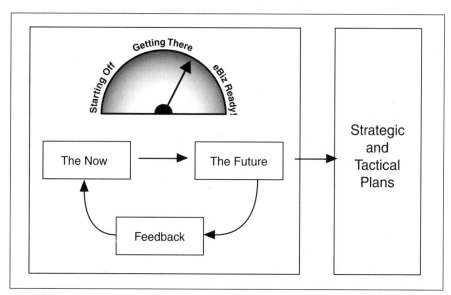

High-Level Overview of the eBiz Readiness!™ Framework

500 companies. It is a modifiable framework that allows you to integrate your own unique industry components and metrics; most importantly it provides strategic direction in e-business.

Can we guarantee that you will be successful by simply following a framework? Of course not. Just like a best-selling book seems to have certain "magic," magic also surrounds the creation of a successful company. The most successful companies exude an aura of great leadership, which is something that no framework can provide. Although this book will not help you with your leadership skills, we hope that it will affect your ability to create "e-business magic." We are giving you the tools to create a sound e-business strategy, assess gaps, and infuse feedback into your e-business readiness efforts. The framework gives you some guidance on creating your directional strategy.

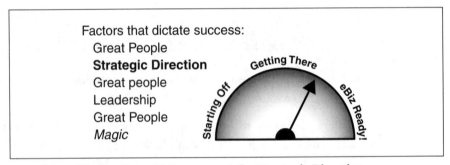

Use of the eBiz Readiness!™ Framework for Strategic Direction

When we wrote this book, we wanted to make sure our customers—you, the readers—would be satisfied with the value it gave you. We found that we needed a balance between the theoretical and practical applications of the framework. We wanted you to be able apply the ideas to *your* situation. We found a balance between the customer value creation theory and practical examples of businesses that are doing the right things in today's e-business space. To continue the customer-focused theme, we present you with scenarios that provide insight into the two e-business perspectives: SME and big business. The challenge facing all companies moving toward or beginning e-business is assessing which infrastructures, functions, business processes, and procedures need to be transformed. We use two fictional example companies in each chapter; one from an established big business with multiple business units and disciplines and another from a small business that just uses a few key components of our framework (and not all its intricacies). "Bob," shown in the following box, is the head of the e-business strategic unit for the big business company (BBCompany). "Sue" runs a small business (SMEBusiness). We provide BBCompany and SMEBusiness in various industries or verticals in every chapter. We hope you will find that some of the information provided by Bob and Sue apply to your situation. The point to remember is that no two companies are exactly the same. We also use examples of actual companies to further explain the points in the book. The examples are woven in the text and highlighted in Doing It Today boxes.

Bob:

CEO of BBCompany

Task: To change his company's traditional business model

Comments: I come from a big business that has moved from being the incumbent company for the sector and must now contend with competition—not only from local firms but also on a global front. It seems like mergers and acquisitions are the only way for us to grow, but I am confident that we can move our business model toward e-business. I interact with customers in various ways; they are starting to use the Internet and e-mail to contact me. The same is true of my suppliers and partners. We have always done business using traditional communication methods—paper and fax machines—but we've suddenly realized that we have to use electronic methods if we are going stay on top of current information and get that information to our customers.

Sue:

CEO of SMEBusiness

Task: To enhance her company's current e-business model

Comments: I come from a small e-business that currently sells to the North American market. I started the business because I wanted to make a career change and focus on the things I love. My company grew from a business that I started in my basement. We now have an office from which we run our operations. Being small means we are nimble, but it also means I wear many hats. I need simple, easy ideas to move my business ahead.

How to Use This Book

This book is organized in a specific way. Most chapters includes the following:

- Getting You Prepared, which sets the expectations for the chapter
- Defining the Horizon, which presents the chapter's core concepts
- Bob's perspective (the big business view) and Sue's perspective (the SME view) of the chapter's subject matter
- Doing it Today, which includes interviews with leaders of actual businesses
- Mini case studies of SMEs and large businesses so that you can read examples of the framework in action
- Are You Ready?, which summarizes the chapter's highlights and metrics

You should read Chapters 1 and 2 first so that you get an idea of the scope of the book. Chapters 1 and 2 introduce the core concepts in e-business, emphasize the need for an e-business readiness assessment framework, and present an overview of the eBiz Readiness!™ framework. The details of the framework are developed in each of the subsequent chapters (Chapters 3 through 10). Although you can read these chapters independently, we recommend that you read them in order. In particular, we suggest that you read the chapter on operational partners (Chapter 6) before the chapter on strategic partners (Chapter 7). Chapter 10 explains how you can create an e-business strategy for your particular situation. It shows how to use the framework to assess your company's opportunities and threats in relation to business, industries, or countries. The book is supplemented with an Internet web site: www.ebizreadiness.com. The intent of this site is to complement the book by creating a community of interest for the readers.

The e-business space is exciting, and it is an exciting time to be *in* the space. We hope that you have as much fun reading this book as we did writing it!

Acknowledgments

This has been such an adventure from beginning to end. Many people gave me strength and encouragement, and they all had such a desire to see me complete this endeavor. The true guiding light for me was my wife, Cathy, who brought me up when I was down, encouraged me to forge ahead, and held down the fort while I was busy. She listened to my joy when I was able to speak to all of the great people that we interviewed for the book and nodded "knowingly" at all of the computer jargon I discussed as I tried out passages of the book on her. I personally wish to extend thanks to each and every one of the people I interviewed for taking time out of their busy schedules to speak with Dawn and me. The wisdom that we gleaned from all of them has been immeasurable; hopefully in this book we passed along the nuggets of wisdom gleaned from those conversations. My parents and family have also been a great inspiration, and I know that they are proud of the work that Dawn and I have accomplished. Dawn has been a joy to work with, and even though she "cracks the whip on occasion" her lamb recipe makes up for any shortcomings :)

I wish to thank Tammy DiPersio for her help in transcribing the many interviews; Stephen Murray for his mentorship, guidance, and insight; and the Telecom Applications Research Alliance (TARA) for enabling me to build the foundation. I would like to thank Gerry Pond for making me believe that Atlantic Canada can make a difference in the global e-business space. The only drawbacks of writing this book were the 20 pounds I gained and the fact that my windsurfing and squash seasons were shortened—but it was all worth it. I look forward to playing baseball and hockey with Owen and spending time with Emily now that I finally have the time. On to the next big adventure . . . voice commerce!

James Craig

The congruence of supporting people, good luck, and overflowing material made our book project smooth sailing. I heartily thank the great people at Saint Mary's University: President Colin Dodds, Dean of Commerce Paul Dixon, and members of the Department of Finance and Management Science at Saint Mary's University for their support—given in so many different and equally important ways. My colleague, Dr. Kathryn Kimery of Kansas State University (she is also known as "Mother-Earth-but-in-a-sexy-way"), gave freely of her time both in proofreading and providing valuable feedback. Thanks, Kate, for your humor and caring. Charity Lees took scrappy, rough diagrams drawn on bits of paper (because as many people will tell you, I can't draw to save my life) and generated many of the digital graphics for this book. I gratefully acknowledge the MBA students (especially Terry Weatherbee) at Saint Mary's University for their ongoing enthusiasm for learning about e-business. Strongly connected to the success of this work is my co-author, James Craig, who is always fun to work with. I especially will miss the chocolate cake slices from his wife, Cathy, now that the book is complete.

I am also thankful for the other wonderful women and men in my life. Thank you, Peter, for your mentorship and strength, and thank you, Serina, the vogue goddess, for a friendship of twenty-something years. Thanks to Joyce,

Eugene, Eldon, and Krista for the special and actively loving roles they play in my children's lives. I am also grateful to Samantha Saltibus (Sam) for providing me with great peace of mind by being a terrific nanny to my kids when critical writing needed to be done. I warmly acknowledge my families, the Josephs (Josephine and Arnold), the Brooks (Molly, Robin, Tamara, Natasha, and Darren), and the Jutlas (Eileen and Hendren), for their encouragement and pleasure they show in knowing that I am always up to something new. Many, many other people make the business that I am in so much fun—Yufei Yuan, Weidong Kou, and a whole host of others that I have forgotten to thank for their many kindnesses. Thank you all. And thank you to the magic of island rain, lemon tea, and Caribbean music.

Dawn Jutla

We thank our reviewers, Peter Bodorik, Professor of Computer Science at Dalhousie University; Jeremy Bernard, E-Business Development Manager at Aliant Communications; Gord Agnew, Professor of Electrical Engineering at the University of Waterloo; Jim Carroll, author of *Yottabits and Lightbulbs,* Chris Fader, Associate Professor in the Department of Economics at the University of Waterloo; Capers Jones, the Addison-Wesley IT series editor; and Marco Parillo, consultant at PricewaterhouseCoopers for the great job that they did reviewing and for the comments that helped us improve the final product.

We would also like to thank the terrific team at Addison-Wesley. Mariann Kourafas, assistant editor, has been behind us all the way, from initial proposal to book completion; we thoroughly enjoyed working with her. Cathy Comer, copy editor, has also been incredibly easy to work with; we thank her for her professionalism and cheerfulness. Mamata Reddy, senior production coordinator, performed miracles in helping us keep her deadlines while we were juggling permission sheets, voice commerce projects, start-up companies, lectures, funding applications, and families. We also thank Kate Saliba, Chris Guzikowski, and Robin Bruce in advance for their marketing efforts.

James Craig and Dawn Jutla

About the Authors

James Craig is president and CEO of diaphonics, a company that develops software applications utilizing natural language speech recognition focused on logistics and distribution. He most recently served as senior manager of e-business development for Aliant, the third largest telecommunications firm in Canada. He oversaw the strategic development of e-business initiatives that created new lines of business. He also sat on the Board of Directors for eResolution, an emerging Internet company focusing on alternative dispute resolution services. Craig has worked with businesses worldwide, including North America, Europe, and Asia and has been a speaker at many conferences throughout North America and Europe. He spent a number of years as a consultant for Deloitte & Touche, working on supply chain engagements in various sectors and was also a systems engineering officer in the Canadian Navy. He has an engineering degree and M.B.A. and is a professional engineer.

Dawn Jutla has worked in the computer science and information technology field for the past 16 years. She has taught university-level information technology courses for eight years. Her publications include "Making Business Sense of Electronic Commerce," which appeared in the March 1999 issue of *Institute for Electrical Engineering (IEEE) Computer,* the IEEE Computer Research Society's key communication vehicle. Nikkei Computer requested that the paper be reprinted for the Japanese market, a sign of the article's wide-ranging impact. She also authored a paper entitled "Developing Internet E-Commerce Benchmarks," which appeared in the journal *Information Systems*. Jutla, who holds a Ph.D. in computer science, has also received several research grants in the areas of database systems and e-commerce. She is the co-author of more than two dozen conference and journal papers in these areas.

CHAPTER ONE

Let's Get Ready: The Big Picture

> The great successful people of the world have used their imagination...they think ahead and create their mental picture in all its details, filling in here, adding a little there, altering this a bit and that a bit, but steadily building—steadily building.
>
> Robert J. Collier, writer

Getting You Prepared

This chapter provides a foundation for understanding the needs and requirements for a framework in e-business. We introduce our approach to e-business, which focuses on the customer as its critical component, and explain how customers are integrated into our framework. We look at the big picture—what has an impact on e-business and how we are transitioning from traditional business practices to e-business. We then drive home the need for a framework in e-business.

Connecting the planet's citizens online. Creating virtual worlds. We may be opening a Pandora's box of social, moral, and economic issues. Some people are excited about this open access to worldwide knowledge and the implications that are associated with it, such as heightened awareness of health and education issues, which inevitably leads to better standards of living. Some are worried they are caught up in a rising tide of technology advancement for which they are not prepared. Some governments have economic concerns; their citizens are connected to the Internet and shopping in countries other than their own. Not only are third-world nations experiencing this trend, but first-world nations are as well. We believe that no country should take the approach of closing its eyes and hoping that a resolution will come forth like a gift from heaven.

Part of the solution should be making your country's businesses more aware of the impact of, ramifications of, and opportunities inherent to e-business. Make your businesses e-competitive! Get your companies e-business ready! Lack of understanding about e-business is exemplified by the results of a survey by the Ekos consulting firm that shows only one third of Canadian businesses think that e-business will have any impact on their success by 2005. A survey by the Andersen consulting firm reveals that even less than a third of businesses in Europe think that e-business is significant.

Although we do not discount the importance of the socioeconomic aspects of e-business, this book is written purely from a business standpoint. Our definition of e-business is as follows:

> *E-business* is using network and distributed information technology, knowledge management, and trust mechanisms to transform key business processes and relationships with customers, employees, suppliers, business partners, regulatory parties, and communities. E-business is about changing business models to create new or increase value for the customer.

In this book, we provide a model for e-business and a supporting framework referred to as *eBiz Readiness!*™ (Figure 1-1), a framework that incorporates the following:

- A macro view, which allows you to see the big picture of e-business
- A micro view, which gives you the ability to identify the details of the big picture
- Feedback, which provides a measure of how effective you are at doing e-business

The eBiz Readiness!™ framework is intended for use by all business companies, ranging from small businesses to lines of business (business units in large companies) to Fortune 500 companies. We concentrate on raising business awareness by showing you how e-business is used to create customer value. A mantra among e-businesses is, "What is value today is commonplace tomorrow." Some people equate value to money, others to time or speed. In e-business, value is all of these things. It is creating and managing "magic." Using the complex entity called *e-business* to truly create something successful is analogous to creating a successful movie. All movies have common components, but that certain something—that movie magic—differentiates the great ones from the wannabes.

The eBiz Readiness!™ framework is a matrix of components that add value to e-business. The framework's high-level view (or macro view) gauges how eBiz Ready! you are. It also has the details to allow you to find out where, how, and why you are excelling or lagging behind in your business. The need for this framework evolved from the simple fact that e-business is complex, and we all need better ways to understand it. Our eBiz Readiness!™ framework is different from other approaches because we take an outward, customer-focused, e-business perspective from governance, partner, agent, and community stakeholder viewpoints and then bring in the internal employee and company perspectives. We

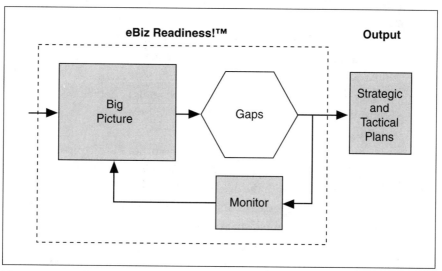

Figure 1-1   High-Level View of the eBiz Readiness!™ Framework

have created an e-business assessment system that is complete, balanced, applicable, relevant, accurate, persistent, and evolved. The framework defines which components and enablers (entities that support the entire e-business infrastructure, such as processes, people, infrastructures, information, procedures, and policies) are essential to e-business creation and successful execution. The framework also defines a set of measures for monitoring and assessing how well you are doing e-business. Chapters 3 to 10 showcase these components and detail the development of the eBiz Readiness!™ framework.

Is creating magic as simple as following a framework of rules? Of course not. Many factors affect whether an e-business will be successful. Although a college degree may give people the fundamental knowledge in their desired area of expertise, many skills that cannot be learned or imitated are needed to form the foundation of an e-business. Executives who are able to explain the vision of where your company is heading and then move the employees in that direction contribute to success. Many examples in the book include companies in which the desire to win is evident—a quality that is brought out intentionally and fostered by the executives. Where does the eBiz Readiness!™ framework fit in? E-business is a complex beast. Regardless, traditional business practices, which are centered on human-to-human interactions, are also complex—you see customers, you see your business (strategic and operational) partners, you see their reactions. E-business has fundamentally changed this process because you no longer see human reactions. You have a much different relationship with your customers, your partners, the communities you build, and the governance that forms the rules about how you conduct business. These changes are occurring at warp speed, and it is the interaction of the stakeholders that constitutes a successful e-business. This is why the eBiz Readiness!™ framework is based on a 360-degree external stakeholder view of e-business. In other words, only when you consider all the stakeholder interactions will you be able to create true value for the customer.

Businesses cannot survive if they cannot see the big picture. They are always told to "focus, focus, focus," which is good advice, but they must also ensure that the focus interacts with the external parts of the business—this is the crux of this framework. It allows you to determine how value is created for the customer. It allows you to determine which components are critical to your success. It helps you choose what you should own and whom you should partner with.

eBiz Readiness!™ gives you a snapshot, a glimpse in time, of your big picture. You can then see your gaps and make decisions about how to overcome them. It allows you to monitor your e-business with measures that make sense for you.

The challenge for you, which was the challenge for the many companies interviewed during the course of writing the book, is picking which key business areas to assess how well you are doing e-business. The eBiz Readiness!™ framework is a good start. It is meant to challenge your thinking about the e-business big picture, but it also gets a layer or two under the covers to ensure that the big picture is correctly formed. The framework is sufficiently flexible to allow successful companies to adapt it to their needs. The companies assess which components make sense for them and add what is missing—most importantly, they act at e-business speed.

Defining the Horizon

In this section, we describe three core concepts in e-business:

- Customer focus
- Customer value
- Value chain progression to value web

Customer Focus

E-business is more than exploitation of information and networking technologies for doing business. It is a business philosophy that concentrates on the *customer*. It is about being prepared for doing business in any way the customer wants. The philosophy transcends all borders and includes *all* the stakeholders who create value for the customer. E-business has an inherent *customer-focused* approach.

Customer Value

Value for the customer may be lower prices, higher quality products and services, a continuous stream of innovative new products and services, speedier responses, convenience, customization of products and services, or even just information about products and services. Customer characteristics have changed. Although value is what customers have always wanted, today's customer has greater access to it. The new customer is fickle, demanding, informed, and in the driver's seat.

Businesses are responding to this customer "demand-pull" of value by squeezing inefficiencies out of their value chains. Demand-pull results when numerous customers "demand" value and "pull" it out of a company. This pull occurs when the overall market is demanding something particular. The traditional value chain (Figure 1-2, *A*) shows the flow of goods and services from one business entity, such as a supplier or a consumer, to another. Each entity adds value to the good or service as it passes through the chain. In e-business the reengineering of business processes and the use of information and networking technology result in reduced transaction costs, increased speed of information flow, and more complete information flow along the links of the value chain. In fact, business information moves in *real time,* or instantaneously. Businesses are passing on these cost savings to their customers and responding more quickly to retain customers, realizing that customer retention is key to their bottom line.

The wireless business is in hypergrowth, with 30 percent growth being the norm. You would think that wireless companies would only be concerned about acquiring new customers, but according to a recent survey of wireless company chief executive officers (CEOs), customer retention was a more important goal than customer acquisition. Continuously creating customer value is paramount

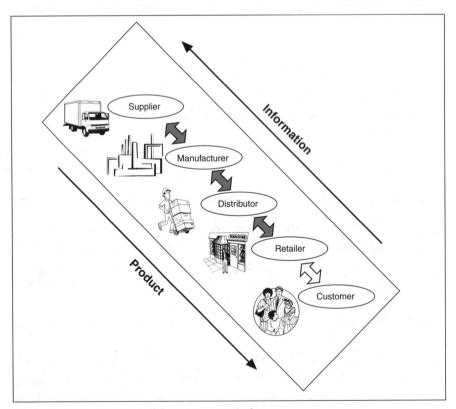

Figure 1-2, A: The Traditional Value Chain

even in hypergrowth areas and is even more important in an established business, for which customer retention is the key to survival.

The Intermediate Value Web

The term *value web* has been in use for numerous years. We were unable to ascertain the originator of the term, but references to a fairly underdeveloped notion of a value web exist as far back as 1997. A 1998 Gartner Group article[1] presented a better picture of the value web underscoring information technology enablers.

Many successful businesses do not stop at the stage of enhancing existing business links. Because of technology and its affects on business process change, some businesses are creating new links in the value chain, giving rise to an *intermediate value web* (Figure 1-2, *B*). The diagram illustrates that businesses are having more direct customer contact.

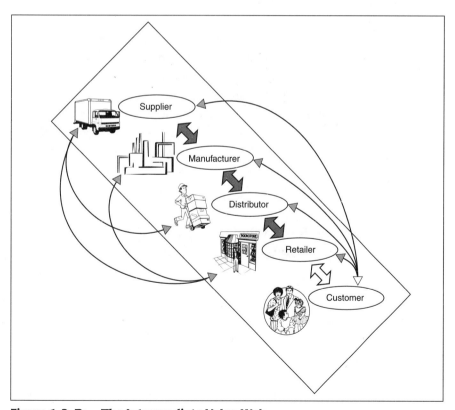

Figure 1-2, B: The Intermediate Value Web

In the intermediate value web, some businesses create new links and deemphasize old links. Dell is a well-known example of a "manufacturing" company that has created a new link directly to its customers, effectively bypassing the distributor and retail links. The new direct-to-the-customer link is possible because of the Web. The reason that businesses did not previously reengineer the value chain is that the cost was prohibitive. Low-transaction-cost Web channels have changed that. Regardless, some companies do not deemphasize existing channel linkages. Their distributors or reseller channels are extremely profitable, and the companies do not want to cannibalize these channels by adding a competing Web channel. Levi Strauss decided to dispose of its Web offering in late 1999 because the company could not figure out a way to stop this type of channel conflict.

Other businesses enhance existing links and add new links. Compaq recently bolstered its Web channel with the acquisition of Inacom's distribution resources. Compaq is now in a position to compete with its resellers in product configuration and fulfillment, making it more like the Dell model. Whether Compaq will cannibalize its reseller channels or support them by complementing them with unique services remains to be seen.

In this book, we focus on showing you how businesses can derive maximum value from their business interactions; in other words, we show you a completely new value web. A holistic view of the value web includes all the business's external stakeholders. External stakeholders include strategic and operational partners and the customer. The external stakeholder view incorporates the traditional entities in the intermediate value web because a subset of the strategic partners is resellers or distributors, and a subset of the operational partners is suppliers. In one direction of the older linear value chain, each entity is a supplier for another; in the other direction, each entity is a reseller for another.

Craig-Jutla Stakeholder Model of E-Business: Creating the New Value Web

The external stakeholders in e-business are customers, operational partners, strategic partners, communities, and regulatory bodies. Figure 1-3 shows e-business from a customer-focused perspective; value is ultimately pulled from each stakeholder toward the customer—creating the customer demand-pull for value. The external stakeholders (customer, partners, community, and governance) are broad categories that can host external business interactions completely. Any other external stakeholders should fit into one of the five categories we have defined. The internal stakeholder is the employee.

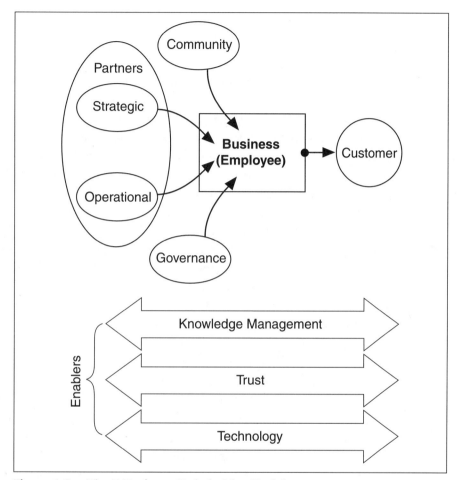

Figure 1-3   The E-Business Stakeholder Model

In this book, we show how each of these stakeholders can create value for the business and ultimately the customer. We think that by the end of this book, you will be firmly convinced that most value is created through enhancing interactions, sharing knowledge, and increasing trust among these external stakeholders and the business entity.

Recall our definition of e-business:

E-business is using network and distributed information technology, knowledge management, and trust mechanisms to transform key business processes and relationships with customers, suppliers, employees, business partners, regulatory parties, and communities. E-business is about changing business models to create new or increased value for the customer.

Apart from technical network and distributed information system infrastructure, the other two major enablers in e-business are knowledge management and trust, among all stakeholders. Knowledge management, trust, and technology are the *common* enablers for all stakeholders.

Our definition of *knowledge management* is management of knowledge that is derived from *any* source; it is not the traditional definition, which merely includes intellectual assets management, particularly assets of the employees. We take wide internal and external perspectives. Knowledge management includes knowledge about factors such as customers, employees, business transactions, business relations, products, and processes. Thus knowledge management encompasses the large areas of business content management, intellectual assets management, transaction management, and relationship management. (We describe these areas more fully in Chapter 2 and develop them in detail within the framework components described in each subsequent chapter.) We define *trust* as a necessary element in a good relationship; trust is confidence in the honesty, integrity, reliability, and justice of another entity. Good relationships among stakeholders create the most value and allow it to flourish. Technology provides infrastructure in terms of communication medium, software applications, and software and hardware solutions to interconnect the business stakeholders, allowing for information and knowledge transfer in real time. For instance, technology can reinforce knowledge management (for example, with repositories) and trust (for example, with digital certificates).[2] We describe other enablers for e-business throughout the book; knowledge management, trust, and technology are important because they include common elements of all e-business components.

The Stakeholders

The external stakeholders are shown in Figure 1-3 and include the following:

- **Strategic partners:** Partners who are planning for the future of your business
- **Operational partners:** Partners who are helping you run your business today
- **Governance:** The individuals applying the rules and regulations that are relevant to your business' stakeholders
- **Customers:** The end-purchasers of the product from business and consumer transactions

- **Community:** The people who are interested in your products and services, people who may or may not include your business customers

Internal entities are implicit to the customer-focused e-business entity (CFBE); they are the following:

- **Shareholders:** The financial investors in your business
- **Employees:** The people who run your business

The New Value Web

The new value web (Figure 1-4) is based on our e-business stakeholder model. It shows interactions among external stakeholders and businesses. Think of the regular entities on the intermediate value web as partner and customer entities,

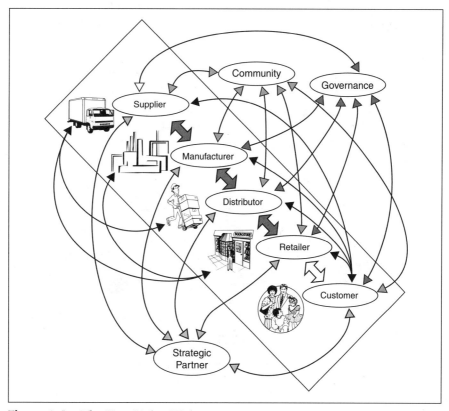

Figure 1-4   **The New Value Web**

then add an external strategic partner, a community, and governance as three other entities, and *then* imagine all of these entities interconnecting—and you have the true new value web. New, enhanced, and closer relationships among stakeholders are formed to create value.

E-Business Models

The value web has given rise to new business models, which can be classified as direct, indirect, or a hybrid of the direct and indirect models. A *direct* e-business model, such as Dell's manufacturer-direct model, is based on the premise that the supply chain entity sells directly to the customer. Figure 1-5, *A* depicts the group of direct e-business models. Categories of direct models include manufacturer-direct, intermediary, aggregator, trading community or net market maker, and auction models.

Indirect business models (Figure 1-5, *B*) include advertising, sponsorship, and community business models. The indirect group either sells to other busi-

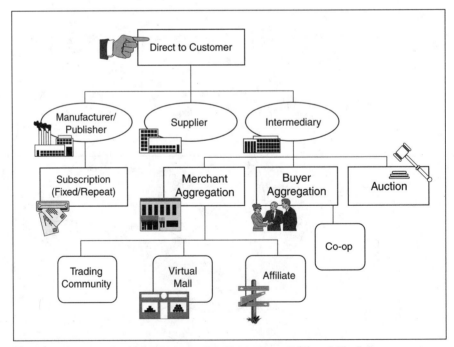

Figure 1-5, A: Moving Closer to the Customer: A Direct Model

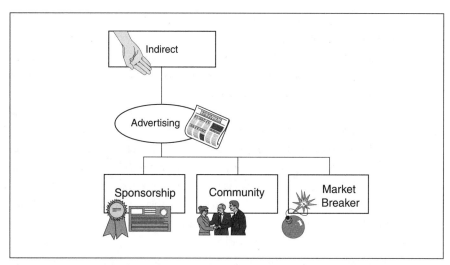

Figure 1-5, B: Moving Closer to the Customer: An Indirect Model

nesses, as do advertisers, or aids in the acquisition and retention of customers, as does the community. Businesses based on the indirect model can provide services to customers for free, or mostly free, and can then, for example, use a pay-per-use system for customers to obtain more advanced features of a product or service. Yahoo.com has features of the advertising and community models; it provides a free search engine, financial information, and web page personalization services to the general public. Market "breakers" use indirect business models. They "break" a market by selling goods or services below cost or giving them away for free. Their revenue is obtained through advertising that draws customers.

Intermediary is an all-encompassing term for a middleman. Intermediaries often offer some service involving interactions between a customer and a business. Subsets include the infomerchants (such as Monster.com and Bargain Finder Online) who broker information (organize, store, and disseminate information, such as jobs and resumes, as a service between two parties), auctions that broker products and services for customers in a setting that is similar to a stock auction market, and infomediaries that store personal consumer information, acting kind of like a person's wallet. Intermediaries may add value through aggregation of merchants in a mall or portal setting or through affiliate marketing (as is done through ExciteStores and amazon.com). Aggregators of buyers, such as Mercata and the MobShop Network, or information, such as Monster.com, are also viable. They add value by bringing together any two entities on the supply and value chains. eBay brings together suppliers and consumers of products and services—and both are eBay customers.

Intermediaries make money by various methods that are often combinations of several other methods. Internet e-businesses such as Charles Schwab's online site and E*TRADE charge fixed transaction fees for Internet stock trading. Others, such as eBay and priceline.com, charge the seller or businesses variable transaction fees that are usually based on the percentage of the selling price. Market makers such as VerticalNet are intermediaries. They bring buyers and sellers together. Intermediaries can also obtain revenue from advertisements (as does webMD), sponsorship, and subscription services, thus using hybrid business models that have a strong middleman characteristic as well as characteristics from the indirect business models.

Thus the third group of e-business models is the hybrid group illustrated in Figure 1-6. Businesses in this group have e-business models with characteristics of direct and indirect groups. We expect that in the future most e-business models will be hybrids. This book explains how the interactions among the strategic partners, operational partners, customers, communities, and regulatory bodies facilitate the development of these new business models.

The keys to the evaluation network for e-business readiness are the processes that occur between the business and the stakeholders. Each of the processes was broken down into its constituent components to develop our eBiz Readiness!™

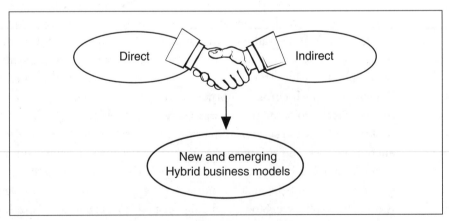

Figure 1-6   Foundation of the New Business Models

assessment framework. Value is derived from enhancing these processes through a customer focus.

Clearing Up Some Confusion: Creating a Common Lexicon

Having a common lexicon of definitions makes it easier to talk about e-business. We have noticed that many people we talk to use the terms *e-commerce, e-business,* and *application service provider* (ASP) interchangeably, but these terms have definite differences (Figure 1-7). E-commerce is a small subset of e-business. It is the small part of e-business that focuses on selling and purchasing goods and services electronically.

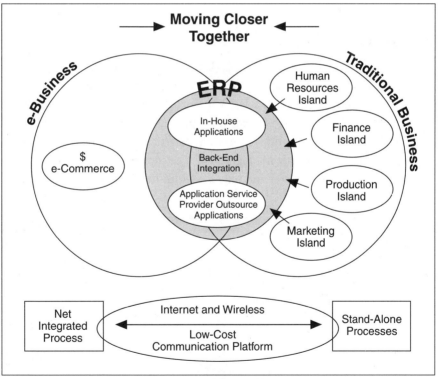

Figure 1-7   **E-Business 2000: Relationships Among E-Business, E-Commerce, Enterprise Resource Planning (ERP), and Application Service Providers**

Application Service Provider

An ASP is simply one option to use for hosting e-commerce and e-business services. The ASP provides a technological infrastructure, such as a server farm—web, database, and other servers—software applications, services, and most importantly connectivity. Businesses outsource to ASPs when they do not want or cannot afford to acquire and maintain the systems infrastructure needed for e-commerce and e-business. Hosted business applications include customer and sales management solutions. ASPs focus on selling business services rather than technology. Companies such as UpShot.com are leading the way in hosting partnership-relationship management solutions for the sales forces of small businesses. Businesses either rent the software for a flat fee or gain access through a pay-per-use model from the ASP. According to the Cahners In-Stat Group, the ASP market revenue is expected to soar from $7 million in 2000 to $7 billion in 2004, mainly from small firms and small office/home office (SOHO) clients. The total number of users is expected to climb from 20,000 to 30 million by 2004.

Enterprise Resource Planning

Enterprise resource planning (ERP) software focuses mainly on the internal processes of a company, such as the financial, human resource, facilities management, production, and sales. The process of moving a business entity into full e-business readiness depends on where the company is starting from and where it is heading. We capture some of these starting and ending points on the e-business continuum illustrated in Figure 1-8. The continuum ranges from companies that are bricks and mortar and only have intranets, to bricks-and-mortar companies

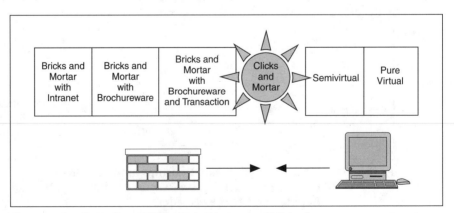

Figure 1-8   E-Business Evolution: Degrees of Virtualness

with brochureware sites, to bricks-and-mortar companies with transactional capabilities, to bricks-and-mortar companies with Internet-specific channel extension (clicks and mortar), to native, semivirtual Internet brand companies, to purely virtual Internet companies. Your company's position on the continuum suggests its physical and virtual infrastructure. The key question is where *should* your company be? The optimum location and model depend on your customer marketing processes. Although ERP software stores external types of information, such as customer information, the packages do not yet have full relationship management facilities. Relationship management is one of the requirements needed to facilitate the flow of stakeholder value from the stakeholder to the business to the customer.

Providing Some Context: The E-Business Spectrum

Bricks-and-mortar businesses usually begin using web-based processes by setting up an internal employee and operation management Intranet, an important stage in their evolution into e-businesses because existing employees become familiar with the Web culture. Bricks-and-mortar companies who launch brochureware sites are taking the first external business step toward using the Internet as a business communication medium for existing physical businesses. A brochureware site simply provides information about the company and its goods and services. This kind of site is not interactive; it lacks support for customer transactions such as *buy, shopping cart, order status,* and user registration transactions. The browse and search functions are the primary functions that are supported. The brochureware sites were some of the most prominent types of Web sites in 1997.

Bricks-and-mortar companies that have an Internet channel for their regular offerings are able to support transactions in their storefront counterparts. The next stage of e-business readiness includes bricks-and-mortar companies offering goods and services on the Internet that they do not traditionally offer in their physical stores. It is not hard to imagine that Barnes & Noble.com could begin selling toys or hosting auctions, as does Amazon.com, although the Barnes & Noble physical stores are primarily restricted to sales of books and music. The end of the e-business spectrum includes the pure Internet companies, companies that are native to and exist only on the Internet, which include Yahoo! and eBay.

The framework presented in this book presents the issues that businesses should consider if they are to obtain complete e-business readiness, regardless of where they are on the continuum. If an infrastructure to support e-business is already in place, the framework can be used to reassess the existing elements as well as direct the focus on the additional elements that are required for total e-business readiness. The framework metrics provide a feedback mechanism to assess e-business readiness.

The Need for the eBiz Readiness!™ Framework

We have been evangelists of e-business for some time. We have helped companies understand the concept of e-business, but our problem was that we had no model or supporting framework to concisely sum up e-business. Sure, we had bits of a framework, but nothing consolidated that said, "This is what e-business looks like. These are the areas you are good in and why." You need to sell your initiatives to executives who do not understand e-business. Most people intuitively understand the concept of stakeholders who surround an e-business. To sell the e-business strategy in the past, we used the e-business stakeholder model and supporting framework to give a high-level overview to people who were not e-business savvy.

A framework is typically needed to give some structure to complex situations. Who would disagree that e-business is complex? A framework breaks the subject into constituent components that can be more readily understood. Frameworks support modularity, reusability, extensibility, and control and may be used as part of a methodology to design or evaluate processes. Frameworks should include monitoring and feedback tools that allow you to reevaluate and potentially change the system being used if required.

Today's businesses are struggling with how to transition into e-business, how to identify all areas that should be addressed during the transition, and determining what types of components comprise an e-business. An e-business readiness assessment framework is needed to answer at least three of the questions commonly asked by people who are talking about e-business:

1. What is the e-business big picture?

2. Which components must be in place to support e-business?
   (a) What are the criteria for an e-business completeness assessment?
   (b) Which enablers are the most important?

3. How do we monitor our e-business and get feedback?

Webster's New World Dictionary defines *evaluation* as the "process of determining the worth or quality of a system." The eBiz Readiness!™ framework forms its evaluation methodology on the basis of providing customer value. The eBiz Readiness!™ framework defines a set of components and provides criteria for evaluating these components within product and service processes in an e-business environment. The components may be within your own business or within other businesses with which you partner. The framework evaluates the overall capabilities of your organization and assists in determining the value and effectiveness of stakeholder interactions. The customer-focused eBiz Readiness!™ framework is based on all the interactions among the business entity, the external stakeholder entities, and the customer focus, or demand-pull, of information throughout the entire framework. The framework defines benchmarks for each stakeholder process interaction and the minimum steps that businesses must take to be competitive in today's e-business environment.

Evaluation systems should have a clear basis of measurement that is easily understood, simple to implement, easy to administer, and clearly cost effective.[3] All the components in the eBiz Readiness!™ customer care evaluation framework are based on a measurement of the degree of indirect or direct customer value, or demand pull, in the system. eBiz Readiness!™ provides the "clear basis of measurement that is easily understood" by clearly defining the components that comprise e-business and clearly explaining the criteria needed to support the components. The framework is "easy to administer" because it has a simple structure. It is "cost effective" because evaluators have a framework on which to base their work and do not have to spend valuable time trying to figure out the components. Monitoring and feedback are also included in the eBiz Readiness!™ framework, which provides definitions of metrics (specific measurements of performance) for the e-business components and their criteria.

The multipurpose eBiz Readiness!™ framework includes three major pieces: (1) the big picture, (2) the details, and (3) a tool for measuring progress, thus it provides the following for businesses:

1. A visual representation of the stakeholder care components

2. Identification of the areas in which a product or business has a weak customer focus
   (a) A flexible, tiered identification approach with criteria that can be modified on the basis of customer-specific and business-specific needs
   (b) Identification and systematic comparison of information about innovative and conventional technologies to meet their customer care needs

3. Defined, consistent, measurable indicators for key criteria that influence selection and deployment of e-business systems with respect to customer care
   (a) Documented, reproducible evaluations that can be updated as needed when information becomes available
   (b) Focused dialogue among major stakeholders

The eBiz Readiness!™ framework gives you a snapshot in time of what your business's overall e-business readiness picture looks like. You can identify your gaps and take the steps to overcome them. The framework allows you to monitor your e-business with measurement tools that make sense for you. It gives you a macro view (a big picture), a micro view (detailed picture), and a feedback loop.

Are You Ready?

Keep the following points in mind as you move on to the next chapter:

- The e-business stakeholder model and eBiz Readiness!™ framework can be used to assess your e-business readiness and formulate a plan to become e-business ready.
- The e-business stakeholder model stipulates that the external e-business stakeholders are the operational and strategic partners, governance, the community, and the customer. Internal e-business stakeholders are employees. Shareholders can be internal or external stakeholders.
- The framework that supports the e-business stakeholder model is referred to as the *eBiz Readiness!™ framework.*
- Three major components comprise the framework: the big picture (the macro view), the detailed picture (the micro view), and a feedback loop that allow you to measure how effective you are at doing e-business.
- Customer focus, customer value, the value chain, and the value web are all important factors in e-business readiness.
- The new value web involves two-way interactions among stakeholders.
- You should distinguish among the terms *e-business, e-commerce, application service providers,* and *enterprise resource planning.*
- The location of your company on the e-business spectrum (for example, whether it is purely a bricks-and-mortar company or purely an Internet company) determines what has to be done to make it e-business ready.
- This book provides you with a comprehensive model and framework that can be used to create a plan to become e-business ready and remain competitive in today's business environment.

References

[1] Schlier, F. and B. Mcnee. "The Virtual Enterprise—The Phenomenon that IT Built," June 1998.

[2] Parillo, M. Personal communication, July 2000.

[3] Myers, B. L. "A Comprehensive Model for Assessing the Quality and Productivity of the Information Systems Function." www.year2000.unt.edu/dappelma/framisrc. htm

CHAPTER TWO

Detailing Up: eBiz Readiness!™ Framework

> **Assess, Enable, Monitor, and Reassess for E-Business Success**

Getting You Prepared

This chapter dives right into the eBiz Readiness!™ framework. Chapter 1 discussed the need for an e-business framework. Now we present you with the higher-level details of the eBiz Readiness!™ framework. We'll walk you through the customer-focused approach, show you the high-level view of the stakeholders, and then explain how it all fits together. We'll show how specific enablers set e-business apart from traditional business and how enablers fit into the framework. This introductory framework chapter prepares you for the remaining chapters, which go into more detail about each stakeholder and how to use the framework.

The eBiz Readiness!™ framework was developed to address a current business need to become e-business ready and decrease the amount of investigative effort required to get there. The framework first gives you a macro, or "big picture," view of e-business, but it also allows you to dig more deeply and identify which components and enablers must be in place to support e-business. Finally, the framework identifies metrics that can be used to monitor and infuse feedback to assess the e-business readiness of an entity.

The eBiz Readiness!™ framework is used as a communication tool at the strategic and operational levels. It is used to answer questions such as the following:

- Which processes should be e-business enabled?
- Where can I create value in the organization?
- Does the executive understand the big picture of e-business?
- Which technologies and applications are important to e-business?
- How do I evaluate e-business applications?
- How do I rank e-business application features?

More formally, as Figure 2-1 illustrates, eBiz Readiness!™ can be used for "snapshot" assessments (assessments of your company at a particular moment in time), gap analysis, and ongoing performance monitoring in an e-business. Furthermore, as we show in Chapter 10, the framework can be applied to not only a business but also to segments of industry, whole industries, countries, and markets.

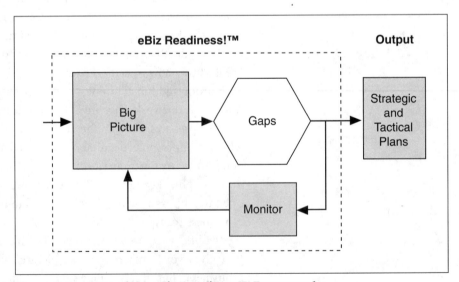

Figure 2-1   Uses of the eBiz Readiness!™ Framework

Defining the Horizon

The eBiz Readiness!™ framework provides a method for assessing e-business functionality. In the context of the stakeholders, the framework defines which components must be in place for e-business and how to assess these components in terms of enablers and metrics. The framework is based on the perspective of an external stakeholder and is customer focused. An external stakeholder could expand a business' horizons to include unprecedented business opportunities.

The Customer-Focused Approach

The customer gets maximum value from combining the value created from each external stakeholder and the business itself. You may recall that the external stakeholders are the community, governance, the customer, and the partners. The *new* mantra of business today is "Stay customer focused." This may not look like such a new idea, yet many companies are too product focused. Even companies that claim to be customer focused find that the majority of product failures are caused by not properly meeting the customer's needs.[1] Being customer focused is correctly understanding customer needs and integrating them into the products and services of the business. It is just as important to target the best customers as it is to keep the products and services customer focused. Following are a few ways that a business can achieve a customer focus:

- Include the customer in the development process. For example, during a joint application design (JAD) session, customer input is integrated into the design process for the development of software applications.[2] A JAD session includes the users, information systems analysts, observers, a session leader, and executive sponsors.
- Provide iterations of the product based on feedback from the customer. National Semiconductor used this method to strengthen its online presence.[3] Although they used a JAD approach for the initial design of the Web site, subsequent customer feedback revealed that customers wanted all the information but fewer graphics because they were slowing down the system. National Semiconductor then removed the unnecessary graphics. By targeting and focusing on the correct end-customers, National Semiconductor has created a world-class online presence that delivers true value to their customers.
- Coordinate technology, business, and customer satisfaction. Roberts Trucking—a 50-year-old trucking company—has reinvented itself through the

astute use of customer-focused processes. The company uses radio frequency communication to interact in real time with truckers who are delivering goods. The system also tracks the location of the trucks using global positioning satellite technology and gives a location signal customers can see in real time so that they know where their shipment is. A computer logistics system computes the optimum balance of routing and loading for the whole fleet of trucks. This is all integrated with an extremely good customer relationship database to give the customers a truly customer-focused experience. The following quote from the consulting firm that tracks the customer satisfaction ratings sums it up: "Satisfaction is so high that there is almost nothing Roberts can do to raise it higher. I know technology is behind it, but that's just a symptom of its philosophy. It focuses on the customer."[4]

Customer Value

A natural extension of customer focus is the value that the customer receives from the product or service. Customer value is a progression from commodities through goods and services to "experiences," with each step progressively adding more value. Value may be obtained through increasing the differentiation of services offered to the customer. Some customers are willing to pay higher prices corresponding to the value of these additional services. James Gilmore writes that "commodities are fungible, goods are tangible, services are intangible, and experiences are memorable."[5] The more successful companies are skilled at transforming the provision of goods and services into customer experiences. At a recent conference, a chef told the audience that today's customers want a "dining experience," not simply a place to eat out. A dining experience includes an excellent meal, a great atmosphere, and good company, which are all combined to make a pleasurable experience. The payoff is that customers are willing to pay much more than they traditionally did in the past.[6] Creating a pleasant customer experience is what companies doing e-business should strive for to deliver value to the customer.

The eBiz Readiness!™ Framework

Our eBiz Readiness!™ framework aggregates the components and enablers that are critical to successful e-business execution. The eBiz Readiness!™ approach is different from other approaches because we consider all the players in e-business: the customer, governance, partners, agents, the community, and internal company stakeholders eBiz Readiness!™ The framework also defines a set of measures for monitoring and assessing how well you are doing e-business. Chapters 3 through 10 showcase these components and detail the development of the eBiz Readiness!™ framework.

We developed the eBiz Readiness!™ framework using an externally focused (customer-focused) view of e-business. An internally focused (company- and employee-focused) approach can negatively affect technology adoption in the marketplace. Many internally focused businesses make the mistake of not integrating marketing the development of new products. In other words, you can build a better mouse trap, but if no one knows about it you can't sell it. The marketing engine must be started before new or enhanced products are released.

We recently worked with a large food services client who wanted to web enable an existing stand-alone PC application. The company hoped that by web-enabling the product, more people would use the service. At the time of this writing, fewer than 2 percent of the customers were using the service, and it was costing the company much more money to support the product than anticipated. The business never had a target market or customer in mind when they were developing and launching the product. Management assumed that because their product was a good one (which it was), all of their customers would flock to it. What they didn't realize was that marketing strategies targeting the early adopters (the buyers who aggressively purchase a product when it first goes on the market)and early majority (the buyers who purchase the product when it is still fairly new but not as soon as it hits the store shelves) can be used to launch a high-tech product.[7] The difficult part is making the transition from the early adopters to the early majority. If the transition is carried out correctly, the product is successful. From a customer-focused perspective, it is important that the e-business understands the external stakeholder—the customer and the potential customer—to market the product correctly.

The eBiz Readiness!™ framework is considered customer focused because your business stakeholders create value to meet the customer's demands and boost outcomes such as customer satisfaction, acquisition, and retention rate outcomes. You may recall that the external stakeholders or linkages are the strategic partner, the operational partner, the customer, the community, and governance. The eBiz Readiness!™ framework defines the enablers and components in e-business that give rise to the value propositions per stakeholder. The framework also provides a measurement tool to assess whether the stakeholder-to-business processes are performing well.

eBiz Readiness!™ Stakeholders

Recall the e-business stakeholder model presented in the previous chapter. The eBiz Readiness!™ framework is built around this model (Figure 2-2). A summary for customer value propositions per stakeholder follows:

The strategic partner allows you to plan for the addition of new markets and new channels, brand awareness, new product and service development, increased speed to market, resource pooling, targeted segments, increased market share, and increased wallet share.

Operational partners add value through lower supply costs, which translate into lower customer costs, on-time deliveries, better product and service availability and reliability, increased product and service quality, shorter lead times, product customization, personalization, noncore expertise (expertise in areas other than core business areas), and provision of technology infrastructure.

Governance stakeholders add trust, privacy, security, and support in policy making; target desirable customers; identify global opportunities; and provide the rules so that e-business can happen.

The benefit the online community brings to the customer is rapid access to knowledge. The community levels the field and allows the member (or customer) to make new and possibly rewarding contacts, aggregate content, obtain access to useful and often free services, and compare a business's services and products with its competitors. The community stakeholder adds team spirit, enhances customer service through offering an extended product and service support knowledge base, enhances trust, empowers members by unifying their voices as they strive toward a common goal, and increases the number of preferred customer profiles.

The customer stakeholder value is primarily a direct or an indirect revenue source. The customer can supply added value by providing feedback, giving input about a product or service development process, adopting self-serve habits, and facilitating negative cash-to-cash cycle times through use of efficient payment systems (Figure 2-2).

eBiz Readiness!™ Components

The eBiz Readiness!™ framework has two main aspects:

1. Identification of *components* and their associated *enablers* to support e-business

2. Measures, or *metrics,* to assess the performance of the stakeholder interaction

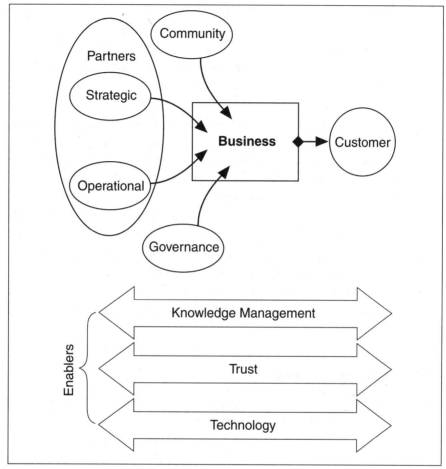

Figure 2-2   Customer Demand-Pull for Value as Depicted in the Craig-Jutla E-Business Stakeholder Model

The components may be whole processes or smaller tasks comprising a business process. Components can also be infrastructure or technology components, cultural organizational components, or people components. Enablers must be present to support the components. For example, an electronic catalog serves as an enabler for an e-business' procurement component. Associated measurement metrics for e-procurement could be catalog availability and accuracy.

Another framework component example is *new market research*, a process that can be carried out jointly between the strategic partner and the e-business entity. New market research that is conducted jointly, or cooperatively, can provide a better understanding of potential market opportunities. Enablers for the new market research component are technology enablers, such as collaborative technological tools for research and instantaneous access to complete, accurate, up-to-date customer and product information.

Yet another e-business component in the eBiz Readiness!™ framework is account planning—a key part of business development. Many partners share information on national accounts. Sales managers use the phone and e-mail to stay involved in the account planning. An enhanced account planning system could include extranets in which true collaboration could take place (for example, white boarding and shared folders within an electronic messaging platform). The enabler is the overall account-planning environment in which customer account information is obtained, assessed, and acted on. The environment includes integration into the customer data warehouse and data mining capabilities, and tools include intranet and extranet feature sets allowing collaboration.

We identify and describe components in the framework in each of the following chapters. Each chapter contains components and enablers for a particular stakeholder.

eBiz Readiness!™ Enablers

The three major enablers that are in common to all stakeholders are knowledge management, trust, and technology. Summaries of these enablers follow. Specific details for each enabler are provided as the framework is developed throughout the book.

Knowledge Management

Knowledge truly *is* power in today's economy. Your business must capture knowledge and allow it to be used throughout the enterprise. Knowledge management is management of all forms of business relationship management, intellectual assets management, and content management. Business relationship management includes customer relationship management (CRM), partner relationship management, supply chain management, trading community relationship management, and regulatory relationship management. Content management includes document management, web content management, media asset management, and syndication of content. Management of intellectual assets includes employee knowledge and expertise.

A key trend in knowledge management is real-time availability and analysis of data. The real-time availability of data is being made possible by relationship management applications such as customer relationship management and partner relationship management software.

CRM is a type of knowledge management. CRM facilitates customer touch point (for example, fax, telephone, e-mail, Web, voice, face-to-face) integration. Future touch points may be voice or machine-to-machine interfaces using artificial intelligence methods, perhaps based on neural networks. Customer touch point integration creates a 360-degree view of the customer and is the most important means of improving customer service. When a customer contacts a company through a touch point, the company can best serve the customer by using knowledge of the customer's past history. Customer history is not only purchase and payment histories but also complaints and service calls problem descriptions. It can be extremely irritating for your customer to constantly repeat the same problem description to various call center personnel during separate service calls in a single day. In addition, any attempts at personalization fall flat when your customer is addressed by the wrong name for the fourth time, especially when the customer indicated during the last three service calls that the name was incorrect! CRM packages have been steadily transforming into "relationship management" packages. Enabling total customer care means you must peek into the management of your supply chains; the better relationship management packages also integrate supply chain management into their core.

Partner relationship management (PRM) is also a subset of knowledge management. PRM is managing the transfer of knowledge and information among partners. Much of the thrust in today's PRM software packages is to support sales channel partners. PRM automates channel product and program management, channel communication, fund management, lead management, partner profiling and partner acquisition, and extended team sales. Automation decreases distribution costs and increases the dissemination efficiency of leads, marketing literature, quotes, and price lists. Knowledge sharing is critical to the success of any relationship, particularly relationships among stakeholders. To integrate distinct suppliers into the product development process, the customer-focused e-business must overcome such barriers as resistance to sharing proprietary information and the "not invented here" syndrome.[8] (The "not-invented-here" syndrome refers to the fact that some people think that no idea, product, or service is good enough unless they create or carry it out themselves; it also refers to the fact that others who think if their company did not create a product or service being used as a component in their final product, then they do not have to provide direct customer support for the product.) Naturally, risk management issues must be addressed when considering knowledge sharing and collaboration among partner stakeholders. The balance between cooperation and competition must be carefully maintained. Each company determines how much knowledge can be transferred safely over to its partner. A critical component in sharing knowledge within an organization is the education and training available to transfer knowledge to others.

Business intelligence is required to glean meaningful information from company data. Data must be retrieved, viewed, analyzed, and managed to get information that can be acted on in real time. The types of data presented to a stakeholder can be significantly different and include customercentric, product-centric, and strategic-financial data. The differences in data presentation may be dictated by the sensitivity of the information, restrictiveness of the viewing platform, or availability (or lack of availability) of the data online. Data are not in short supply for many companies in this networked IT age. We have plenty of data but no easy way to find the right type of information.[9] Only when the right tools for knowledge sharing are available and data are properly structured can relevant information be gathered and insights be gleaned. British Columbia's Ministry of Environment, Lands, and Parks has found that its business intelligence efforts have paid off, not only by integrating disparate information sources but also by fostering better communication and cooperation among departments and branch locations.[10]

One enabler for knowledge sharing among stakeholders is the available, sophisticated business intelligence tools, such as data mining capabilities and viewing features. Business intelligence applications are currently primitive in their functionality and integrative abilities. Microsoft offers some analytical functionality in its structured query language (SQL) server product and Excel 2000 extensions. Another knowledge management enabler is available data that can be integrated for partnering. The data may be related to research and product development, customers, resources, or schedules. Oracle Express and SAS offer superior product functionality but currently lack the capability to integrate with business data that reside on other vendor platforms. This problem is also associated with enterprise resource planning (ERP) business intelligence offerings.

Knowledge transfer is an overlooked area of knowledge management. Today's companies are filled with knowledge resources—people. They not only have many trade secrets, but they are the source of most of their institution's knowledge, and thus form the bulk of the assets of companies in the information age. Knowledge transfer is an attempt to garner the information the employees have and store it in an infrastructure that the organization can use to educate others and ensure the proprietary information is captured. Knowledge transfer is especially important when dealing with strategic partners because products may be developed that do not incorporate the knowledge of the employees—the originators of the ideas. Critical knowledge can be lost permanently when employees leave a company. Employee knowledge is being captured in corporate portal products, such as enterprise information systems packages offered by companies like HummingBird and Autonomy. As users read and write data in documents, spreadsheets, databases, or e-mail, a knowledge base of employees' skills and interests is created for later mining. Managers can quickly determine which employees add the most value to each situation. Knowledge transfer is facilitated as the program automatically points the user to similarly themed documents and people with similar interests. The user can decide whether to use the information. A common theme that emerged from all companies interviewed for this book was that the "right" employees are the key element in the e-business success equation. The Big 5 and New Age consultants, such as NerveWire, Zefer, and Scient, possess the focused skills needed to supply the vision, time, and people to companies like Hewlett Packard (HP), Sun Microsystems, and Cisco as they create and execute their e-business strategies.

The metric to assess how well knowledge transfer is being carried out is the *breadth of shared information,* information that can be captured and reused for others. The information is obtained through reports, courses, documents, and project assessments. Many service industries have distinguished themselves through the use of knowledge management software. Examples include consulting firms such as Andersen Consulting, Deloitte & Touche Consulting Group, and Ernst & Young, which use a knowledge repository to store "lessons learned" and project benchmarks to facilitate rapid customer solution deployment.

Content management synchronizes companies' data among various sites and ensures that it is updated and current. Timely and accurate content is critical to the success of e-business. Content drives traffic to Web sites. It provides value by building mind share (knowledge sharing) and customer loyalty. Fresh and accurate content maximizes the time that users spend at a site and is an externalization of the e-business brand. Good content increases page views and click-throughs, essential for e-businesses that depend on advertising revenue. Content updating considerations for an e-business include issues such as content migration, new content authoring, replication, and syndication. Content reading considerations include issues such as personalization, search effectiveness, categorization, and contextual selling. All of these activities require sophisticated knowledge management tools.

Trust

The *Oxford English Dictionary* defines trust as "a firm belief or confidence in the honesty, integrity, reliability, justice, etc. of another person or thing; faith; reliance on the person or thing trusted." None of these definitions are easily quantified, but they are all an integral part of the selling equation. Customers need to trust the business before they will open their wallets. Furthermore, the more trust they put in the business, the easier it is for the business to retain them as customers. A good example of trust in the bricks-and-mortar world of customer acquisition and retention is an experience the author had while looking for an automobile repair shop. The author heard about the shop from a personal friend, which promoted trust in the business. Once the job was done, the author was satisfied and more trust was established. Now that the shop has performed many more jobs well, the author has implicit trust in the garage. This is an example of the level of trust that e-business should strive to create to get and retain customers. The "switching cost" for customers who want to switch e-business companies is extremely low—they are just a "click away" from the competitors. One e-business company that has successfully earned customers' trust is a construction company called Bidcom. Customers enter the site and use free services such as a project estimator and business lead generator. As they see other tools, they try them because they are gaining trust in the company. Customers then start to use the workflow mechanisms in the project management tool because they truly trust the site. They're hooked. They were a click away from competitors when they entered the site, but trust was established as they used tools such as the managed project collaboration space, which also created a switching cost for the customer. An interesting note about Bidcom is that they are not using any external seal ensuring they are treating customers' data in a trustworthy manner. (An external seal is issued by a third party such as the Better Business Bureau or Verisign. The seal provides a level of trustworthiness.) An unbiased third party that validates their use of customer data could enhance Bidcom's customer trust. This highlights how complex the concept of trust is, especially in e-business. No one formula creates trust. It is earned by a series of interactions with the customer that build it over time.

The components that create trust form a customer-care continuum that ranges from community to one-on-one interactions. Community trust components include the ability to listen to unbiased comments about your company and its products, the ability for a customer to interact with other customers to build a community, and the ability to resolve issues from a community level to increase trust. At a more fundamental level, customers' lack of trust regarding online transactions with e-businesses is a barrier to their acceptance of online purchasing. Distrust can be created through concerns about privacy as well as the legitimacy of the e-business. In the Internet domain, everything is public unless businesses use security technologies and create privacy of information policies that assure the consumer, community member, or business partner about the integrity of the transaction and business. E-business legitimacy is addressed by trusted certificate authorities and online assurance seal providers. Consumers are also concerned about whether they can prove that they have made a payment online, as well as whether their online instructions are being accurately interpreted and documented. In other words, nonrepudiation of interactions and transactions is needed for the customer or partner to trust the e-business.

Technology

The "low cost" Internet communication platform delivers functionality that makes it the most strategic killer technology application for business in the twenty-first century. Its low transaction cost, global reach to multiple markets, ability to deliver data anywhere, and platform scalability in terms of the numbers of participants it can intimately handle make it extremely useful to the entire human race. Sharply decreasing computer and network hardware prices, increasing power of hardware servers, increasing universality of common standards, and increasing network bandwidth have made business and consumer connectivity to the Internet possible.

Accompanying Internet-enabled software applications such as ERP packages from SAP, Peoplesoft, and Oracle; e-commerce applications from Microsoft, BroadVision, CommerceOne, and Ariba; relationship management packages from Siebel, Onyx, and ChannelWave; and enterprise portal applications from HummingBird and Autonomy, have caused business to change processes, adopt best of breed practices, slash costs, and introduce efficiencies into supply chain, CRM, and internal operations. Basic TCP/IP store and forward applications such as e-mail and news expedite collaboration, information flow, and information use.

Semantic agreement standards unify the meaning of business concepts, creating a common vocabulary. Multiple standards for semantic agreements, such as BizTalk, Commerce One, and Open Applications Group; integration standards, such as extensible markup language (XML), RosettaNet, EDIFACT, and MOMA; and component interface protocols, such as CORBA, COM+, Enterprise, and JavaBeans, are the heart of the application integration market. A primary challenge is to integrate new e-business applications with existing legacy systems and expand overall systems over time. The standards enable e-business to scale and integrate with multiple marketplaces and procurement systems. The XML standard is more widely used by vendors to tackle the integration problem. The common function, which is provided by many integration vendors, is a means of taking XML data from various companies and translating it into a format that can be processed by your business' internal systems. The other side of the coin is translating data into and XML exporting it to your partner and customer processes. The component interface protocols allow for interoperable and reusable software applications across systems. If universally adhered to, these standards are expected to allow vendors to deliver e-business software application functionality quickly and economically.

Network systems management is an essential area for an e-business. This area is responsible for ensuring that the e-business's network is functioning correctly and for monitoring its performance. Technical issues in network systems management encompass quality of service items such as response time, transactional throughput, and network availability, reliability, security, and video and sound quality. Vendors such as Tivoli, HP, and Computer Science Corporation have promising products for network systems management. These products are essential for application service providers (ASPs) to offer and comply with terms in service level agreements (SLAs) written in business contracts. Current SLAs are full of loopholes because required measurement tools are not available and the metrics are not commonly defined. However, technology vendors are working hard to remedy the situation. A study from the Cahners In-Stat Group estimates that ASPs will spend $1 billion on technology infrastructure to handle the increased business in the next year. They will be tapping a $23 billion market by 2003 according to a DataQuest estimate. Network equipment providers and solution application providers such as Cisco, Nortel, Sun Microsystems, IBM, Oracle, and Microsoft are continuously developing, acquiring, and partnering to provide a stream of innovative technology products to this market.

Today's high bandwidth Internet is currently accessible through cable and asymmetrical digital subscriber lines (ADSLs), offering data transfer rates of up to 1.5Mbps. A very high speed digital subscription line (VDSL) is currently being deployed, with rates up to 7.5Mbps. Current Internet satellites offer 400Kps speeds, but in the future, we expect speeds in excess of 200Mbps. Applications such as video on demand need the future bandwidths to become viable. Astrolink, partnering with big-name players like Lockheed Martin, has a geo-stationary broadband project that proposes transmission to a satellite at speeds up to 20Mbps and receipt of data at up to a whopping 226Mbps. Optical networks present the promise of cheaper and faster networks. Software products are in the pipeline that will boost network capacity higher than optical networks in days, as opposed to months, and eventually in real time.

The mobile market, referred to as the *M-commerce* or *wireless* market, is making heavy inroads in business. Sales agents are reporting that the mobile handhelds, personal digital assistants, and cell phones are time savers, cost savers, and very convenient. These devices can interface with the Internet and hence gain access to business data in real time. Applications for convenience abound. General Magic's Portico product allows you to use voice activation to check, compose, and send e-mail messages while driving in your car. The functionality is enabled through use of known keywords. Natural language processing issues such as incorrect recognition of correct context still exist. Voice extensible markup language (VXML) is a new proposed standard for enabling voice recognition and text-to-speech conversion over the Internet. A future application of VXML would be to use a phone to obtain VSML-tagged information that is stored on an Internet-connected device such as a server or personal computer. Obtaining e-mail, stock quotes, and weather forecasts are preliminary applications. One challenge is updating off-site computers that are not always connected to a network. However, technology products that exist today are able to manage file distribution, data synchronization, and data distribution for your mobile workforce.

Implementations of research from the artificial intelligence field provide intelligent agents to perform time-consuming, continuous monitoring, and highly repetitive types of tasks for you. These intelligent agents are very useful in user interfaces, which take the form of avatars and natural language response engines. Corporate Jeeves is deployed at many Web sites to answer questions that are asked in a free-form language format. English is the predominant language, but you should expect it to have multilingual capabilities soon. Other common uses for intelligent agents are to do comparison shopping, to carry out a sophisticated search, and to look for entertainment. Agents are also being deployed for e-mail management, mobile workforce applications, and e-appliances.

The Internet appliance market includes handheld devices, Net TVs, Internet gaming consoles, screen phones, and web pads from which users can run standard Internet browsers and even access streaming media. Mobile phone software applications are becoming available that can intercept a phone call while you are browsing the Internet or reading e-mail and allow you to indicate online whether you would like to accept the call. Technology vendor InfoInteractive has announced its products for wireless systems and already has call manager products for wired phone systems in the North American and European markets. The company has partnered with Intel to add features to future Internet appliances.

As mobile workforce integration and rental of applications from operational ASP partners become more common, technical security solutions are in more demand than ever. Software- and hardware-based security products from Certicom and Cyberlink are available for mobile devices and Internet transmissions and access to address Internet privacy and security. Security measures deployed by ASPs for some clients include the segregation of public and private networks. Network availability is also an issue. One method that businesses use to help maintain network availability is to have fully redundant and routing hardware and backup power supplies, as well as several ISP and ASP providers.

Firms are using technology to stay ahead of the curve. Distributed information and database, multimedia, artificial intelligence, cryptography, biometric, and software technologies are being vigorously applied to e-business by the best minds in the world. In the future, we will have computers with no keyboards and accurate information that can be obtained anywhere and at any time in real time. For a business to successfully use such technology and knowledge management infrastructure, the business must have the customer's trust!

Metrics in the eBiz Readiness!™ Framework

Benchmarking

Benchmarking and proactive analyses of business processes metrics help you stay ahead of innovation, revenue, and cost curves. Under-spending for networking infrastructure and software applications and consistently spending more than budgeted for systems are some of the symptoms of ill-defined e-business strategies. Benchmarking is a special application of performance management. Benchmarking compares the results of a standardized core set of measures with those of other enterprises in the same industry. The definitions of the measures are the same for all the enterprises. As you may well imagine, it is difficult to benchmark e-businesses. No industrywide agreements exist to define which metrics to use. We hope that this book will help establish a standard core of measurements to enable benchmarking in e-business.

In 1999 the European market for IT measurement and benchmarking was valued at $1.5 billion, accounting for approximately 2 percent of the total IT expenditure. Performance measurement and benchmarking are recognized as important mechanisms for communicating whether tactical execution is aligned with corporate strategic goals and vision. Metrics can be used to gauge changes in performance, costs, and effectiveness of business processes. Equipping your business with the policies, procedures, and software needed to measure its performance allows you to understand its strengths and weaknesses and detect emerging trends that contribute to the effective management of your e-business.

In the early 1990s, Harvard University professors Kaplan and Norton proposed a balanced scorecard approach for identifying key business performance measures from financial, customer, internal, and learning and growth perspectives. The approach is balanced because external customer-focus and internal employee and financial measures are used to assess the business. Certain components of the execution of the balanced scorecard approach have been criticized; for example, the metrics identification is incomplete because each business creates its own scorecard, leading to long delays in implementation. Regardless, it remains one of traditional business's more comprehensive measurement tools. However, measurement tools for e-businesses must incorporate other stakeholder perspectives. In February 2000, NCR announced that it would join forces with Gentia Software to deliver balanced scorecard solutions to Teradata-based CRM solutions and data warehousing customers, initially in European markets. Steve Fluin, chief executive officer (CEO) of Gentia Software, claims that "the resulting solution will bridge the current gap between CRM execution and strategic planning, fulfilling the vision of the truly customercentric organization."

Ariba's Keith Krach measures his company's success by its customers' success. Each week, Ariba applies a 60-component rating index for customer satisfaction concentrating on how Ariba impacts the customers' bottom line in lowering costs, raising revenues, and adding value services. Boeing is another example of a company that places emphasis on customer measures. The company has developed a measurement instrument that *suppliers* use to evaluate Boeing as the *customer!* Boeing also gives awards to suppliers for superior performance.

Customer Metrics

Measuring e-business using a customer focus makes sense; increased customer satisfaction and retention rates are tied to key e-business components. Satisfied customers bring increased revenues through higher sales or more products per order. Regardless, what the dotcom companies have been doing with their revenues has shaken the foundation and challenged the validity of purely financial metrics (such as profits). Many of the new dotcom companies are plowing 60 percent to 80 percent of their revenues back into customer acquisition activities, such as marketing and research and development of new products and services.

The eBiz Readiness!™ framework is driven by the following core customer metrics.

Customer Metrics

Customer Retention

Existing customer loss rate (just for repeat customers), customer retention rate (including old and new customers)

Customer Satisfaction

Lead times, on-time delivery, continuous stream of innovative products and services, anticipation of emerging needs, product customization, personalization, convenience, team spirit (community), cost to customers as compared to competitors (reduced through pricing or lower cost to acquire and use product or service through all stages: ordering, receiving, inspecting, storing, handling, rescheduling, reworking, and paying), product or service availability

Customer Acquisition

Change in look-to-buy ratio, change in number of viewers

Customer Profitability

Ratio of customer cost per market segment, percentage of preferred customer profiles, market and wallet share in targeted segments

---

Shareholder value is driven by customer value expectations. The bottom line depends on whether the company's offerings continuously and repeatedly sell well. From the elevator speeches for stakeholder value propositions presented at the beginning of this chapter, it is clear that each stakeholder's performance is tied to customer metrics.

Certain metrics, such as customer satisfaction, are directly affected by various business components. That is, some metrics are functions of other metrics. For example, the change in the customer retention rate depends on the change in the ratio of actioned feedback (feedback that is incorporated in planning and not simply ignored), ratio of missed deliveries to on-time deliveries, rate of new product or service introductions, and degree of price innovation. Retention rate is referred to as a *higher-level aggregate metric* because is affected by other, lower-level metrics. The customer satisfaction aggregate metric depends on research and development processes, since one of the factors that contribute to customer satisfaction is affected by the introduction of innovative products and services. Value, such as reduced costs to customers, may be affected by changes to procurement processes; for example, the introduction by the supplier of business models based on price innovation, as well as innovations to supply chain or manufacturing processes affect procurement processes and therefore value.

A standard set of core low-level metrics also exists for time, quality, price, and cost (Table 2-1). These metrics are used throughout all business components when you break down the higher level metrics into two or more low-level, core metrics to find the root of the problems. These core metrics are often integrated into higher-level business strategy, process, or goal metrics. Tables 2-2 and 2-3 summarize metrics for the knowledge management, trust, and technology enablers.

Financial Metrics

This book does not focus purely on traditional financial measures because they are (1) generally well understood and (2) more important for companies in the "sustain" stage with mature markets. E-business is causing companies to move into a growth phase in which the emphasis is decreased with respect to the traditional financial measures affecting cost reduction rates and increased for alternative measures such as sales growth from new customers and markets and new product and service offerings. These factors should always be taken in consideration, whether they are emphasized or not. Their impact was highlighted by the market corrections of many of the technology stocks in the year 2000.

Table 2-1   Standard Metrics for Quality, Time, Price, and Costs

Quality	Time	Price and Costs
• Reliability and availability of network service	• Speed to market	• E-transaction cost
• Availability of e-commerce channel	• Cash-to-cash cycle time	• Price innovation
• Availability of products and services	• E-commerce channel response time	• Competitor pricing −Costs ratio = Our product or service price + Costs to acquire and use product or service (competitor's product or service price) + Competitor's cost to acquire and use the product or service
• Availability of e-business channels	• Sales call response time	
• Transaction throughput rate	• Mean response time to inquiry or service calls	
• Response time	• Lead times and reliability of lead times	
• Video and audio quality (such as frames per second)	• Percentage of time equipment is successfully in operation (up time)	• Cost savings ratios in all processes
• Return rate	• Mean time taken to correct or resolve problems	
• Number of warranty claims		
• Number of customer product and service complaints	• Mean time taken to locate relevant information	
• Percentage of defect-free products or services	• Ratio of missed deliveries to on-time deliveries	
• Number of field service requests	• Ratio of processing time to throughput time	
• Usage of service guarantees		

Table 2-2   Summary of Metrics for Knowledge Management

- Integration of business data index
- Level of integration of all systems containing content
- Employee productivity, satisfaction, retention, loyalty, and profitability
- Customer satisfaction, retention, loyalty, and profitability
- Quality of service, which includes availability of services, transaction response time, transaction throughput, video quality, audio quality, and video rate
- Interoperability of transaction management components
- Data consistency
- Data currency
- Speed of update
- Search response time
- Search accuracy
- Interoperability with external systems
- Increase in productivity
- Growth in volume of knowledge base
- Frequency of access to knowledge base
- Frequency of access to collaboration work areas
- Knowledge access time
- Number of tasks that are self-service
- Time per task or per call
- Cost per task or per call
- Number of corporate information collections
- Number of employees per project
- Number of projects per employee
- Number of instances of non-owner access to documents
- Average utilization rate of knowledge base
- Percentage of employees using knowledge base
- Knowledge accessibility index
- Knowledge transfer speed
- Amount of knowledge transfer
- Management of all types of data (unstructured and structured)
- Cost savings in business process
- Increased business benefit in service

Table 2-3   Summary of Metrics for Trust and Technology

Trust	Technology
• Abandonment ratio	• Customer satisfaction
• Employee and customer satisfaction	• Innovation index
• Employee and customer retention	• Cost savings
• Employee and customer acquisition	• Time savings
• Employee and customer loyalty	• Scalability index for product or service
• Brand awareness	• Quality of service index
• Privacy index	• Access speed
• Dispute resolution index	• Functionality index
• Consumer protection index	• First-to-market advantage
• Degree of customer interaction with community	• Communications cost
• Transactional nonrepudiation index	• Network capacity
• Service completeness	• Percentage of sales from product or service enhancements or creation
• Quality of service	• Time to develop next generation of products
• Service level agreement compliance	
• Security index	
• Transaction integrity index	
• Number of disputes	

Return on capital employed (ROCE) monitors how a company uses physical and financial capital to create value for shareholders. Return on investment (ROI) is the most commonly used measure for corporate performance because it is based on profits. ROI=net income divided by total assets. Its main advantage is that it shows the use of existing assets and the value of new assets. ROI is thus popular for measuring improvement in asset utilization. The ROI measure is blurred by book value, depreciation policies, and short-term operating conditions. However, because ROI is profit based, it is influenced by all factors and provides a total bottom-line summary statistic. ROI is an overall indicator of the success of a company's financial strategies to reduce costs, increase revenues, and increase asset utilization.

Targeting asset utilization, cash-to-cash cycle time specifically measures the efficiency of working capital management. Cash-to-cash cycle time is calculated as the number of days cost-of-sales are in inventory and the number of days sales are in accounts receivable minus the days that purchases are in accounts payable. Business entities on the value chain buy goods as input to value-added operations, which means that capital is tied up in inventory. It takes time to pay for the goods (accounts payable) and collect money for subsequent sales of the value-added goods (accounts receivable). The goods also sit in inventory before they enter a manufacturing process or before they are sold again. Negative cash-to-cash cycle times occur when customers pay you for your product before you pay your suppliers for inputs to the product.

Other broad metrics are return on equity (ROE) and earnings per share (EPS). ROE is calculated by dividing net income by total equity; ROE is thus affected by equity. EPS is net earnings divided by the amount of common stock. EPS can be calculated using alternative accounting principles and like ROE can have different values.

Economic value added (EVA) is the after-tax operating profit minus the annual cost of capital. EVA is strongly tied to stock price. Reducing the amount of capital used to earn profit or investing in high-return projects are obvious ways to improve EVA values. EVA sums all of a company's capital and reclassifies expenses such as research and development expenses as investments in future earnings. Some costs of capital are interest charges. Market value added (MVA) is the difference between a company's market value and the capital invested in it. Current share price is another financial measure that continuously monitors business performance.

The metrics that are identified for business performance throughout the rest of this book are nontraditional, customer-focused measures that corporations are beginning to focus on more and more. Kaplan and Norton's text on the balanced scorecard method provides sound arguments and examples of why financial metrics are not sufficient for measuring business performance, especially in the e-business era.

eBiz Readiness!™ Internal Rating and Weighting Scales

eBiz Readiness!™ supplies rating and weighting scales for components and metrics. The *component* rating and weighting scales are used for snapshot assessment and gap analysis. The *metric* rating and weighting scales are used for monitoring and feedback.

How to Apply the eBiz Readiness!™ Framework

Let's consider two cases as we discuss how to apply the eBiz Readiness!™ framework. The first example involves one enabling component from each stakeholder interaction with a business, which gives us a macro view of the pieces of the business. The second example involves a single component for one stakeholder, the strategic partner, but in more detail than in the first example. The second example provides a micro view of a targeted part of the business. Although we have not yet justified the stakeholder components that we present to you in the following two examples, we will do so in the relevant chapters and ask that you take a leap of faith for now. We present all of the components, enablers, and metrics for all of the stakeholders in the appendix, which is intended to be a quick reference for information.

Macro View

The first example application of eBiz Readiness!™ is at a broad level so that you can qualitatively assess the strengths and weaknesses of your overall business or targeted areas of your business. One component per area (customer, governance, strategic partner, operational partner, and community) that is being assessed is targeted. The presence, functionality, and interoperability of the enablers are qualitatively assessed, and the component under study is assigned a rating. We use the component rating and weighting scales given in Tables 2-4 and 2-5.

Table 2-4   Rating Scale for Components

Rating	Description
0	This is not a part of this system.
1	This has rudimentary features of the component available but does not have the "common" features.
2	All available enablers are present but are administered differently.
3	All enablers are present and interoperate with each other. This is the benchmark to aim for when evaluating systems.
4	Flexibility for additional enablers and interoperability are available (indicating future growth). This is the target for companies that are pushing the envelope!

Table 2-5   Weighting Scale for Components

Weight	Description
0	Not required
1	Could be in the system
2	Should be in the system
3	Necessary (must have)
4	Necessary and essential (absolutely must have)

Example 1: Assessment of Business Components Stakeholder Processes

SME Perspective: It is always more challenging for small businesses to build brand awareness and enter new markets than it is for large companies.

SMEHiTech is a small startup that sells Internet service products to the North American and European markets. SMEHiTech's focus has been on customer value innovation, early mover advantage, and operational partnering for information systems infrastructure. The culture is forward oriented, meaning they quickly take advantage of new opportunities and are not resistant to change. The employee base is 85 percent technical—designers, programmers, and support employees—15 percent administrative. SMEHiTech is a knowledge-based business.

This example focuses on a cross-section of business components in SMEHiTech. One component per stakeholder is selected. All selected components are important to SMEHiTech, so they have been assigned a weighting of 4.

SMEHiTech has not launched its media campaign for its new service. It has a few customer contact points that are well documented internally but not very well known from the customer perspective. Therefore customer support gets a rating of 1; the rudimentary features of the component are available, but it does not have the necessary features.

SMEHiTech's community interaction level rates poorly because it does not yet have a community established. The assumption is that another system will provide the community, or the business will provide a marketing plan that will build a community. Because of this, the area achieves a low score, lower than the benchmark because the company is still trying to create a sense of overall community for the Internet service but has not yet accomplished the task.

The governance system has two of the three components needed to create trust. SMEHiTech has a privacy policy for information usage and a security policy that covers physical and logical aspects of security. It does not provide consumer protection other than through traditional processes (such as working with the Better Business Bureau or communicating with the company). Therefore the governance component has two of the three components needed to create trust—privacy and security—but because it does not have the third component—consumer protection—it does not achieve the benchmark (3) and thus scores lower.

The transaction management component rating score is 1. The company has so many disparate billing platforms and customercentric data locations that it is difficult to get a consolidated view of the system. A single ERP would be beneficial for the company, but the organization has acquired best-of-breed systems that do not easily talk to each other. Therefore the level of ERP integration is considered rudimentary. The system is good in some niche areas but across the board is not complete.

The account planning environment is bare bones. The data kept is only on historic buying habits of Internet-related services but gives no insight into buying habits of emerging services. The collaborative environment consists of e-mail and a simple information-based intranet. Many initiatives are underway in this area because of the strong account team planning structure that is currently in place. SMEHiTech is aggressively trying to augment the capabilities, so it is assigned a rating of 2.

A few internal processes are being reengineered to reduce cycle time. Employee health and pension plans are still handled in house. No current plans are in place to deploy a corporatewide knowledge portal. A lot more can be done to electronically facilitate knowledge transfer. A rating of 1 is assigned to the firm's efforts to boost employee productivity.

Table 2-6 provides a summary of the weightings and ratings per component. A component's overall score is obtained by multiplying the assessed component rating and the level of importance (weight) assigned to the component. The overall benchmark for the component is obtained by multiplying the benchmark rating by the component weight. Consider the customer support component shown in Table 2-6. It has an overall score of 4, which is derived from multiplying the component rating (1) by the weight (4). The benchmark rating for the component is obtained from multiplying the benchmark rating for the component (3) by the weight of the component (4). The benchmark rating represents the

Table 2-6 Example of Assessment for One Component Per Stakeholder

Component	Enabler	Overall Rating	Benchmark	Component Rating	Component Weight	Benchmark Rating
Customer						
Customer support	Customer data integration Access to customer data at all touch points	4	12	1	4	3
Community						
Community interaction	Interaction tools	4	12	1	4	3
Governance						
Trust	Privacy Security Consumer protection	8	12	2	4	3
Operational Partner						
Transaction management	Systems integration	4	8	1	4	2
Strategic Partner						
Account planning	Account planning environment	8	12	2	4	3
Internal						
Employee productivity	Process reengineering Employee plans automated at source Knowledge portal	4	12	1	4	3

industry standard for the components. The industry standard is normalized to the rating scale shown in Table 2-4. Currently the industry standard for each component in our example is 3—indicating all enablers are present for the component, and all interoperate.

The graph in Figure 2-3 plots the overall scores for each component and illustrates the overall assessment of certain e-business components as compared to their respective benchmarks. Consider the axis for customer support that is shown in Figure 2-3. The axis has graduations (0, 2, 4, 6, 8, 10, 12, 14, 16) emanating from the center. SMEHiTech's overall customer support score is a 4, which is shown on the axis for customer support. Connecting the points for overall component scores reveals an inner polygon. Each point on the polygon represents the assessment for customer support, community interaction, trust, transaction management, account planning, or employee productivity. The benchmark for each

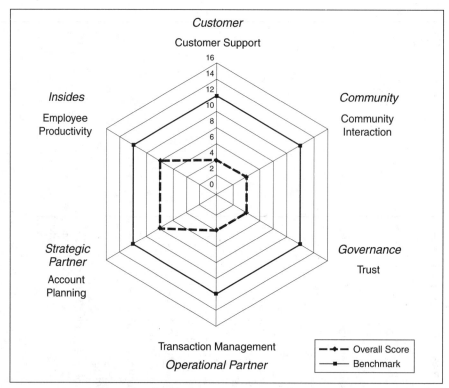

**Figure 2-3   "Snapshot" Plot of One Component Per Stakeholder
                        for SMEHiTech**

component is shown on the points of the outer polygon. In some cases a company's assessment of a component exceeds the industry benchmark or standard, so the benchmark point is closer to the center of the plot than the company's equivalent score.

The Feedback Loop

eBiz Readiness!™ can be used to monitor the progress and success of e-business strategies. When the eBiz Readiness!™ metrics are used, it should be clear who is responsible for the collecting and reporting tasks. The process should be a highly collaborative application process involving many key personnel from multiple business units or functions. Metrics data can be collected using in-house instrumentation of software applications or off-the-shelf performance software or with a performance measurement partner.

In the following example, we show how you can use the eBiz Readiness!™ framework to examine the new alliances process interaction with the strategic partner stakeholder in an small business setting.

Example 2: Assessment of SMEHiTech New Alliances Business Component

Since SMEHiTech's unique product was introduced to the market 2 years ago, another player has "tripped" into their market space. Although the competitor is a big business that concentrates on other products other than SMEHiTech's, SMEHiTech has realized that it cannot not ignore the threat and needs to actively adopt measures to reduce risk. In the past 6 months, SMEHiTech has aggressively executed partnering strategies to meet a diversification objective.

eBiz Readiness!™ identifies which features to consider as you form new alliances, such as resource complement and brand name lending. Examples of resource complement are new markets access, new technology access, expertise access, and new product creation. Metrics for new alliances are collected and include the following:

- Customer acquisition, retention, and profitability rates
- Number of new products and sales
- Degree of resource complement
- Degree of cultural fit among companies

- Level of team chemistry among partners
- Market share per employee in partner company
- Number of new markets penetrated
- Level of feedback from partners

SMEHiTech has targeted a large computer chip manufacturer with an international reputation, as well as national and British Internet service carriers, for co-product bundling. These alliances have given SMEHiTech immediate access to new markets through brand name lending and adoption of a percentage of their partners' existing customer base. SMEHiTech's customer base has climbed from 10,000 to 3 million and its current share value has quintupled since these alliances were executed. Other alliances have been made to improve research and development of new products and services. The eBiz Readiness!™ metrics for research and development performance include the following:

- Percentage of past products and services that were successful
- Percentage of sales from new products and services
- Introduction of new products and services to competitor
- Ratio of new product and service introduction
- Capability and capacity of research and production
- Sales performance for new products and services
- Knowledge levels of products and services and accessibility of that knowledge
- Level of team integration
- Availability and sophistication of project management and team interaction tools
- Speed to market
- First mover
- Cash-to-cash break-even time

If your company collects metric results, you can use the eBiz Readiness!™ framework's rating index (Table 2-7). The rating index is used to normalize the collected metric results. For example, if your company sent out a survey to assess customer satisfaction using Likert scale types of questions (5 is excellent and 1 is poor), the overall result of the survey would need to be translated into a rating. The metric rating index could also be used, for example, if your company decided to collect results for a lead time metric. If 20 percent of the time the lead time exceeded a set customer acceptance threshold, but the other 80 percent of the time the lead time fell within the threshold, you would need to assign an overall rating to this result. This result may be negative if only 10 percent of customers experienced long lead times in the previous measurement period. On the other hand, your company may consider this a very poor result if it thinks that it stands to lose one fifth of its customers.

The metrics for each component are weighted (Table 2-8). Some metrics are less important than others for meeting targeted business objectives. The weights essentially allow your e-business to factor the relative importance of each constituent in the whole picture. We use the eBiz Readiness!™ framework to weight the new alliance component at 4 because it is an essential strategic component in SMEHiTech. Each metric is then weighted in the context of business objective relevance. The ratings are assigned after the collection of metric results. To make the table concise, we have omitted some metrics that were not as important to SMEHiTech. We show the assignments in Table 2-9.

Table 2-7   Metric Rating Index

Rating	Description
0	Negative
1	Poor
2	Fair
3	Good (benchmark)
4	Excellent (ahead of the curve)

Table 2-8   Weighting Scale for Metrics

Weight	Description
0	No importance
1	Lightweight
2	Middleweight
3	Heavyweight
4	Sumo

In the appendix, we show one method to calculate overall benchmarks and ratings for the components and enablers when you have feedback in terms of actual measurements. We use the ratings and weightings as multipliers, but in reality a company may devise other calculation schemes for showing the gaps.

The overall rating for the new alliance component is calculated at 44. The benchmark is 48. One of the benefits of the eBiz Readiness!™ framework is that it is highly flexible. It easy to imagine SMEHiTech using eBiz Readiness!™ to assess how much value one alliance brings as compared with another.

The overall assessment in Figure 2-4 illustrates the strength of the company in forming new alliances. The area enclosed in the solid line with points marked by an X is the plot of the SMEHiTech.com's internal assessment; the area enclosed by the dashed line shows the benchmark—the desired values that should be within the analyzed system.

The results of the analysis show that SMEHiTech has been successfully promoting brand awareness. Resource complement in terms of finance needs work. The capital infusion rate and return on capital employed does not meet the

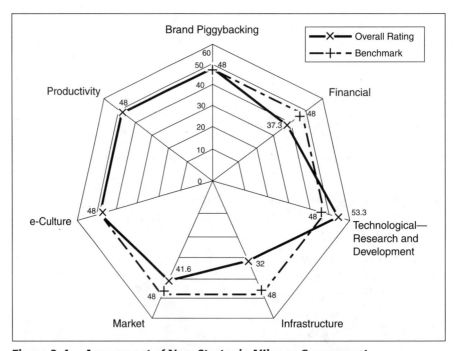

Figure 2-4   Assessment of New Strategic Alliance Component

Table 2-9 Assessment of New Alliance Component

	Overall Score	Component Rating	Component Weight	Metric Weight	Metric Result
Brand Piggybacking	48	48	4	—	—
Brand awareness	—	—	—	4	3
Financial	37.3	48	4	—	—
Capital infusion rate	—	—	—	4	2
Return on capital employed (ROCE)	—	—	—	4	2
Budget allocation	—	—	—	4	3
Technological (Research and Development)	53.3	48	4	—	—
New products and services	—	—	—	4	4
Research and product capability and capacity	—	—	—	4	3
Product and service knowledge levels	—	—	—	4	4
Ease of access to knowledge	—	—	—	4	3
Speed to market	—	—	—	4	3
First mover	—	—	—	4	3
Infrastructure	32	48	4	—	—
Availability	—	—	—	4	2
Reliability	—	—	—	4	2
Scalability	—	—	—	4	2
Market	41.6	48	4	—	—
Cost savings ratio	—	—	—	4	3
New market penetration rate	—	—	—	4	3
Customer acquisition rate	—	—	—	4	3
Customer retention rate	—	—	—	4	2
Customer profitability ratio	—	—	—	4	2
E-Culture	48	48	4	—	—
Leadership quotient	—	—	—	4	3
Productivity	48	48	4	—	—
Team interaction level	—	—	—	4	3
Market share per employee	—	—	—	0	—
Revenue per employee	—	—	—	0	—

benchmark. Partnering for research and development has been extremely successful. The company exceeds the benchmark in this area; Figure 2-4 shows that the overall score exceeds the benchmark rating for research and development. Infrastructure is clearly a problem area and needs to be addressed. Customer retention and profitability ratios are too low. The company's e-culture is very future oriented and matches that of many of its partners—forward thinking and aggressive. The team interaction and market share per employee metrics indicate that employees are working well together as a team and are producing marketable products.

Following are calculations that can be used to derive the figures in Table 2-8. Other methods can be used. (For example, the choices of *m* and *n* as divisors were arbitrary.)

The benchmark (B) at enablers level (benchmark for the enabler *i*) is

$$B_i = \left\{ W * 3 * \sum_{k=1}^{m} M_k \right\} / m$$

where
m = Number of metrics for enablers
3 = Standard benchmark rating
W = Weight assigned to enabler
M_k = Weight for k^{th} metric

The overall rating (R) at the enablers level (overall rating for enabler *i*) is

$$R_i = \left\{ W * 3 \sum_{k=1}^{m} M_k * I_k \right\} / m$$

where
I_k = Normalized result for k^{th} metric
m = Number of metrics for enablers
W = Weighting assigned to enabler
M_k = Weight for k^{th} metric

The benchmark (B) for the *component* is $B = \left\{ \sum_{i=1}^{n} B_i \right\} / n$, where n = number of enablers.

The overall rating (R) for the *component* is

$$R = \left\{ \sum_{i=1}^{n} R_i \right\} / n, \text{ where } n = \text{number of enablers.}$$

To illustrate the calculations of the overall rating score and benchmark scores, consider the financial enabler shown in Table 2-9. Assuming that the metric benchmark rating is 3 for all metrics, the overall benchmark score is calculated as follows using the previous formulas:

B_i = [4 (which is the metric weight) × 3 (which is the metric benchmark rating) + (4 × 3) + (4 × 3)] × 4 (which is the weight of the enabler)} ÷ 3 (which is the number of metrics for the enabler) = 48

The calculation for the overall rating score for the resource complement enabler is as follows:

R_i =[4 × 2 (the metric result rating) + (4 × 2) + (4 × 3)] × 4 (weight of the enabler) ÷ 3 (number of metrics for the enabler) = 37.3

Are You Ready?

We have covered a lot of ground in this chapter. We show the requirements for performance measurement systems and how they are meant to measure and manage key success factors for a business. We show some generic measures; your task is to start identifying the key success factors for your business. We identify and explain many of these factors and associate metrics with them throughout the book in more detail with each stakeholder group. We give examples of the eBiz Readiness!™ framework usage in the case studies at the end of Chapters 3 through 10. Two case studies are found toward the end of each chapter—one for an SME and the other for a big business. These chapters contain a summary of key metrics for the e-business linkages under study in the Are You Ready sections. A complete listing of the metrics from all chapters can be found in the Appendix. Keep in mind that in today's e-business economy, "What is excitement today is expectation tomorrow!" To accommodate this mindset and facilitate rapid progress, the eBiz Readiness!™ framework is not a rigid code of rules but rather a framework of components, enablers, and metrics that evolve in response to changes in the business environment.

eBiz Readiness!™ Framework Strengths

- Enables snapshot analysis, gap analysis, and performance monitoring to assess metric results
- Defines which business *components* must be present for successful e-business creation
- Defines which *enablers* support these business components
- Supplies metrics for business component enablers
- Provides a level scale for metric results
- Has flexibility in application; can assess or monitor (1) individual or multiple stakeholder interactions and (2) subsets of business components from across or within stakeholders, which allows focus on business goals
- Is extensible and allows additional components, enablers, and metrics for your specialized industry vertical
- Provides a methodology that can be used for internal scanning of your business's capability and market sensing, in addition to external stakeholder interaction processes
- Focuses on the outcomes; is a tool for assessing your business's strengths and weaknesses
- Contributes to an action plan for the remedying of problems or advancing ahead

The eBiz Readiness!™ framework provides a method (a snapshot analysis) for you to quickly identify the weak points and strong points in your e-business's interactions with its stakeholders. The snapshot analysis provides a "big picture" of your company's readiness to engage in e-business. Gap analysis is facilitated through assigning component benchmarks or the standards-to-achieve for business components and examining the difference between the benchmarks and the actual assessment of the business components. Performance monitoring and feedback are supported through metrics definitions for the e-business components. The metric results are fed into the eBiz Readiness!™ framework to calculate the components' ratings. Metric results can be used to validate qualitative snapshot assessments. As in most business initiatives, the use of the eBiz Readiness!™ framework in your business must be initiated by an executive-level leader.

References

[1]Levitt, T. "Marketing Myopia." *Harvard Business Review* July–August 1960: 54.

[2]Flaaten, P. et al. *Foundations of Business Systems,* 2nd ed. Fort Worth: The Dryden Press, 1992.

[3]Seybold, P. *Customers.com: How to Create a Profitable Business Strategy for the Internet and Beyond.* New York: Random House, 1998.

[4]Salter, C. "Roberts Rules the Road." *Fast Company* September 1998: 114.

[5]Gilmore, J. "Welcome to the experience economy." *Harvard Business Review* July–August 1998: 97–105.

[6]Panel discussion. *New Product Introduction.* Atlantic Food Processing Conference, Prince Edward Island, November 1998.

[7]Moore, G. *Crossing the Chasm: Marketing and Selling High-Tech Products to Mainstream Customers.* New York: HarperBusiness 1999: 17.

[8]Ragatz, G. L. "Success Factors for Integrating Suppliers into New Product Development." *Journal of Product Innovation Management* 14, no. 3 (1997): 190–202.

[9]Gill, P. "Building Intelligent Enterprises." *Oracle Magazine* July 1999. www.oracle.com

[10]Gill, P. "Empowering an Environment." *Oracle Magazine* July 1999. www.oracle.com

CHAPTER THREE

Your Reason for Being: Your Customers

> Knowledge *is the broadest category; it includes facts and ideas, understanding, and the totality of what is known.* Information *is usually construed as being narrower in scope than knowledge; it often implies a collection of facts and data.*
>
> www.dictionary.com

Getting You Prepared

This chapter introduces you to doing e-business with your customer. The power has shifted heavily in the favor of the customer, so we help you understand ways to manage them. We'll also show you the critical role channel partners can play in your business and how they can improve the overall customer equation. We then break down the complex issues and integrate them into the eBiz Readiness!™ framework so that you can see how to measure your strengths and weaknesses in the customer stakeholder area.

Understanding your customers is having the ability to know their history with your company, what they may do in the future, what they are doing in the industry currently, and what events may affect them. Good salespeople always tell you they know their customers. They know who makes the decisions in a company and what drives the decisions. Most importantly, they know where their customers' business is going and how their industry is doing. They have a thorough understanding of the issues. Those are the good ones. The bad ones don't understand the issues and will not be successful until they start knowing their customer intimately.

E-business has raised the standard for "getting to know your customer." Customers want precise billing information and timely service—they want it all. If they don't get it, they go to the competitor who *does* give it to them. Sure, some customers are more profitable than others, but customer retention is the key to success, so we need to understand the customer.

Introducing the Customer Stakeholder

Total knowledge derived from the customer, supply chain, partner, governance, and community is what drives the strategic business decisions that create the most value for your customer. Customer relationship management (CRM) is a broad term for managing a business's interactions with customers. Effective CRM is about acquiring, analyzing, and sharing knowledge about and with your customers. Total CRM includes your direct business contacts with customers, your channel partners' indirect contacts with customers, and customer contact management in your supply chain.

Typical interactions between a customer and a business occur through marketing, sales, and service interactions. *Marketing* is the process of targeting and acquiring new customers or retaining existing ones, *sales* is persuading customers to buy your products or services, and *service* is taking care of the customers after the sale so that they will keep doing business with you. Marketing, sales, and service are part of any customer touch point at a business. Combined, they create an overall customer experience. The online experience hurdles include fear, disappointment, and lack of incentives. Fear can be alleviated through awareness, security, and trust programs. Disappointment can be alleviated through better experiences, personalization, and good customer service. Lack of incentives can be alleviated through convenience, loyalty programs, and better prices.[1]

CRM is not just "knowing your customer," it is the ability to enhance your business process based on their requirements. You must own the customer's experience. Land's End, which has retail and online clothing and merchandise stores and catalogs, has a CRM system with built-in intelligence. For example, some Land's End online customers recently ordered some products for their 4-year-old using the sizes they had used the previous year. Land's End pointed this out and suggested that they might need a larger size. This is a great example of knowing your customer and using product knowledge and rules to give a customer a better experience. The GAP, a retail clothing store, is one of the standout companies that has used its online presence to combine virtual and real-world elements to provide a seamless experience for customers. Customers can return goods purchased from the Web to physical retail stores; this procedure not only resolves a Web returns policy issue but also creates another opportunity for a sale.[2]

Cross-sell and up-sell opportunities arise in the marketing and service areas, not just the sales areas, of a customer-focused business. An example of cross-selling is suggesting that customers buy a can of leather protector when they purchase a pair of leather shoes. Offering midsize rental car to a customer who shows interest in a small rental car is an example of up-selling.

The term *customer service* means many things to many people. It can mean every aspect of selling and providing service to a customer or it can simply be processing funds and doing exchanges and refunds. Good customer service is a requisite for retaining profitable customers. Unprofitable customers cost the company more money than they bring the company in revenue. Customer attrition, also known as *customer churn* or *customer turnover,* refers to the loss of customers to a competitor. When unprofitable customers move to competitors, customer attrition is not necessarily a bad thing, but it is unacceptable to lose profitable ones. A recent study in *Forbes* magazine showed that the number-one business imperative among Fortune 500 chief executive officers (CEOs) in the new age of e-business is customer retention. Customer acquisition (marketing) costs for traditional and dotcom companies are extremely high compared to the costs of customer retention strategies (8:1). Therefore once you get new profitable customers, you must do all you can to keep them satisfied! Customer satisfaction is a significant challenge for e-businesses.

Customer retention strategies include marketing strategies, such as quickly and efficiently letting troubled market segments or the whole market know about differentiated services such as special promotions or incentives. A popular retention strategy is using customer differentiation service levels. Pivotal, a vendor in the small-to-medium CRM market, captures this strategy succinctly with the "treat different customers differently" strategy. The strategy is based on giving all customers superior service and then giving extra perks and incentive programs to the more profitable customers.

E-business merchants have generally used only rudimentary tools to keep in touch with the customer, and sometimes the communication is solely for the resolution of problems. Many emerging customer service tools focus on new strategies, such as e-mail management, workflow management, chat, call back, and Internet protocol (IP)-telephony. Businesses realize that investing in proactive customer service is required to create brand loyalty and cultivate future purchase opportunities. The savvy e-business merchants use every customer contact as an opportunity to promote products tailored to the customer's needs and requirements. The industry that has had the highest success rates of converting shoppers to buyers is the financial services sector. A recent report from Jupiter Communications revealed that 16% of people browsing through the financial services area became customers.[3] Other industries that are enjoying similar success are the travel and retail industries. Different points of customer contact, including the Web, e-mail, phone, fax, and kiosk, require different types of content and are integrated with traditional points of contact, such as face-to-face and regular mail. Commercial products are available to help integrate many of the mediums. For example, the Vignette multichannel server provides content for the Web, interactive voice response (IVR), e-mail, and fax applications from one common database.[4] IVR enables users to respond to voice prompt menus using a phone or other voice-enabled device.

This chapter focuses on how CRM can be used to deliver customer value. In e-business, effective CRM uses all sources of customer data. The number-one enabler in CRM is the extraction and integration of customer data from all sources, including hard copy, e-mail, stand-alone databases, spreadsheets, accounting software applications, and text files. A good CRM implementation either has the capability to extract customer data from databases of many different vendor products and place it in one database or to intercept and direct data from all customer contact points (such as phone, fax, call center, Web, or walk-in contact) to one customer database.

The low-cost, standardized, universal communications infrastructure is the key to electronic CRM. We take a life-cycle view of electronic CRM—we examine e-business support for engage, order, fulfill, and support processes in the marketing, sales, and service functions.

Defining the Horizon

Contact Points Integration

The knowledge management enabler is critical to getting, retaining, and providing service for the customer. Knowledge management results in superior service because it provides an opportunity for contact points integration, also known as *touch points integration.* A company with contact point integration does not have separate databases or logs for communications such as faxes, e-mails, voice mails. All customer or business partner interactions are recorded in one centralized customer repository, regardless of the touch point and its input format (for example, phone, e-mail, fax). Contact points technology enablers include e-mail, computer telephony integration (CTI), IVR, call routing switch, fax, Web chat, and machine-to-machine interactions.

Your business must consider customer segmentation and the overall value of the customers, factors that determine the types of systems to be used for each contact point, potentially reducing the cost of supporting customers. Gartner Group has estimated that an interactive Internet site for customer service can cost from $500,000 to more than $35 million. The cost depends on the level of system integration, the types of touch points being used (such as phone and e-mail) and the level of integration in your e-business strategy.[5] Other estimates include a 3-year investment of $2 to $4 million for a 15-seat contact center (in other words, 15 software licenses) and $4 to $6 million for a 75-seat contact center that integrates all touch points. Whether all possible service touch points are used may be contingent on the costs and communications plan to the customer. Customers who are aware of the service promote use of the contact points.

CRM software solutions need to interact with a multitude of input devices: personal computers, scanners, telephones, and handheld devices. In recent years, we have seen the mobile sales and field service forces embracing the use of wireless devices such as the PalmPilot. Large CRM vendors are ensuring that these wireless devices can interface with their platforms. Siebel Systems, a leading CRM vendor for large businesses, formed an alliance with Palm so that they could jointly market and sell handheld e-business solutions. They hoped to streamline the collection of information on the field; allow users to get into corporate systems to acquire real-time sales, marketing, or service data; and maintain the integrity and completeness of the corporate data. Even pizza delivery persons use handheld point-of-sale devices to process debit and "smart cards"; smart cards have embedded microchips and can act as credit or debit cards and store various types of information. In North America, it may become more commonplace for credit cards to be swiped through handheld card readers at restaurant table as it is in Europe. These handheld devices must be able to interact and integrate with your corporate information system.

Contact Points

When a customer calls the company's contact center, CTI allows a customer service representative (CSR) to view the customer's information simultaneously on a computer screen. CSRs are able to immediately scan the customer's service history and be more helpful to the customer. They may also identify or create a sales opportunity. Some CSRs have access to marketing campaign information as well. The computer interaction allows CSRs to search knowledge bases to get product recommendations or solutions to problems so that they can respond to the customer quickly and knowledgeably.

IVR allows customers to respond to voice prompt menus (such as, "Press 1 for Sales," "Press 2 for Finance") using the phone buttons or their voice. IVR allows customers to find information such as a company's business hours or their accumulated air miles through this self-service method. IVR can be used for placing orders or making inquiries as well. Voice recognition technology is used to take spoken customer requests or responses and create a text script of the interaction. The text script equivalent and voice data are then stored in the customer database. The script allows you to easily and quickly search the database. If requested, the record of the voice data may be played back to the customer for confirmation. The voice record can also be used for security purposes. Technologies that are embedded in Web pages, such as voice buttons (also known as *call me buttons*), allow CSRs to quickly call back a customer. The customer enters the phone number and clicks the voice button, which activates the call center number. A CSR then calls the customer, initiating instant service.

Voice over Internet protocol (VoIP) will be the next wave of Web customer service. In the future, the customer will be able use a computer instead of a phone to initiate an intelligible verbal conversation with a company. They will also be able to use their phone to have an actual verbal conversation with business computer systems—without any human intervention on the computer server side—thus forming another customer touch point.

E-mail is one of the most pervasive interaction tools used in e-businesses. E-mail response management systems (ERMSs) are software programs that fully or quasi-automate responses to customers. ERMSs classify and sort incoming messages according to predefined categories such as requests for information or complaints and customer priorities. Some intelligent systems respond automatically to the customer based on keyword identification. For quality assurance, ERMSs may automatically suggest a written response and send it off to a CSR for approval. The CSR can then review the response, add to or correct it, and forward it to the customer. Many Web sites provide a "contact us" button that when clicked brings up a Web form with the company's e-mail address and structured fields for certain types of information. The Web forms are easier for the ERMS to process than freely written, unstructured e-mail because form fields give the data context.

Instant messaging and chat room interactions enhance the online customer contact experience. Chat bots are interactive software applications that can "talk" to people. They simulate natural conversations. Avatars are online proxies of people that are represented in 3-dimensional graphics. They often represent an alter ego or a mood. Virtual facial expressions on avatars are programmed to depict a range of human characteristics such as cheerfulness or puzzlement. Chat bots and avatars can welcome customers to the customer service site, and supply delay, product, or other self-serve information through natural language or voice interactions. They then pass the customer on to the CSR. A log of the chat bot-customer and CSR-customer interaction is added to the customer's record in the database.

In the impending world of network-connected appliances, machine-to-machine interaction may be another potential customer contact point. When "smart refrigerators" are running low on certain items, they will be able to send a message to a food service company telling it to deliver groceries to the customer's home. A washing machine may be able to put in a service call for itself; a receiving machine would run remote diagnostics and e-mail the owner about the problem, service, and cost details.

Metrics are required to measure the effectiveness of CRM systems and can also be used for alerts or control. Onyx Software, a leading provider of CRM business solutions, provides an eMetrix module that reports on call response time, number of sales opportunities, close rates, and marketing campaign effectiveness. Numerous calls for product or service problems at any touch point (such as e-mail, phone, or fax) can alert a company that something may be wrong with a certain process. An example of a control system is the military command, control, and communication system used on navy vessels to detect power loss, which triggers the automatic shutdown of noncritical power-draining components.

This is an example of machines autonomously monitoring and taking action to decrease the hazards of a situation.

Companies like Onyx are providing portals to all the company data so that a user such as a CSR can have access to customer information as well as product, sales, marketing, and service information. Sales personnel also use the portal to examine sales lead information and submit expense reports. Enterprise portals usually have task management capabilities so that users can prioritize and categorize tasks and activities.

Bob:

We have a lot of different types of information coming from various contact points. We know it's necessary, but it will take a major integration effort to get all of our lines of businesses talking. Integration will improve our customer service, which *already* sets us apart from other companies and has allowed us to compete.

Sue:

We need to see the big picture—our interactions with our customers, partners' customers, and partners! We need to have accurate and useful information to give our customers a great experience or we will lose them.

eBiz Readiness!™ Components for Customer Stakeholder

The e-business process for the customer (Figure 3-1) comprises four main components: engage, order, fulfill, and support.

Engage

"E-businessing" the engage component means network-enabling the process of enticing the right customers to buy a product or service. Some forms of proactive engagement are having your product or service appear prominently in the results of a popular search engine or through advertising banners on an idle cell phone display. The CRM aspect of e-business is not just online marketing, sales, and

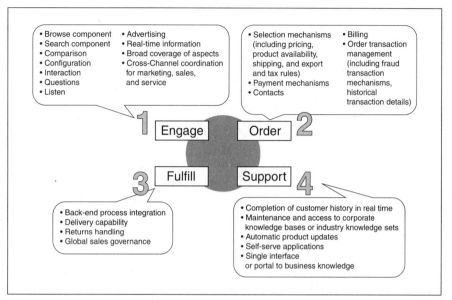

Figure 3-1   Components and Enablers for Customer Stakeholder

service but also supporting these functions in traditional channels (such as through a retail store or reseller) through use of Internet and wireless technology. Here we focus on Internet-supported enablers for engagement. The discussion applies to businesses ranging from purely Internet dotcom companies to companies with actual retail stores and a Web channel (clicks-and-mortar companies) to net market makers and breakers.

Software companies like Netscape used an effective engagement strategy: they gave a product away "for free." Their plan was to obtain revenues later through another product, ideally one that was tied to the free product. In Netscape's case, it is the suite of XPert e-commerce tools that costs more than $250,000. RedHat made millions by increasing their share price! Some companies give away "teasers," or stripped-down products or services. After the customer is engaged, the company obtains revenue by offering billable add-on features. These strategies complement other marketing campaign strategies such as time-limited price reductions or sale or clearance signs.

Interactive marketing effectively "tracks" customer actions and pushes suggestions or advertisements on each customer. Online interactive marketing uses customer profiling, personalization, and contextual advertising extensively. The amazon.com company is very good at interactive marketing. When you search their site for information on an item of interest, you encounter a button that reads, "If you would like to read more about this topic . . ." embedded next to the search results. When customers start looking for product or service information, whether online or offline, they browse, search, compare, configure, interact, question, and listen. Your e-businesses must support these activities as well as identify customer needs and solve customer problems. Throughout these stages, use advertising to get the customers to look at your product. A scary statistic, one that is probably not far off the mark, estimates that Generation Y-ers will spend about a third of their lives using the Internet!

Browsing online is promoted by interactive content that allows the customers to find certain products and services. Interactive content has multiple data indexes so that a customer can drill down (focus in on) to the product of interest and visual merchandizing tied to the customer's platform capabilities. Great content draws traffic to a site. Browsing can be aimless or targeted; regardless, browsing gives you an opportunity to engage the customer.

Searching is the interactive process of using a search engine to find information. Customers interact using language and numbers as the search mechanism. Customers should be able to use links to relevant terms based on localized contextual language. For instance, the Ask Jeeves search system allows customers to submit queries in a natural language format and then choose from multiple search engines, which gives the customer a range of options.[6] The Neuromedia system takes this one step further. Using an artificial intelligence-based system, it allows a search for product attributes, thus bringing the automated customer care experience closer to an experience that can be provided by a real CSR. Finding a product online is often much easier than thumbing through pages and pages of catalog material. Customers of companies like Grainger are finding Web channels to be extremely useful.

Comparison shopping allows customers to research products from several suppliers at once. Customers enjoy being able to see similar types of products and services so that they can compare attributes. Good comparison shopping sites display product and service specifications such as price, discounts, and warranties. The Computer Warehouse and Buy.com sites allow customers to compare prices of many suppliers.[7]

Interacting, configuring, listening, and questioning help a merchant personalize views for the customer. These characteristics compose the themes for personalization and trust, marketing, and content for points of contact. The themes range from picking and choosing products to pushing specific information to the customer. Personalization during a search involves tailoring information to the specific user, which includes localization of content, contextual presentation of data, and iterative learning based on user input. Localization of content is the ability to tailor content to the customer's requirements at each customer location. Business globalization (reaching a wide range of customer groups) makes content localization more difficult. For example, localized content is required to present a true price to your customer, one that reflects all of the pertinent costs, rules, and regulations. Localization dictates how your customer interacts with your business. The customer may speak another language or be visually impaired—two significant localization issues. Clearpicture is a small firm that specializes in multilingual human resource surveys. Terry Norman, CEO of Clearpicture, was able to conduct a global online survey of IBM employees that could process multiple languages and included computer-generated speech programs for persons with visual impairments.

Best-of-breed CRM systems include products that localize and present content to customers in any language according to a "learned" or configured set of preferences. The first version of these systems presents content based on the customer's Internet address and Web site; for example, a person with an Internet address that included ".ca" (JohnSmith@ISP.ca) would receive Canadian content.[8] Hooking in the customer with devices such as Web page voice buttons to increase human contact is another "engage" enabler.

Identifying needs and solving customer problems using engage enablers means describing the product or service to fit the customer. You want to make an ad for a toaster read like that of a BMW! Marketing during the engage stage can provide a conduit for new product or service development.

Access to a common customer database allows regular brick-and-mortar businesses to more effectively cross-sell and up-sell. Complete access to customer information can create a richer customer experience. Another aspect of engaging a customer involves coordinating efforts with channel partners. Your customers do not want to have to say "no" to multiple companies offering the same product or service in a short time. To avoid annoying your customers, share and manage lead information on prospects or potential customers with your channel partners. Direct online prospects to the channel partner that can offer the best service to the customer. All online prospects are automatically recorded in a database, and the leads are then available for follow up by your company's or its partners' sales personnel.

Dotcom companies also use traditional media such as newspapers, radio, and television to engage new customers. PriceLine periodically takes out full-page ads in local newspapers advertising hotel room availability in various cities in the United States. On the game show Jeopardy, Priceline.com is announced as one of the companies that donates prizes for runner-up contestants. In fact, it is well known that dotcom companies reinvest from 50 to 85 percent of their revenues in marketing to build brand awareness. Clicks-and-mortar companies use their Web channels to complement traditional engagement methods. Both companies (Internet and clicks-and-mortar companies) advertise their Web sites through hard-copy media such as brochures. E-business has actually been great for the brochure-making companies, despite initial fears that the online distribution channels would cut into their revenues. Exactly the opposite happened—they are making more money from winning e-business company accounts for offline promotions than from their former revenue sources!

All types of businesses use profitability and competitor analyses to target the right prospects, customers, and partners in the first place. Data mining the customer data warehouse supports these types of analyses and allows the business to effectively create marketing campaigns. Full knowledge management allows personalization and one-on-one marketing. Sales order history can be used to create and personalize a customer service offering by allowing customers to view their previous transactions. Best-of-breed examples include full customer care suites that have integrated sales order histories with their marketing systems.

Information required for customer care is derived primarily from (1) a customer data warehouse for linking to multiple touch points and (2) a marketing knowledge base or encyclopedia. These factors must be integrated with (1) enterprise resource planning (ERP) systems, (2) partner relationship management systems, (3) supply chain systems, and (4) external sources (for example, mapping, economic statistics, weather). Finally, use of intelligent agents for comparison shopping and personalized experiences also need to be considered.

The rental car company Hertz has a successful integrated strategy for retaining its customers. They have made it easier for customers to do business with them by establishing loyalty programs and tracking customer preferences, information that is accessible to the entire dealer network. It's easy for customers to do business with Hertz, so they keep coming back, a program that is reinforced through tremendous customer service and commitment.[9]

In summary, the engage enablers are browsing; searching; comparing; configuring; interacting; questioning; listening; interactive marketing; real-time information availability; broad coverage of prospects; cross-channel coordination for marketing, sales, and service; and reduced cost or "free" products and services. A metric for the engage component is the *level of integration of the engage enablers.* Your company's level of integration is low if you only have one or two of the mentioned factors; the level is high if you have all of the factors and they are integrated into a comprehensive customer care "engage" service. How well the engage component is performing can also be measured by the customer acquisitions ratio, customer profitability ratio, the number of new and effective marketing campaigns in the last 6 months, and the number of new interaction methods. Useful range metrics are indexes such as the convenience index (low—inconvenient, high—very convenient), pricing index (low—poor pricing, high—competitive pricing), and usability index (low—difficult to use, high—easy to use).

The listed metrics are a mix of leading (a priori) and lagging (after-the-fact) indicators. Leading indicators are known as *performance drivers,* new initiatives or changes that are expected to improve performance. Examples of performance driver measures are cycle times or level of integration of engage enablers. A lagging measure is an outcome measure; it is used to measure something that has already occurred. For example, customer satisfaction, which is usually measured through surveys, is a lagging indicator. Other lagging measures include the customer acquisition ratio, improved sales, and higher asset utilization.

Bob:

We have several strong advertising campaigns on the go using multiple media sources (television, radio, newspapers, and the Web). Web advertising is very different—on an ad, your company's logo pops out of nowhere in a contextual setting! It's quite a challenge to consider the number of complementary places our ads can go on the Web!

Sue:

My business needs to get easy-to-use, analytical tools to create good customer profiles. Right now, we collect lots of customer data at our Web site, but we haven't been using it for anything.

Mark Ingrich and SIEMENS

DOING IT TODAY

Siemens is a world leader in electrical engineering and electronics. Situated in the corporate communications office in Munich, Germany, Mark Ingrich is responsible for corporate development for e-business, and at the time of interview he was responsible for the project management for the Siemens Internet portal. When asked about Siemens and its e-business strategy and e-culture orientation, Ingrich said, "It was a big step ahead to look from the customer's point of view and not from the inside out. That was the most important point to discuss with the various business groups in Siemens. That was the hard task, to make them understand that we *do* need to look from the outside inward, not the other way around."

Ingrich addresses issues such as what the user (consumer or supplier) looks for in a company Web site in his work with media agencies and as a consultant for large and small companies doing e-business. Market research was conducted in the United States, Germany, Denmark, and Portugal, countries thought to be generally representative of the Siemens market, and was combined with information gained from first-hand experience. Siemens wanted to have a good overview of developments over the globe. "The United States was chosen because of the Internet craze; the trend is coming from there," said Ingrich. "We think they are years ahead of Europe in Internet years. Europe is speeding up a lot—you can just see the development. We chose Germany because Germany is our home market and we want the company to meet its market expectations. Portugal and Denmark were chosen because they are good examples of smaller countries, trends, and customers in smaller companies. Denmark is the representative for the Scandinavian countries, which are very Web savvy and know how to deal with the Internet. Portugal represents South America and parts of southern Europe. They are not as well equipped with lines and networks."

A big improvement for the Siemens Internet portal is its easy-to-use product finder. Siemens sells more than 1,000,000 products in 50,000 product families. The company is trying to make it easier for customers to find what they're looking for. The portal's product finder offers product, service, and solution groups. Among the categories are Siemens' e-business solutions (including Siebel- and

SAP R/3-based solutions), energy, and transportation. The product finder also lets the customer find a product from an alphabetical list. As of March 2000, only 300 product groups were accessible through the portal. This starting point showed Siemens' customers how the portal works. Siemens has two areas in its portal—a seller area and a buyer area. The seller, or supplier, area is the port of entry for e-procurement.

Ingrich also discussed business integration issues. "A company as large and decentralized as Siemens has dozens of independent, decision-making business units," he said. "Thus each business unit has its own ERP system and bolt-on applications. A challenge is to integrate all these systems so that Siemens can get a common customer database. Without the common database, it is impossible to implement cross-marketing, cross-selling, and personalization. Moving information transparency is achieved when a customer from one part of the company wants to become a customer of another part of the company. The sharing of the whole range of products across sites is also facilitated through integration."

Siemens set its flagship Internet portal site up in less than 3 months. It's a great start—and is focused on the customer. It will take Siemens some time to implement real electronic business strategies for the whole company—which is understandable for a company with more than 450,000 employees in 193 countries!

Order

Ordering is the process in which a customer selects and makes a commitment to purchase a product. Ordering includes various selection and payment mechanisms and order management. The ordering process has traditionally been a sales process; however, interactive marketing can weave its way into this process, and an opportunity for excellent customer service exists as well. Your customer doesn't distinguish among marketing, sales, and support—they experience the whole business. Web channels blur these borders because customers expect the unified experience all at once.

Real-time shopping environments help customers select products or services by giving them consolidated views of prices, availability, shipping and tax rules, and any other pertinent information that expedites the ordering process. Customer ordering ties into the ERP or back-office system for dynamic pricing, just-in-time (JIT) inventory control, and other logistical and customercentric mechanisms. A back-office system refers to the hardware and software server systems that make up your core information system. They normally comprise your business database systems. Supply chain visibility is obviously important to CRM. Customer expectations are more realistic because the customers receive accurate delivery dates and order status information. Customers are also able to see their previous order histories. In the future, it may become cost effective to allow customers to make incremental changes to their orders until they are shipped.

Ordering systems must go beyond simply taking orders if they are to create real value for the customer. They must access real-time supply chain management data—demand planning and forecasting, manufacturing planning and scheduling, distribution and deployment planning, transportation planning, and scheduling data. Supply chain management *optimizes* the delivery of goods, services, and information from supplier to customer. Based on this real-time supply and demand data, a business can distinguish itself by creating dynamic pricing, offering nimble product or service configurations, promotion, and product mix optimizations. Global sales drive the integration of other information such as custom and excise duties and governance rules for export to a country in the order management systems for e-business. When e-commerce sites were in their infancy, little of this back-end integration occurred. Expenses were wasted on hiring personnel to rekey data into the back-end system; slower process cycle times were the result, creating little value at the front end. In addition, data entry errors eroded customer trust.

A good example of a company with systems integration is Dell, which has customized links to suppliers, enabling materials to be located in real time. By collecting data on market patterns and purchasing trends, Dell has been able to respond rapidly to changing customer needs and more effectively manage their products.[10]

The payment mechanisms for business-to-customer (B2C) e-commerce include credit cards, micropayments, electronic funds transfer, and other types of noncash settlements such as contracts and invoices. These mechanisms must allow for nonrepudiation of the transaction. Micropayments are relatively new methods for transferring funds. They have a much lower cost per transaction than traditional credit cards. Best-of-breed mechanisms can handle multiple types of micropayment structures.

Contracts and quotes are agreements made between trusted parties and are used more in business-to-business (B2B) e-commerce transactions to allow for the purchase of goods and services. Best-of-breed companies can handle multiple customer contracts and accept full or partial quotes based on customer requirements. Invoices are payment mechanisms that are commonly used to start the payment process. Invoices come with an inherent level of trust that implies the account will be paid within a certain length of time. Companies using invoices should have an audit process that is reconcilable by both parties to ensure prompt payment. "Other-cash" is a flexible payment selection category that includes alternative or deferred payment processes.

Order management refers to the management of the details of a customer's order. It can vary from details about a single consumer's order to details about an entire corporation's order. Dell has created a good order management process. They have multiple order management information systems for personal and corporate use that show order details and statuses.[11] An order entry system must address service orders, not just product orders, which means that warranty management—the types of available warranties—should be integrated into the order management system. Warranty management is critical for companies that sell no digital goods and have warranties that include the policies for handling defective products and returns. Obtaining customer information at the point of purchase can be difficult and challenging for online businesses, yet customers must have a proof of purchase for returns and service. Keeping sales receipts is annoying to most customers—obtaining customer information at the point of sales means that customers don't have to keep their sales receipts.

Siebel Systems, a leading CRM vendor for big businesses, recently formed an alliance with Aruba so that they could offer complete sell-side and buy-side e-commerce. The interface to Aruba's online Internet catalog is displayed on the user's desktop—the buy side. The user selects the product, and control is transferred to Siebel's e-sales supplier software—the seller's side. Siebel's e-sales facilitates product configuration and other marketing assistance. The information is then transferred back to the buy side—Ariba—which automatically produces a purchase requisition and sends it to the supplier.

To recap, the order process enablers are selection mechanisms (including pricing, product availability, shipping, and export and tax rules), payment mechanisms, contracts, order transaction management (including fraud transaction mechanisms and historical transaction details), and billing. The quality of order management depends on the level of integration of order process enablers. A company with less integration would only have rudimentary features available, whereas a company with higher level of integration would have best-of-breed features.

Metrics for the order component are order accuracy rate, revenue per channel ratio, number of products per sales order, integrated pricing, inventory control availability and accuracy, number of payment mechanisms available, usability index for product or service selection and payment mechanisms, percentage of cross-sell sales, percentage of up-sell sales, order tracking availability, order tracking accuracy, fraud checking mechanism reliability, historical transaction details availability, billing availability and accuracy, billing error rate, availability of credit card verification services, availability of electronic funds transfer, and product or service customization index. Supply chain metrics such as inventory turns and order fill rates apply.

Bob:

Our company handles order management well. The most commonly used payment mechanism is still the credit card. The service level agreements (SLAs) with our contractors need work. We usually need stronger and more comprehensive guarantees. Some of our partners meet us halfway, but I believe that they have difficulty with the SLAs too because the systems performance monitoring tools are not sophisticated enough to determine what we need to do to create a robust system.

Sue:

We *do* know the importance of order management in our company; we've been burned before. To leverage our early-mover advantage, we released a pay-per-use service to the market, but our billing system wasn't set up to handle it. Many users that downloaded the product received our hosted services for free! Even worse, it confused our customers more when we started billing them weeks after they had begun to use the service.

Tom di Marco and BOEING

DOING IT TODAY

Boeing is a customer-focused organization in the business of selling airplanes. Customers need to have parts to run their aircraft, and Boeing must do everything it possibly can to ensure that the customers have a great experience with the company. One of the challenges of a global customer base is that customer problems are very diverse. Compare running a jet at 40,000 feet that crosses the Atlantic once a day with an aircraft that operates in Hawaii, making many trips a day but never getting above 10,000 feet. There are huge differences in corrosion and wear-and-tear on the two aircraft. Depending on the operator, some aircraft may be kept in service for as long as 35 years, whereas others may be retired much earlier. Customers also wanted Boeing to react quickly. It was no longer an option to take days getting a spare part to a customer—it was wanted in a matter of hours! The model was changing with the customer. Customers wanted things to happen in real time versus using batch and forward methods that were more consistent with older business practices.

Boeing had no ubiquitous access for its global customer base that was cost effective to run, that is, until the World Wide Web. The company recognized the capabilities of the Web, that it could be the customer-facing portion of their Spares Ordering Non-stop Inventory Control (SONIC) program. Boeing's Part Analysis and Requirements Tracking (PART) Page complements SONIC.

The Federal Aviation Administration (FAA) dictates how the products are to be handled and stored, and Boeing adheres to the regulations closely. The distribution centers can be repositories for frequently moving parts and also for very large parts. The SONIC system knows where all the parts are in the world, where the order originates, when a customer receives his or her order, what customers typically want to buy, any alternatives that may be available, and where the customer must go to get the part. It then generates all the appropriate shipping information. Boeing's team of programmers is focused on this system, which was developed in-house. It uses bar code technology to track the parts through the entire process from picking, packing, over-boxing, and shipping. The customer can log into the Boeing PART Page and see the status of the order at any stage.

continued

The future is in new aircraft, which create a whole new set of challenges for spares support. As an example, the Boeing Business Jet introduces a new type of customer into the equation. These customers may not have special departments for ordering parts for the planes—they do the ordering themselves. However, their primary touch point for information is through a cellular telephone. Now they want Web access on their phone so that they may have the same rich information normally obtained through traditional browser interfaces. Future thoughts about where the Boeing PART Page initiative could go is that sensors in the plane can detect when parts need repair or overhaul. The plane would "place the order," and the parts would be there on the plane's arrival. Now that's integration!

Fulfill

Fulfillment involves managing information on product or service movement. It is a subset of knowledge management because it requires knowledge of product movement or supply chain information. Many businesses only track orders until they are shipped, not until they are delivered to the customer. In addition, some products require installation, configuration, and testing after delivery. Fulfillment refers to the product delivery process, which is based on the nature of the goods (in other words, whether they are digital or nondigital). It is important to determine the nature of the goods and therefore the fulfillment process—ensuring customers get their product or service is the crux of e-business. *Fulfillment* is sending a product, delivering a service, or any situation in which the terms of an agreement are completed with a customer. Your customer wants you to get the right product to the right place at the right time, and you want to do this at the lowest possible cost. A fulfillment strategy may involve your supplier delivering your product directly to your customer instead of to your business. *Returns* are an iterative loop between fulfillment and support and are used when the customer has a problem and needs to send products back and possibly get replacements. Many online businesses overlook the returns process.

The critical enablers in the fulfillment process are back-end process integration, delivery capability, and global sales governance. Back-end processes are those business processes that are not visible to the customer. Integration of business processes means that a company's processes are seamlessly connected—and it affects customers' access to information about product availability and lead times. Businesses that start out with a good understanding of e-business have an advantage because they design their entire business from a customer's perspective. All the systems interact with common databases to gain access to requested data. A good example of a true e-business that has tied all its systems together, from order processing to order management to fulfillment to support, is amazon.com. In contrast, the online company Chapters has different hardware and software servers for each of its online businesses, which include chapters.com and chaptersglobe.ca. The customers have difficulty using the site because the businesses operate autonomously and do not cross-reference their customer data warehouse. In addition, customers who purchase from one of the online stores are not allowed to return books to the bricks-and-mortar (physical) store, which creates problems because customers often don't differentiate between the two types of businesses.

Many enterprises fail to realize the true cost of fulfillment, and they think their Web-commerce transactions are profitable. However, they are actually often unprofitable because they don't change their back-end fulfillment process.[12] You must plan a strategy to sell products using multiple mediums and develop a strategy for back-end fulfillment. For example, Clearwater Fine Foods hired a director of e-commerce to develop a fulfillment strategy, develop a customer facing system, and ultimately tie the new system into the back-end system. The company tied in its existing customer-focused fulfillment strategy from telesales and face-to-face sales.

Delivery is *how* the products or service orders are fulfilled. Delivery can range from using a computer server to deliver electronic goods to physically delivering tangible goods. The digital goods are the easiest to fulfill but may be tied to an e-commerce transaction engine. The entire procedure for digital goods delivery should be totally automated. When goods are nondigital, delivery becomes more complex. Enterprises in a B2C model may have to employ a "pick-and-pack" strategy for their product fulfillment processes. Retail music Web businesses that allow you to pick a series of songs by various artists, download them, and burn them to one CD are using a pick-and-pack model for delivery of digital goods. B2B businesses may have to ship partial pallets instead of full loads.Companies ship partial pallets when they don't have enough material to ship a full load. In the past, customers paid for the unused space. Now customers can share containers. Special shipping needs have given rise to container aggregation shipping models and e-business shipping companies such as iShip.com. Many companies use outsource fulfillment agencies such as United Parcel Service (UPS) and FedEx, which have shipping capabilities that the firm does not have.

Integrated resourcing (IR) encompasses fulfillment, customer communication, and flexible manufacturing and distribution of products. The key to IR success is having multimodal transportation systems, integrated communications networks, and enterprise knowledge about the product.[13] Agile manufacturers are invaluable to operational partners because they incorporate all the customer-driven principles, including IR, seamless business environments, and an environment that is conducive to continuous innovation. The IR system must be able to handle sales as well as returns, a task that is a challenge for virtual Internet businesses as well as traditional brick-and-mortar stores that have an Internet presence.

Multimodal transportation systems include interfacing with many types of transportation components, including containers, trucks, trains, planes, and others. Materials handling systems serve as intermodal integrators, providing seamless connections among different transport modes and the manufacturing and distribution facilities. Integrated communications networks form the backbone that allows all components of the virtual integration team to communicate with each other. Unlike a proprietary network, the openness of the network provides interoperability for all. Enterprise product knowledge should focus on establishing a knowledge management system that allows the entire enterprise to tap into the information about the product, such as design, support, and upgrades. Access to product information is important for IR success because it helps dictate which types of delivery and returns fulfillment options are available.

Global sales present fulfillment challenges. Many businesses get very excited about the possibility of selling products and services to customers throughout the world. The difficulty is that some businesses don't have all the policies and procedures needed to export globally. They often expose themselves to a significant risk of violating customs or trade compliance laws, which can lead to fines and negative publicity. Global export capabilities involve integration of the governance stakeholder functions. If the back-end integration, delivery, and governance factors are not considered, the operation could decrease profitability and permanently damage customer relationships.

The metrics for fulfillment are the back-end integration index, delivery capabilities index, and governance rules knowledge index. The delivery capability is also measured through a customer-added value index, a rating that is used to determine whether the delivery method increases value for the customer (for example, by giving them exactly the songs they ordered when they used a pick-and-pack model to order a CD), whether value increases as a result of lower transportation costs, or whether value increases through availability of stocks that are always on hand because of continuous replenishment programs. A low index rating is given to companies with limited enabler capabilities, whereas companies that receive high ratings have all of the enablers and are "pushing the envelope" in terms of their fulfillment capabilities. Metrics also include missed deliveries, average time to commit an order, and elapsed time between order receipt and delivery.

Bob:

We sell and deliver tangible goods. IR is a very important part of our delivery equation. Sites that allow us to rent spaces in container loads (rather than requiring us to rent an entire container for a few items) provide us with enormous value.

Sue:

We are considering fulfilling some of our product and service orders over the Internet. We worry mainly about security, bandwidth, and most importantly, our customer's desire to use the Internet in this way. We plan to keep our finger on the pulse of new technologies to address our concerns.

Support

Historically, the term *customer service* referred to providing service to customers after they had made a purchase. Merchants now realize that well-executed, proactive customer service can convert shoppers into buyers, turn buyers into repeat purchasers, and even increase the incremental purchase value of each customer. *Self-service* incorporates personalization and trust and encompasses the ability of the company to handle its customers' desires. Trust creates a feeling of belonging and privacy; compliance with governance rules engenders customer trust. Best-of-breed companies have all of their information available in a customer-accessible, Netcentric environment in which customers are able to modify and update their information. Order tracking is one of the best-known self-serve applications.

As an e-business merchant, you must get the most out of all the points of contact with your customer, business partners, and business partners' customers. The CRM areas that are required are based on a continuum of customer service ranging from high-volume, low-value calls to calls requiring human intervention to calls requiring a third-party arbitration or mediation. The customer service levels can also be based on the your company's customer segmentation and could factor in the customer's value to the company; for example, the higher-value customers may receive extra attention, or perks, from the company. Of course, the customer support standard should never be low—it should always foster the transition of a low-value customer into a high-value customer. You should incorporate a method to receive and track customer feedback so that your company can continuously improve its customer service.

A critical enabler of good customer support is knowledge management—in the form of customer contact point integration—because this enabler includes strategy, technology, and most importantly, customers. *Contact point integration* is important because customers communicate with an organization in many ways. For example, Stora Forest Industries in Sweden developed its first Web site in 1996. The company set up the site to keep customers informed about which products were being offered, not realizing that the site would become a conduit for customer service. Like many initial Web sites, the site's builder was its maintainer and wore many hats. The company was swamped with e-mail, and the poor IT professional who was in charge tried to answer all of the customer inquiries. The response time was abysmal, some times as long as 10 days. The response was routed through to the appropriate CSR and dealt with accordingly. It took the company a year to recognize its problem. One company who *has* carried out the integration well is Charles Schwab. The business handles more than 8,000 messages per week using an integrated response system that only requires 35 CSRs. An automatic response system combines e-mail, brick-and-mortar brokerage offices, and toll-free numbers into one common customer service area. CSRs must answer each e-mail within 24 hours but normally respond within 6 to 8 hours.

Synchrony Communications, a CRM vendor for small and medium enterprises, takes e-service a step further. The company has created e-relationships by having its customer deal with the same CSR or CSR team regardless of the contact point being used by the customer. In addition, Synchrony's e-CRM solution improves customer interactions in multiple channels; they receive an e-mail, respond by fax, and follow up with a phone call.

Customer contact information that is stored in your company's database should be used to inform customers of product updates and upgrades. Keeping customers informed is yet another way to engage and support the customer.

Current contact management software features include collaborative white boarding, real-time application demonstrations and sharing, text chat, voice chat, form sharing, and Web site co-navigation. Web site co-navigation, or "follow-me browsing," allows each Web page that is viewed by a customer or agent to be visible to both parties. Collaborative white boarding allows customers, business partners, and agents to draw diagrams or to circle and highlight points in real time over the network, whereas form sharing allows agents to help customers fill out fields. Assessment features included in contact management software include assessments of presentation tools and performance, integration of multiple media, security, ease of use, management, online help, archiving, and reporting. Many vendors offer supersets of these collaborative services. Among them are PlaceWare, Active-Touch, Centra, Contigo Software, Envoy Global, SneakerLabs, Cisco, and Lotus.

Hewlett Packard (HP) uses PlaceWare's PlaceServer Technology Framework in its virtual classroom for training and education. Businesses can use the classroom for training customers and employees. Pivotal Corp. uses ActiveTouch's WebEx Meeting Center services, which provide powerful collaborative meeting tools to its customers who use the Pivotal e-Relationship 2 CRM package. Pivotal users can schedule and conduct live (audio- and voice-integrated) Web-based meetings or sales presentations with customers or other business partners. Software demonstrations, document sharing, document annotation, and Web site co-navigation are supported.

Cisco offers an intelligent contact management (ICM) product that interfaces with CRM solutions software provided by companies such as Siebel, Vantive, and Clarify. It can handle multiple contact centers and hundreds of customer or business participants. One nifty feature of ICM is its contact routing ability, which matches agent profiles to customer profiles so that appropriately skilled agents handle the customer calls. Companies without this type of service can result in problems for customers who need assistance. One customer had the frustrating and time-wasting experience of calling for assistance with a software product and being routed to a totally unsuitable help desk CSR. Even though the customer was a representative from another software company (and therefore obviously a very knowledgeable user), the company's first contact point was a frontline service representative who had only been trained to handle low-level users of the product. Situations like this get even worse when a customer who needs to speak with a product expert gets this type of frontline CSR, and the CSR insists on trying to find the solution in a database.

Knowledge management enables support through the provision of complete customer history in real time, maintenance, and access to corporate knowledge bases or industry knowledge sets. For example, IndustrySupport.com contains problem resolution descriptions and suggested e-mail responses. A company with a low knowledge management enabler level would have contact points with disparate systems and inconsistent interfaces, and a high-level company would have total integration across all customer contact points with one consistent interface to the information.

Successful customer support is affected by the level of customer interaction that is built into the system. For example, if you call Dell's customer service center, they provide all levels of service, including external supplier (third-level) support. Success is measured by the seamlessness of the customer support continuum.

High-level measures for the customer support component include the customer retention ratio and customer satisfaction level. A personalization index assesses the "warmth" of the business relationship with the customer. A low value indicates an impersonal relationship, and a high value suggests a close relationship. A knowledge access index measures how easy it is to access enterprise and external knowledge such as customer or product information and expertise in newsgroups. Other metrics are e-mail response system availability, average response time to service a call, abandonment rate (the number of customers who make a service call and then hang up before being served), elevation or transfer rate, and call duration. Numerous calls about a product or service may indicate potential product or service problems. The quantity of customer feedback can be used to measure customer loyalty. The company's response to customer feedback is its "customer listening quotient."

Bob:

Good service is very important to our business, and we are always looking for new ways to improve it. We don't have a good method to evaluate our existing and new customer services. The eBiz Readiness! framework is a good launch pad from which we can create and implement a metrics program for customer service.

Sue:

I'm interested in the new service software offerings for our small business. We are limited by our budget, and I'm hoping an option will be to rent the software. I don't know all the implications, but I hope outsourcing the software services is as easy as outsourcing my payroll services. I will use the framework to try to find out where my customers are heading and to ensure that the company we buy from has high standards and has all their bases covered.

Steve Ehrlich and NUANCE

DOING IT TODAY

Nuance Communications is a leading provider of natural-language speech-recognition software for self-service applications. Nuance currently sells three technologies, one of which is voice recognition. Voice recognition technology identifies which language a person is speaking and what is being said. Natural language understanding is the second; this technology allows people to speak naturally and is able to interpret the information. The third technology is voice authentication, a technology that uses a voice print to identify each unique person. These technologies are being used in a wide variety of ways; they are used in call centers to improve customer service, and voice dialing and voice portal services are used by telecommunications companies. Speech recognition is typically used to replace or augment the CSR or agent. Companies are not just thinking about what to do for their Web site customers but what to do for their phone customers as well.

A service call typically costs between $1 and $16 per call per CSR. Nuance's voice products reduce complex calls to about a tenth of the cost ($1 to $1.50 per call). Companies also use Nuance's products to provide better customer service. Lengthy phone wait times are an increasing problem because as people shop more online, they are using the phone more to buy. These calls are queued because only a certain number of CSRs are available to handle them. Customers get frustrated by long wait times, and some companies exacerbate the problem by using touch-tone systems—customers just hate this! Many of them just "press 0 for the operator" but still end up in a queue anyway. Voice technology products allow companies to handle many more customers simultaneously and thus effectively decrease wait times.

"A customer's experience on the Web is very different from the one on the phone," said Steve Erlich, vice president of marketing. "They go to the Web site, which is very personalized. They come to the phone, and it's 'press 1 for this, press 2 for that'—a big letdown. I think companies are realizing that they have to provide consistent Web service regardless of whether the customer wants to interact with them through the Web, through a personal digital assistant (PDA),

continued

or through the phone. And the commonality is that the applications, business rules, and database have to be the same for all touch points. Thus Nuance addresses the problem by providing a voice interface to the same rules engine that is powering the Web site. Companies can create voice commerce applications by building on their e-commerce investment."

Nuance has a vision that involves having interconnected voice sites, a vision called the Voice Web. "You can think of a site as a mirror of a Web site, except that certain things don't make sense," Ehrlich said. "For example, you can't see pictures. There are certain things that are appropriate for the phone. And the opposite is true. There are certain things you can do on the phone but can't on the Web site. I might get to a voice site and want to call customer service. The functionality of the voice site could be to direct me to the right department to get my problem solved. I might use a voice browser to browse different voice sites, much like I use a Web browser today, except that the voice browser only has a voice-user interface and runs in the network. Over time, we will see the merger of Web and voice. The compelling and productive interface of the future is really a combination of both; it is a lot easier to talk than type and easier to read than listen."

Regarding his vision for Nuance and its industry, Ehrlich said, "The day is coming when I will pick up the phone and won't get a dial tone—I will get, 'How can I help you, Steve?' An intelligent dial tone! I could then call a buddy, call a business, connect to my favorite voice portal, or search for information. Today, when I go to the Yahoo! site to look for furniture, they don't know which furniture store I am searching for, but when I pick up the phone in the future, I will be able to search in the same way by voice. Today I wouldn't pick up the phone unless I knew who I was calling! We have a different model emerging. We are trying to bring the Internet model to the phone for the first time. You will pick up the phone and say, 'I need a ticket to New York,' and your voice browser will say, 'Okay. I'll connect you to your preferred travel agent on the Voice Web.' That kind of model is definitely worth investigating!"

Questions You May Want to Ask

Overall

- How do *you* define CRM?
- Which of the CRM vendors you evaluated impressed you the most and why?

- What types of measures did you take or will you take to accommodate globalization in your sales, marketing, and service?
- How do you measure your organization's sales, service, and marketing capabilities and compare them to other organizations?
- How are you effectively working with your customers?
- Sales are often a stand-alone entity. How do you get marketing and service (people and processes) involved so that you can integrate touch points?
- How do you support team selling?
- How can you move from a transactional interaction view to an extended lifecycle view of the customer?
- How do you plan to keep the loyalty of your existing customers?
- How do you measure customer erosion?

Leverage of Multiple Channels for Selling

- How many sales channels do you support?
- Are your customer touch points integrated? For example, if a customer were to cross channels by using the phone as well as the Internet to report a problem, would both these contact points be aware that the other was contacted by the same customer? Can salient customer history be viewed electronically at each touch point?
- How do you combine inside sales with the Internet? Call centers with field sales? Do you or will you support multichannel sales?
- Do you use sales compensation technology to mitigate sales between internal and external sales agents?
- How do you distribute knowledge that is generated *beyond* as well as *during* the sales process?

Engage

- What does *engage* mean to you? Does it cover both new and repeat sales? Does it involve customer acquisition or retention or both?
- How do you target the "right" customers for your company?
- Did you redefine your engage process to be suitable for e-business?
- What types of technologies do you use to support your engage process?
- What roles do mass customization, "one-on-one marketing," and personalization play in your engage process?
- Do you use agents in your engage process (such as MyVirtualModel at Landsend.com)?

- Landsend.com also uses technologies such as Click2Talk to enable a Web user to speak directly to a CSR. Does your company use similar technologies? What are they?
- How do you extend the customer's relationship?
- How do you use your business community to support your engage process for new and repeat sales and promote customer loyalty for customer retention?
- How does your business sell to, market to, and service the community?
- What type of technology do you use to store and analyze information about your customers?

Order

- Does your business have point-and-click, real-time shopping environment support? Does it include accurate, up-to-date pricing, product features, and product delivery times?
- How many payment systems (for example, micropayments, credit cards, cash, flooz [an online form of currency]) are available?
- Is your order management fully or quasi-automated?
- Does your back-end system facilitate access to product availability, pricing and information about lead times, and order status?
- Can the customer view historical transaction details online?
- How many billing mechanisms (for example, pay per use, total purchase) does your business support?
- If you have multiple billing mechanisms, does your business support multiple billing systems, or does one billing system handle the different billing modes?
- Is your fullfillment process or channel visible throughout the process to your customer?
- How mature is your delivery infrastructure? What are its components?
- Does your enterprise have all the policies and procedures in place to support global export?

Support

- What is your online store's returns policy?
- In what ways do you personalize service for your customers?
- Are all service support touch points integrated?
- What types of channels are used to provide service? What are the costs per channel?

Using the Evaluation Framework

To use the framework, you must determine which components are most important by weighting each independently, assessing the systems, plotting the results, and evaluating the resulting plot. The framework allows you to assess whether your e-business is strong enough in the areas that are most important. The gauge brings an overall perspective to the e-business readiness, whereas the details are contained within the plots.

Recall that the rating scale is the qualitative score given to the assessed system for each component. Each component has one or more determining factors composed of criteria that can be judged. The weighting scale essentially allows the e-business to factor the relative importance of each constituent component. (See Chapter 2 for details on the scales.)

Small-Business Perspective: Customer Stakeholder Assessment (SMEDistributor)

Sue:

We are investigating companies that provide small businesses with CRM solutions. Pivotal, SalesLogix, Onyx, and Upshot are under review. We are analyzing the investment and maintenance costs of a CRM package and are considering our options. Many of the CRM software packages have more features than we need.

SMEDistributor is a company that distributes business machines—fax machines, photocopiers, computers, and typewriters—and is currently selling to the Latin American and Caribbean markets. The company's motto is, "People, Solutions, and Commitment to Service." SMEDistributor also sells software packages and provides software training packages for its customers. The company is small; it has an annual revenue of $10 million. Its financial systems are computerized. Present points of contact are fax machines, telephones, marketing representative visits, and Web pages. The distributor has a mobile sales force and two reselling channel partners. Together, they mainly sell to seven industry verticals—manufacturing, oil and gas, retail, insurance, education, media, and government.

The service department has a mixed customer service history. Customers are often unhappy because it takes multiple service calls to fix their problems. They are also unhappy because the equipment breakdown rate is high, resulting in frequent service calls. Some customer differentiation and prioritization exists—the managing director ensures that the service reps are aware of who the big customers are. Missed service appointments are also a problem. Rescheduling occurs at times because parts have not arrived on time, leaving customers with inoperable equipment for long periods.

The company receives sales leads from various sources. Sometimes a sales lead comes from an inquiry that a secretary writes down on a scrap of paper and puts on a sales rep's desk. Whether this lead falls into a black hole or is pursued depends on the sales rep. SMEDistributor would like to have more management control over leads. Lead accountability and management are a requirement of any CRM package in which SMEDistributor invests. Sales personnel often complain about accidentally using old price lists and the amount of time it takes to create quotes for customers. A sore point for SMEDistributor's mobile sales force is the lack of real-time access to up-to-date price lists and new marketing information.

When salespeople follow up a lead or receive a call from a customer, they should be able to quickly pull up all pertinent customer information on a screen. A scan of a customer's buying history can quickly identify cross-sell or up-sell opportunities. If customers are online, the opportunity to obtain and record more knowledge about themselves should present itself.

The distributor routinely sends new price lists and marketing literature to its resellers. The marketing literature sent is usually a subset of what actually exists. The sales personnel selecting which material to pass on to the resellers must make subjective judgments about what is important enough to send and whether it is cost effective to distribute all of the marketing literature. Unfortunately, the indirect channel partners then complain that they don't have as many marketing resources to work with as the distributor. SMEDistributor recognizes that it needs to address this concern because knowledge or content needs to be present at every customer contact point. Another issue that needs to be addressed is targeting customers. Sometimes the distributor and reseller target the same customer, so salespeople from different companies compete against each other to sell the same product.

Orders from other countries are faxed to SMEDistributor. The information must be entered twice: once in the fax and again in the order system. SMEDistributor has its own "customs" department to deal with the rules and regulations of import and export to the countries that are part of the business' market. Delivery capabilities are well developed, and delivery lead times are rarely a problem. Although the stores and delivery process systems are computerized, they are stand-alone processes. Items can be tracked on the phone using confirmation numbers. Because SMEDistributor has no dedicated CSRs, customers often tie up the time of accounting personnel with calls to verify bills and terms of agreements.

SMEDistributor wants to improve its overall customer satisfaction, customer retention, and customer profitability ratios. The company aims to accomplish the following:

- Resolve customers' problems after their first service call
- Integrate supply chain management with service so that replacement parts will arrive on time
- Identify customers who cost the company a lot of money in service costs in comparison with the revenue they bring in
- Identify customers who might buy service packages
- Increase revenue through higher sales
- Improve the ratio of accurate quotes
- Improve the ratio of accurate orders
- Use the computer software support calls as opportunities to sell software training packages

The eBiz Readiness!™ framework analysis of the case reveals that the engage, order, fulfill, and support components are all equally weighted as a 4 (very important). Customers can browse through product catalogs and price lists. Sales agents are available to help with comparing, configuring, and interacting, as well as just to listen. Up-selling is relatively easy, but cross-selling is more difficult because the company has no common customer database. The ignored sales leads and use of outdated price lists indicate the urgent need for real-time access to information that is available to sales reps as well as customers. Cross-channel coordination has some of the requisite pieces, but others are missing, such as full distribution of material and customer assignments. Collectively, the engage component is assigned a rating of 1—rudimentary features are available but not all common features are present.

The outdated pricing lists and other information affect product and service selection. Otherwise, taxes and shipping procedures are excellent because SMEDistributor has its own customs department. Payment and billing systems are working well. Transaction details are all being logged. Collectively, the order component is assigned a 2—all requirements are present but are separately administered.

The fulfill capability is a stand-alone process. The stores and delivery processes are not integrated in the back-end financial systems. The fulfill governance is well done because of the customs department. Collectively, the fulfill component is assigned a 2—all criteria are present but separately administered.

Support is the lowest ranked component at SMEDistributor. Customer information is maintained solely in the financial system. The data are not available to the marketing or service representatives. No common database stores records of customers' interactions with the business. Phone conversations about products and services and complaints are often unrecorded. No automated knowledge bases exist. Collectively, the support component is assigned a 1—rudimentary features are available, but not all common features are present. Because the components are all equally weighted, it is sufficient to plot the evaluated ratings versus the benchmark ratings.

According to the eBiz Readiness!™ RadarScope, the company's overall customer readiness assessment (Figure 3-2) shows that SMEDistributor is just starting out. They have many gaps to fill according to the framework. The plot in Figure 3-3 shows that the weakest areas are "engage" and "support." The standard CRM packages on the market thoroughly address both these components. The spines of the polar plot, which are labeled with component names such as *engage, order, fulfill,* and *support,* are all axes. The score for each component is plotted on its corresponding axis.

To solve the time problem created by customers who call in to verify bills and credit terms, SMEDistributor has decided to put the process on the Web. The company will allow customers to log in to a secure site to review their billing history and payment terms. SMEDistributor further plans to automatically alert

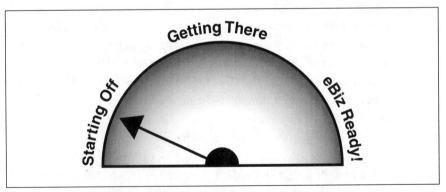

**Figure 3-2   RadarScope View of SMEDistributor's Customer
                Readiness Level**

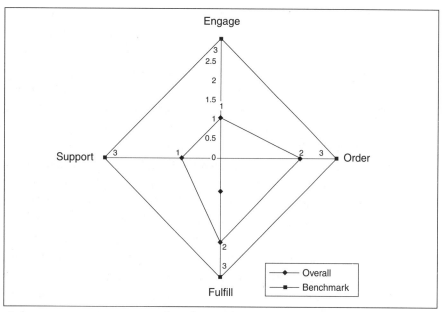

Figure 3-3   SMEDistributor Customer Stakeholder Readiness Assessment

its customers a few days before their preferred terms expire by sending reminder e-mails. Customers will be happy to be reminded so that they can save money by either paying no or lower interest amounts. SMEDistributor is satisfied because it may reduce its overall average cash-to-cash cycle time (the time from SMEDistributor's payment for an item and the receipt of the customer's payment for the same item). They also plan on allowing the customer to view current lead times and track the status for their ordered products—a handy self-service feature.

Big-Business Perspective: Customer Stakeholder Assessment (BBFinance)

Bob:

If you would like to see how other banks stack up to BBFinanceOnline, go to www.scorecard.com and www. bankrate.com for ratings on the effectiveness of the bank's e-initiatives.

Big Business Finance Online (BBFinanceOnline) uses technology to continuously offer new and innovative services to its customers. It is expanding its old and very established bricks-and-mortar bank with online banking services. The company would like their clients to able to do their banking from any spot in the world at any time—365 days a year. BBFinanceOnline inherits trust from its bricks-and-mortar counterpart. Customers know that when the network is down, the local branch doors are usually open!

BBFinanceOnline engages and retains clients through its easily accessible account services (for example, savings, loan, line of credit, credit card), convenience, numerous options, and flexibility. From simple funds transfers and bill payments to complex trade finance transactions, customers can carry out many banking activities. Integrated account information and transfer capability allows Web-initiated, same-day transfers between brokerages and banking accounts and shows balances for trading and regular accounts. Instant credit approvals and mortgage preapprovals, check reorders, and account transaction statements are standard services. Other services include check return and electronic bill presentation. Check presentation allows customers to view their processed checks online—a function that is supported by optical scanning technology. Electronic bill presentation allows customers to view and pay all bills online and includes automatic bill and debit reconciliation options. Savings are tremendous for the biller (because there are no mailing expenses), and the client benefits from the convenience. Transactions are easy to execute and secure. Fulfillment is mainly carried out in the digital medium, although checks and statements are mailed through regular post office mail.

BBFinanceOnline outsources credit card processing, check processing, and other payment documents; custodial and payroll activities; document management for mortgage loans; and technology infrastructure management. To access cash and perform debits, customers can use a card, wireless point of sale devices, Web phones, cell phones with "smart card," and the telephone. All contact points are fully integrated.

BBFinanceOnline has formed alliances with others to share the costs of administrative office operational processes, including check verification and presentation, and make them more efficient. Online customer service support is limited. Many companies' Web pages immediately transfer the client to a CSR in certain situations (for example, when a user is having difficulties logging in). Currently no natural language agent is available online that allows customers to ask finance-related questions.

BBFinanceOnline achieves the benchmark rating of 3—all factors are present and interoperable—in all four customer component categories (Figure 3-4). The engage component is assigned a rating of 4, exceeding the benchmark because the building blocks for future bolt-on services are present. The results of evaluation using the eBiz Readiness!™ framework are plotted on a polar plot chart showing all of the components for the customer stakeholder. Figure 3-5 illustrates the results

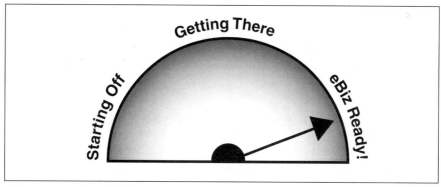

Figure 3-4   RadarScope View of BBFinanceOnline Customer Readiness Level

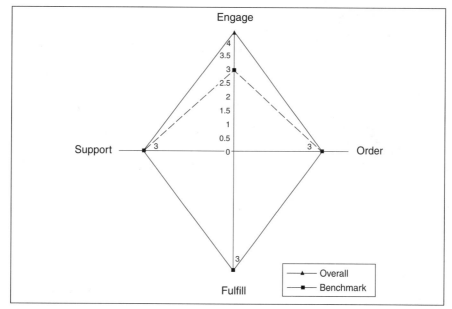

Figure 3-5   BBFinanceOnline Customer Capability Assessment

within an overall polar plot for BBFinanceOnline's business. The figure shows that the e-business already has strong engagement, order, and fulfillment components but needs to strengthen its Web customer support. Every customer component is very important and is equally weighted as a 4, thus the rating score for BBFinanceOnline is plotted versus the benchmark rating.

Are You Ready?

Table 3-1 provides a snapshot of all the components, enablers, and metrics essential for successful interaction with the customer stakeholder. Some customer metrics have indexes. A low index value is a poor rating; a high index value is a good rating.

Highlights from this chapter include the following:

- Total CRM covers your direct business contacts with customers, your channel partners' indirect contacts with customers, and customer contact management within your supply chain. It integrates aspects of supply chain management and partner relationship management.
- Channel partners may plug gaps in areas such as fulfillment, market development, market presence and penetration, and implementation and execution capabilities.
- Customer contact points are face-to-face, e-mail, CTI, IVR, call routing switch, fax, Web chat, and machine-to-machine interactions.
- For total customer data integration, you need to technology-enable your face-to-face customer contact points and store information on customer interactions.
- The eBiz Readiness!™ measurement framework shows your e-business's level of readiness, weaknesses, and strengths in regards to customer support.

Table 3-1   Components, Enablers, and Metrics for the Customer Stakeholder

Components*	Enablers	Metrics
Engage	• Browse function • Search function • Comparison • Configuration • Interaction • Questioning • Listening • Interactive marketing,real-time availability of information • Broad coverage of prospects • Cross-channel coordination for marketing, sales and service	Channel partner coordination index Comparison shopping index Convenience index (low—inconvenient, high—very convenient) Cost of adding new products and product options Customer acquisitions ratio Customer loyalty and satisfaction indexes Customer profitability ratio Customer wallet share Customer win back ratio Customer win/loss ratio Lead routing and tracking time Number of new and effective marketing campaigns in the last 6 months Number of new interaction methods Partner loyalty and satisfaction indexes Pricing index (low—poor pricing, high—competitive pricing) Speed to market with new products or services and product or service options Usability index
Order	• Selection mechanisms (including pricing, product availability, shipping, and export and tax rules) • Payment mechanisms • Contracts • Order transaction management (including fraud transaction mechanisms and historical transaction details) • Billing	Accuracy of point-of-sale information capture Availability of credit card verification services Availability of electronic funds transfer Billing availability and accuracy Close ratio Cost of governance compliance Selling quality consistency index Costs savings (clerical + training + overhead) Customer loyalty and satisfaction indexes Fraud-checking mechanism reliability Historical transaction details availability

99

Table 3-1 Components, Enablers, and Metrics for the Customer Stakeholder (*cont.*)

Components*	Enablers	Metrics
Order (*cont.*)		Integrated pricing and inventory control availability (that is, pricing agility)
		Manager selling/mentoring time ratio
		Number of payment mechanisms available
		Number of products per sales order
		Order cycle time
		Order error rate
		Order tracking accuracy
		Order tracking availability
		Partner loyalty and satisfaction indexes
		Percentage of cross-sell sales
		Percentage of up-sell sales
		Pricing accuracy
		Pricing customization index
		Product/service customization index
		Quality assurance (need for third-party price review) index
		Inventory accuracy
		Quote accuracy
		Revenue per channel ratio
		Sales commission administration cost, time, and accuracy
		Sales forecasting accuracy
		Selling time ratio
		Time and cost to prepare quote
		Usability of product/service selection mechanism
Fulfill	• Back-end process integration • Delivery capability • Returns policy • Global sales governance	Back-end process integration index
		Customer-added value index (low price, convenience, satisfaction)
		Customer loyalty and satisfaction indexes
		Delivery capability index
		Global sales governance index
		Integrated resourcing index (that is, multimodal fulfillment)

Table 3-1 Components, Enablers, and Metrics for the Customer Stakeholder (*cont.*)

Components*	Enablers	Metrics
Fulfill (*cont.*)		Partner loyalty and satisfaction indexes
		Missed deliveries
		Average time to commit an order
		Elapsed time between order receipt and delivery
Support	• Complete customer history in real time	Abandonment rate
	• Access to corporate knowledge bases or industry knowledge sets	Average response time
		Call duration
	• Automatic product updates	Chargeable call duration
	• Self-serve applications	Chargeable/nonchargeable service problem ratio
	• Single interface or portal to business knowledge	Community index (for example, access to expertise in newsgroups)
		Customer feedback availability
		Customer retention ratio
		Customer satisfaction level
		Elevation and transfer rate
		E-mail response system availability
		Knowledge access index
		Noncharageable call duration
		Number of incident reports per product
		Personalization index
		Product or service knowledge levels
		Partner loyalty and satisfaction indexes
		Customer loyalty and satisfaction indexes

*Recall that the knowledge, trust, and technology enablers are common to all components (see Chapter 2).

Statistics and Numbers

- 49 million: according to BizRate.com, the number of orders that were placed online during November 1999 and December 1999
- $1.1 billion: according to NPD Group, 1999's online apparel sales, which were double that of 1998; $2 billion: expected online apparel sales in 2000
- $40 million: the price Mark Cuban paid for a Gulfstream jet through an online purchase on Yahoo!
- 51 percent: according to the Boston Consulting Group, the number of Internet users who have purchased goods or services online (survey of 12,000 Internet users in North America)
- $14 billion: the amount that the International Data Corporation (IDC) estimates companies will spend on e-support by 2003

References

[1]"Evolving Online Shopping Strategies: From Customer Acquisition to Customer Retention." October 1997. www.jup.com.

[2]"The Experienced Customer." Fall 1999. www.fastcompany.com/nc/001/024.html.

[3]Swerdlow, F. "Customer Service Online." *Digital Commerce Strategies.* Jupiter Communications, 1998.

[4]www.vignette.com

[5]Amuso, C. "Spending to Save Money: Interactive Service Web Sites." *Research Note.* Gartner Group, August 1999.

[6]www.askjeeves.com

[7]www.buy.com and www.compwarehouse.com

[8]www.canada.com

[9]Seybold, P. B. *Customers.com: How to Create a Profitable Business Strategy for the Internet and Beyond.* New York: Times Books, 1998.

[10]www.killer-apps.com.

[11]www.dell.com

[12]Enslow, B. "The Fallacies of Web Commerce Fulfillment." *Inside Gartner Group Report* March 1999: 1.

[13]Kasanda, J. D. "Innovation Infrastructure for Agile Manufacturers." *Sloan Management Review* Winter 1998: 76.

CHAPTER FOUR

Get Everybody Working: The E-Business Community

> A business community—whether it is a collection of strategic partnerships, closed or open, asynchronous or synchronous—represents access to common services, human expertise or knowledge, and content—providing us with a means of working together.

Getting You Prepared

We have introduced you to the concept of community in e-business, so now we are going to investigate the factors that comprise a community—why a community is so critical to the e-business equation and what can be done to build one. You need to understand the many types of communities and the circumstances in which you need one type versus another. By the end of this chapter, you will be able to determine the types and composition of the communities that can serve your needs, allowing you to build the proper community for your e-business.

Our first experiences with online communities were in chat rooms, where we talked to virtual citizens about windsurfing and other topics. These initial community interaction tools have been augmented, so now we can find communities rich with knowledge about topics of interest at whatever good site we go to. Previously we could only ask questions about books that we wanted to buy; now we can go to industry verticals (companies that focus on a specific segment of an industry, such as steel) to find information from "our" virtual community—our common bond. The community makes purchasing easier and also makes us want to return because we have good experiences. Communities definitely have a "method to their madness"—methods that motivate people to stay online longer and join in discussions repeatedly.

You are going to learn about the details of communities: what constitutes them, how you use them in e-business, and the challenges they pose. At the end of this chapter, you will be able to assess a community for its strategic and tactical planning needs. Detailed examples will show you how the framework applies to communities for big companies and smaller companies. These are the starting points, and you can then incorporate your own unique perspective into the eBiz Readiness!™ framework.

All of us come from real-world communities. Whether your home, your school, or your workplace, each collection of people represents a real-world community. The dictionary's definition of *community* is, "a social group of any size whose members reside in a specific locality, share government, and often have a common cultural and historical heritage."[1] However, note that in this chapter, we are referring strictly to business communities. We are not referring to social communities such as The Well (www.thewell.com). The Well is one of the oldest virtual communities to be created purely for the congregation and interaction of individuals who exchange ideas and data.

A good definition for the *e-business community* would be, "a constantly changing group of people collaborating and sharing their ideas over a network."[2] E-business takes this definition one step further by incorporating the reason you would want a community within a customer-focused business. Communities help you retain customers by offering a comfortable atmosphere and acquire customers through marketplace expansion, increasing loyalty, and developing stronger relationships between the business and customer. The aim of any business is to increase site stickiness, which is how long and how often a customer visits a site. Communities allow potential purchasers to draw on the experiences of other shoppers for product knowledge and advice. Participants can offer each other far more believable and personal opinions than a storeowner or advisor.For example, the amazon.com community members post their own comments about the books they have purchased. This is a truly great selling point that stimulates and maintains interest and gets people buying!

E-business has definitely changed organizational charts—the Vice President of Community is a new position in many companies. The person oversees the business community regardless of whether your company owns the community or is in a partnership with a community aggregator to establish a community presence. Online communities have convening power, offer economies of scale, provide an interested audience, and are instantaneously and cost-effectively reachable. The online community provides the customer with fast access to knowledge, new (and sometimes formerly unreachable) contacts, content aggregation, access to useful services, and the ability to compare a business's services and products with a competitor's.

Communities are the audiences of a business. A specific benefit that a community presence brings to a business is the acquisition of more complete customer and business partner profiles. Businesses use these profiles for generating leads, targeting advertisements and promotions, and personalizing member services. Hi-tech corporations such as Microsoft and Egghead use communities for tech support, product launches, and software deployment. NetPodium's Intervu collaboration tool uses audio and video streaming technologies to enable the business to demonstrate products or give corporate or sales presentations to hundreds of community members over the Internet simultaneously. Cheap and effective product launches, internal and external training, and education can be targeted to specific community members.

Infomediaries are customer communities that present unprecedented opportunities for e-businesses. An infomediary is a site that acquires and stores customer profile information. For example, a customer can create a profile at the infomediary site and then reuse the profile at different Web sites that request customer registration information, whether the sites are shopping or downloading sites. The customer can view and modify the profile at any point, adding or reducing privacy options. This application is convenient and consistent for customers. If the customer trusts one site more than another, the customer can modify the profile for that particular site. PopularDemand, an advocate of "consumer-in-control" marketing, provides a service that allows customers to declare their preferences for receiving or not receiving different types of direct marketing material. The service includes an option to restrict the e-mail that arrives in customers' inboxes. PopularDemand effectively serves two masters: the customers, who gain increased control over their marketing preferences, and the companies, who target the right customers without alienating others and in turn benefit from improved sales and marketing effectiveness.

Yahoo! and America Online (AOL) are types of infomediaries because of what they were initially structured to do. Their primary focus is generating traffic—bringing people to a specific online place. When they get their customers, advertisers pay. Many of the free services (such as chatting, e-mail, finance, and news) offered by the sites to increase stickiness also collect customer profile information.

The economies of scale derived from middleman community aggregators such as eSteel, Chemdex, VerticalNet, FreeMarkets, and DoubleClick are developed through amortization of the trading partner's cost to connect to all its relevant companies and amortization of technology infrastructure costs. The infrastructure supports the efficient exchange of e-commerce transactions among all community members. Another benefit of being a trading partner is that you don't have to worry about upgrading technology or making decisions on using new technologies, a task that is carried out by the community aggregator.

Defining the Horizon

Terms you hear repeatedly in reference to types of Web business communities are *horizontal* and *vertical, business to customer (B2C), business to business (B2B),* and *business to partner (B2P).* Trading communities such as aggregators, auctions, and exchanges are being hailed as the foundation of the next Internet commerce frontier. AOL scored an advertising run rate of $1.5 billion in 1999. In comparison, the New York Stock Exchange (NYSE) pulls in less than $110 million in income each year.

Broad-and-Shallow Versus Narrow-and-Deep Portals

Portals are collections, or "windows" of online community information. They are classified as either Internet portals or enterprise portals. Successful Internet portal strategies are described as being either *broad and shallow* (horizontal) or *narrow and deep* (vertical). Enterprise portals provide a source of information, processes, and systems about an enterprise.[3] An example of a broad-and-shallow Internet portal is AOL,[4] which has created a community for the masses. An example of a narrow-and-deep Internet portal, which is sometimes referred to as a *vortal,* is Chemdex,[5] a company that creates a community in which scientists, researchers, purchasing managers, and life science suppliers can purchase scientific products. The effectiveness of each strategy is affected by the value of the content provided by the community. Broad-and-shallow portals need general content, whereas narrow-and-deep portals need focused content.

AOL and Yahoo! are broad-and-shallow portals that have multiple commerce partners who pay to belong to their portals. The commerce partners hope to get some of the traffic that is coming to the portal through the producers' sites or sales channels. The partners also intend on developing awareness of their brand names and increasing customer retention.[6] On the Internet, customer acquisition is very costly for companies, but switching costs (the cost, whether in time or money, for a customer to switch to another competitor) are very low, often nothing. Because customer acquisition is so costly, the portals must also play a role in customer retention. They personalize data from the commerce partners to create an overall personalized package for each customer.

Businesses usually approach the task of building a community from one of two main angles in mind: vertical or horizontal. Vertical communities harness and leverage industry-specific knowledge and content and then provide value to the customer by offering services to the community members. Horizontal communities, such as those based on search engines, offer services first and gather content and knowledge second. The community services tend to be diverse and applicable to numerous interests and themes. News, sports, entertainment, and finance information commonly appear on horizontal sites. Community service prices range from free to per transaction fees to flat fees.

A business can have many types of communities: an external customer (B2C) community, a business partner (B2B) community, and an internal employee community. Each group may be serviced differently, and the groups can be large or small. Lockheed Martin has thousands of employees but hundreds of customers. Microsoft can have thousands of employees but millions of customers.

VerticalNet, a B2B community, obtains its main revenue from the transactional services required by its community members to communicate and do business. It aggregated the audience first and then supplied them with services. Garden.com is a vertical B2C community that attracts people with its content and knowledge. The free services create stickiness by giving customers further value. Typically, when community services are free, business advertising, affiliate shopping revenue, and lead creation activities are important.

Business-to-Consumer Communities

B2C communities can be built by an individual company promoting its brand name or by several companies that are blending within a community site. Some businesses do both, and some form only partnerships because of cheaper costs, increased audience size, or better marketing capabilities. Building a community based on a particular brand gives your business more control over access to and possible use of customer data. Regardless, your company risks experiencing brand erosion resulting from privacy issues surrounding use of customer data. Partnering with an established community aggregator such as Yahoo! GeoCities, iVillage.com, WebMD, or VerticalNet gives your business a much wider audience; the privacy concerns have been removed indirectly, and the technology infrastructure and updating issues are someone else's headache. The risk that comes with forming partnerships is loss of control of your customer's data. The control is subject to community governance rules, which can, and do, change. Even so, limiting your community to a single brand means that you fragment your market sensing capability, meaning you can only track your customers' purchasing patterns on your site. A blended community can offer wider market sensing capabilities if the community aggregator allows companies to share complete customer profiles. The profiles may contain purchasing patterns at competitor sites as well.

People spend a long time online with other community members, which helps your company get more details about its potential customers. People who share information about their upcoming and ongoing projects can provide your company with useful hints about the consumers' possible upcoming purchases. *Knowledge management* is your business's management of its information.[7] Knowledge management overlaps with the enterprise portal because the enterprise must manage its information based on the stakeholder with which it is interacting, including internal resources, suppliers, partners, and customers. Personalized knowledge management creates consumer stickiness; customers are reluctant to switch because the personalization allows them to find information more easily.

When developing a community strategy, your business needs to determine (1) the economic potential of the community, and (2) the sort of competition you will face. The responses will help you form a community strategy that will have the right blend of community components but not expose the company to a significant economic risk. Your company will also have to meet the challenge of combining its new online virtual community with a real-world community to exploit all customer touch points. So far, we haven't seen any models that are doing this yet.

Various companies interact differently with consumers and businesses. People are the root of consumer and business communities, and people want to interact with each other. Community interaction and trust are part of the equation—the development of the trust required to retain customers. Communities are gold mines! Your business needs to acquire the right prospecting tools and stake its claim but still retain its customers' trust.

Bob:

We need to keep on top of the new technologies to facilitate business community interactions. Collaborative technologies are starting to mature, and we predict some exciting possibilities. We can certainly save money through virtual meetings if our customers or business partners are comfortable with the technology. We will always have face-to-face meetings for our more critical business interactions.

Sue:

I like the strategy of community blending. One of our concerns is reaching a larger audience. The fact that we may be able to access a service to view customer profiles is a bonus because it would allow us to target the right consumer segments. It would save marketing money and be less annoying for customers who don't care about our products and services!

Business-to-Business Communities

Trading communities, also known as *net market makers, e-marketplaces, trading e-hubs, vortals (vertical portals),* or *intermediaries,* provide services for buyers and sellers. According to Forrester Research, the three main categories of marketplace communities are aggregators (such as Grainger), auctions (such as eBay), and exchanges (such as CheMatch). Some hybrid trading communities fall into more than one category. Further classifications include vertical or horizontal and B2B or

B2C. Vertical communities are for individual industries, whereas horizontal communities, such as Monster.com, provide services for numerous industries. Metal-Site and Asiansources are vertical B2B auction sites, whereas Bid.com and eBay are horizontal B2C auction sites. Companies often use B2B auction sites to get rid of excess inventory. PaperExchange and ChemConnect are exchange sites. Exchanges are based on the stock market model. They create spot markets or last-minute markets in which the price fluctuates according to supply and demand.

Trading communities bring buyers and sellers together on the Internet. They add value by facilitating the buy-sell transaction, which includes the engage, order, and in some cases the fulfill components of a typical customer interaction (see Chapter 3). The facilitation of the buy-sell transaction takes two main forms: content aggregation or dynamic pricing support.

Content aggregation benefits the sale of low-cost items that have high purchase order transaction processing costs, markets with many suppliers, and the sale of items from suppliers that can be switched easily and cost effectively. The creation of a common product catalog must be feasible. Imagine you are procuring ballpoint pens, paper, or staplers for your business. It doesn't matter to you whether BIC, 3M, or Office Depot are the suppliers. The switching costs are insubstantial.

Communities that support dynamic pricing mechanisms allow businesses to negotiate prices in real time. These communities provide infrastructure enablers for auctions and spot markets. Examples of such communities are BusinessBots, i2i.com, Intelligent Digital, Moai, Tradeum, and Viewlocity. Commodity goods such as oil, power, gas, chemicals, and bandwidth typically require spot markets and have special fulfillment requirements. For example, corrosive acids require special carriers and cannot be shipped by air. Oil and gas require the rental or acquisition of a pipeline infrastructure. Commodity goods tend to be sold in very large volumes.

Although trading communities were initially created for big and midsize businesses, small business communities are also springing up. Examples include allBusiness.com, BuyersZone, Demandline.com, EqualFooting, KillerBiz, Onvia.com, SmartAge, and SmartOnline. Some small business communities such as FOB.com use reverse aggregation mechanisms that traditionally have benefited buyers more than sellers. The buying power of the small business is aggregated through the trading community, which then makes one large purchase from one or more distributors or suppliers. In this way the small business benefits from distributor and supplier discounts for large-volume purchases. Trading communities that use reverse auction mechanisms also favor the buyer, which is particularly important to small businesses.

Mark Walsh and VERTICALNET

DOING IT TODAY

According to Mark Walsh, president and chief executive officer (CEO) of Vertical-Net, the great strength of the company's approach is that it is based on an audience perspective. Companies like AOL, Yahoo!, and other grand names in the consumer space know that if you consider the audience first, the other parts fall into place. The typical things that you look for when building a company are a good product, good technology, an infrastructure, good delivery, good marketing, and a good audience—and the audience is the key. Getting and understanding the audience first and then flushing out the technology platform and commerce model is the more defensible long-term approach. If we appeal to the full panoplies of the audience of the specific vertical, industrial, or technological marketplace, then (Content + Community + Commerce) × Strategic partnership = VerticalNet. If you have the first two C's, commerce develops more naturally, is more defensible, and produces a margin for VerticalNet and its partners to demand, expect, and count on.

It is romantic to think of the Net as a disintermediator (an entity that cuts out the middleman in the factory to customer supply chain); in fact, a lot of the B2C behavior has been associated with disintermediation. Charles Schwab, amazon. com, and consumer markets that sell fungible or commodity goods are naturals for disintermediation. The B2B side is different; disintermediation is a lovely theory but is not the same. The B2B market has far fewer opportunities for true disintermediation.Why? Information is important and is used by buyers and sellers during the sales process. Buyers and suppliers want to continue having a relationship in the B2B environment in the future. They interact and use the Internet as an informational platform. B2B transactions are not as simple as consumer transactions.

The B2B transaction occurs in three phases. First, the buyer or specifier gathers information about the products that are available and about the companies

continued

selling them. They investigate numerous vendors, gather information, and compare the companies. Businesses allow consumers to do a lot of this today by providing search mechanisms and virtual storefronts.

The second phase begins after the buyer has found the product; a whole new set of features kicks in. For example, I, the hypothetical buyer, have decided to purchase 3,000 pollution control valves. I have to decide whether I want to buy new or used valves, create instant request for proposal (RFP) or request for quotation (RFQ), initiate my order, or go to a chat room and talk to people who are using my product (whether it is a member-generated or an owner-generated discussion).

In the final phase, I need you to give me the tools that allow me to make the purchase. Integrate the buying process into my systems. Use VerticalNet's Net Effects with online customer service, and use Yantra Web and the telephone. Invest and team up with Ariba or Commerce One. All software must interact with enterprise resource planning (ERP) systems. VerticalNet uses an Isadra Web-based catalog normalization engine for its products. We ensure normalization, information integrity, and integration with legacy systems. Howard Samms has hundreds of legacy systems. We purchased NECX, an electronics distribution company, to enable fulfillment—to physically take title to, or own, the product. NECX serves as an intermediary for 18,000 trading partners—it understands the logistics of an exchange market. The problem with many exchanges is that they forget they may be dealing with tangible goods that are being distributed, some of which have a shelf life. We can't fax pizzas! We need to know how to get a pizza (the tangible good) from the oven (the supplier) to a house (the customer). Digital market makers forget that shipping pizza is a lot different than shipping, for example, a book—pizza is more messy and gross!

In the next two years, VerticalNet will take several steps. We will change our current model by continuing to attract people with content, but we will also allow them to perform other transactions such as buying and selling within vertical markets. People will be able to drill down—do research on and perform comparisons of products—and then make a decision about what they want to buy. VerticalNet will trim some of its sectors and will be a number-one or number-two market maker, content provider, and source of community for its buy-supply neighborhood.VerticalNet will also have localized (geographically customized) versions in its new European and Asian (Japanese, Korean, and Chinese) markets.

> The Fortune 50 companies are rapidly trying to get their businesses on the Web, but some of their initiatives will seem silly. Building a community is not about getting their products on the Web and saving money; it is about a company joining other communities to bring together buyers and sellers—it's about letting their products speak for themselves.

eBiz Readiness!™ Components for the Community Stakeholder

The part of the eBiz Readiness!™ framework that addresses the community stakeholder contains four fundamental components: engagement, interaction, services, and governance (Figure 4–1). The engage component involves turning a community member into a customer. The interaction component involves the creation of a community. Interactions make people feel like part of a group. Services are essential for attracting people to a community, which is different from engaging members so that they will buy something. Services also play a significant role in member retention. The governance component involves creating a feeling of trust within the community.

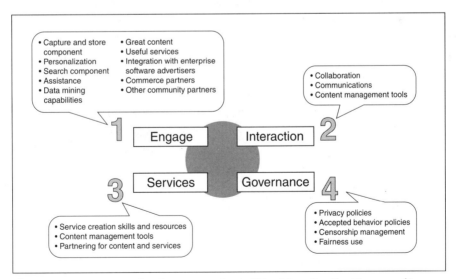

Figure 4-1   Community Components and Enablers for the Community Stakeholder

Engage

Engagement is turning a community member into a customer and then keeping the person as a customer for life. How is the *community* engage component different from the *customer* engage component described in the previous chapter? Engagement in a community involves learning as much about a customer before a transaction. You should try to get the type of valuable information that allows you to make relevant product and service offers. Members of a community share far more information with a business than do regular business customers. Consider the Garden.com community. Members can use the site to plan a garden, which provides the business with far more information about them than would have been obtained if the members were merely shopping. Garden.com can learn the entire scope of a customer's project—whether bricks, trellises, or top soil are needed as well as how much of them the customer needs. Contrast this type of customer with a customer who makes periodic purchases at an online gardening store. The store can only statistically estimate whether that particular customer will make another purchase at the store again in a predetermined time frame. Garden.com can more accurately predict what its members will purchase and when because it knows their plans. Armed with knowledge like this, community-based businesses can suggest products (for example, through contextual banner ads or promotional e-mails) or offer deals on customized packaged products and services that the customer will very likely explore.

Community sites can use short, unobtrusive questionnaires to find out more about its members' lifestyles and create more in-depth profiles. Garden.com briefly hosted a questionnaire based on the theme, "How do you celebrate your garden?" Some of the answer choices include, "By chronicling my garden layout, bloom cycles, and events in my garden journal," "Celebrate? I forgot to celebrate my garden last year! This year, I'll turn over a new leaf, though," and "Call me a garden party planner." We don't know Garden.com's motives for hosting the questionnaire; it could have been simply for entertainment. However, the members' selections may have allowed the business to further profile its members: the careful planner, the short-term enthusiast, or the long-term enthusiast. Careful planners are predictable; these customers enjoy being shown selections of tulip bulbs in autumn or appreciate preferred pricing on fertilizer in spring. The long-term enthusiasts are high-value customers; the short-term (or busy) customers will buy sporadically in bursts.

Data mining capabilities allow businesses to identify novel, useful, valid, and understandable data patterns. It gives businesses the ability to predict how certain community members will respond to a marketing campaign, predict the impact on sales of bundling and promoting certain products, and estimate how likely it is that a particular member will switch to a competitor. Chapters.ca recently bought gardencrazy.com. Using customer profile information, buyers of more than two gardening books were targeted for a particular marketing promotion. Chapters offered 20 percent off of its bulbs and other garden products through gardencrazy.com. The result was an amazing 70 percent take rate! That is, 70 percent of all targeted customers bought a product through gardencrazy.com. In the field of marketing, a promotion with a 3 percent take rate is considered a success! Rick Segel, Chapters CEO, says that his target market for business communities is the late majority (customers who wait to purchase a technology until it has proven itself). Not the early adopters (customers who buy a technology as soon as it is on the market), early majority (the large group of customers who buy a technology a little later than early adopters but when it is still fairly new), or laggards. The late majority is a huge group and will be for a few more years.

Personalizing tailors the information that the knowledge management enabler maintains, which creates an overlap in the actual customer area. In the community area, customers who may not have purchased anything yet may still want information that is tailored to their needs. Personalization builds trust and loyalty and increases a member's potential for becoming a purchasing customer. For example, certain features on Yahoo! and Ask Jeeves allow the personalization of the site's content and layout, resulting in MyYahoo! and My Jeeves. Knowledge management tools allow for content management and the application of business rules. Business rules are dictated by the businesses that are participating in the community. Some rules are wrapped around public processes (interactions between two or more companies) and other rules are wrapped around private processes (internal company processes). Business rules include the information that you trade, the information's format, and the type of trade credit you are using. Internal rules often include workflow (authorization) rules but can also address issues such as spending limits.

Knowledge management is important because different types of information are presented to different users, such as internal users, partners, suppliers, and customers. When such a wide array of information is being presented, the information must be easy to find, logically arranged, and rendered for the user's interface (for example, the Web, the phone, a wireless device) based on how the user will be interacting with the content. Some information is also time sensitive, such as current stock prices.

Community localization also plays an important role in personalization. Mark Walsh, VerticalNet CEO, says, "B2B e-commerce is by nature more global than consumer e-commerce. Businesses are more accustomed to buying products that have been made far away. Businesses buy from a local distributor who has taken title to (ownership of) the product and has the product available. The product may have been manufactured from very far away. Everybody likes to buy from people they trust. We have large, well-financed efforts in many nations and form partnerships to localize the content with language and the verticals that make sense. We use the partners as the original sales forces that visit the local companies. We've created a place on the Web where you can buy and sell within your localized VerticalNet and with the click of a button bring or source (search for) information from global sources such as customers and sellers. We have some cross-traffic promotional efforts similar to those of AOL. We are repurposing content and repurposing product data for individual nations that buy online storefronts that have been localized to the country. For example, we can provide the metric version of a pump that a customer in Germany needs. Information and stock-keeping units (SKUs) are localized."

Providing a site in which members can easily find what they are looking for is an essential part of the engage process. Just as traditional bricks-and-mortar businesses such as grocery stores have supremacies (strategically placed products—for example, at eye level), trading communities offer an analogous deal. The placement fees used in the grocery business are similar to fees paid to search engines. When you go to a grocery store, you tend to gravitate toward products that you can see easily, not towards the ones you have to search for on the top and bottom shelves. The same thing is true of search engine results; you probably only try the first one or two pages worth unless you search other pages. A placement fee places a supplier's products earlier in the search range, increasing the chance that someone will click on them. Businesses that can buy lots of product placement space are in essence buying the "end cap"—the premium end-of-the-aisle locations—because more space allows members to find products more easily using the search mechanisms. In other words, if your items are the first three results in a search, it is likely that the customer will click on one of your links. "For companies that can afford to have supremacy at an Internet site, search engine space and banner ads that capture the attention of the buyers are the most successful," Walsh says. "However, the Internet allows the customer to drill down with one or two clicks and see other vendors. This is easier than it is in the real world—sometimes it can be hard to get to the far corners of the trade show and visit the 'small' guys. On the Internet, you can rapidly search and compare lots of products—drill down. We may have the ability to sway where the visitors are going, but the Internet is a leveler, making it easier for customers to compare many products. A good example is the SABRE system, which is owned by American Airlines. Forty percent of all travel bookings were made from the first screen of the results listings, and of course, American Airlines was the first entry that appeared. The travel agents could drill down and look at the Northwest, SAS, and other entries, but many didn't because they were 'lazy' and stopped. Good buyers and good sourcers (people who are locating the products) use the Internet correctly to find the best deal."

The community can "normalize" content for the member by translating keywords or product tags and descriptions from different sources into common terms. Doing so also enhances the community's engagement power. Members have less work to do to find what they need. A community actively searches for content suppliers, which include its members. In a B2B community, the companies provided would be suppliers of goods and services. A buyer can then choose from a larger number of suppliers and as a community member has a larger selection of people with which to communicate.

Community engagement processes involving commerce should include the ability to contact a real person. Assistance is the "helping" component of the community and involves searching, solving, and recommending. A Boston Consulting Group report stated that "no access to real-time help" was a reason that customers gave for leaving and not buying anything from a site.

People love free stuff. Giving away something "for free," whether it is a product or service, is a strategy that some communities use to attract members. Diamond Technology Partners wrote a book called *The Killer App* they actually placed online so that people could read it for free. Diamond provides interaction tools for the customers and supports a forum for fans and critics of the book. Diamond took a traditional medium, a book, and created an e-community that may buy services from Diamond Technology Partners or buy future books from its authors. Putting the book online allows you to assess the company's value to you and raises your confidence level in them as you learn of their employees' intellectual expertise.

Communities have an enormous potential for generating live feedback from and forming relationships with members or customers. Communities can then increase brand awareness and provide information that drives transactions. Many community sites support sponsors, advertisers, and commerce revenue links. Sponsors of a business and its community help members trust the business. Advertisers and commerce partners extend this impression because they are investing in the power of the site to attract customers. eBay promotes trust among its more than 6 million users by adding features such as buyer and seller ratings.

Internet malls alleviated parking concerns and brought a world of products to customers' computers. Internet malls had high expectations but could not live up to them because people buy things differently over the Internet. Bricks-and-mortar stores are trying to extend their channel to the Internet—and portals are the "malls" of the Internet. High-value portal commerce partnerships with Yahoo! or AOL can clearly drive sufficient traffic to a virtual storefront. Obtaining spots on these sites is beyond the reach of the average small business, but other online locations, such as regionalized community sites, offer communities a head start on generating customer loyalty. Doug Hall, director of the Canadian Information Highways Committee, is spearheading an initiative to create local online communities that are associated with geographical districts throughout Canada.

In summary, enablers for the community engage component are capture and storage of member information, personalization, search function, human assistance, data mining capabilities, service provisioning, free service or content, and portal partnerships to drive traffic to the site. Metrics for the engage component include number of unique visitors, number of repeat visits, member acquisition rate, member retention rate, customer acquisition rate, number of successful marketing campaigns in a given period, take rates per campaign, ratio of change in community content, usability and data currency indexes, and level of brand awareness.

Bob:

Our community members are an enthusiastic bunch. They create a wealth of content, sharing expertise with one another at an incredible level and rate! We have gotten customers from our community membership through product launches and beta product testing. We have many volunteer moderators for our news groups. They're thrilled that we host this type of forum for them!

Sue:

Our community membership is dynamic and growing! We are having so much fun creating specific, targeted market campaigns. We used to send mass mailings out to huge lists of people, and we will continue to do so for some campaigns. We use simple database query tools on our community member and customer databases to filter and create campaign audiences. We see a difference in the take rates for our offers already, and the new process has cut our mailing costs.

Community Interaction

Online communities are not self-supporting. They require individuals with special skills, as well as specialized processes and tools to make them succeed. The management of an e-business community requires archivists, usage analysts, product developers, and an executive team. Interaction tools are used to help the community members and sponsors communicate and interact with each other. Two laws help explain the importance of community tools. Moore's Law states that will double every 18 months while costs remain constant. Increases in processor speeds coupled with decreases in prices and increases in speed of access to memory give more power to users and facilitate community growth. More power means quicker access to more content and scalable collaboration sessions—community interaction sessions in which many community members participate at once. Metcalf's Law states that the usefulness, or utility, of a network equals the square of the number of its users. For example, phones wouldn't be very valuable if only a few people had them, but they are in fact tremendously valuable because they are so widely used.[8] The most commonly used tools are those that are available to the most people. Prevalence also depends on access technology and operating system requirements. Community tools also depend on the access technology (speed) and operating system requirements. The best community tools are ones that don't require a lot of horsepower to run (access or operating system) and have ubiquitous interfaces for the community members.

Collaboration and content management tools for member-business interactions are important if your company wants to create a successful community infrastructure. The extent of the interactions depends on the requirements of the customer and the business's relationship with the community member or customer. The interaction tools should be as technologically simple as possible so that they are easy for the customer to use. Some tools are limited by the human factor. For example, managing a chat session with more than 10 concurrent users is difficult. Scalability is important because some sites manage thousands of chat sessions simultaneously. Chat rooms, message boards, and e-mail are commonly used online interaction tools.

Community members have the capacity to generate an enormous amount of information, so Web sites must consider community content size and type as well as the size and type of other business content when purchasing content management tools such as search engines and catalog managers. A community that becomes too big or diluted can be dissected into subcommunities. Other tools, such as those provided by Well Engaged LLC, enable sites to instantaneously create virtual subcommunities. Well Engaged offers an all-in-one package that includes conferencing software, host servers, and consulting services.

Depending on the target audience, interaction tools may be multilingual. In fact, the Internet's global reach makes it fairly certain that multilingual capabilities will eventually be required on many sites. In addition, multilingual interaction tools must incorporate an understanding of the culture. With so many permutations and combinations of communication tools, the selection of interaction tools should be based on the target audience's needs, language, and culture. Language translation tools help sites manage the multilingual aspect of community. Authorware from a content management tool called MacroMedia places all natural language components into one folder, facilitating the change from one language to another.

Collaboration tools can help create cooperative environments in which people can work together. Some collaboration tools are aimed at business users, whereas others are aimed at consumers. Collaboration tools, such as calendars and meeting tools, allow other community members to share schedules and common information, enabling them to work together more easily.

Many of the customer interaction tools (see Chapter 3) are also used in communities. Companies that make interaction tool's include PlaceWare, Centra, and Cisco (which makes the collaboration server). ActiveTouch, Inc. has a "portal" solution that vertical companies such as sales.com—a professional sales community—use to make their sites interactive. In many cases, interactive meetings increase productivity and reduce face-to-face meeting and travel costs. Users and prospective customers meet in real time, carry out transactions, and collaborate instantly through their browsers.

Community members can interact passively by creating content. One member posts a message, and another reads it and provides feedback. When a community member is given resources to create the content of a site, it creates a sense of ownership and hence increases loyalty to the site. Community members of amazon.com create content through postings of online book reviews. Thus a factor that affects community interaction is the level of content management given to the member or customer. One content management tool, Vignette Story Server, was built from the ground up to support content, structure, and navigation. It delivers content based on browser type, operating system, and language. The level of content integration is based on the business application being run.[9] Examples of content include knowledge, product information, news, all of which can be tailored to the user's language. Examples of structure and navigation include taxonomy rules, indexing, and sorting functions. Examples of integration include real-time pricing, inventory, and other areas.

An aggregate enabler is the level of community interaction that takes place between the customer and business community. The primary enablers for the community interaction component are collaboration and content management tools. Component metrics are response times and the availability and scalability of the interaction tools. Additional metrics include the abandon rate of tool use and ease of access to content and services.

Bob:

These new conferencing and collaboration tools will save us enormous amounts of money in travel and employee time. We can do beta testing of our products on our enthusiastic and product-savvy members. We already support standard chat and forum technologies for our members.

Sue:

We chose a blending strategy to develop our community, so our partner community maintains all the community collaboration tools. However, we acquire and support our own content management tools, which are essential to keep our community information current on the larger portal.

Community Services

Bolt-on services are the rage in e-business. New and established B2B portals, as well as businesses undergoing consolidation, need to have ways to make their portals stand out from the others. By continually offering innovative and useful services, they can provide value to the customer and create stickiness at their community site. Common and often free services that are offered by horizontal sites are news, financial, and sports information. Community services can be used to engage new members and customers as well as retain them. Some communities charge for services. For example, some financial trading communities charge for online expert advice and bleeding-edge research. B2B communities charge for various aspects of a buy-sell transaction. Some communities use subscription, mark-up, membership, or storefront fees, and many provide auction services. The growth of third-party services for community sites is expected to explode. Bolt-on services such as alternative dispute resolution (ADR) and assurance services are needed to engender trust in communities.

Claimed to be the largest community in cyberspace even before the Time Warner merger, America Online, Inc.'s AOL Services has 21 million members. It provides services in 15 countries and seven languages. AOL hosts 50 million ICQ (instant messenger) registrants, 2.2 million CompuServe members, and 20 million NetCenter registrants. AOL frequently strikes strategic alliances to continuously offer its customer base new services, a strategy that ensures site stickiness and customer retention.

The Time Warner alliance with AOL brought customers brand name content in various categories such as Warner Brothers movies and television, Cable News Network (CNN), and Time. Time Warner has an audience of 1 billion and has access to a CNN service, 35 million Home Box Office (HBO cable TV) subscribers, 120 million magazine readers, and viewers of three of the top five basic cable networks. AOL Time Warner let their community members be the first to see the 2000 *Sports Illustrated* swimsuit issue cover and facilitated chats with the swimsuit models. An alliance with Monster.com, a leading global careers network, brought job search services, including live chats with career consultants, to AOL's members.

A service called GovernmentGuide provides an online guide to government resources and benefits. The service provides a one-stop complaint center where users can immediately register complaints with the appropriate agency about particular products or services. An "Ask the White House" feature gives visitors a virtual seat in the White House press room. Visitors get answers from the majority and minority parties to the five most frequently asked questions.

AOL claims that two thirds of their members have shopped online. During the 1999 Christmas shopping season, AOL members spent $2.5 billion in retail sales with partner merchants. All the partner merchants support AOL's 100 percent money-back safety and satisfaction guarantee, addressing consumer security concerns with shopping online. AOL has an annual run rate of $1.5 billion in advertising and commerce revenues.

AOL's alliance with Onvia.com taps into the small business community opportunities. Onvia.com provides an e-marketplace for small-business buyers and sellers and supports its own community as well. It is a good example of a site that builds community around its brand as well as blends with larger communities. Reading the exchanges in its marketing forum allows you to see how this community facilitates networking and builds relationships among small business stakeholders. For example, one community member with a Web design company may post a request for marketing services. Another community member who is in urgent need of Web design services may see the message and e-mail the Web designer—instant business!

Microsoft's bCentral is a dedicated portal offering services to the global small business community. The site provides services such as search engine listings, free banner networks through ad swaps with other businesses, and a privacy wizard that creates privacy statements in 30 minutes. Commerce affiliates offer free credit analyses and tax filing.

In January 2000, Microsoft invested $100 million in the previously mentioned VerticalNet. The companies entered into a strategic alliance to deliver B2B services and content to the small-to-medium enterprise (SME) market. The B2B services provided by the trading communities include certifying suppliers and obtaining committed volumes and discounts, handling international trade logistics such as export document creation with appropriate customs duties, and quick-pay services in which the companies take title to increase liquidity. Some communities provide application service provider (ASP) services. Ariba and Commerce One are transitioning into this type of model so that they can enter the midsize procurement market.

We do not describe how to create great services in this text—mainly because our imaginations are surely too limited to touch on the enormous possibilities that exist. However, a rule of thumb to follow when creating services is to address a widely unmet need, one that has always existed or one that you have identified yourself. Think about the audience you can reach with the Internet and whether it could be used to change the way a particular service works. Partner to create the service if necessary. Knowledge about an industry, a market, or a customer segment greatly facilitates the creation of useful services.

In summary, enablers for the services component are content management tools, service creation skills, and partnering for the provision of content and services. Metrics for the service component include the rate of introduction of new services, revenue per service, cost per service, member satisfaction, personalization index, and feedback from each service.

Bob:

I am the CEO of a trading community. Our main service is enabling the buy-sell transaction, which involves providing a stringent order management capability. We also provide the necessary infrastructure and governance.

Sue:

We are in the clothing tailoring business. An application provider hosts the community and enables small businesses in the industry to join. Together we offer free dress, fabric, and store-window design services. Our latest service allows customers to "try on" clothes using a virtual model based on their body type.

Community Governance

Good community governance engenders trust and confidence. E-businesses need to create trust if they are going to carry out transactions with members or customers. More consumer privacy issues exist in a Web community because people spend a long time online sharing information and using services. Community sites collect knowledge about the members based on the sites from which they are coming, what they are doing on the system, how long they are on the system, and the site they are going to when they leave. To provide customizable and personalized services, many Web sites collect "click trails" or "click streams" along with registration and survey information. Click trails identify which pages you have visited in a merchant's store, track the number of visits and business carried out at a store, and monitor shopping basket contents. The information is often stored in cookies on your computer's hard disk. The cookies are continuously updated. Uses of cookie data include estimates of audience size, traffic patterns, and promotion tracking.

Communities share information with third parties when the consumer uses co-branded services, click-on promotions, advertisements, or community Web site links. If the community offers a service in conjunction with another partner, as does AOL with Monster.com, then both parties share the customer data. External sponsors of promotions, advertising networks that provide ads for the community, and affiliated merchants also collect customer profile information from the community. Many community sites such as Yahoo! analyze the collected consumer data and share the results of the aggregation with advertisers and other business partners, which are often referred to as *trusted third parties.* Users can find out when and what type of information is being collected about them by reading the community's published *terms of service or use agreements.* Different services on the same community site may have different forms of these agreements.

Consumer privacy is currently a significant issue and includes concerns about emotionally charged items such as medical health, family history, child safety, and exposure of financial information. People worry when their names are sold on consumer lists and insights about their purchasing behaviors are shared with partner or affiliated companies. People sense that they lose more privacy on the Internet than through the selling of customer data in direct mailing and telemarketing businesses. The telemarketers and direct mailers obtain the data from trusted companies to whom the customers freely give information. Consumers generally find telemarketing and direct mailing annoying rather than really intrusive. On the Net, customers may be providing a vendor with personal information without being aware of it, so the sense of intrusion is greater. Although most businesses have not implemented data mining solutions to use the customer data that they capture, people believe their data is actively being examined and thus their privacy is being abused. Some communities have more privacy concerns than others. Members of health-related communities want strong privacy policy statements from the sites because of fear of reprisals from insurance companies and employees.

In contrast, the B2B communities' privacy concerns are nowhere near those of the consumer sector. Intimate knowledge in the business sector is different from personal information in the consumer space. Publicly held companies have transparency of information—in other words, they must disclose certain facts to their shareholders such as annual sales data and costs. Privately held companies are not required to disclose the numbers. However, the publicly accessible Dunn and Bradstreet databases show a company's purchasing history and the payment history of privately held companies. Businesses are also experienced with outsourcing, so corporate data are managed by third-party service organizations. Banks may outsource check processing, and entire industries may outsource human resource functions, payroll processing, and health plan processing. Businesses are more experienced than customers with interbusiness contract law. Which B2B interactions are affected by privacy issues? One is the analysis of competitive bidding information. Some communities such as online exchanges store the complete electronic transactions that take place among trading partners. The businesses then have the ability to peek inside transactions and comprehend how community members make purchasing decisions. More importantly, they know from whom you have purchased products. Audits of these transactions can reveal whether a company always awards contracts to the lowest bidder or quality plays a role in the decision. For example, according to VerticalNet CEO Mark Walsh, if NASA were using an online exchange to obtain certain nozzles, members of the exchange would be able to examine the details of the transaction and determine whether the purchase decisions were based on quality, or NASA simply purchased the nozzles from the cheapest supplier.

Communities create key positions to examine content, facilitate discussions, and assist in dispute resolutions. The mitochondrial genome community at Emory University (www.gen.emory.edu/mitomap) has a full-time qualified scientist who performs quality assurance checks of the result findings submitted for posting by biological scientists around the world. AOL censors and employs governance rules to prevent libel suits. Highly trained facilitators ease the path to greater community interaction productivity by keeping members on the topic. Additional resources for community management include personnel for archiving, analysis, and product development.

Governments play a critical role in the success of large-scale communities. The Canadian government initiatives to get its citizens "connected" are exemplary because the initiatives remove the digital divide between the "have's" and the "have not's" by providing computer access in public places like malls and libraries. Every citizen should be connected to the Internet by the end of 2000. The government has already successfully connected every school in Canada to the Internet. This is an example of fairness of use—making the technology equally accessible to all. In summary, the enablers for community governance are privacy policies, accepted behavior policies, censorship management, and fairness use. Metrics for the governance component include security, privacy, dispute resolution indexes, and cost of censorship.

Bob:

We have published our privacy policy. We use member data to personalize member services. We also use the data for targeted marketing. We share the data solely with commerce partners.

Sue:

Our customers don't seem to worry too much about privacy at our site. They have known us for years in a more personal capacity. We assure them that our site is secure. Their personal statistics are kept behind a firewall.

Community Questions

While building your communities, you may find it useful to consider the following questions as you determine which types of communities meet your needs.

Overall

- What are your community goals?
- Which community creation strategy will you use—build or blend?
- Is the strategy of building a virtual community aligned with your business strategy?
- Will your community be horizontal or vertical?
- Do you plan to host two communities—one for customers and one for collaboration among business partners?
- Is the community going to be an aggregator of content and/or buyers and sellers, an auction community, or an exchange?
- Can you think of vertical market exchanges that fulfill your enterprises' spot needs—as alternatives to strategic partnerships, predefined contracts, and electronic data interchange (EDI) implementations? (You make spot purchases when you need something and have to search around to buy it. Having a standing contract offer is different than spot purchasing because you know who to turn to when you need something.) Do you have any alternatives to spot purchasing, or is it only used to fulfill your spot needs? Does the vertical market expose you to more or less risk?
- What are the benefits and savings for customers who join or use your community? Which core business processes between companies and customers will your community facilitate? Can you quantify the reduction in cycle time for some of these processes? Can you qualify some of the value-added features?
- How will *you* obtain value from your community? How will your members and customers obtain value?
- If you will obtain revenue from your community, list all methods you will use, such as transaction fees, list fees, advertising, fee per service, or fee per usage.
- How will you measure your success? By the revenue your sellers make through listing in your community? By the level of customer loyalty or brand awareness?
- What will be the most frequently executed transaction or process within your community? Arthur Armstrong did a study on communities and identified four distinct types of communities according to the types of needs they serve.[10] (1) *Communities of transaction* facilitate the buying and selling

process, (2) *communities of interest* bring together similar people, (3) *communities of fantasy* bring together people for the creation of a new virtual community, and (4) *communities of relationship* bring together people who want to meet people with similar experiences and make personal connections. Do you plan to facilitate the creation of the four community types?

Engagement

- How do you plan to attract people to your community?
- Do you intend to organize your content in a way that is easy to find? What useful services will you provide? Can you provide services that are not found anywhere else? Which sites will compete with yours?
- Do you plan to do a launch of your Web channel in the traditional media, including a launch of your community site?
- Will you give away free services or products?
- If you host a trading community, what will you do to attract small enterprises to your community? (For example, some e-markets digitize sellers' content at no charge.)
- Which community transactions have a long cycle time? Can you build business relationships from these transaction interactions?
- What is unique about your content management capability? How do you manipulate your sellers' content for maximum usability to the buyer? Do you make recommendations to the sellers you host?
- Do you see scalable content management as a critical success factor? Do you think that your technology partners are capable of providing you with the tools you need? What tool would you like to see developed for content management?
- How many people and what percentage of your overall staff will be assigned to content management tasks?
- How many staff members will analyze your data? Will they be a team of people? What will some of their job titles be?
- What are the key questions that must be answered in the data analysis exercise?
- Which knowledge mining tools will you use?
- Will you use an ERP package? Which back-end process integration will be the most important?

Interaction

- How sophisticated will your knowledge management infrastructure be? What are the most important things you will keep track of with regard to your sellers and buyers?
- How will your community address globalization issues? How will you support multilingualism?
- What communication tools will you use within your community? Which do you think will be the most frequently used? Which do you think will have the most promising use in the future?
- Do you support or plan to support tailored extranets for client groups?
- Community applications and services are used to address internal and external corporate needs. The applications and services include virtual sales teams, software deployment, channel enablement, product launches, training and education, online tech support, collaborative designers, interactive tours, corporate presentations, sales and marketing presentations, and seminars. Do you plan to install tools, such as real-time collaboration tools, to enable these applications (for example, Centra, Learnlinc, Sametime)?

Services

- Will you provide member personalization services? Give an example of a service that you are excited about.
- How often do you plan to introduce new services on your site?
- Are you planning on following an aggressive partnering plan for the creation of new services?
- How often have you previously provided new personalization services on your site?
- Will you allow your business customers to view their transaction and interaction histories in a secure area, or will this data only be used for the business?

Governance

- What role will your site play in creating *trust* among members? How will you facilitate the interactions needed to build customers' (the participating businesses') trust?
- What mechanisms will you support so that the users (buyers) within the community can provide feedback?
- What mechanisms will you have in place at the *community level* to resolve issues? Will they be ADR measures?

Small-Business Perspective:
Community Stakeholder Assessment (SMEDistributor)

Sue:
We want to create a virtual place where people with common personal and professional interests can engage in dialogue, share ideas and industry tidbits, and help each other feel connected to a group and our business. We want to localize our community to the Caribbean and South American regions.

The following case study continues the story of SMEDistributor.com, the small B2C enterprise mentioned in Chapter 3 that sells fax machines, photocopiers, computers, and typewriters to the Latin American and Caribbean markets. SMEDistributor also sells software packages and provides computer training packages for customers. We will show you how SMEDistributor can use the framework presented in this chapter to create an e-business community strategy.

Recall that the company's motto is "People, Solutions, and Commitment to Service." The company is small; it has an annual revenue of $10 million. Present points of contact are fax machines, telephones, marketing representative visits, and the Web. SMEDistributor has a mobile sales force and two reselling channel partners. Together, they sell mainly to seven industry verticals—manufacturing, oil and gas, retail, insurance, education, media, and government.

The management wants to mount a full-fledged B2C community component on the company's Web site for the following reasons:

- To build brand awareness
- To build site traffic for new customer acquisition
- To increase numbers of repeat visitors
- To obtain more complete customer profiles
- To provide an indirect level of customer service through community members
- To create an advertising revenue stream
- To obtain content at lower cost
- To hold online software demonstrations and seminars
- To conduct product launches

- To increase members' spending by having them share common interests and enthusiasm with the community

The management wants separate B2B and business-to-employee (B2E) communities for its internal and external sales force and reselling partners for the following reasons:

- To train sales personnel
- To allow sales personnel to help each other
- To establish best practices and keep the quality level of all sales personnel consistent
- To pitch internal presentations
- To hold virtual sales meetings
- To provide one interface for dissemination of internal corporate information such as policies, procedures, and documentation

The strategy for building communities boils down to one question: "Should we build around our own brand, blend into a larger community, or both?" SMEDistributor decides to do both. It intends to join major Caribbean and Latin American portals as a merchant store. It will advertise on the portals and "join" other communities that specialize in the software that it sells. Joining may include sponsoring events at the community site or moderating a discussion forum in the area. SMEDistributor will host its internal and B2B community at its Web site.

SMEDistributor already has some community interaction tools in place. The company has a communitywide bulletin board and white-boarding facilities for sales personnel. To achieve its community goals, SMEDistributor will at least need to provide Web conferencing and chat rooms in addition to its bulletin board technology. The engage component enablers—capture and store functions, personalization, search and assistance, and back-end data mining—must be part of the community software. Search engines, help features, software to collect click histories, databases and data warehouses, personalization templates, and data analysis tools will facilitate engagement.

The services that the SMEDistributor will offer at its community site will be the key to attracting repeat visitors and creating site stickiness. The blended community is an advantage because it already has a suite of services. A brainstorming session produced the following list of services that SMEDistributor would like added to its community site. A service called *MachineTips,* which provides tips on office machines regarding usage, longevity, and legal issues (such as photocopier counterfeiting), as well as services providing industry-focused news, business news, finance news, and e-business topics. The service wish list for the B2B community includes strategies, sales tools and tips, competitor information, customer information, product information, and a forum for sharing best practices.

Community governance rules will include (1) content that infringes on copyrights, patents, or trademarks cannot be transmitted, and (2) no impersonation, irrelevant postings, unlawful content, spam, collection of other users' personal data, violation of laws, or creation of content encouraging criminal conduct are allowed. Privacy policy rules will address many issues, including the proper use of customer profiles. SMEDistributor wants to own its content and plans to request a license agreement before the member (whether a business or a consumer) can join the community.

Big-Business Perspective: Community Stakeholder Assessment (BBFoodCompany)

Bob:

We find the components of engagement interaction, services, and governance very useful in assessing what we have. We'd like to add one more framework component—social behavior. We want to understand more about making a person feel like a member of a group. We will hire a consultant in sociology or anthropology to help us with this aspect of our community site. It's fascinating how easily we can expand the eBiz Readiness!™ framework to suit our needs!

BBFoodCompany is an international supplier of baby and toddler food. The company is experienced in using Internet technology to communicate with its suppliers and customers. Over the years, it has developed an online community that it wants to expand. BBFoodCompany believes that it can leverage its brand on a community site to create two new sources of revenue, from online advertising and percentages of transaction costs from affiliated commerce partners. The management is using the eBiz Readiness!™ framework to assess its existing community and then identify the important community components.

Currently, BBFoodCompany has a few interaction tools for its members. They can post to a bulletin board, and the company has two full-time staff members who monitor postings for quality assurance and compliance with company guidelines for "acceptable behavior." No privacy or security policies exist. The company keeps its links to research articles on babies current. Feedback from members indicates that individuals spend a lot of time looking for specific information. Better tools are needed to increase the relevance of search results and search at a more detailed level. The consensus is that the site has good content, but it is poorly organized and its access tools need improvements.

The company has never publicized its community site, but users of its Web channel "discovered" the community by clicking on links at the top of the site's home page. The community model is completely impersonal. It offers no special services—only a site search engine. The community site is mainly a type of browser. Customers can use the provided e-mail address to send comments about the community to the business. To a large extent, the company has done nothing with the member profile data that has been collected from the community site. Most of the company's management does not know that this data even exists.

We used the eBiz Readiness!™ framework to analyze the company's community component. We used the generic weighting and rating scales provided in Chapter 2. We assigned a rating of 1 to the engage component—rudimentary features are present, but it does not have all common features. Recall that the engage enablers are search and assistance, recommending and solving, data mining, trial product or service, and a community communications program. BBFoodCompany does no data mining, search tools are inappropriate, and no communications program exists.

The interaction component was also assigned a rating of 1. The company supports passive interaction through postings, but no interactive support services are available. The services component is assigned a 0—it is not part of the current system or community site.

The governance component was rated as a 1. The site has censorship and quality control but no privacy or security policies.

Figure 4-2 illustrates how poorly BBFoodCompany is performing in the community area. They have a lot of potential for growth. We did not modify the ratings with weightings in the plot because each component was equally weighted.

We then used the framework to quickly brainstorm a list of ideas for the community site. The components were examined one at a time.

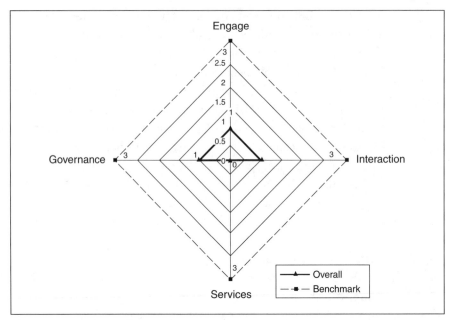

Figure 4-2   BBFoodCompany Assessment

Engage

- Target child care workers and parents.
- Launch the community site using newspapers, television, and radio.
- Have dynamite and current content.
- Localize the site to each customer in terms of language, visual impairment considerations, and local activities for parents and their young children and babies.
- Provide opportunities for visitors to chat with child-behavior and child-rearing experts.
- Syndicate content from other related communities
- Allow parents and child care workers to create content.
  - Let them post anecdotes concerning developmental milestones, odd behaviors, and solutions for problems.
  - Include a tip center with tips on topics such as nap time, bath time, meal time, and play time, and organize it by topic.

- Allow commerce partners (for example, merchants of toys, books, baby furniture, and baby accessories) to create content.
  - Allow them to host syndicated content on your site.
  - Let them post recall information.
  - Create a safety center where they can post safety tips about items such as car seats, strollers, playground equipment, baby furniture, and baby clothes.
- Allow researchers and trade publications to post articles.
- Allow related local communities such as recreational centers to post information about weekly activities.
- Allow members to contribute to a recipe section for homemade baby food.

Interaction

- Create chat rooms.
- Host online workshops.
- Host small seminars for members—allow up to 100 participants per seminar.
- Include sophisticated search and sort functions.

Services

- Partner with health organizations, and provide a search function that allows members to search for the nutritional information of any food item.
- Create (or partner with another site to create) a service for members that allows them to design a playroom, child care center, or playground online.
- Partner with another site and create a day care center search service.
- Provide comparison shopping agents for baby items.
- Host charitable auctions.

Governance

- Establish privacy and security policies.

This list was created in half an hour using the community components in the eBiz Readiness!™ framework as a guide. The next challenge for the company is to forecast its potential revenues and expenditures. It could cost them hundreds of thousands of dollars to create and maintain a community site with all these items. However, AOL draws in $1.5 billion a year in advertising and affiliate revenues—and parents all over the world are ready to spend money on their children!

Are You Ready?

Table 4-1 provides a snapshot of all the components, ancillary enablers, and metrics essential for successful community assessment. The key enablers—technology, knowledge management, and trust—are threaded throughout the components. Some customer metrics have indexes; a low index value is a poor rating, and a high index value is a good rating.

Consider the following points as you move on to the next chapter:

- A company can either build a community around its brand, blend into other communities, or do both.
- Once a company decides to build, it can either do so in house, outsource the task, or both.
- The three main types of business communities are business-to-customer communities (B2C), business-to-business (B2B) partner communities, and B2B trading communities.
- The benefits of building an online community for a business are numerous. Online communities help the business build brand awareness, increase site traffic and therefore new customer acquisition, generate repeat customers, obtain more complete customer profiles, provide an indirect level of customer service using the community members, create an advertising revenue stream, obtain content at lowered cost, hold online product launches and software demonstrations, and increase members' propensity to spend.
- Customers benefit from joining an online community. The benefits include access to aggregated and normalized content about topics of interest, useful services, expertise, and a network in a new group or market. Communities also provide their members with quick knowledge access, level the field for making new and possibly rewarding contacts, and give them the ability to compare a business's services and products with its competitors. The community stakeholder adds team spirit, enhances customer service through an extended product and service support knowledge base, enhances trust, and increases the number of preferred customer profiles. Organized community members can also influence governance policies more effectively than can one individual.
- In future decades, trading communities will enhance the relationships between buyers and sellers to such a degree that strategic partnering processes (for example, in account planning, new market research, joint research and development; see Chapter 6) will become important. The challenge will be to

Table 4-1   Metrics for the Community Stakeholder

Components*	Ancillary Enablers	Metrics
Engagement	• Capture and store function • Personalization function • Search function • Assistance • Data mining capabilities • Great content • Useful services • Integration with enterprise software advertisers • Commerce partners • Other community partners	Customer acquisition ratio Customer profitability ratio Customer retention ratio Member acquisition ratio Member retention ratio Duration of site visit Number of unique visitors Number of repeat visits Number of successful marketing campaigns Take rates per campaign Ratio of change in community content Personalization index Localization index Usability index Data currency index Level of brand awareness Number of languages supported Advertising revenues Commerce revenues from community members Commerce revenues from affiliated sites Traffic from affiliated sites
Interaction	• Collaboration, communication, and content management tools	Interaction tool response time Availability of interaction tool Scalability of interaction tool Abandonment rate Product or service knowledge access
Services	• Service creation skills • Resource content management tools • Partnering for content, services, or both • Privacy policies	Rate of introduction of new services Revenue per service Cost per service Member satisfaction with service Personalization index Feedback from service
Governance	• Accepted behavior policies • Censorship management • Fairness use	Security index Privacy index Dispute resolution index Cost of censorship

* Recall that the knowledge, trust, and technology enablers are common to all components (see Chapter 2).

exchange business data without losing trust, reliability, relationships, quality, or anonymity. Knowledge and data are valuable in a community. You must expose some of that data to the member companies within the community. The portal collects data on customers coming and going to the businesses within the site. The businesses want access to this information so that they can more effectively design their Web sites for participating customers. If you give out too much information though, you may violate the trust of the actual customer. It is a balancing act. One-to-one marketing is the panacea but only works if someone wants to opt in and share their data.

- Using the eBiz Readiness!™ measurement framework shows you your e-business level of readiness, weaknesses, and strengths in regards to your ability to build and support an online community.

Statistics and Numbers

- Commerce One offers auction services for 1 percent of the value of the purchase order processed and $1 per purchase order processed.
- The NYSE trades billions of transactions and trillions of dollars but generates less than $200 million annually.
- FreeMarkets was the first B2B reverse auction market maker.
- Internet portals, Internet infrastructure services, and B2B software and commerce companies rank first, second, and third, respectively, in terms of the magnitude of their market capitalization. Portals are more than 300 billion, Internet infrastructure (for example, network routers) are more than 240 billion, and B2B software and commerce companies are more than 200 billion in market capitalization.

References

[1] www.infoplease.com/ipd/A0381720.html

[2] Gill, R. "Online Communities—Building Content From Collaboration." *Research Note*, Gartner Group, May 1998.

[3] Harris, K. "Important Distinctions Between Enterprise Portals and Knowledge Management." *InSide Gartner Group*, Gartner Group, August 1999.

[4] www.aol.com

[5]www.chemdex.com

[6]Swerdlow, F.S., Cohen, E., Patel, V. "Portal Deals: Forecast and Metrics for Acquiring Customers through AOL, Yahoo! and Other Portals." Research Study, Jupiter Communications, July 1999.

[7]www.oracle.com

[8]www.killer-apps.com

[9]www.vignette.com

[10]Armstrong, Arthur. "The Real Value of On-Line Communities." *Harvard Business Review* May/June 1996.

Starting Off | Getting There | eBiz Ready!

CHAPTER FIVE

Going Against the Flow: Operational Partnering

> In every operation there is an above the line and a below the line. Above the line is what you do by the book. Below the line is how you do the job.
>
> From A Perfect Spy *by John Le Carré, espionage novelist*

Getting You Prepared

In this chapter, we further explain the concept of *operational partners:* the partners who are helping you run your business today. We explain the continuum of partners, a concept that is critical for understanding how to manage the mix of companies. The historical roots of operational partners stem from traditional supply chain management functions, but e-business has introduced many more functions that we explore in detail. All of the components are specific to the partners who are helping you run your daily operations and include the areas of knowledge management, trust, and technology. We also show you the enablers of the components and the metrics so that you can assess whether the components are working properly. We then show you how to use the framework in both small-to-medium enterprise (SME) and big business settings. The point to remember when reading this chapter is that we are giving you some tools to determine your effectiveness in dealing with the partners who make your business hum. You probably have some partners that are strategic partners and are helping you plan for tomorrow; we explain those concepts in Chapter 6.

A consulting engagement that we had with a very large food retail company highlighted the wide range of business partners that is available. The company has a whole continuum of suppliers, or operational partners, that it must manage differently. The company uses integrated e-business initiatives with some partners and uses more traditional means with others. Our client company works with large suppliers and embraces many e-business initiatives for cost-cutting measures that increase profitability. The margins in the food retail industry are extremely low. If you shave a penny off the cost of a case of goods, then you can save millions of dollars for the organization over the course of a year. On the other side of the coin is a strategy that involves using local goods from local suppliers, which makes the company's stores stand out from the competition. The local suppliers are usually very small businesses and have not embraced e-business. The small guys don't have IT departments, extranets, or many of the normal tools that can be used to keep the costs down. What it boils down to is that all parties have to be *creative*. The food distributor's challenge, like your challenge, is to find the right management equation for its operational partners—one that will deliver true value to the customer in the end. The food company's solution is to buy computers for their small supplier and communicate with them in a batch store-and-forward mode on an as-needed basis. Although sending purchase orders takes a few hours, it's quicker than traditional paper mail, or "snail mail." In addition, customers have access to local specialty food products, which enhances their shopping experience.

Introducing the Operational Partner

Novell's chief information officer (CIO), Sherry Andersen, jokingly calls herself the "chief information outsourcer." Rob Almeida of the Canadian Imperial Bank of Commerce (CIBC) substantiates the importance of outsourcing: "A business can strategically outsource everything but the management team to operational and strategic partners." Indeed, the role of the CIO is turning into one of information outsourcer. CIOs must manage the unprecedented rate of introduction of and changes in Internet application models, architectures, and software applications for e-business. Outsourcing is conservatively a $100-billion-per-year worldwide industry. The current IT labor shortage is contributing to IT outsourcing as firms experience difficulty finding and retaining qualified personnel. Firms want to rely on a partner whose core competency is taking care of IT headaches! In addition, the Web distribution channel brings unique challenges to bear on a firm. Undoubtedly, e-business will cause the outsourcing industry and operational partnering to grow at an unprecedented rate.

Operational partners help you run your current business. Outsourcing partners are only one type of operational partner. Suppliers, consultants, system integrators, hosting providers, and trading communities are other candidates for your operational partners. KPMG has a catchy commercial for e-business partnering that goes something like this: "No e-strategy, no online brand, your supply chain does not take advantage of the Internet . . . unless you partner with the right business to integrate with the Internet, your business could very well end up in here (garbage can)."

In e-business, *external service provider* (ESP) is the relatively new umbrella term for the consultant, system integrator, hosting service provider, outsourcer, or application service provider (ASP). Typically, businesses use operational partners for the following:

- To acquire necessary materials in a reasonable time and at a reasonable cost
- To reduce and control operating costs
- To reduce lead times and therefore improve product and service quality
- To allow the business to focus on core competencies
- To simplify maintenance and change management tasks
- To manage out-of-control IT budgets
- To compensate for a lack of in-house expertise
- To limit IT asset acquisition
- To increase the operational infrastructure and provide wider geographic coverage
- To create opportunities to supply a new customer service or product

E-business takes "the typical" one step farther. Operational partners are used to overcome Internet-specific challenges such as developing Internet equivalents of cash or network security. Flooz.com, a small Internet company founded by Spencer Waxman and iVillage co-founder Robert Levitan, provides an application for and the implementation of a system for online currency called *flooz*. Flooz.com has more than 50 affiliated companies, including Barnes &

Noble.com, drugstore.com, and Dean and Deluca, which all accept flooz gift certificates as currency. Flooz.com and its affiliates are considered operational partners because the company handles part of its affiliate companies' payment processing functions. Flooz.com takes a percentage of the transaction purchase price in return for its services. Accelerated growth strategies, lack of technical infrastructure, limited human resources, and round-the-clock support demands also prompt e-business companies to outsource.

Operational partners exchange detailed information for the execution of daily operational tasks. Some of the most commonly outsourced tasks in e-business are applications infrastructure, application hosting, human resource tasks, Web site hosting, customer service and support, distribution and order fulfillment processes, transaction and payment processing, and security. Operational partners such as ASPs are investing in these maturing application areas. Forward-thinking and leading ASPs such as USi provide total customer relationship management and data warehousing solutions as well. Companies are also outsourcing networking and hardware and software infrastructure. ASPs remove the difficulties associated with staffing and maintaining customer relationship management (CRM) centers. ASPs make it easier to warehouse data by providing state-of-the-art infrastructure and expertise.

SMEs that are long on vision but short on resources are relying on the ASPs for affordable e-business infrastructure and application hosting. Upshot.com, a start-up ASP, provides a scaled-down customer lead management (customer relationship management and partner relationship management [CRM/PRM]) and sales application free of charge to small businesses. Companies such as Telcos, a mature industry that is currently declining because of its outdated business models, are rapidly redefining themselves as ASPs. ASPs have three obvious advantages: SME market penetration, brand names, and deep pockets. Consultants see an opportunity to provide total e-business solutions by extending their operational partnering efforts to address infrastructure needs. For example, KPMG, a global consulting company with known outsourcing expertise, entered into a joint venture with Qwest, a brand-name telecommunications company, to create an ASP service called Cyber.Solutions.

ASPs provide value as operational partners by providing change management, application management, and application support services. The International Data Corporation (IDC) estimates that the ASP market will be worth $2 billion in 2003. Businesses are also forming partnerships with companies that provide dedicated services, such as those provided by Web designers, traffic builders, marketing specialists, merchant banks, and content providers.

Defining the Horizon

Interactions with partners can be limited or extensive. The key to e-business is to build partnerships in which you create better relationships with others. Boston University's Dr. T. Waters presents the continuum of partners[1] that follows:

- Market exchange: short transactions based on preset interactions and standard rules
- Performance contract: interactions in which both parties have negotiated expectations
- Specialized relationships: interactions that have characteristics of partnerships but are not long term and do not share common measurements
- Strategic partnerships: long-term, mutual relationships with shared benefits and goals

All of these partnerships are based on the independence and duration of the interaction. Dell is involved in all these various relationships, and they are formed based on the longevity of the technology involved—short-term relationships for short-term volatile technologies, long-term relationships for non-volatile, long-term technologies.[2]

We present a continuum of e-business partners in Figure 5-1. External service provision paradigms include one-to-one, one-to-many, and many-to-many models. Locked-in suppliers depend on one or two large, powerful customers. Consultants customize extensively for each business and hence use a one-to-one model. Infrastructure hosts and ASPs use a one-to-many model because they amortize the hardware and software across many customers. Online electronic marketplaces or trading communities use a many-to-many model. VerticalNet uses a many-to-many model; the company brings suppliers and buyers together regardless of the technology infrastructure in the individual companies.

At one end of the spectrum, management, IT, and technical consulting address the creation of a corporate business strategy and vision, business reengineering, systems design, organizational planning, and technology assessment. Consultants may have space at a customer's site and tailor the processes and applications to the business' needs. Systems integrators provide assistance in the design, creation, and installation of architectures and applications and integrate new and existing hardware, software, and communications.

Companies also outsource hardware and software applications to keep the business running. Infrastructure outsourcing includes partnerships with hardware manufacturers such as Hewlett Packard (HP), IBM, and Sun Microsystems. CIBC

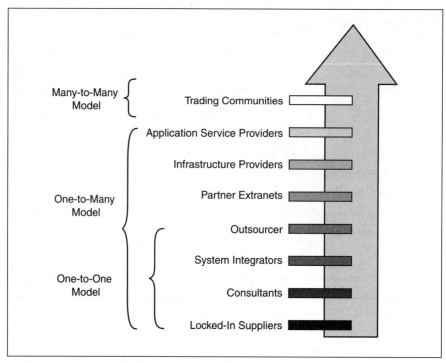

Figure 5-1   Operational Partner Continuum

spun off its back-office processing to INTRIA, Items and INTRIA HP. The partnership with HP helps manage the network and servers for technologies to distribute personal computer (PC) banking. Network hardware manufacturers such as Nortel and Cisco are operational partners with many telecommunications companies. Other infrastructure providers include software tool vendors, network management and monitoring product vendors, Web technology vendors, and enterprise application integration (EAI) product vendors.

Operational partner extranets allow for the efficient reengineering of many business processes. Novell employees can change their health plan options directly with Aetna, the company's health care plan provider. The process is much easier than filling out forms at Novell, which must be approved internally before being sent over to Aetna, where they are rekeyed. Partner extranets also facilitate supplier-manufacturer collaboration in the product design process, often leading to higher output quality. Firms hoping to improve the efficiency of their supply chains through partnering with suppliers and customers are moving toward forming strategic partnerships rather than maintaining purely operational relationships.

Whole-business process outsourcing is well established in financial areas such as payroll and payment processes. Banks have been outsourcing their check processing functions for years. Human resources is another area that is widely outsourced. Logistics, procurement, and accounts are beginning to outsource more and more. OrderTrust[3] is an example of a company that provides outsourced order processing systems, including merchandising management, order management, customer management, and financial management.

ASPs differentiate themselves from other operational partners by taking responsibility for customization and change management services—the design, implementation, operation, maintenance, and management of the applications they host for the businesses. The responsibilities include upgrading technology platforms to offer competitive business solutions. The ASPs offer service level agreements (SLAs) that require the continuous testing and monitoring of applications, hardware, and the network at the operational level. USi, a leading ASP that has 34 percent of the ASP market share in North America, sells its services by "assuming *total responsibility* for an application solution, providing the level of service to meet and exceed your business goals." The most valuable proposition to businesses is how quickly they can benefit from the services because of the ASPs' expertise in deploying e-business solutions.

Trading communities, also known as *market makers, e-marketplaces, trading e-hubs, vortals,* or *intermediaries,* are also types of operational partners because they provide services for buyers and sellers of products. In the future, online marketplace or trading communities will go beyond simple transactional data exchanges. They will exchange various types of analytical data such as actual sales, forecast sales, and inventory in real time. They will become more like strategic partners than operational partners.

eBiz Readiness!™ Components for the Operational Partner Stakeholder

The important customer-focused components within the operational partners are centered on the e-business enablers of trust and knowledge management (Figure 5-2). The trust enabler addresses identification and security mechanisms, as well as contract management. The knowledge management enablers include

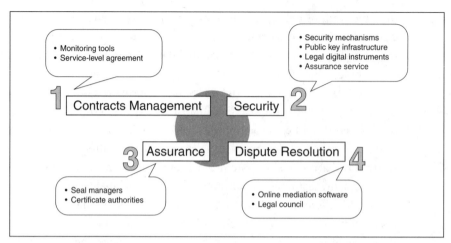

Figure 5-2, A: Components for the Trust Subset of the Operational Partner Stakeholder

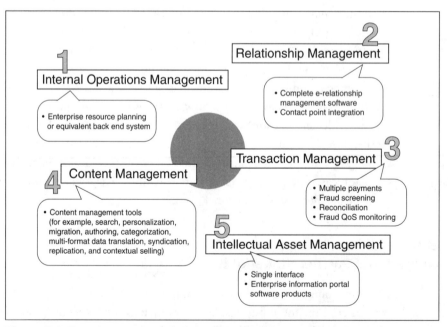

Figure 5-2, B: Components for the Knowledge Management Subset of the Operational Partner Stakeholder

internal operations management, transaction management, relationship management, intellectual assets management, and content management. Solutions for knowledge management and trust activities are available for all industries and may be specifically tailored to individual industries. Patient billing is an example of a vertical knowledge management application for the medical services industry.

Partnering for Trust Services

Partnering services for establishing trust in e-business fall into one of four categories: (1) assurance services, (2) security mechanisms, (3) contract management, and (4) dispute resolution mechanisms.

Assurance

E-business assurance services provide a statement of guarantee for the security, integrity, and authentication of electronic transactions and communications. Numerous organizations provide these services to businesses to make consumers more confident about carrying out electronic business transactions. One such organization is VeriSign, the seal manager for the WebTrust assurance service. A company that successfully applies for and receives a WebTrust seal of assurance displays a seal icon on its Web site's home page. The seal denotes that a certified public accountant or chartered accountant has confirmed that the company's e-business principles and controls conform to WebTrust principles and criteria. As a WebTrust seal manager, Verisign also independently examines whether the business complies with the criteria for obtaining a WebTrust seal. A user can click on the seal to view the details of the digital certificate, which include the type of certificate, compliance results, to whom the certificate is issued, and where the company awarded the seal is located. Having reputable accounting firms representing the logo can create a perception of a higher level of credibility and integrity than a self-regulated program. Some assurance providers carry limited insurance for certified sites.

Verisign is a leading provider of public key infrastructure and digital certificate solutions. The company provides products that allow Web sites to transmit encrypted data and authenticate the source and destination of the data. Verisign itself does not ensure merchants and customers of privacy, business policies, or transaction processing integrity.

The Better Business Bureau Online (BBB Online) assists in resolving consumer disputes and provides consumer information about business policy issues related to business advertising ethics and responses to consumer complaints. The

BBB requires that disputes be handled by binding arbitration. The BBB Online seal does not yet apply to security practices. The BBB Online Privacy service, launched in 1999, awards seals to e-businesses that follow good information privacy practices, such as clearly posting privacy policies. Privacy practices include informing the customer about the intended use of the information, disclosure of how customer information will be used, allowing a customer to "opt in" or "opt out" of mailing lists or plans, customer access to personal information and security of that information, monitoring of the commerce site by a third party, and consumer dispute resolution.

TRUSTe, founded by CommerceNet, Electronic Frontier Foundation, and the Boston Consulting Group, provides assurance of privacy for customers. The e-business must prominently display a privacy statement that addresses what information will be collected, for what purposes, and with whom it will be shared. TRUSTe does not examine business policies and transaction integrity. As it stands, e-businesses are commonly using one assurance provider and complementing the provider's assurances with technology acquisition or policy statements for issues that are not addressed by the seal provider but are deemed important to the customer and e-business. Measures for good assurance services include changes in consumer confidence, customer acquisition ratio, and indexes for security, privacy, transaction integrity, and business validation.

Bob:

We use WebTrust to verify the integrity of our business and related policies. Their services are a simple extension of the audit and accounting services provided by our Big 5 accounting partner. We're doing everything possible to minimize the perception that consumers face more risk doing business online than anywhere else. We want to maintain as much transparency as possible.

Sue:

We went with TRUSTe because it's a relatively inexpensive assurance mechanism but still provides consumers with the certainty that they are interacting with a reputable business.

Security

Your business needs to create security policies for all online and offline scenarios. Will you allow a computer with a hard disk containing sensitive business data to be taken off site for repairs? Even if the machine is repaired on site, what precautions should you take so that the data is not appropriated? Nondisclosure agreements between business parties are the norm. Awareness and education on issues that require security measures are necessary in the business setting.

A business analysis of security needs defines the service requirements, the impact of losing the services, and the benefits of implementing the security policy. For databases that contain highly sensitive data, such as some military and personal medical data, keeping the data in isolation is always an option. In this chapter, *data in isolation* refers to data that cannot be accessed remotely on or off site. Protection mechanisms may include restricting the list of users and requiring sign-in authorizations with a third party. The risk and business benefits tend to be low for this scenario; risk to the data is low because of the physical security measures, but the business benefits are low because the data is not accessible to a wide range of users that could create value from using the data. Another form of isolation can be created through islands of networks. The networks are independent and do not interact, thus virus transmission rates decrease. This type of isolation only works for functional and data-independent applications, otherwise the security defeats the purpose of having networked information in the first place.

Security protocols must address which entities the systems need to authenticate, define the communication paths between authenticated entities, state which entities need to be controlled, identify the access privileges of the entities, and specify encryption and data integrity mechanisms.

Denial-of-Service Attacks

The Yankee Group market research firm estimates that the denial-of-service attacks in early February 2000 against eight popular Web sites, including CNN, ZDNet USA, Yahoo!, and eBay caused lost sales, reductions in market capitalization, and increased spending on security measures totaling $1.2 billion.[4]

Denial-of-service attacks occur when an organization's Internet servers are overloaded with bogus requests for data or from wasteful process time outs caused by malicious users. The extra load on the system consumes central processing unit (CPU) and expensive database processing cycles, degrading the site's response time to an unacceptable level and sometimes leading to server failure. The attacks in February 2000 were allegedly caused by a hacker with the handle

"Mafiaboy" who managed to launch a simultaneous attack that was distributed from hundreds of machines belonging to unsuspecting users. Thus hundreds of user machines connected to the Web repeatedly requested Web pages from the attacked sites, generating heavy loads on the servers incredibly quickly.

Lower-level attacks are possible through SYN flooding and smurf attacks. SYN flooding occurs when the final acknowledgment to the server's synchronize-acknowledge (SYN-ACK) response is not sent, which causes the server to keep polling for the acknowledgement until it eventually times out. A smurf attack is accomplished by sending ping requests to a broadcast address on the target network. The return address (the address given for the response) is changed or spoofed to the victim's address.

Personal firewall products are available to detect and protect user machines from being hit with coordinated network attacks. ZoneLabs provides a free firewall called ZoneAlarm for home users of personal computers, and Network ICE offers a firewall product called BlackICE. A site called Shields Up allows users to have their machine ports scanned by the site's service to determine whether user file systems could be accessed remotely over the Internet. Compromised data present an ominous threat to companies and personal users alike. Compromised data can even be rolled into backups, so after a while the old, clean data become unrecoverable. What a waste for a company to use expensive data mining software on bad data—garbage in, garbage out.

SofaWare offers a solution to prevent data compromise that involves embedding firewall software in cable and digital subscriber line (DSL) modems. In April 2000, Juniper Network and MetroMedia Fiber Network announced the creation of a high-speed filter chip, the Internet processor II that filters 20 million packets of data per second, a rate much higher than its software equivalents.

Some ASPs and Internet service providers (ISPs) furnish antivirus software and firewalls as add-on services. These service providers are also doing more to educate users about security issues, especially since December 1999, when a lawsuit was filed against Pacific Bell alleging that the company did not provide adequate protection against Internet intrusions and did not inform customers that the DSL line was not secure.[5]

E-Commerce Security Technologies

Implementing a security policy involves technical knowledge, common sense, and business sense. Technical knowledge of good software engineering techniques ensures that all files made available for Internet access are screened for possible security breaches. Recently, systems administration personnel who were implementing a popular e-commerce tool inadvertently provided general Internet access to clients' order databases, databases that contained their personal credit card numbers in a public order_log.dat file. The irony is that the e-commerce tool was advertised as "secure." People who were aware of the flaw could access the site's order_log.dat files and view the credit card information simply by using a search engine. Businesses can detect security breaches in network-accessed databases by monitoring and periodically auditing their systems. For example, monitoring for repeated login attempts that occur within seconds could indicate that someone is using an automated tool to try to crack the password protection.

Technology-based Internet security methods invariably use some form of authentication, encryption, certificate schemes, or all of these methods. Access control and transmission control are two traditional technologic security categories (Figure 5-3).

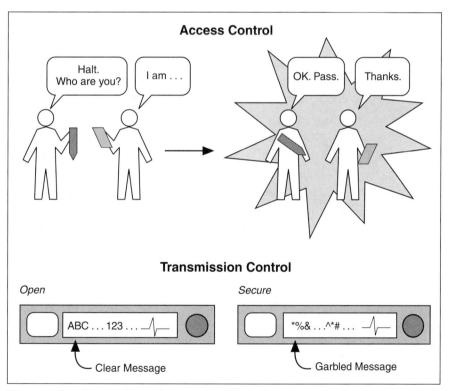

Figure 5-3   Access Control versus Transmission Control

Access control schemes involve authentication and authorization. Common forms of access control mechanisms are password schemes and other generic authentication schemes that can be characterized as "who-I-am," "what-I-know," and "what-I-have" schemes. Smart cards and credit cards use the who-I-am (name and signature) and what-I-have (the card) elements. The what-I-know element is used for more extensive credit queries (such as calling the credit card company with a question about a bill). Password protection uses who-I-am and what-I-know schemes. The more expensive biometric methods, such as those involving fingerprints or eye characteristics, in conjunction with access codes integrate all three schemes.

Keyware Technologies partnered with biometric technology providers such as Veridicom, Visionics, and Authentec to deliver biometric security solutions to the e-market. Biometrics are measurable physiological or behavioral characteristics that are used to identify an individual. Fingerprinting, retinal and iris scans, voice pattern recognition, facial recognition, and hand geometry are some of the biometric technologies. Signature recognition biometrics monitor the amount of pressure applied during a pen stroke, as well as the height and width of the pen strokes, which is more accurate than other security measures. Voice biometrics can be used for cellular telephone security, and encryption is regularly used for access control. For example, CD contents can be encrypted, and then only authorized users who have decryption keys can access the information.

Encryption is also one of the most popular methods used for packet transmission protection. The secure sockets layer (SSL) is the most widely used security protocol for Internet transactions by commerce service providers.[6] SSL incorporates public key cryptography, a technique that involves a pair of asymmetric keys (a public key and a private key) for encryption and decryption. The public key is distributing widely, but the private key is always kept "private" by its owner. Data that are encrypted with the public key can only be decrypted with the private key and vice versa.

Transmission control includes authorization, encryption, and data integrity components and is used when data are transmitted or transported over a network. Many companies partner with public key systems providers such as Certicom and Cylink to offer enhanced security in their products and services. Certicom's elliptical curve cryptography is used in 3Com's PalmPilot organizer and Palm computing platform, in 724 solutions for wireless banking and brokerage financial services, in HP's OpenView network management product line, in Sybase's SQL Anywhere mobile computing solution, and in DigitalOwl's content distribution solutions, to name just a few. In February 2000, Cybersafe and Certicom created a partnership so that they could develop secure payment systems for e-business that provided transaction and identity protection, which in turn provides consumer privacy and eliminates online fraud opportunities. The Brazilian government uses Cylink Corporation's PrivateWire product to ensure the security of online tax filing transactions. In 1999 the product helped six million Brazilian citizens securely file their 1998 income tax returns.

The primary obstacle to the widespread deployment of public key systems is the lack of a support structure—a *public key infrastructure (PKI)*.[7] A PKI associates authentic public keys with authorized users; administers the management of the keys, including their generation, distribution, and deletion; and stores, retrieves, and archives keys. The status of the keys, whether valid, lost, revoked, stolen, or expired, needs to be monitored. A PKI can also provide an archive of security violations. The PKI is composed of a set of communicating trusted certificate authorities (CAs) because no single governing body can manage all the potential users in the world. Thus the individual CA, such as Verisign, administers the usage of a subset of user keys. The digital certificate, issued by the certificate authority, contains data such as an identifier of an owner of the certificate, an identifier of the organization that issued the certificate, a public key, and an expiry date. The certificate is signed using the certificate issuer's private key. Everybody knows the certificate issuer's public key. Certificates are a standard way of binding a public key to a name. The commercially available Certicom TrustPoint consists of a line of flexible cross-platform PKI products that allow original equipment manufacturers (OEMs) to develop applications with built-in digital certificates.

The U.S. Postal Service sums up the public key infrastructure technology with the following definition: "[It] is a system of digital certificates and certificate registration authorities that validates each party involved in an Internet transaction. CAs guarantee and confirm that the individuals exchanging information online are who they claim to be." In 1999 the U.S. Postal Service partnered with Cylink Corporation to put a PKI platform in place to provide new communication solutions to postal service customers.

Metrics for identification mechanisms include the strengths of the guarantee for nonrepudiation, authentication, and scalability of the solution mechanism.

Bob:

We want to allow our accountants online access to the company's financial data. Biometric-based electronic authentication methods will be implemented by the year's end. We're very keen on using digital signatures to speed up some of our contract process. However, we are awaiting government legislation to ensure that the digital signature will be accepted in a court of law.

Sue:

Our small business e-commerce needs are provided by our ASP partner. We made sure we knew what level of security we needed and used this as a major criterion for selecting our ASP partner. Our final ASP choices had the right levels of security and control to allow us to feel comfortable about outsourcing the program.

Contract Management

Contracts are very important because they define the terms and agreements with the operational partner, the e-business, and ultimately the customer. They address issues such as terms of payment and SLAs.

Vendors tend to make more profit from longer contracts, but e-businesses must be aware that unforeseen opportunities may be on the horizon, so they shouldn't lock themselves into long contracts. Former 5-year contracts are being replaced by shorter 2- to 3-year terms. Advances in technologies and competitive pressures are also reducing the length of the terms. Who would have thought 5 years ago that e-mail systems could be as inexpensive and bandwidth prices could be as low as they are today?

Service level agreements

SLAs are very important contract inclusions. E-businesses and their operational partners need to agree on the business and technical metrics to be used for service level assessments. All parties must have common definitions for what constitutes the attainment of the service levels. For example, stipulating and obtaining an average response rate of 3 seconds could mean that for 25 percent of the time, the response rate is 4 seconds and the rest of the time it is 2 seconds. However, that fourth second could be the second that causes customers to go to another site.

An e-business must have an almost 100 percent guarantee of network and application availability. In 1999, eBay's market capitalization decreased by $2.25 billion during a 22-hour down time. Other large companies have reported annual losses of $4 million resulting from local area network down times. Vendors have difficulty guaranteeing service levels because an SLA must be derived from the SLAs of the various components that deliver the overall service. The overall SLA is determined by the SLA of the weakest component. For example, nGage, a payment service for Aliant's e-commerce service, has an accompanying contract stipulating that service levels must be maintained. The Aliant customer network is robust, hence it is assigned a good SLA. In contrast, the nGage component runs across a variety of networks to get to the gateway (of the customer network provided by Aliant), and other networks throughputs are not timely in comparison. The SLA for customers using the nGage payments is based on the nGage component, not on Aliant's network. The overall customer SLA is based on the worst SLA in the virtual organization.

Network system monitoring tools are slowly being put on the market. Currently the main vendors of these tools are Tivoli Systems, Computer Associates, and HP. Technical assurances for quality of service address transaction throughput, response time, video and audio quality, reliability, and availability. Security levels and compliance rules should be stipulated along with these quality-of-service meters.

Payment model

Another important component of the contract is the payment model, which can take various forms. *Cost plus contracts* are based on the actual cost of service and a fixed vendor. *Time and material fees* are based on hourly rates and incurred expenses. *Fixed-price contracts* give businesses more control over project budgets, although vendors may use junior staff members to save costs when they think they may have to make a lower margin or lose a contract. *Business-benefit contracts* are harder to negotiate because payment is tied to the project's contribution to the business's value (such as how much it decreased costs or increased revenues). *Shared risk and reward contracts* are more commonly used with strategic partners. The businesses share development costs and expertise to create a product or service and then share the revenues. *Fee-for-service contracts* are based on service usage. They can follow pay-per-use models or charge a flat monthly fee. Regardless of the payment model chosen, e-businesses reap the biggest benefits when their objectives are aligned with those of the ESP, supplier, or trading community with whom they are contracting.

Contract completeness criteria address issues such as customization management, product or service upgrade management, platform management, and training and support. Penalty clauses serve as incentives for enforcing vendor timelines, and convenience clauses serve as useful methods for canceling the contracts with no penalty. Termination clauses must stipulate the full recovery and security of the business's data. In summary, the contracts should address the completeness and level of the services to be provided to the e-business.

Bob:

We have many operational partners and hence manage many contracts. We use systems to monitor our network, but now we need a system that can help us control the contracts. Each one has SLA terms that we must manage and maintain. If our operational partners don't live up to their SLAs, we take a harder bargaining stance; if they perform poorly, we have other forms of recourse.

Sue:

For us, any operational partner is a major extension of our business. We don't have too many partners because they are too difficult to manage, but we know what our standards are and emphatically insist that they are met. Our customers expect quality and nimbleness—and that's what they get. If an operational partner keeps us from meeting our customers' expectations, the partnership quickly becomes history.

Dispute Resolution

Governments throughout the world advocate the use of alternative dispute resolution (ADR) to resolve business-to-business (B2B) and business-to-consumer (B2C) conflicts. *ADR* refers to any method used to settle a dispute outside of a courtroom. The two most common forms of ADR are arbitration and mediation; other methods include early neutral evaluation and conciliation. Arbitration is a simplified trial with a mutually agreed-on arbitrator or panel. The "trial" has no discovery process and uses simplified governmental rules. Mediation is the cheapest, most informal method of ADR. Mediators attempt to create a win-win situation for both parties. Trained mediators work with the parties to reach a settlement or agreement that both parties accept. Companies such as clickN-settle.com, eResolution, and Resolve Mediation Services provide e-businesses with ADR services over the Internet. These programs try to settle claims more quickly and more cheaply than traditional legal means—with no resulting adverse publicity—at any time, day or night.

Some types of consumer claims are suitable for online ADR. Cheaper costs result from lower (or the lack of) travel expenses, lower litigation fees, and the elimination of the need to physically host the involved mediators and parties. The time saved by simply eliminating travel and face-to-face meetings allows a mediator to resolve more cases in a given period, also resulting in a lower cost per case. People may really latch on to this type of quick, online dispute resolution because traditional litigation is so unsettling and disruptive to the parties involved. Online resolutions may also provide more valuable and appropriate settlements to the parties involved, such as apologies, job offers, or future business—none of which are outcomes in formal courtroom cases.

Being judged by the media and the overall adverse publicity that can be generated in a courtroom are no longer problems when you use online ADR. Demands and offers are confidential; only the final settlement amount or agreement is revealed. The insurance industry is particularly good at using ADR. An insurance company can have tens of thousands of claims being disputed at any one time. Departments that handle liability claims for businesses can effectively use ADR to reduce the cost of handling disputes and resolve most of their cases more quickly than they would if they used traditional forms of litigation. Every area of law is addressed: contracts, commercial liability, construction conflicts, employment practices, environmental issues, medical malpractice, and personal injury. E-commerce exacerbates multijurisdictional claim issues and multiparty cases. The online ADR companies are tapping into the $160 billion spent on litigation each year in the United States.

clickNsettle.com's business model works like an auction. Once both parties agree to use its services, they must agree to the final amount that is negotiated by the company. The plaintiff submits a settlement demand amount online. clickN-settle.com electronically notifies the defendant of the amount, and the defendant can give a counter offer. The negotiation takes place entirely online. When the demands and offers sufficiently converge, clickNsettle.com's system notifies the parties that the settlement is near resolution.

eResolution recently partnered with RealNames, a service provider that helps Internet users more quickly and easily find brands, companies, and products on the Web using the products' familiar names instead of their complicated Web addresses. EResolution currently provides domain name ADR and Real-Names Internet keyword dispute resolution.

Metrics for operational partnering for dispute resolution include cost per case, case close rate, average settlement amounts, credibility (the experience of the providers and their arbitrators or mediators), and general satisfaction of both parties.

Bob:

We have an established legal framework that spans our global trading routes. We are used to providing service in multiple countries but see ADR as a means to augment our legal process. We have ADR written into our contracts so that it's always an option. Whether ADR is used for a particular case is a judgment call made by our senior legal advisor and the legal department.

Sue:

We finally sold our product to a market outside of our domestic trading area! We made sure to write ADR into our sales contract because I don't think that we can afford to pay for the traditional legal process if something goes wrong. I know ADR may not be as binding as going to a judge, but that's the compromise we're willing to make. We feel that online ADR empowers us to trade on a global scale—fairly and competitively.

Partnerships for Knowledge Management

Operational partners for e-business knowledge management fall into one of five categories: (1) internal operations management, (2) relationship management, (3) transaction management, (4) intellectual assets management, and (5) content management.

Internal Operations Management

A fair amount of company data from which knowledge can be gleaned are stored in databases through enterprise resource planning (ERP) packages and in several application repositories or in stand-alone digital and nondigital islands. The challenge for companies is the extraction of useful information out of the disparate areas that store the internal operations data. Nondigital formats are being put into digital form so that the content can be managed like other assets. Although the data include information about the internal operations management, parts of internal operations management are often outsourced to many different vendors with their own specific hardware and software platforms, thereby increasing the complexity of data interoperability.

ERP packages focus on the internal components of a company—finances, human resources, and materials and facilities management. VerticalNet uses Corio's ASP services for its ERP. Corio hosts PeopleSoft software for enterprise management. Most companies outsource their payroll processing. CIBC outsources check processing and infrastructure hosting. Many of the better ASPs offer a service to customize ERP installations for clients—a high-end service because ERP implementation and support are the most costly and complex of software installations, requiring significant client customization. Customization may entail writing new code and hooking it to the ERP. A large amount of enterprise data for small businesses are stored using accounting packages and one of the numerous stand-alone PC applications. Managemark, a leading producer of B2B applications for small and medium businesses, offers management Web applications. Managemark's Internet subscription services give access to ExpensAble and TimetrakAble. ExpensAble is used for expense report creation, submission, and review, whereas TimetrakAble is used for time tracking and reporting, which helps increase the efficiency and productivity of the mobile workforce.

Internet e-business applications have successfully penetrated the procurement area, which is more commonly known as *e-procurement*. Ariba was the first company to offer an Internet-based operations procurement system. Ariba sells software to companies that allows the companies to connect to Ariba's online catalog of office supplies. Company suppliers are asked to join the Ariba network of suppliers so that each supplier can see the other suppliers' offerings. Commerce One is similar to Ariba in that it provides tools for building e-procurement marketplaces. The advantages of trading in e-marketplaces include access to more suppliers and the creation of a transparent market, which leads to procurement of higher-quality product and services, better product availability, and in some cases better prices.

Both Ariba and CommerceOne are moving toward using an ASP model for procurement. Instead of licensing the procurement software to the business for use with clients, Ariba and Commerce One will host all the software for the business. This move will enable the procurement software companies to penetrate the midsize enterprise market.

Metrics for internal operations management include the following:

- Cost savings for procurement items
- Changes in the perceived "business benefit" of the service
- Changes in productivity, such as the number of people it takes to do a task in a given time

Sheri Anderson and NOVELL

DOING IT TODAY

As we mentioned previously, Sheri Anderson is the CIO at Novell, which she jokingly says stands for "chief information outsourcer." Here is what she had to say about her approach to managing information systems.

"It is a framework for thinking about what the IS department does. They set up services instead of devices or things. So rather than asking, 'Can we outsource these servers or this human resource application box,' we want to think about the tasks as services. We want to outsource to obtain additional capabilities but we don't want to outsource our control. Novell's network directory service (NDS) is one of the key elements in our framework, especially because we have human resource services as one of the first points of outsourcing. We don't want control of employee information to be outside the company, but we do need the outside capability.

"We took our information architecture document and the process map that we had built for the whole company and turned the process map into a services map. We asked ourselves some questions. What are the services that we supply

continued

in terms of supporting the business? In terms of business profits? What are the services that we provide as the IS department?

"We assessed how much we were currently outsourcing, which was more than people thought. We assessed which services were likely candidates for outsourcing and identified the barriers to doing so. We put the services in a typical two-by-two matrix, with one dimension as 'simple versus complex' and one as 'generic versus proprietary.'

"The initial thought was that the simple and generic services were the most obvious candidates for outsourcing. This turned out not to be the case. We began to run into some state-of-the-art issues that we had to incorporate into our findings. For example, we considered the fact that our business is a global business, and some ASPs who were providing services in the United States (and Canada) really could not effectively serve the whole world.

"We outsource our 401K processing to an American company called *Fidelity*. They provide account access to our employees, and we have built a link between our intranet and the external Internet to allow the data to go back and forth securely. Employees can go to the Interweb [Novell's Web-enabled information portal], identify and authenticate themselves, and then see data on Fidelity's Web site. This is a good example of how we aren't outsourcing a device or a system. We didn't go to Fidelity and ask for an application. We asked for a certain update frequency, certain availability, and other factors. We defined the service rather than the implementation. So when I am talking to people about the process of outsourcing in a high-tech company, I am constantly saying things like, 'It isn't about outsourcing PeopleSoft. *Right?* It is about outsourcing a service—hiring more employees or managing benefits. It isn't about a server box and application.' I don't care what Fidelity runs their 401K applications on. I only care about my service level. Because we are in the business of selling software, thinking in terms of software applications turns out to be a hardened mindset. I constantly have people telling me things like, 'I read about this company that will outsource Oracle for you.' Well, we don't want to outsource Oracle, we want to outsource the *services*—keeping the general ledger, financing, staffing—instead of getting server boxes.

"In a nutshell, we looked at this matrix of candidates for outsourcing. We thought about how we could structure things as services instead of boxes, how

continued

much has already been done, and the candidates for continuing the process. For example, to nobody's surprise, a high percentage of human resource tasks such as payroll were already outsourced. We are in the process of outsourcing stock option management, which is a task that we had been doing internally for a long time. It will cost more, but outsourcing will provide enormous additional business capabilities that we could never have provided internally. Thus we are making a good business choice. Now in some cases, we found that outsourcing costs more and doesn't provide any better business benefits; those tasks aren't good candidates for outsourcing yet. One of the things we like about the service perspective is that it allows us to look at the cost per service and the cost per service level. Because, of course, as IT people, we have to explain to our customers that *better* isn't necessarily cheap.

"The services map process has resulted in numerous good things. Although as the 'chief information outsourcer' I must be doing a lousy job, because only about 10 to 12 percent of our current services are outsourced!"

Relationship Management

The focus of a majority of today's e-businesses is marketing, sales and services, or CRM. Results are already pouring in regarding the transition from publishing information on paper to publishing it on the Web, as well as input regarding business contact information integration. CRM companies such as Siebel Systems and BroadVision partner with ASPs such as USi and Corio to provide e-businesses with hosting options to satisfy this market.

Small businesses that would like to outsource relationship management can consider ASP vendors such as Upshot.com and Salesforce.com for e-sales hosting solutions. The software tracks prospect leads, manages contacts, shows current sales forecasts, creates reports, and shares best sales practices with other sales team members. The hosting services are provided at a low monthly fee. The fee varies according to the number of users. Siebel provides a community resource site at Sales.com that offers tips for salespeople and software tools for individuals. Although SalesForce's offerings for sales has only a fraction of the functionality of Siebel's e-sales, the 80-20 rule applies for small businesses—20 percent of the functionality is used 80 percent of the time. Small businesses do not usually require the complex, function-rich features needed by larger businesses. Marc

Benioff, chairman of SalesForce.com, sees a SupportForce.com, ServiceForce.com, or FinanceForce.com on the horizon. SalesLogix launched Interact.com, a site that provides e-business services to midsize business sales forces. Scheduling a sales demonstration in an out-of-town location through the Interact.com site immediately triggers the presentation of airline reservation and hotel choices.

Service provisioning, from the ESP's point of view, is the process of implementing, or "turning on," a service for a customer. It can be as simple as clicking "yes" in a software program to as complex as the business provisioning needs dictate. Forming partnerships to provide services is entirely plausible. Companies such as Support.com offer a comprehensive support platform for Internet infrastructure products; they can provide immediate support for users through the Web. Support.com provides technical support for products such as Microsoft Windows. Corporate IT departments, outsourcers, and ASPs can use Support.com's database on the Internet to identify and resolve problems. Corporations can increase PC usage levels without adding extra support personnel to the IT department. A company called Everdream is using Support.com's platform to provide support services to small businesses through the Internet. The company states that for a small business the monthly cost of supporting a PC is approximately $250. The company offers its services at a substantially lower monthly fee.

Another popular outsourced application is e-mail management. E-mail is the most commonly used Web-enabled point-of-business contact. Managing e-mail falls under the area of relationship management, particularly CRM, in which high volumes of e-mail are appreciable. Gartner Group estimates that the volume of inquiries sent through e-mail channels will increase about 100 percent annually through 2002. E-mail response management systems (ERMS) manage and track e-mail from arrival through receipt, autoacknowledgement, routing, queuing, and response. The e-mail response can be a fully automated response, which suggests that quality assurance is good, or a partially developed e-mail, sometimes called an *autosuggestion*, that is sent to a customer service representative (CSR) for checking. The autosuggestion program generates a suggestion by looking in a predefined response library. Stand-alone e-mail systems will not stand the test of time because as we explained in Chapter 3, contact point integration is mandatory. Therefore e-businesses that form operational partnerships with outsourcers that have dedicated e-mail services or ASPs that are dedicated e-mail providers should find out the outsourcers' or ASPs' plans to integrate e-mail into larger relationship management applications. The e-businesses may then want to negotiate a short-term contract.

Solutions exist for strategic business partners and professional service management. Niku automates obtaining, managing, and delivering professional services. The company offers a package that manages business development, project management, resource management, time and expenses, project billing and accounting, and knowledge management. ASP USi hosts iNiku.com, Niku's business portal for consultants, contractors, and professionals working individually or in small businesses. USi also partners with Siebel to provide sales force automation and customer care to increase productivity for field sales, telesales, telemarketing, call centers, help desks, customer service operations, and third-party reselling operations. ChannelWave is another vendor whose application for PRM is hosted by leading ASPs.

Another e-business term gaining popularity among partners is *collaborative e-business.* Sainsbury, a large British supermarket operator, and Nestle, the world's largest food company, use collaborative e-business processes for efficient promotion planning and product launches between the two companies. Efficient Consumer Response United Kingdom (ECR UK), an organization that officiates efficient customer response principles, estimates that $4 billion can be saved annually in the European market through more efficient promotions. Collaborative e-business processes mean tying of back-end supply chain to the front-end customer processes such as marketing, sales, and service. Retailers, manufacturers, and suppliers will be able to synchronize dynamic supply chain data. Regional advertising, launches of new product lines, simplification of the feedback loop by instantaneous access to consumer likes and dislikes, improved customer service, seasonal promotions, returns processing, or any project that needs to be managed will benefit from collaborative e-business. Partners will be able to track consumer sales and trends in real time and plan accordingly. Basket analysis and marketing management data can be shared. Collaborative partnerships have roots in operational partnerships, but once planning for the future enters the picture, operational partnerships gain strategic value!

The customer focus is evident in efficient consumer response (ECR) initiatives based on the principle of providing the best quality service to the customer through integrated partner collaboration, information sharing, and efficient supply chain operations. ECR depends on other initiatives such as just-in-time (JIT) inventory management—which ensures that products are available when and where the business needs them. ECR cannot be implemented by one company; the supply chains of others must also use JIT management (also known as OrderTrust) and have visibility. ECR and JIT initiatives are continuous replenishment programs. ECR initiatives benefit product promotions. Retailers and suppliers are able share information on the performance of previous product promotions, allowing retailers to better estimate levels of product in stock and suppliers and therefore better estimate production levels. Sharing information about new product lines or promotions can also allow suppliers to respond more quickly to consumer demands.

Another supply chain initiative, *collaborative planning, forecasting, and replenishment (CPFR),* was developed by Logility Systems in partnership with Heineken. CPFR builds on continuous replenishment programs and advanced planning and scheduling (APS) systems. APS systems focus on the planning component of an organization and include tasks such as forecasting the demand of customers, suppliers, and organizations. Incorporating and integrating CPFR tools with CRM programs and back-end ERP programs gives an organization insight into its operations. This insight helps the management to make accurate and informed business decisions and decreases the cycle time for getting accurate information to marketing and sales personnel. Logility's products—Demand Chain Voyager and Supply Chain Voyager—are used by Heineken USA and Eastman Chemicals facilities worldwide. Essentially, the product bolts on to existing systems such as SAP R/3. Heineken has reported a 50 percent reduction in cycle time for determining a customer's need, delivering the product or service to fulfill that need, and finally receiving a customer satisfaction report.

How else is relationship management changing? E-businesses are forming closer relationships with their customers. Traditionally, operational partners obtained indirect customer feedback from their companies but rarely received it from the end-customer because of complex channel and multistage distribution networks. Companies are slimming down their distribution networks and forming much closer relationships with the end customer.

For example, Clearwater Fine Foods, a Canadian seafood company in Halifax, Nova Scotia, has formed a partnership with United Parcel Services (UPS) to create a major distribution hub in Louisville, Kentucky. Live lobsters that are caught in Nova Scotia are shipped to and kept in Kentucky. They are then shipped to continental locations via overnight air freight—directly to the customer rather than to supermarkets or fish markets. This type of close interaction with customers, which has been facilitated by IT, is allowing companies to use new, innovative ways of doing business, as well as form new types of relationships. These include make-to-order (manufacturing products that have already been ordered) versus make-to-stock (predicting future sales to determine the amount of product to be manufactured), dynamically linking to ensure continuous product improvement, and creating the community that will bring together the customers.

The overall metric for measuring relationship management is the level of integration of all its pieces. Thus CRM must be integrated with supply chain management for supply chain visibility, PRM must be integrated with CRM for quick and accurate customer responses, and CRM must be integrated with internal systems or ERPs to derive the extent of the customer demand-pull.

Bob:

Our company has many products and services that are sold throughout the world to customers with a very diverse set of requirements. We also have thousands of suppliers for the goods we need. Relationship management allows us to manage the whole mix from customer to supplier and ties in our ERP system. Our customers and supplier relationships span the whole spectrum—some are complex and others are very simple. Whatever the case, we have a very good picture of our relationships.

Sue:

We sell a very specific mix of products to a very specific customer base. We use relationship management mostly for the customer relationship aspect. We need to ensure that we don't miss anything, because we are only as good as our last order. We are looking at integrating relationship management into our ERP, but it isn't a necessity today.

Transaction Management

Transaction management includes management of information such as acceptance of payment, fraud screening, business rules, and reconciliation processes. The reconciliation processes are necessary because some e-businesses serve as infomediaries rather than e-commerce storefronts. Transaction management differs from transaction processing because of its extra features. Basic transaction processing functions include credit card verification, fraud screening, and electronic funds transfers from consumers to merchants. Transaction management functions include additional features such as order management and notification, management of customer information, creation of shopper communities, and reductions of the technology load on the servers of commerce service providers. For example, Cybercash[8] offers transaction processing and management services—they recognize that the extra features will help them stand out from the competition and add customer value to the virtual value chain.

Several companies, such as ClearCommerce, OrderTrust, and Calico Commerce offer products for transaction management and processing from the point of order to the point of shipment. Their products integrate sales into ERP systems and trusted third parties such as payment processors and shippers. Security mechanisms, taxes, shipping, fraud detection, payment processing, and transaction recovery procedures are established. Customer notifications of order completion and shipment are also transaction management functions.

Most companies that provide transaction processing solutions rapidly get companies' products on the market so that businesses can quickly achieve a marketplace presence. Asia-Links, a portal for business between Asia and the United States, recently formed a partnership with Calico Commerce and created an online marketplace in 90 days. ClearCommerce also offers transaction processing hosting and professional services such as product customization and application development, system integration, preimplementation planning, and training. OrderTrust, a company used in leading trading communities such as VerticalNet, manages the entire life cycle of an order. Management of the process does not stop when the product is shipped to the customer but continues through the delivery of the product or service to the customer's establishment. OrderTrust's architecture allows the supplier's inventory to be monitored in real time. The supply is checked when the customer places the order so that customers can receive real-time notification of out-of-stock or back-ordered products. The OrderTrust network translates orders into the vendors' receiving format (such as e-mail, EDI, extensible markup language [XML], or file transfer protocol [FTP]). OrderTrust is highly flexible and allows vendors to use various storefront technologies to connect to the trading community. OrderTrust monitors issues such as falling under the threshold of stock reorder levels, discontinued items, and price changes. The company handles return updates and refund requests as well. OrderTrust is an applicable solution for many industry verticals.

Calico Commerce offers customized solutions for specific verticals: telecommunications, financial services, hi-tech manufacturing, industrial manufacturing, and retail companies. GE Global eXchange Services has services for telecommunications, retail, transport, and manufacturing verticals.

ASPs offer template B2B e-business solutions. Leading ASP USi hosts Broad-Vision for e-business transaction management. Its capabilities include a personalized shopping experience, order processing and management, customer support, payment, fulfillment, content management, dynamic marketing, advertising, community building, and integration with front- and back-office systems. USi offers the Microsoft Site Server to smaller companies. Verio rents products that increase businesses' Web site e-commerce capabilities—such as virtual shopping carts, catalog management, merchant account services, and back-room services.

Other companies provide parts of the transaction processing equation. Internet Billing Company (IBill) provides secure transaction processing solutions for B2C and B2B e-commerce. It enables companies to receive payments for goods and services over the Internet through online checking, credit card billing, and phone billing. IBill maintains payment interface, payment processing, and ancillary management services. More than 10,000 online businesses use IBill's products. IBill advertises that it has a rapid setup time (2 days) and no setup fees.

Interoperability of the transaction processing platform components is the key to proper functioning. Metrics that may be used to evaluate how well the transactions are being managed include transaction response time, transaction throughput, reliability, availability of transaction management services, catalog availability, and index for integration of front- and back-office systems.

Bob:

We have an entire department that looks after our transaction services. Currently, online sales are only a small fraction of our business, but we recognize that the fraction will grow. Parts of our business require additional processes such as fraud detection and online credit checks. One plan we've considered is to let our channel partners use those non-integrated functions first and then work on integrating them some time in the future.

Sue:

Our provider gave us all the transaction management tools we needed—we sell 80 percent of our goods online. We needed integrated tax codes, especially for North America, and fraud and credit checks. We also needed a smooth process for refunds. If a customer is entitled to get money back, we must make sure that the process of doing so is simple. Customers are the key to the success of our business.

Intellectual Asset Management

Enterprise information portals, also known as *corporate portals,* are considered critical technology for intellectual asset management. Examples of intellectual assets include employee expertise, reports, patents, and corporate documents. HummingBird Systems and Autonomy provide corporate portal products that allow a smooth transfer of knowledge among employees and partners. As documents (such as e-mail, word-processing, database, and ERP files) are read or added to, the information is simultaneously catalogued. When an employee opens a report, the system automatically lists two or three of the most closely related documents or employees or partners who have some degree of expertise in the subject area.

Another intellectual asset area is personnel training. gForce Systems is a leading supplier of corporate learning portal solutions in the e-learning marketspace. gForce products enable the rapid transfer of knowledge. gForce software—eLearn Author, eLearn Publisher, and eLearn Manager—is used to produce, manage, and deliver personalized Web-based training for employees, partners, and customers. The products enable users to add streaming media to PowerPoint slides, edit synchronized media, and sort and catalogue material into a learning repository. The system also tracks content usage and user feedback.

Tools that can facilitate knowledge transfer are categorized as *collaborativeware.* GroupSystems products include online tools to help users create methods and processes so that partners, customers, and employees can work together, any time and any place. Companies such as PlaceWare support virtual conferencing, virtual presentations, and "follow-me" browser features to enable group work while reducing costs by "virtually" bringing people together.

Workforce management and retention are completely automated in Deploy Systems' comprehensive Employ! product. It facilitates hiring and retention of top-notch talent. E-businesses can also outsource recruitment activities or buy services from human resource sites such as Monster.com.

Metrics for intellectual asset management include an accessibility index, speed of knowledge transfer, "amount" of knowledge transfer, and usefulness of the knowledge assets. The accessibility index refers to how easy or difficult it is to get access to the knowledge resources. The speed of knowledge transfer is defined as the length of time that an individual takes to become familiar with all of the company's knowledge on a particular topic. The "amount" of knowledge transfer refers to how well the company captures knowledge online. The usefulness of knowledge assets indicates how helpful the knowledge-management initiative has been.

Bob:

We have recently re-vamped our corporate intranet so that information is more accessible and useable. One of the areas that we focused on was the proposal area. A lot of company information is buried in those proposals. We now use an Autonomy program to get access to all kinds of unstructured data. This increases the value for the customer because we can put much more pertinent information together.

Sue:

Our company only has a handful of developers, so we recently ran into difficulties when one of them left. Each of them has a wealth of knowledge. Our business' value is based on people rather than physical assets. We have decided to try to capture as much information as we can and put it in an intellectual asset program. I hope that we can get an outsourced service so that we can focus on our business.

Content Management and Data Warehousing

Content management

Timely and accurate content is critical for a successful e-business. Strong content brings traffic to Web sites. It provides value and builds mind share and customer loyalty. Fresh and accurate content maximizes the quality of time that users spend at a site and is a reflection of the e-business brand. Good content increases page views and click-throughs, which are essential for e-businesses that depend on advertising revenue. Gartner Group states that a poorly maintained Web site results in lost opportunity, brand erosion, and potential legal liability issues. Content consists of text, graphics, multimedia, executable code, and information retrieved from databases. Sites may have to manage hypertext markup language

(HTML), JPEG, graphics interchange format (GIF), C++, common gateway interface (CGI), active server pages, JavaScript, Shockwave, XML, virtual reality modeling language (VRML), and perl scripts. Banner ads, links, and executable code for new services are examples of content that need to be managed in online communities. Managed content for retail Web sites is similar: ads, product pricing, image graphic updates, and updated links.

Managing large amounts of Web content, such as store or auction catalogs, requires tools to develop, categorize, and index the information. Companies have a lot of data (such as customer, partner, employee, product, sales, service, production, and shipping data) that are viewable or accessible on the Web. The heart of the content management process is triggered by a user request to obtain data or store data in the repository. *Viewing data* involves data retrieval, data normalization, and presentation formatting. Data can be retrieved from one database or many company or partner databases. *Data normalization* is the translation of data into a predetermined standard format like XML. Data can be retrieved from several databases that use different data formats. Normalization converts all formats into a standard format. *Presentation formatting* refers to placing the data in a contextual Web page for user viewing. The data that are added to or changed in a repository—for example, when a supplier updates a catalog or an employee updates company information—must also be categorized according to their attributes and placed in the appropriate databases.

Companies such as Vendors Interwoven, OnDisplay, Versifi, and Vignette offer content management solutions for publishing large volumes of content in a company's intranet, extranet, or Internet site. Most of the products include marketing tools for content that is being viewed, facilities to integrate with external systems, and some decision-support system for understanding the relationships between the customer and content. Web content managers are "bolt-on" tools that can be integrated with CRM, ERP, and human resource systems.

Updating content for an e-business involves issues such as content migration, new content creation, replication, and syndication. Many e-businesses have home-grown Web applications and content that are buried in files in inefficient areas and need to be under the control of a content manager. Content creation is no longer just the domain of the IT department; material is being written on-the-fly by subject-matter experts. Some e-businesses support global content development teams who publish any time and anywhere. With easy-to-use tools that provide automatic versioning and archiving, the authors can directly store updated content in the repository, effectively taking the responsibility off the shoulders of the IT members.

Replication issues arise when an e-business supports different development and production servers or has multiple independent and mirror sites. Development servers are like sand boxes; developers build and test solutions in them. The sand box is forever changing; software code and other data are continuously being fixed, added to, torn down, and reworked. Employees can verify their content changes and test them at any time. After the authors are satisfied with the results, applications are moved, typically with a content manager, to a stable environment on production servers. Sometimes the directory structures on the development and production servers are different, so the content manager uses appropriate mapping to resolve them.

The time and money that can be lost during down times make it essential for e-businesses to have mirror sites. Mirror sites are also necessary for disaster recovery and efficient performance. Regular Internet users know that download sites closer to home can offer better download rates; for example, customers can be offered two geographical options, such as American or Australian. Replication issues can be complicated in many large e-businesses because they have numerous Web sites. For example, Condé Nast hosts several of its magazine Web sites, including *Vogue, GQ,* and *Condé Nast Traveler.* The content throughout the sites has to be consistent, which means that all sites should be simultaneously updated. Another issue for an e-business with multiple sites is a consistent "look and feel," which can be achieved with content manager templates.

The syndication business model is a relatively new aspect of content management in the online world. Just as newspapers receive information from services such as Reuters and then extract and edit the content for local presentations, the same can be done on Web sites. You can host a franchise on a portal by "owning" a few portal pages that have parent e-business content targeted to the portal's community. Each franchisee customizes content for another target audience. Interwoven defines syndication best: "Syndication provides the opportunity to franchise Web assets to all types of end users who will add value on the way."

Managing copyright material is another aspect of content management that must be considered. Intellectual property is a key issue in e-business because many companies' assets are based on intellectual property (IP) rather than tangible assets. Content management for copyright materials is a new business area that includes materials such as music, software titles, and videos. Traditionally, you loaned or purchased the content and put it in a collection for your own use. E-business opens up a whole new, very accessible method for moving and trading intellectual property to others without paying the proper copyright fees.

Reading content involves issues such as personalization, search effectiveness, and contextual selling. By monitoring customer interests and habits, content managers can personalize content to the targeted end user. Search engine integration is an obvious feature—users need quick access to content.

Contextual selling integrates content and commerce. Customers showing interest in a certain product can be sent ancillary material such as ads, videos, or audios about the product. For example, you could enhance the buying experience for a customer who wants to purchase a CD online by providing streaming audio snippets of all the songs on the CD or reviewers' comments about the CD. Contextual selling triggers these mechanisms when customers request more information about or show interest in a product.

Content management in e-marketplaces is more challenging than management of a single Web site in terms of scale, format differences, and response performance. A single integrated suppliers catalog must be displayed to the buyers. Numerous suppliers operate in a marketplace, and all have nonstandard product and service codes. The formats of the initial supplier catalogs (some of which are paper catalogs) are translated into XML. Product codes are unified so that they are seamlessly integrated into the marketplace. You also must manage and synchronize individual supplier changes. Suppliers tend to retransmit their whole catalog instead of just updating their old ones. The marketplace content manager needs to extract the updates and apply them to the integrated supplier catalog. Cardonet is an example of a company that provides a comprehensive content management suite for e-marketplaces.

In summary, a content manager can ensure that the contents of the Web sites hit the market on time and within budget. The manager facilitates the development and testing of content and provides a high-quality, personalized Web experience. Content management solutions must be able to handle the global network of development and production servers and remote server farms.

Data warehousing

Whereas the content managers keep operational data moving, *data warehouses* provide tools to quickly analyze business data and glean the business intelligence out of an e-business data repository. Sagent software, a leading data warehouse solutions company, provides extraction, transform, and load (ETL) tools, and Web analysis and access capabilities. Similarly, E.piphany addresses the relationship management market by allowing employees and partners to securely access data in real time. E.piphany solutions provide extractors for major enterprise systems (such as SAP, Oracle, and Baan), major front-office systems (such as Clarify, Pivotal, and Siebel), and major e-commerce systems (such as BroadVision, Vignette, and Microsoft Site Server). One E.piphany application provides analytic, campaign management, and real-time personalization solutions using data that it has compiled from many diverse sources and then integrated. E.piphany products support data mining capabilities for customer profiling and behavior pattern recognition, as well as forecasting features for various analyses and projections. Its estimated set-up time is less than 16 weeks. E.piphany recently acquired the Octane software company and was ranked by Gartner Group as a first mover for total electronic relationship management (eRM) applications (the first company to produce and market eRM). Octane products complement companies' existing systems because they give users the ability to perform service, sales, and support activities from a single system and using any of the customer touch points—whether Web, e-mail, telephone, chat room, or fax.

It is disturbing to consider how much of a company's collected data are drastically underutilized. For example, grocery stores can collect vast amounts of point-of-sale (POS) data about customer buying habits, such as frequency, amount, and types of purchases, but they don't do anything with the data! In 1995, Sears still could not analyze its customer purchasing data details. Even obtaining summary information required dedicated state-of-the-art systems. Companies' systems should continuously capture and archive data it so that in the future they can work with operational and strategic partners and utilize the information. The stored data could actually help determine strategies such as the types of products that are available in the store and which complementary products should be advertised together and so on. Thus an index of data usage is a measure of how well a business is using its content to glean useful information.

Metrics for measuring content management are data consistency, data currency, speed of data update, search response time, search accuracy, and interoperability with external systems.

Bob:

Our hundreds of offices alone generate so much information that managing external sources of content exacerbates an already difficult situation. We chose Vignette Story Server to manage our content because we can integrate workflow (and authorization) with the content to make our jobs much easier. We now have the freedom to repurpose some of the data for use in other areas.

Sue:

Our external content management efforts focus on our community. We are too small to create our own community site, so we formed a partnership with an established portal and are providing and managing some of the content. We use Internet access to get into our partner's content management system. We don't have a content manager for our internal Web site—we find that version control is a big challenge. We want to buy a lightweight, trimmed down content manager or outsource the function.

Small-Business Perspective:
Operational Stakeholder Assessment (SMEManufacturer)

SME Perspective: We weren't sure whether we could afford to outsource to an operational partner. We investigated the business benefits—and found that we *couldn't* afford *not* to outsource!

Local beer maker, SMEManufacturer, has been brewing beer for the last 100 years. Brand recognition is high. Business is brisk. In addition to its manufacturing plant, the business owns a quaint, old, defunct brewery, which they open to the public during the summer tourist season.

The management at SMEManufacturer has been investigating how they can introduce a Web channel. They would like to use the Web to sell to local pubs and liquor stores, and they want to build a larger export market. The brewery plans to form an online beer community for their brand to create site stickiness (in other words, increase the time people spend on the site and how often they visit). They plan to have a link to the community from the larger, generic beer.com site. Additionally, they plan to provide real and virtual tours of the old brewery. They will market and sell general merchandise, such as t-shirts, mugs, and sun visors with embroidered or printed brewery logos, from the Web site and the actual old bricks-and-mortar brewery.

The main office currently has an IT staff of four employees. They are busy all year round maintaining the financial, manufacturing, and mobile sales force systems. The management would like to get the Web site up and running before the opening of the old brewery this summer. They have determined that they will need a person with Web design and development expertise and an IT infrastructure platform to host the Web site. From past experience, they know how difficult it is to hire and retain good local IT personnel. They also realize that they need assistance with the platform purchasing decision. They can either bring in a consultant and do the project in house or have the Web site designed by a local firm and hosted by another company. A third alternative is to use a single vendor who would be responsible for designing and hosting the site. The management has hemmed and hawed over the first option because they don't really want to use their limited resources to acquire new IT assets and employees. However, they are aware that an integration problem may arise if they use one of the other two options. For the best overall system function, the Web site should be connected to the rest of the back-end system. The management is concerned about maintaining the security of the corporate data that will be moving over the network, as well as about the inherent network delay in connecting the back-end and front-end systems. They decide to send requests for proposals to ASPs nationally to assess the options more completely.

After receipt and review of the proposals and an assessment and summary by the management, SMEManufacturer proceeds with the third option. They like the idea of having one vendor who is responsible for the entire project. Costs per month are lower than if they used the in-house option. The ASP vendor has expertise, a good track record in the hosting business, and a reputable Web design firm as its operational partner. The SLAs also guarantee 99.99 percent up time, rapid response rates, security, and around-the-clock support. The agreement incorporates business value metrics for assessing contract performance. The ASP will customize its offerings for integration with SMEManufacturer's existing systems, which the ASP will host as well. Best of all, the Web site is scheduled to be online in 30 days!

Big-Business Perspective:
Operational Partner Assessment (BBGovernment)

Bob:

I'm a consultant with the local branch of a large consulting company. BBGovernment has many services that need to be transferred online. Because of space constraints, we have restricted our attention to two services. The following case illustrates how we can use the eBiz Readiness!™ framework to analyze proposals from vendors or ASPs.

Government strategists have recognized that their agencies and departments are gold mines of content. They have developed an overall initiative to go online, so each department is given a mandate to move their services to the Web.

BBGovernment is the department responsible for regional town and planning activities. (In some countries it is known as the Department for Housing and Municipal Affairs). BBGovernment oversees registries of land lot surveys, architectural building plans, and deeds. It is responsible for property assessments; tax inquiries; aerial photos; property maps; topographic maps; survey information; land development; and related programs such as loan payments, mortgage payments, and land leases.

BBGovernment identifies a small subset of services that it will move online. It examines its options for executing the transfer and continuous maintenance of online content. BBGovernment first identifies its simple services. One is providing deed, property maps, and survey information online. Currently, people who want a copy of a deed must actually go to the department's office and provide their last name to a clerk, who electronically looks up the tome for the deed. The indexes for the paper copies are on the department's internal computer system. The clerk provides the tome identification and relevant page numbers, and the people have to go to a room to retrieve the deed information. The relevant pages are then photocopied for a fee of $10. Three salaried personnel handle these tasks.

The Department of Works wants to create a service for simplifying the process of obtaining bids from contractors who maintain roads and clear tree growth away from physical overhead lines such as telephone and power lines. BBGovernment plans to share its geographic information system (GIS), which contains current digitized maps and aerial photos of the region, with the works department to make the service possible. Contractors will access the GIS system, target the maintenance area, and submit online bids to the department for the contract to maintain the area. The GIS system allows the contractors to view new flora growth or dilapidated road conditions without having to drive out to the sites. The cycle time for the bidding process will be reduced.

BBGovernment does not have the resources—staff or expertise—to perform the conversion exercise. Several issues must be addressed.

- The executives do not have expertise in information systems; they don't know what transferring services online involves.
- The hardware and software infrastructure to support the service applications is not available. No supporting government agency is available to assist in the process of evaluating what may be necessary.
- The company needs teams of people who can physically key or scan in the reams of content in some realistic time frame.

The top executive recognizes that the company needs to outsource the online transition and services. BBGovernment hires a consulting firm to help the executive create a request for proposal (RFP) document for the two services described. The firm uses the eBiz Readiness!™ framework as a guide for determining what the ASPs need to address in their responses. After a few weeks, several ASPs respond with in-depth proposals, and the company gets a good idea of what it will cost for an ASP to host the two services.

The consultants then use the eBiz Readiness!™ framework to assess the thoroughness of the ASP proposals. For the deed access service, the consultants consider how the ASPs address content management, relationship management, and SLA issues. For the shared service for the contractors, the consultants consider the ASPs' attention to transaction management, content management, relationship management, and trust components. The consultants assess whether the enablers for these highlighted components are present in each ASP proposal. They assign ratings to each component based on the rating scale given in Table 2-2. They weight the identified components at 4; other components in the framework such as intellectual asset management are weighted at 0. After the assessments the consultants present the executive with gap analyses of the ASP proposals. Their presentation includes accompanying polar plots to thoroughly clarify the findings for the executive. The eBiz Readiness!™ framework clearly identifies the reasons that the consultants are recommending hiring a particular ASP.

The consultants help the executive with contracting out the data warehouse and GIS designs to other operational partners. In their responses to the RFP, several of the ASPs had recommended *their* operational partners because of their expertise in design. Finally, the consultants negotiate the contract terms on behalf of their client—BBGovernment.

Are You Ready?

Table 5-1 provides a snapshot of all the components, enablers, and metrics essential for successful operational partnering. Some partner metrics have indexes. Low index values are poor ratings; high index values are good ratings.

Table 5-1   Metrics for the Operational Partner Stakeholder (*cont.*)

Components*	Enablers	Metrics
Contract management	• Monitoring tools for expiry of contracts and quality of service • Service level agreements (SLAs)	Service completeness Quality of service SLA compliance Term length suitability Speed-to-market index Expertise level Service level Service cost Resource index Business benefits
Security	• Algorithms and mechanisms • Public key infrastructure (PKI) • Legality of digital instruments • Assurance services	Authentication index Nonrepudiation index Privacy index
Assurance	• Seal managers • Certificate authorities	Consumer confidence rating Customer acquisition Security index Privacy index Transaction integrity index Business validation index
Dispute resolution	• Online mediation software • Legal counsel	Case close rate Cost per case Settlement amounts Customer satisfaction

Table 5-1   Metrics for the Operational Partner Stakeholder (*cont.*)

Components*	Enablers	Metrics
Dispute resolution (*cont.*)		Business satisfaction Confidentiality index Credibility of provider and mediators
Internal operations management	• Enterprise resource planning (ERP) or equivalent back-end systems	Cost savings in business process Increased business benefit per service Increase in productivity
Relationship management	• Complete e-relationship management software • Total capture of business information at each contact point	Overall integration index Relationship management integration index (customer relationship management [CRM], partner relationship management [PRM], and supply chain management [SCM]) ERP and relationship management integration index Metrics for customer Engage and Support in Chapter 3
Transaction management	• Multiple payment, fraud screening, and reconciliation capabilities • Capability to monitor the quality of service during transaction execution	Integration of front-end and back-end systems Overall quality of service Availability of services, transaction response time, transaction throughput, video quality, audio quality, video rate Interoperability of transaction management components Metrics for customer Order and Fulfill components in Chapter 3
Content management	• Content management tools • Full functionality: search function, personalization, migration, creation, categorization, multiformat data translation, syndication, replication, and contextual selling	Level of integration with all systems containing content Data consistency Data currency Update speed Search response time Search accuracy Interoperability with external systems Full functionality index Usage of analysis results index
Intellectual asset management	• Single interface to all pertinent data • Enterprise information portal software products	Accessibility index Knowledge transfer speed Knowledge transfer amount Knowledge asset usefulness Management of all types of data (unstructured and structured)

*Recall that the knowledge, trust, and technology enablers are common to all components (see Chapter 2).

Highlights from this chapter include the following:

- Some of the reasons companies seek partnerships are out-of-control management of new technology, accelerated growth strategies, multiple projects, new enterprise solutions for e-business, accelerated time lines and around-the-clock demands for support, resource shortages (for example, of capital or qualified employees), and perceived dilution of core competency.
- Channel partners may plug the gaps in areas such as fulfillment, market development, market presence and penetration, implementation, and execution.
- Types of operational partners include suppliers, consultants, system integrators, outsourcers, infrastructure providers, ASPs, and trading communities.
- Interactions between operational partners and customers have traditionally been limited to feedback from the company—rarely did it include feedback from the end-customer because of the levels of indirection inherent in complex channels and multistage distribution networks. Companies are slimming down their distribution networks and forming closer relationships with the end-customer.
- Integrating ASPs into the customer value chain allows the experts to handle the e-business operational and you to focus on your core competencies. ASPs are responsible for around-the-clock support, change management, hosted product upgrades, and platform infrastructure, including hardware, software, and personnel.
- The operational areas that can be outsourced or hosted are transaction management, content management, intellectual assets management, relationship management and internal operations, ADR, and other trust mechanisms.
- Operational partners can be valuable for providing trust services, as do CAs and security product providers.
- SLAs are the core of contract management between operational partners.
- Using the measurement framework shows areas in which high-level operational partners can be useful. We take an e-business-solutions focus and consider high-level operations.

Statistics and Numbers

- IDC estimates that the electronic support industry will grow from $3.1 billion in revenue in 1999 to $14.2 billion in 2003.
- Cahners-In-Stat Group states that small businesses with annual revenues of less than $10 billion and fewer than 20 employees spend $57 billion annually on computer-related expenses.
- A 22-hour failure of the eBay site cost the company $5 million in revenue and reduced market capitalization by $5 billion.
- Gartner Group estimates that 60 percent of e-business Web channel expense is for content development, 15 percent for software, 20 percent for support, and 5 percent for hardware.
- Nike has outsourced 100 percent of their athletic footwear manufacturing to numerous production partners throughout the world.

References

[1]Waters, T. "The Importance of Developing and Managing Business Relationships." *Inside Gartner Group* July 1995: 2.

[2]Magretta, J. "The Power of Vertical Integration: An Interview with Dell Computer's Michael Dell." *Harvard Business Review* March/April 1998: 75.

[3]www.ordertrust.com

[4]Niccolai, J. "Web Attacks Could Cost $1 Billion." *IDG News Service* February 2000. www.pcworld.com/pcwtoday/article/0,1510,15219,00.html

[5]Spangler, T. "One in Four Broadband PCs at Hack Risk." *Inter@ctive Week* April 2000.

[6]Hidgins-Bonafield, C. "The Electronic Crane: E-Commerce Infrastructure Builds Upwards." *Network Computing* December 1998: 44.

[7]Agnew, G. "Security, Cryptography, and Electronic Commerce." APICS'99, Saint Mary's University, Halifax, Nova Scotia, Canada.

[8]www.cybercash.com

CHAPTER SIX

Hand-in-Hand into the Future: Strategic Partnering

> Strategy is a style of thinking, a conscious and deliberate process, an intensive implementation system, the science of ensuring future success.
>
> Pete Johnson

Getting You Prepared

A major factor in today's business equation is how closely you must work with your partners, your customers, and even your competitors. This network of alliances is what we call your *strategic partnerships*. This chapter will give you the ability to define the areas in which you need strategic alliances and how you must change to effectively manage strategic partners in the e-business space. We explain the component framework that you can use to analyze your business. We apply it to certain situations and show you what some companies with strategic partnerships are doing today.

The beauty of this chapter's opening quotation is that Pete Johnson's comment is so true! Coming up with an idea is a small portion of solving a problem in a business. How well you implement that idea is the key to success. To ensure that your company is not a "flash in the pan," enjoying rapid success and then rapid demise, you must plan your future—and then strategize and create that plan. It's simple to plan within the confines of your organization, but it gets much more difficult and is critical to your success to engage external entities that will help you to ensure continuance and growth.

We currently work with companies that are trying to become e-business enabled. These companies hired people to bring new thinkers into the organization, but their biggest influences come from their strategic partners. The strategic partners are already e-business enabled and are teaching organizations new ways of thinking, new ways of doing business, and most importantly, ensuring that they become e-business enabled. The e-business initiatives do not come about by blind chance. Your board of directors and senior executives must recognize that forming strategic partnerships is the only way to change your business quickly and achieve success in the process. You must lay the groundwork for successful partnerships to bear fruit in the marketplace.

Introducing the Strategic Partner Stakeholder

Strategic partners are those partners whom you think hold the key to your future success. Forming a strategic partnership is not just a simple transaction, such as buying a service or product. You are linking an outside business to your customer value proposition to help you plan the future of your business. In the simplest terms, good customer value is why your customers want to do business with you.

Businesses either *build* or *acquire* strategic partners. Regardless of which method is used, you must understand part of the core operational issues of your partner companies. Many partnerships are moving from strictly operational to strategic partnerships because of business goal alignment among the partners and the ease with which knowledge can now be shared through e-business network applications. The newly acquired strategic partners will want to interact with and learn about your company's operational capabilities as well. For example, integrated resourcing, billing, and order tracking are frequently used process in all these companies.

More and more, large and small companies are entering into strategic alliances to meet the ever-broadening range of *immediate* customer needs, adapt to technologically induced change, diversify, and ultimately increase revenues and shareholder value. A strategic alliance allows large investors to outsource the research and development of new markets to smaller, agile e-businesses. For example, Delta Airlines invested in Priceline.com to tap the Internet market for airline seat auctions. The small start-up companies' benefits also include short time to market for products and services and new technology. The larger companies provide brand names, channels, and financing.

An interesting by-product of some alliances is the accompanying rise in the stock price of the partner companies, particularly of the older, more established partners. When Time Warner announced its merger deal with America Online (AOL) in January 2000, the stock price of both companies increased. Time Warner's rose $20 per share, and AOL's rose but then decreased slightly a few days later. The merger of the technology firms, eTek Dynamics and JDS Uniphase, resulted in a $42.50 increase in share valuation for eTek and $3.50 for JDS. Both firms offer high-bandwidth fiberoptic backbone products.

Strategic alliances are becoming so critical in the Internet economy that new positions such as "vice president of strategic alliances" are appearing in organization hierarchy charts. Responsibilities of these new positions include strategic planning, design and execution of complementary tactical business plans, channel strategy management, identification of new products and services, and the execution of growth objectives and strategic partnerships.

Traditional interactions with strategic partners include cross-colonization of the board of directors, product managers, and other key business positions to facilitate the information exchange. In e-business, extranets are typical tools used for interactions among strategic partners. The extranet is different from a simple Internet site because only trusted partners have access to the extranet; the general public uses the Internet site. Extranets are convenient, provide rapid access to information, and reduce communication costs for e-business.

This chapter identifies the important components that you should target to support your strategic alliances. We provide a framework for measuring the success of your e-business alliances with your strategic partners. We explain the key strategic partner interaction methods, as well as discuss the key terms used in a customer-focused e-business.

Bob:

We have a lengthy annual business-planning process that involves a top-down view, starting out with the executive and including all the business units and their business plans. Strategy is critical to our future success, and our shareholders demand it. Our strategic planning process now officially includes some of our strategic partners. Our strategy is implemented at all levels of our organization, and we plug teams in to work with external partners wherever it makes sense.

Sue:

My strategic planning process involves putting my thoughts down on paper and then bouncing the ideas off my business partner and mentor and the rest of my family. I see strategy as critical to my success because it forces me to think of the future. A lot of my strategic direction is driven from my strategic partner's direction. Before I formed the partnership, I had to make sure that I believed in the strategic partner's direction because I didn't have the clout to influence it significantly.

Defining the Horizon

Businesses need to determine whether they are ready to form successful partnerships, as well as whether their potential partners are ready to do so. We define the term *strategic partner* using the strategic partner continuum that follows.

Strategic Partner Continuum

Many levels of strategic partnerships exist. Some examples are partnerships for technological research and development and the creation of processes and product, purchase-supplier alliances, joint ventures, equity investment partnerships, and licensing partnerships. Long-term marketing agreements for marketing, distribution, and production with other companies are also strategic relationships. A value-added reseller (VAR) is a strategic partner. An online affiliate is a modern example of a strategic alliance in which a site supports links to numerous partner businesses or affiliates. The company brings in revenue by obtaining a percentage of the money made from customers who were directed to the affiliate site and purchased products. For example, amazon.com and marthastewart.com use the affiliate model.

The continuum of strategic partners (Figure 6-1) ranges from majority investors, who integrate tightly into the e-business, to loosely integrated suppliers. The stakeholders shown are not an exhaustive list of all the types of strategic partners but represent some of the main groups. Majority investors hold more than 50 percent of the voting shares, and minority investors hold less. The allied strategic partners within the continuum are partners who have added value to their businesses through partnerships. The value may be increased market share, new market penetration, or decreased costs for new customer acquisition and customer retention. Enhancing the supplier relationship leads to strategic partner programs such as just-in-time (JIT) inventory management. At the bottom of the continuum are suppliers who traditionally represent the "old school" and conduct business transactions at an arm's length.

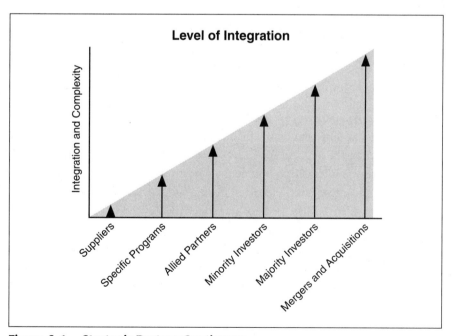

Figure 6-1   Strategic Partner Continuum

Bob:

Our strategic partners are companies with whom we've had loosely formed and contractual relationships for years. They recently collaborated with us formally to plan for the future, and I think it's critical that we do everything to incorporate them into our business. Some of our newer strategic partners are helping us transition into e-business. We are all working hard, but the strategic partnerships help us accelerate the process.

Sue:

We defined our strategic partners in our original business model. However, I find that defining new strategic partners is a continuous process in the Internet economy. The partners I find most useful are those that help my business launch into new markets. It can be difficult to get the attention of the bigger companies, but it is getting easier now that my business is growing. I only have enough resources to monitor a couple of relationships closely, so we must be careful as we choose our strategic partners. If we put too much time and energy into the wrong partner, it could break us.

Allied partners are used for customer acquisition and market expansion. The Canadian Imperial Bank of Commerce's "CIBC Inside" strategy is an example of allied partnering. Although not as pervasive as "Intel Inside," the CIBC Inside strategy is intended to double the current customer base (8 million) of Canada's second largest bank. Thwarted in an effort to increase its customer base through a merger with Royal Bank of Canada, CIBC turned to the U.S. market. They have formed an alliance with the Winn Dixie grocery store chain, which is based in Jacksonville, Florida, to offer financial services. They are tapping into Winn Dixie's existing customer base of more than 1,200 supermarkets.

VerticalNet, an online business-to-business (B2B) marketplace, has a strategic alliance with Microsoft. VerticalNet promotes Microsoft's products and services throughout its industry-specific community Web sites. VerticalNet's formula for success is combining good content with community building, commerce support, and multiple strategic alliance agreements ([Content + Community + Commerce] × Strategic Partnership = VerticalNet). In the partnering arrangement, Microsoft is to use its BackOffice and FrontOffice software to create the VerticalNet community solutions. VerticalNet will subsume Microsoft's trading community plans. Furthermore, VerticalNet will use other Microsoft services as part of its e-business Web platform. In the coming years, Microsoft has planned to place more than 80,000 storefronts in the various vertical markets. Planning for the future is clearly an important element in this partnership because the use and value of online marketplaces are predicted to explode during the next 5 years. VerticalNet's online marketplace gets validation from Microsoft, which is now a huge Internet player. Microsoft can widely demonstrate the effectiveness of its e-business software solutions and build community in a new business forum. Businesses recognize that online marketplaces such as VerticalNet will be a powerful medium for customer acquisition and retention in the future. VerticalNet has an international community of millions because of its alliances with portals and content providers such as Yahoo! and Deja.com.

An important strategic partner in the sales, marketing, and service side of business is the VAR. Integrating and optimizing the mobile sales force, e-sales, channel partners, and retail partners' sales channels are customer-focused e-business priorities. Benefits to selling through multiple channels include increased revenues from enhanced market reach, reduced time to market, and enhanced customer service at lower cost. Most customers use more than one channel for obtaining customer service and sales or marketing information. Customers often find themselves reaching for the telephone when a company's Web site is performing too slowly or they need human assistance. Sometimes they leave messages or try to get assistance from both channels for the same problem. Companies such as ChannelWave Software, Allegis, and Partnerware focus on providing solutions for managing channel partners. You can think of your mobile sales force and e-sales team as partners to maximize the benefits of these packages. Because more than 50 percent of vendors provide leads to their VAR partners, lead management is a standard feature in support applications. Other features include support for joint business planning, and quick and targeted marketing, sales, and service information dissemination.

At the lower end of the strategic partner continuum, alliances exist for co-managed and vendor-managed inventory. In extreme cases, some of these alliances may exhibit captive-buyer and captive-supplier features. In a captive-buyer relationship, the buyer has no choice but to buy from a particular vendor.

Because the vendor's products are so highly specialized and the level of competition in the upstream market is low (as it is for some technology products), suppliers are hard to find. The captive-seller relationship is often defined by the strength of the customer. A large customer may dictate how the seller does business. The vendor then invests a lot in infrastructure to service that customer.

More partners are working more closely with each other through specific programs such as continuous replenishment management of supply chains. Initiatives like continuous replenishment enhance the relationship and often evolve into new or tighter strategic partnerships. Quaker Foods, a global food manufacturing company, provides goods to Sobeys, a national grocery chain in Canada. Quaker and Sobeys instituted a continuous replenishment management system. Quaker transitioned from being an operational supplier into strategic partner. Quaker handles inventory at the Sobey store level and gains intimate knowledge of the point-of-sale (POS) information for all Quaker-produced items that consumers purchase. The alliance enables the partners to coordinate specials and bundle like goods for the end-consumers. The two companies have built this relationship up to the point at which they share the expertise for the enterprise resource planning (ERP) software, SAP R/3, which is convenient because both companies are going through a revision upgrade of their SAP systems.

Detailed information is exchanged among strategic partners, and the information is then used for planning for the future; information that is exchanged between operational partners is used to plan simple, day-to-day operational tasks. Corporate information includes marketing, customer, security, and financial data.

The following examples show that a strategic partner can be a superset of an operational partner, and the lines defining the two types of partnerships can become blurred.

- Hutchison Telecom, Cable & Wireless HKT Mobile Services, and SmarTone Telecommunications Holdings intend to develop a common security standard for mobile e-commerce transactions. "M-Cert," the initiative being carried out by Hong Kong's three largest mobile phone operators, is aimed at promoting development of mobile e-commerce in Hong Kong by facilitating the adoption of a single standard for all public key infrastructure (PKI) based mobile e-commerce services. The three companies, fierce competitors in Hong Kong's crowded mobile phone market, said they would jointly invest HK$10 million during the project's first year and could increase the sum later if necessary. They said the M-Cert standard would ensure the authentication, integrity, nonrepudiation, and confidentiality of electronic transactions.

- The small Internet company Flooz.com, founded by Spencer Waxman and iVillage co-founder Robert Levitan, is the source for an online currency called *flooz*. Flooz.com has more than 50 affiliated companies, including Barnes & Noble.com, drugstore.com, and Dean and Deluca, that accept flooz gift certificates as currency. Flooz.com and its affiliates are operational partners because Flooz.com handles part of the affiliate companies' payment processing functions.

- Telecommunications Applications Research Alliance (TARA) is a springboard for new Netcentric products and services. TARA assists many small organizations with financing, research and development, and partnering. Companies within the TARA framework consider TARA as a strategic partner because growth synergies are created for both partners. Planning for the future is necessary for the success of both partners, success which has been attained by small companies such as ClearPicture.

- General Motors' auto-parts suppliers are considered strategic partners within its integrated supply chain. General Motors involves each supplier in the design process to identify how to manufacture the goods correctly and forecast the facilities that will be required to meet the demand of the product. All of the automotive suppliers and strategic partners have been involved in an initiative called the Automotive Network Exchange (ANX). This extranet service allows the strategic partners of the Big Three auto manufacturers (General Motors, Chevrolet, and Ford) to communicate securely. One of the key network service providers for the Canadian ANX network is Bell Emergis, a company that has worked very closely with its American counterparts to produce the robust, secure network required to exchange information. The network allows all types of business information to be transmitted and can turn operational partners into strategic partners.

- Shaw Cable is a partner of Rogers Cable, the major cable provider in the United States. Rogers Cable partners are able to use the "@home" and "@work" programs within their business. The partners do not develop the products and services but do serve as channels for them. An alliance formed as a resource complement allows companies such as Shaw Cable to have services that they could never afford to develop. "Fast and furious partnerships" could be the mantra of today's businesses.[1]

Market exchanges, which are located at the bottom of the partner continuum spectrum, are relationships in which no specialized assets have been developed that can work in a proprietary way with a single partner. In a marketplace a
company can switch partners at low cost and with minimal consequences. Highly
standardized products and services created with stable and mature technologies
are commonly traded on market exchanges. Popular market exchanges are
e-steel, VerticalNet, Chemdex, and FreeMarkets. Monster.com and the British
start-up First Tuesday host online job marketplaces. Digital Gem brings together
Canadian small-to-medium enterprises (SMEs) and facilitates the mergers and
acquisitions process. InsWeb Insurance aggregates multiple insurance providers
and sells insurance policies online. Biztravel.com brokers for business travelers
and agencies.

Bob:

Our company has many
blurred strategic/opera-
tional partnerships—they
used to be operational in nature,
and now they are very strategic.
Even some of our competitors have
become our partners—kind of like
the "co-opetition" environment that
we read about. Our future depends
on how quickly we form partnerships, so we are working out how a
business our size can accomplish
that feat.

Sue:

I like the incubator model,
in which the investment
firm brings together facilities and resources to build the business. I used it to get my business off
of the ground. It gave me access to
resources that I would not normally
have had, including financial,
people, legal, and other types of professional services. More importantly,
it gave me access to successful men-
tors. The incubator model was the
key to our success, and two of our
strategic partners were brought in
from the "early days" of the model.

Partner Relationship Management

Channel partners responsible for customer-facing processes such as sales, supply
chain, and service processes are benefiting from a new class of software applications for indirect channel management called partner relationship management

(PRM). Today, PRM mainly concentrates on the reseller partnership. We expect that in the future, PRM functionality will include support for research and product or service development and integrator relationships. Integrators are parties that resell a company's product or service by integrating or bundling it with one of the party's own products or services or a third party's products or services.

Processes and activities that today's PRM automates are channel product and program management, channel communication, fund management, lead management, partner profiling and partner acquisition, and extended team selling. Automation decreases distribution costs and increases dissemination efficiency of leads, marketing literature, quotes, and price lists. Lead management facilitates lead tracking and forecasting. Each salesperson that takes responsibility for a lead is held accountable for that lead. The accountability results in increased sales performance because leads don't fall through the cracks. Partner profiling allows an e-business to target the most appropriate partners. Profiles within a PRM system are kept to manage partners' data such as expertise, contacts, and services. Partner information such as sales information and lead close rates are also maintained in the profiles. Fund management allows for the request, distribution, and tracking of market development and co-op funds. Channel program management enables program launches and tracking and the evaluation of return on investment (ROI) per partner-specific marketing programs.

Tom Di Marco and BOEING

DOING IT TODAY

Tom Di Marco is proud of Boeing's Part Analysis and Requirements Tracking (PARTS) Page initiative. Boeing has improved customer satisfaction by cutting the lead times to get replacement parts to airline customers from 30 days to 10 days and then to 2 hours. The PART Page is complemented by the Spares Ordering Non-stop Inventory Control (SONIC) system. The SONIC system is not just a data repository and presentation interface, but a whole logistics system that enables parts to arrive to a customer quickly. Boeing has eight distribution centers; three are in the United States, and the rest are located in strategic places worldwide. The distribution centers can be repositories for higher moving parts but may also

continued

store very large parts. The SONIC system can locate where all the parts are in the world, from where the order comes, when a customer receives an order, what customers typically want to buy, alternatives that may be available, and where the customer must go to get the part. It then generates all the appropriate shipping information. Bar code technology is used to track the parts through the entire process from picking, packing, over-boxing, and shipping. The customer can log into the PART Page and see the status of the order at any stage.

The strategic partner interface to the SONIC system allows suppliers to manage interaction with Boeing. Suppliers can get Boeing's inventory levels and actually forecast requirements up to two years in advance. Production schedules are based on the forecast, and it is critical to the success of Boeing's partners to have accurate information. One major difference in the aircraft industry over other forms of transportation is that it is highly regulated. There are regulations dealing with certification, handling, storage, and other aspects of spares support. The SONIC system captures all this regulatory information and provides the customer with access. The value chain for the customer is the richness of information presented, ranging from real-time inventory to historical manufacturing information.

Boeing has about 200 strategic partners who manufacture airframe parts. The SONIC system and the manufacturers' interface allow a rich exchange of information. Highly complex machined components are produced by a subset of suppliers. Boeing uses these suppliers for difficult parts that need only small runs. The SONIC system enables the customer to be closer to the design process of these types of suppliers.

Additional value is provided to the customer through the provision of on-line maintenance manuals, service manuals, and fault detection manuals. Customers use illustrated parts catalogues to find out what part(s) they need. The systems are separate today, but future plans call for integration of the PART Page with all the manuals and information stored in other Boeing sites. This consolidated view of the spare parts, obtained through enhanced knowledge sharing between Boeing, its suppliers, and its customers, is a critical step in giving rapid, useful information, as well as more *value*, to the customer.

eBiz Readiness!™ Components for the Strategic Partner Stakeholder

Customer touch points are the links between the customer-focused business entity (the e-business) and its stakeholders. The stakeholder we are examining in this chapter is the strategic partner. The links provide high value if they are used to their fullest capacity, but they provide low value if they are simply not used. Your e-business must make strategic decisions about which links to emphasize as you balance issues such as cost, resources, strategic importance, and the loss of previously proprietary information.

The eBiz Readiness!™ evaluation framework is customer-focused, meaning that it is based on the customer demand-pull of information—they demand something, and the company responds (rather than the company initiating the exchange, or "pushing" information). Recall that the framework facilitates, guides, and provides a context for how a business interacts with others in the e-business environment. The components to fully support a strategic partnership may be within your company or may be within other businesses to which you outsource. This framework evaluates the capabilities of your overall organization and helps you determine the value and effectiveness of your outsourcing components.

The high-level overview of the strategic partner components and enablers is shown in Figure 6-2. The following sections give more details about the

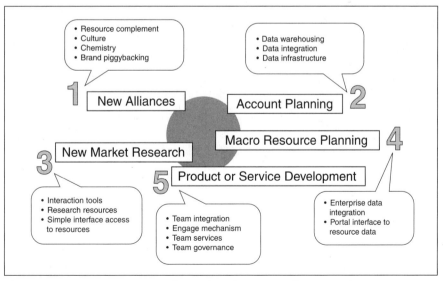

Figure 6-2   Components and Enablers for Strategic Partnering

components, explain why they are important, and show their determining factors with examples. The components are numbered; the enablers are boxed.

Strategic partners collaborate on business development. The partners move the business forward as they create plans for operating in the marketplace. Business development helps you build and maintain a successful business by focusing on the stakeholders and creating the right products or services to match the customers' needs. Each stakeholder's capability can be leveraged through joint business development. Joint business development can include all the strategic partners but usually involves various subsets of business partners, depending on the project or goal. Development tasks include account planning, macro resource planning, new market research, and product development. The key to successful business development is appropriate knowledge sharing; a central theme in e-business is that greater value is obtained through increasing depth of knowledge and increasing the speed with which that knowledge is used.

The strategic partner process cycle includes identifying strategic partners and carrying out joint business development.

Bob:

This framework is critical for us because although we have separate divisions doing these tasks, we all have to work together. I see this as a way to give us one vision that we can share.

Sue:

I actually wear all of these hats—chief executive officer (CEO), vice president of marketing and sales, chief information officer (CIO), clerk, and "chief bottle washer"—as do my business partner and mentor. I find the framework useful because it forces me to think of all the components that are involved with dealing with strategic partners.

New Alliances

Businesses form new alliances for numerous reasons—to increase their customer base, develop new products or services, complement resources, gain new expertise, offer new services, retain customers, innovate, and lower the cost of entry into new markets. Your business must form new alliances with the right companies to gain strategic value.

Targeting an allied partner may allow you to use *brand piggybacking* to increase the size of your customer base. Partnerships with well established portals such as Yahoo!, AOL, and amazon.com and communities such as iVillage and VerticalNet almost guarantee new customers. Partnerships with companies such as Sprint and Regional Bell Operating Carriers that have well established services do the same. Businesses must be aware of how much their allied partner customer base overlaps with its own client base and be informed of their allied partners' growth rates. Overlaps are tolerable when the partners sell multiple noncompeting products to the same customer.

For Internet companies, innovation establishes brand names. For example, amazon.com never stops innovating and has truly established its brand. Useful metrics for measuring an alliance that has been established for brand piggybacking are *new customer acquisitions, creation of new product or sales offerings* for the entire customer base, and *change in sales.* Recall that companies can either sell tangible goods directly, resell them through a channel partner, or integrate products or services with others to create new or enhanced products and services.

Another reason for forming an alliance is to *complement your resources (resource complement)*. Resources can be in the form of human expertise, knowledge, financial expertise, communications, technological and transport infrastructure, and new or enhanced channels. A good example of partnering for brand piggybacking and resource complement is Microsoft's alliances with European firms such as Deutche Telecom of Germany, NTL in the United Kingdom, and UPC in the Netherlands. Deutche Telecom is the largest telecommunications carrier in Europe. UK cable television infrastructures are among the world's most modern and make a good test bed for high-speed interactive communications services. Tapping into these companies' infrastructures and foreign market penetration allows Microsoft to rapidly position itself as a key enabler of the next generation of interactive services. Another example is the British Toys R Us alliance with easyEverything, which is reputed to have the world's largest Internet café. The alliance will provide Internet access to kids and families at Toys R Us locations throughout the United Kingdom. Wal-Mart and AOL formed a similar alliance. The initiative provides Internet access to remote and small-town Wal-Mart communities; co-branding and cross-marketing opportunities are created for both companies.

German based BROKAT Global and Finland's Nokia teamed up in January 2000 to deliver wireless application protocol (WAP) solutions to the financial services industry. BROKAT has a presence in 14 countries and is a leading supplier of software to the financial industry. BROKAT's list of more than 2,000 clients include Deutche Bank and Cooperative Bank UK. The alliance's goal is to give customers the ability to offer secure transactional services with WAP-enabled mobile phones. Nokia also signed an agreement with Malaysia's leading mobile phone operator, Maxis, and begins trials in February 2000 using WAP services with Nokia's technology. The partners in this trial are local and big-name global content providers such as Reuters, Bridge Financial News, and Orktopas. Services include news, e-mail, games, access to stock information and indexes, and foreign exchange prices. Jamaludin Ibrahim, CEO of Maxis Communications Berhad, explains: "The Maxis WAP services will eventually mean easy access to the Internet at the click of a mobile phone button and will keep end-users abreast of the latest information through the selected services offered, such as stock and financial updates and news services—any time and anywhere."[2] Forming an alliance for a resource complement includes financial considerations. Is the proposed alliance able to share the financial risks fairly? Is the potential partner fiscally healthy? Financial statements for established companies should be examined. Venture capital funding for start-up companies should also be evaluated. Communications, technological, and transport infrastructure are examined for best-of-breed ratings (the best that a company could do in this area). A useful metric is *the degree of resource complement* that the potential partners bring to the table.

For companies with deep pockets and established brand names, outright acquisitions or mergers are sometimes made for resource complements. In 1999, Cisco acquired Selsius Systems, providing them with much-needed voice technology expertise. Cisco also acquired GeoTel Communications and Fibex Systems within the same month. GeoTel provides high-end call center voice processing, and Fibex provides ATM voice and data integration. The acquisition of Shasta by Nortel enabled Nortel to offer uniquely different service levels for voice and data flow. In 1999, Ariba announced plans to purchase e-market platform vendor Tradex Technologies. The purchase allowed Ariba to complement its materials, repairs, and operations offering for internal business effectiveness with software and services for B2B electronic marketplaces. Ariba now has the capability to collect fees from both suppliers and buyers. The merger and acquisitions process is longer and more detailed than a partnering process because it requires full integration of businesses. A partnering process only focuses on the integration needed to achieve a few business goals. Cisco maintains a set of metrics for mergers and acquisitions at www.cisco.com.

The degree of internal e-business readiness of your partner also contributes to the success of an alliance. This factor can be measured using the framework specifications in Chapter 4. The question you should ask your potential partner is, "How do your business' processes affect my business' processes?" The answer to this question affects the back-end integration of partner systems that directly affects workflow efficiency and possibly data integrity. The back-end integration of various business systems can take months and may be costly. However, e-business cannot be treated as just another IT project. Being effectively wired drives and enables change. E-business changes business models.

For partner systems integration, businesses need to determine how much format translation, how many changes to its own or its partners processes, and how much effort are required. Most time system integrators (SIs) carry out the integration exercise. Knowledge transfer must be effectively carried out. Online access to internal service and knowledge databases is essential among partners. Use of standards such as extensible markup language (XML) needs to be in place, especially if the software infrastructures are not the same.

E-culture match also contributes to successful alliances. Your company culture could be defined as "the way we do things around here." Cultural differences are evident in business processes and factors such as profit sharing, timing of market releases, obtaining permission to move ahead with plans, levels of bureaucracy, and level of conformity to procedure. A cultural mismatch can be particularly damning when products and services need to get to market in "Internet time." Peter Fabris[3] cites an example of a cultural issue that emerged during the late stages in the partnership formation between Corning and Samsung. The two companies formed the alliance of Samsung Corning to manufacture cathode ray tubes for the South Korean market. Difficulties developed when Corning wanted to issue dividends, not knowing that Korean companies plow their profits back into their businesses. Fortunately, they reached a compromise. They issued smaller dividends than originally planned for. If the companies had agreed on a dividend policy in advance, they could have prevented this situation from developing. Businesses must be flexible about their specific definition of an alliance because of external and internal corporate factors. Therefore a relevant metric for measuring new alliances is *the degree of cultural fit among the companies.* The *degree of rigidity and flexibility* in the partnering corporations is another metric.

"Chemistry" among key individuals has a tremendous impact on alliances and may be the most important factor determining the success of the strategic

partnership. In other words, management and technical personnel from all the businesses must be able to interact well. Upper management neglect of the company, egos, miscommunication about the alliance's goals, and insufficient commitment are common barriers to successful alliances. Using teams of people for specific business activities mitigates some of these problems. Providing additional compensation to the alliance managers often promotes successful cooperation. The key metric involves how *smoothly* the teams interact with one another. The dispute between Toronto-based Open Text and Netsys Technology Group is an example of how an alliance can break down because of miscommunication and legal lack of clarity of alliance goals. Initially, the two companies agreed for Netsys to have exclusive rights to sell Open Text's Livelink product in Scandinavia. However, licensing disputes quickly emerged when Netsys began selling Livelink over the Internet. Even worse, Netsys announced that it would compete with Open Text for the U.S. market by selling Livelink for 80 percent less than Open Text's U.S. price! E-commerce laws are directed toward the source of a business rather than where the services or products are being consumed. Companies exploit this by moving their servers and other business mechanisms offshore to circumvent the laws. The *dissolution of a partnership* is a factor that needs to be evaluated before you sign an alliance agreement.

A partnership breakup is like a divorce. Who keeps which assets? Do you get to keep customer information or product development information? These issues should be addressed before you enter an alliance. In some cases, certain corporate information must be concealed from the beginning of the process so that both companies are protected. The 1992 alliance between Northwest Airlines and KLM Royal Dutch Airlines is an example of a relationship that soured. KLM invested $400 million in Northwest, allowing them to link the Detroit and Amsterdam hubs and increase the transatlantic market share by 4 percent. However, the companies began to disagree about who had control, and the partnership soon dissolved. However, on a positive note, at the end of the relationship KLM had made a billion dollars on its Northwest investment, and the previously near-bankrupt Northwest had turned around its finances.

The metrics for new alliances are the following:

- New customer acquisitions
- Creation of new product and service offerings
- Degree of resources complement required
- Degree of cultural fit among the companies
- Dissolution of partnership issues

- Degree of rigidity or flexibility
- Team chemistry
- Market share per employee in the partner company

Bob:

We have many divisions that run in our global business, and each line of business runs like a separate company. The challenge is to create alliances that benefit the entire company even though we have decentralized deal-making capabilities. We need these capabilities for speedy processes in our market, but they can cause problems if we don't perform thorough due diligence during the selection of our partner alliances. The tradeoff is that we need new alliances to get into new markets—we aren't as agile as we would like to believe!

Sue:

I try very hard to pick the right alliances. My criteria are quite straightforward: the alliances have to give me new revenue opportunities. If a particular alliance jeopardizes my existing revenue streams, I have to have a very good reason to go after it. I also see new alliances as increasing the trust level with my existing clients because they see me growing, and it gives them confidence in my small company's abilities.

Monty Sharma and NOVELL

DOING IT TODAY

Monty Sharma, vice president in charge of the ASP portfolio at Novell, sees strategic partners as important stakeholders in their business. The types of partners range from Internet service vendors (ISVs) to customer solutions integrators (CSIs). Companies in the ISV space, such as Lucent, Nortel, and Intel, are strategic partners because they extend product offerings by integrating Novell's products with the ISV's products. A senior vice president is personally dedicated to each

continued

ISV to ensure partnering success. A great example of strategic partnerships in action is Compaq and Novell. Compaq uses Novell's caching technology in its headless servers—servers that are dedicated to caching functions. One of Novell's claims to fame is that it owns one of the fastest caching routines in the world. Compaq provides value to its customers by offering enhanced application performance obtained by use of Novell's superior caching algorithm.

Novell is a good example of a company that can smoothly break an alliance. When one of their employees leaves the company, Novell uses its "Digital-Me" initiative to ease the transition. Employees who work at Novell have personal and work profiles. When they leave, employees can take their personal profiles with them. These profiles may include membership information for professional organizations such as an Institute of Electrical and Electronic Engineers (IEEE) society. The employees may want to maintain their memberships. They can have the IEEE use all the personal registered information from Novell. The only piece of information the employees would need to update at the IEEE organization would be the employment information. Employees' work profiles remain with Novell and are managed by Novell's network directory structure (NDS) services. On resignation, employees' privileges to corporate information, from extranets for example, are automatically revoked.

Novell also manages partnerships with the NDS product. For example, if Novell partners with an Indian company that does not have sufficient bandwidth access for the work the companies are doing, Novell would create a mirror site in India. Partial work profiles of employees on the Novell team are then uploaded to the mirror site. Partial profiles only include the information that is necessary for the partnership.

Account Planning

Account planning involves monitoring customer accounts and having a good understanding of the information shared among the strategic partners and the customer-focused e-business. Account planning is a key component of business development. It focuses efforts toward understanding the needs and requirements of the end-customer, which is the function of account planning (not simply sharing information). Account planning could involve customer-focus groups (real or virtual), needs analyses, continuously updating and understanding the customers to be able to push their customers into new products and services. This continuous innovation is critical for the success of a business.

BCE Emergis and Aliant, who are strategic partners, have excellent shared account planning. They share information on national accounts; the senior account manager, who monitors the BCE Emergis main office, heads the customer accounts. All of the sales managers are involved in the account planning somehow, whether through e-mail, phone, or another method. An enhanced system might include extranets, which would allow true collaboration such as white boarding and using shared folders.

The IT infrastructure supports for capability are the following:

- Integration into the customer data warehouse and data mining capabilities
- Tools including intranet and extranet feature sets, such as shared folders within an electronic messaging platform, that promote collaboration

Allegis offers one of the few PRM software packages that include account planning support. The package's business planner facilitates alignment of partner goals and creation of partner-specific marketing programs. Marketing programs can be tied to specific business objectives.

The useful account-planning metric is the overall *account-planning capability* for obtaining, assessing, and acting on customer account information.

Bob:

Account planning is a crucial activity for us. We have many lines of business that focus on some of the same customers. The planning becomes even more complex when we introduce our strategic partners into the mix because we end up making uncoordinated promises from all directions. We're considering using sales tools that will allow our internal and external partners to focus on customers, especially our most important customers.

Sue:

My joint account planning with my strategic partner is usually done over coffee during lunch. I have to make sure that my partner does not promise things to our shared customers that I can't live with, but my partner usually speaks with me before making any promises. Mind you, that doesn't always happen—which can put a strain on our relationship.

New Market Research

New market research is conducted jointly, or cooperatively, so that the partners can gain a better understanding of potential market opportunities. The organizations assess new markets through collaborative efforts rather than through account planning—new market research is a typical business development task. Methods of conducting research include primary and secondary research. Many companies outsource research to firms who specialize in the task. New market research must be conducted during the business development process because it helps you gauge the climate for new products and services. Research can also help you pinpoint a particular market segment that make up the early adopters of your new products or services. Market research focuses on the customer to increase the organization's knowledge of the customer needs and requirements, thereby enhancing the company's ability to deliver true customer-focused products.

A metric for assessing joint new market research capabilities is *the level of research interaction* between the strategic partners, the customer-focused e-business, and the research firms for researching and assessing new markets. For example, a company called Clear Picture conducts online surveys for corporate customers such as IBM and assists in the analysis of the feedback. Motorola formed a partnership with the Ministry of Information Industry (MII) of the People's Republic of China to share technology and research efforts for third-generation (3G) mobile communications. The joint effort involves the market research, development, and implementation of 3G technologies in China. Motorola's network solutions sectors (NSSs) in England and China will form an alliance with the Research Institute of Telecommunications Transmission (RITT) under MII. Each partner will contribute about 10 researchers. The alliance's goal is "to gain a better understanding of the unique 3G needs of the Chinese market, including applications, standards, network design, and implementation."

Another metric that can be used to evaluate new market research capability among firms is the number of new markets that partner companies have successfully penetrated in the last year—*the new market penetration hit rate*. The hit rate includes both successful and failed attempts at market penetration.

Elements that could be included in facilitating research capabilities are the following:

- Access to detailed information on the customer, culture, and country; ideally, ensure that all of the pertinent data is captured, not just from the company but also from the key decision-makers with whom the company must interact

- Maintenance of extremely detailed information to make sophisticated searches and analysis easier

The metrics for new market research are the following:

- Level of research interaction
- New market penetration hit rate

Bob:

We set up a research facility that is used for our research and development and marketing departments so that we can work with our strategic partners when we are conducting new research. It makes it much easier to coordinate our efforts. The challenge is coming up with the right data focused on the right customer base. It's not bad working with some of our partners, but others find it challenging to define new markets—the partners who are good at the technical tasks but really look to us for direction for the market.

Sue:

The majority of my primary research for new markets is generated by my strategic partner. A lot of the secondary research that I have used in my new market research has also come from my partner because it can afford all of the analyst services. I use my history with my incubator as a good starting point for new market research because many of the firms that I know are also targeting similar geographical markets.

Macro Resource Planning

Macro resource planning involves resource allocation and scheduling at a very high level—a macro level—in the new business development exercise; it includes the ways resources are shared among strategic partners. Resource planning is even more important as more companies are going global but are still maintaining a very narrow focus that requires more careful and aligned strategic resource planning. The traditional approach to resource planning between strategic partners is to hold quarterly or annual meetings in which each partner attempts to plan for the short, medium, and long terms. Partners need to know what they have (or don't have) to work with. Resource planning is being facilitated with IT; strategic partners are collaborating at every stage, from preliminary planning to implementation and support. Partners need to have assurances that the business can carry out macro resource planning correctly and is thus able to run the business properly. Macro resource planning is customer focused—the customer ultimately benefits from the innovative products or services placed on the market through reduced production time and amortized costs resulting from efficient cooperation among partner companies.

The metric for evaluating macro resource planning success is the *macro team-planning capability,* which includes access to past and forecasted corporate information, planning and forecasting tools, and actual versus predicted data for feedback. In short, resource data integration is required.

Xwave Solutions, Canada's second largest IT company, plans its resource requirements based on the requirements of its strategic partners. Xwave and Aliant, its strategic partner, have an intimate knowledge of one another's business; both have access to corporate information and both use collaborative tools, such as shared folders and an intranet, during the planning process.

Elements that could be included in the macro team-planning environment are the following:

- Human resources integration among firms, including skill sets, availability and scheduling, and prioritizing
- Equipment availability, scheduling, license acquisitions and expirations
- Project scheduling tools
- A collaborative work environment with extranet capabilities, some of which may be very rudimentary capabilities whereas others may be full, broadband, feature-rich capabilities

Product or Service Development

Product or service development for this part of the eBiz Readiness!™ framework is the development conducted by the customer-focused e-business and its strategic partners. Product or service development is another critical component of moving a company into the future. A *product* is anything that is the result of *effort.* The term encompasses not just physical products but includes systems, procedures, processes, organizations, people, services, courses, hardware, and software.[4] The product development process integrates marketing, project management, and technical development into one process, the sole purpose of which is to develop or enhance new products and services. The strategy for developing new products and services is tied into the strategic purpose and blueprint for the business. The executives must be able to clearly explain where the company is heading so that the vision can be translated into the proper products and services for the marketplace.

The pace for introducing new products and services to the marketplace is often what differentiates one industry from another. In faster-moving industries, such as telecommunications and finance, 3 to 6 months is the norm for new product development—any slower development and the competition beats you by coming out with a new product. For other industries, such as biomedicine, new product development might take years from inception to implementation. IT facilitates the development process by allowing access to more valuable information, allowing for more robust collaboration methods for the diverse teams and providing newer methods such as simulations and configuration management.

MCI formed a product development partnership with WorldCom. WorldCom fought off bids from GTE and British Telecom and finally joined MCI. WorldCom saw that the future was in IP networks—not switched services. WorldCom and MCI quickly developed new products and services for the marketplace, a task made possible because of their ubiquitous 100 percent IP-based data network, a sound vision created by the executives, and IT for their development teams.[5]

A Dun and Bradstreet Web site called Supplybase.source highlights how Internet technology can be used in the product development cycle. The site brings together corporations with the companies that meet their product development requirements. The current database includes more than 15,000 companies involved in the design and manufacturing industries.[6]

Metrics for assessing a company's ability to carry out joint product development include the *percentage of past successes* with jointly developed goods and services and the *expected potential of the new product or service. Expected* and *actual performance of the new product or service, product or service knowledge levels,* and the *ease of access to the knowledge* are other useful metrics.

Team interaction is crucial for getting actual work done. Many of the previous components have emphasized teams (sometimes virtual) working together in nontraditional settings to accomplish a task. Traditional project management approaches may be unsuitable for today's environment. Traditional approaches focus on order and structure to minimize risk and maintain schedules and budget (which is not necessarily a bad thing). The traditional approach is based on the assumption that staff members are widely available, the planned time scale is acceptable, and risk reduction is key.[7] JIT project management turns the project management model around—the project manager's task is to find tasks for the company's resources (such as staff members or strategic partners), instead of finding resources to do the tasks. Changing this model focuses on the IT requirements in the project interaction schema.

Project management processes enhanced through the use of IT are used by Nortel from Kanata, Ontario, Canada. Nortel has development teams in three major world centers: Canada, the United Kingdom, and India. One team works on the project at the beginning of their workday. They hand off the project to the next team who is just starting its workday as the first team's ends, and the second team hands off to the third team. Nortel gained a competitive advantage by using IT in their project management process.

Therefore another metric for measuring allied partner product development is the *level of team integration;* various skill sets and expertise must be used together for a product's development to be successful. This integration metric includes such elements as team dynamics, education, and training, factors that enhance the team experience. Collaborative tools must be able to support the team efforts. The main use for IT applications in Netcentric new media projects still appears to be the dissemination of information rather than the provision of a collaborative work environment. Version control problems indicate a lack of support for collaborative efforts. For instance, if file transfers tend to arrive in bursts near project deadlines, they could lead to version control difficulties because so many files are arriving so quickly.[8]

A metric for project management is the *availability and sophistication of the project management and team interaction tools* in the system. The tools include the scheduling, coordination of resources and version control capabilities and the availability of viewing tools. Team interaction tools will become very important in the future as so many virtual teams develop among the strategic partners.

Elements that can be included in product development team integration are the following:

- *Workflow process integration.* Some larger firms have approval processes for authorizing capital expenditures. The approval is based on a business case and goes through some form of executive approval based on its complexity, strategic alignment, and cost to the company. Highly integrated firms are integrating this process in the company workflow to expedite the product development cycle.

- *Knowledge repository for customercentric data to determine product requirements.* Companies should do some form of account planning and capture information about the customer so that they can enhance product development from a customercentric viewpoint.

The metrics for product development team integration include the following:

- Percentage of past successes
- Expected potential for the new product or service
- Actual performance for the new product or service
- Product or service knowledge levels
- Accessibility of the knowledge
- Level of team integration
- Availability and sophistication of the project management and team interaction tools

---

Blair Lacorte and VERTICALNET

DOING IT TODAY

Blair Lacorte, chief strategy officer of VerticalNet, claims that the core competency of VerticalNet is partnerships. Backed by the Internet Capital Group, VerticalNet was able to view 50 to 60 markets simultaneously, as well as the patterns that exist among them. The company identified the applications that could be used across the various markets or communities of interest (COINs). The goal is to create scaleable communities; ones that can easily handle content growth, transaction volume growth, service offerings growth, and membership growth. VerticalNet needed to form a partnership to achieve this goal.

VerticalNet entered into a partnership matrix that includes many-to-many integrating partnerships with the following partners:

- Vertical communities: partners in markets
- Suppliers and people who want to sell: partners in selling
- Core technology providers: partners in technology
- Bricks-and-mortar companies: partners in markets, selling, service, and technology

continued

"We have tiers of strategic partners," said Lacorte. "We don't form major partnerships unless we have an economic reason to do so. Strategic partnerships may take the form of investments or acquisitions. VerticalNet has already made more than 17 acquisitions and invested in over six companies."

VerticalNet targets three different types of investments: core technology, community, and service. For example, TradeEx is a technology partner, Neoforma is a healthcare market partner, and Zelocast is a service partner with on-demand video.

VerticalNet targets three different types of acquisitions. The first type is an existing vertical company that has a lot of content but has not made any money (perhaps because of an inability to scale—to grow its processes so that the company can grow). The second type of acquisition is of a horizontal service, such as training applications that can be used across all communities. The third type of acquisition is of existing bricks-and-mortar verticals that are in the process of moving to the Internet; for example, NECX, the transaction-based market place that VerticalNet acquired and then helped move to the Internet.

VerticalNet currently uses stock for making its deals. VerticalNet makes the investment, integrates the company into its core business, and then grants access to the newly added functionality to the 3,000 companies that sell through VerticalNet. Because the company has so many partners, it has to funnel and assess the best acquiring and investing opportunities. VerticalNet gives its partners a lot of latitude so that they can still go after opportunities, even if they do so without VerticalNet.

Lacorte explained how VerticalNet assesses its partnerships: "VerticalNet has a strength in the many-markets model. Advertisers want to be able to hit many markets, and we have synergisms with technology and vertical companies. VerticalNet can partner with anyone."

Following are VerticalNet's criteria for picking industry verticals (VerticalNet had 57 verticals as of September 2000):

1. We look for industries with companies that have organic growth models and unstructured data for how they purchase products. Look for companies who have made capital goods purchases and production purchases. VerticalNet's role may be that of a trade show, trade journal, industrial represen-

continued

tative, or a trade organization—a role in which information transfer is very important. VerticalNet can provide a way to get asymmetrical information from suppliers to buyers because the buyers need the information to purchase the products.

2. Pick markets that the industries could acquire (such as Gov.com or textileWeb.com)—individual markets that may be doing well but could never scale large enough on their own (but could within a VerticalNet environment).

3. We look for areas in which a partnership makes sense because the other companies have a head-start advantage.

VerticalNet's partnership model translates to the following nine pitch points:

1. A partner that increases the traffic and usage of VerticalNet (for example, Yahoo!, Excite)

2. A partner that has knowledge of the buying process (for example, of sourcing, specifying, browsing, researching, and buying)

3. A partner that has deep vertical knowledge (for example, Neoforma)

4. A partner that has unstructured data capabilities for content (for example, trade journals)

5. A partner that has structured content (for example, buyers guides, catalogs, cash registers)

6. A partner with tools that can be used in the buying process (for example, purchase orders, request for quotes, request for proposals, and other documents); a partner with cross-functional tools that businesses use

7. A partner that has tools that plug into VerticalNet's base infrastructure, such as the Microsoft and IBM architecture

8. A partner that has information it is disseminating to other companies (for example, Grainger and Westco, who are leaders in the maintenance, repair, and operations [MRO] distribution and disseminate product information to customers)

9. A partner that can bring standards to VerticalNet

We have three tiers of partnerships. The Level 1 tier represents the partners who meet one of the nine criteria mentioned, Level 2 partners meet a couple of

continued

the criteria, and Level 3 partners meet three or more criteria and are higher-value partnerships.

One caveat you should consider when using the model: look for simplicity and focus the relationship. You must have three touch points and a simple relationship—complex is not good. The rule of thumb used to be that start ups never did business with other start ups. They needed an economic incentive. Start ups today are clearly stating in their business plans that their mission is simply to survive. Partnerships must have a financial incentive to survive. The rule for new alliances is "plug and play"—the best alliances are the ones that provide the best fit. If your alliance dissolves, make sure it doesn't take you down. If the alliance is essential for running the business, then put in place the rules needed to make it work.

VerticalNet facilitates about 90 percent of the physical goods trading among its participants. The company has two ways to make money. It can be a merchant of record and take possession of its goods, as well as incur the overhead costs of inventory and carrying charges. This is the amazon.com method. The other way is to be an agent who facilitates the transaction between buyers and sellers and then takes a portion of the proceeds from the transaction. This is the eBay model. VerticalNet uses a combination of these two models but concentrates on the latter. Using the first model, VerticalNet takes title of fungible goods (goods that can easily be substituted such as pens) across lines of business. The company is responsible for the costs associated with factors such as warehousing and inventory because it owns the goods. Using the second model, VerticalNet acts as an agent and receives money from fees levied for their transactions; the company does not own the goods but does facilitate the transaction.

Regarding customer value, Lacorte said, "VerticalNet wants to 'overproduce' customer value. The company has operational partners who provide products but are actually customers too." VerticalNet created value by introducing a flat-fee advertising rate of $7,000 to advertise in the industry vertical. The fee is not based on the CPM fees that are standard for the industry. Customers appreciate the fact that a fixed fee does not waver.

VerticalNet obtains $25,000 per transaction for the sale of a lead. This sounds high, but B2B transactions can be in the millions. Are they leaving a lot of money on the table? That is, could they get more money per transaction? "Store-

continued

fronts versus lead generation. The customers are thinking, 'When I do start to sell online then I will do it with these guys [VericalNet] because I trust them.' That is debatable. VerticalNet is trying to create customer value through lead generation and online sales. The company gives the traditional bricks-and-mortar operational partners and customers a migration strategy for doing e-business today. Making the services that VerticalNet's customers will use, getting customers to try the services that VerticalNet is providing, and building the trust with customers results in a 90 percent retention rate for the partners who advertise through VerticalNet. Relationships earn us the right to do business.

"Customers pay the money. The storefronts and the people who create the communities are the customers. VerticalNet focuses on both types of customers because they are both critical to its success. The storefronts pay VerticalNet's bills, but the community's customers pay the storefront's bills. We have storefront customers who subsidize the unstructured content on the site. We have a tightly integrated relationship with these customers. We give them tools so that they can monitor the site and have access to lots of information. We are very attached to these customers.

"The community's customers are in a more passive relationship with Vertical-Net. They may look at the site one day to look at press releases, the next day to find information, and the next day to look for jobs. We have a very different relationship with these customers, but they are also critical to the success of Vertical-Net. A passive relationship is more broad and shallow. On the back end, we have a more active, deep and narrow relationship with the community customers." VerticalNet's communities currently have about 2 million active relationship community customers who have a narrow, deep relationship with VerticalNet. The company does not charge them to be in the community but does charge them for transactions. The communities bring users to the storefronts. The VerticalNet content is what draws customers. The continuity relationships, which are on the back end, are the companies that provide the information. For example, the front-end customers would be the Microsoft and Microsoft Network (MSN) customers who can get the right industry vertical information. The back-end customers make up about 80,000 companies that can get involved with that community. VerticalNet's partnership with Microsoft, which placed its BizTalk product into VerticalNet's infrastructure in return for SMEs that are driven to

continued

VerticalNet communities by Microsoft, is its largest investment in an Internet company and second largest investment overall to date. The largest investment they've made has been with a telecommunications company. Microsoft is the pinnacle of the flexible partnership model. "These guys are going to build the biggest network ever, and VerticalNet wants to be involved with them. Vertical-Net also has partnerships with Yahoo! and Alta Vista that will drive the right traffic to the our site."

When asked about VerticalNet's value to the suppliers, Lacorte says, "One third of VerticalNet's suppliers uses VerticalNet as their only Internet space, one third of them uses VerticalNet as their number one spend (the company on which a customer spends the majority of its e-business budget), and one third uses VerticalNet as their strategic partner in market building.

"We are developing different markets—SME and lines of business (LOB) or a division within Fortune 500 companies," he says. "We will help them to get spot and open market buys. Do these markets overlap? Yes."

The next steps are partnerships with the big-buyer consolidators such as PeopleSoft, Ariba, and CommerceOne.

VerticalNet's job is to help you get some more exposure:

- VerticalNet will get you on the Web in a community of interest. We give tools to suppliers so that they can belong to the community.
- VerticalNet will provide you with marketing information and RFI, lead, RFQ, and RFT information to buyers and suppliers.
- VerticalNet can go one step further and integrate the actual transaction. We can upgrade your relationship with VerticalNet. We can be a merchant and sell your products, be an agent, and be an exchange and take a fee—these are different methods. Production and nonproduction products require different models. Production goods use exchanges, whereas nonproduction goods may require auctions some we may never do on-line and just take a fee for linking the buyers and sellers.

For our RFI leads, 20 percent of the transactions are closed within 1 month at an average price of $50,000. Fifty percent of businesses do new business with people with whom they have never done business before.

Regarding the issue of buyer's trust, Lacorte says, "We haven't had any issues

continued

arise yet. Buyers do their research. The leads never leave the community. Our knowledge management infrastructure will get more sophisticated as we go along. We get to see the customers' buying patterns and how people search. NECX is going to do about $400 million of bookroom services. This means we will have a huge risk management department and guarantee that customers will get what they expect. We bought the mechanisms for customer service support."

Regarding the global scale of VerticalNet, Lacorte explained, "Forty percent of our traffic is from outside the United States. Whether we enter a particular local market is decided on a country-by-country basis. In Asia, we are setting up Softbank in Kanji for Japan. We are building networks and tying them in to ours so that they will run off the same base. A lot of business is done in English. Sometimes it's not as imperative to localize."

The executives at VerticalNet perform self-assessment exercises. They hold architectural meetings and examine the company from the inside out—what they are doing, what they have done, and what they are doing right. The meetings address scalability, migratability, and performance. They also hold meetings to address external issues, such as market conditions and trends. They see that the procurement side of the business is strong; however, they have a series of product development initiatives that exists.

Lacorte's 3-year vision for VerticalNet is to bring in half of its revenue through transactions and the other half through other sources. Business development will then work with developing strategic partnerships and drawing new customers. Within 3 years, the revenue mix for VerticalNet should be half from transactional services and half from all of the other services. The ratio will shift by vertical. VerticalNet will have flexibility and scalability. Application services will be the key to its scalability. VerticalNet will create partnerships as it recognizes that its core competency is strategic partnerships. It will create a liquid supply for midsize and small companies and LOBs within Fortune 500 companies.

Summary

Bob:

We need to identify the multiple subcomponents (such as account planning and new market research) that are part of business development. Our business is complex, so although a simple model will not suffice, this framework gives us the flexibility to apply it to our situation.

Sue:

Some of the components of the framework are too detailed for my purposes. I need to understand *some* of the constituent components, but it would be too cumbersome to include everything in my planning. As my business grows I can include the extra planning components.

You can form many types of strategic partnerships, and the eBiz Readiness!™ model may only touch the surface of the components that describe your situation. We have tried to make the framework as generic as possible so that many types of businesses can identify with the identified components. The next section poses questions that you can ask that may open up some other considerations for your situation.

Questions You May Want to Ask

We provide overall, thematic, and strategic partner process questions to help you evaluate your strategic partner.

Overall

- Which joint tasks are performed with partners?
- How do you use channels and partnering to create new customer segments and market opportunities?
- How do you work with independent software vendors as development partners, and how can you leverage them as value-added channels?
- What are the most important emerging and alternative channels in your sector? How will you use them?
- How do you manage new channel conflict created by extension of partner channels?

- Have you encountered or do you anticipate competition among partners?
- Do you do joint billing and pricing of products or services with your partners?
- What are the most effective approaches for partnering with ASPs?

Knowledge Sharing

- Do your company and your partner's company engage in joint data mining exercises, or is knowledge shared at an aggregate level?
- Is there any integration of data among partner companies? How do you facilitate it? Do you plan to facilitate it?
- What partner's data would be useful for your company to have and vice versa?
- How do you transfer knowledge to and from your partner?
- Do you offer joint training courses for employees of the virtual team?
- Is the information you need easily accessible and online?

New Alliance

- What is the value of this alliance for all partner companies?
- Are the cultures of the partner companies similar?
- Are the companies equally rigid or flexible?
- Are the companies' goals aligned?
- How do you assess whether the key personnel in the partner companies will be able to work well together? Who are the key personnel in your partner company? Who in your company could make or break the alliance?

Account Planning

- Do you share account planning with your partners? How? What information do you share?
- If you share account planning with your partners, what new value have you been able to offer to the customer?
- Is the shared customer database online and accessible to your partners?

New Market Research

- Does your new market research complement that of your partners? How do you share research?
- How many new markets have you been able to enter because of your partners' input or presence?
- Do you and your partners share market information through an extranet application?

Macro Resource Planning

- Do you share resources with your partner? Which resources?
- How do you share resources and scheduling tasks with partners?
- What types of corporate information do you reveal to your partners during resource sharing?
- How do you and your partners alert each other of new requirements?

Product Development

- Have you co-developed products with a partner?
- How do you work together? In what ways do you depend on each other? What are the resource complements (for example, skill sets, technology)?
- How do you host virtual teams? What infrastructure is put in place to support them?
- Which team interaction tools does your company use?

Thinking about your answers to Questions You Should Ask will help you use the rating and weighting portions of the eBiz Readiness!™ framework.

Using the Evaluation Framework

Using the framework involves determining which components are most important by weighting each independently, assessing the systems, and evaluating the pictorial output from the plot to assess whether the e-business is strong enough in the most important areas. The gauge gives you an overall perspective of your e-business readiness and includes the details in the plots.

Small-Business Perspective: Strategic Partner Assessment (SMEGiftBaskets)

Sue:

I identify most with SMEGiftBaskets because its is an SME that is trying to expand. The following case highlights the importance of strategic partners. I have gone through the same trials and tribulations!

SMEGiftBaskets is an online gift basket e-business (SMEGiftBaskets.com) that currently sells its products to the North American market. The owner has read this chapter and is planning a strategic alliance strategy based on business development, knowledge sharing, and team interaction. Business development is weighted the heaviest. The "executives" (all three of them!) think that targeting new partners, market research, product development, and account planning are essential to expanding the business. They want to use marketing to expand throughout the world as well as strengthen their current customer base in the North American market. The company currently has excellent knowledge-sharing practices. It has no strategic partner teams in place, thus the team interaction component is missing in this e-business.

SMEGiftBaskets presently has no business alliances. Because they are a small e-business, the management determines that using an affiliate model to attract allied partners may be their best bet. Allied partners would get a small percentage of each sale resulting from directions from their sites. Possible allied partners include companies that sell items or offer services for occasions such as births, weddings, holidays, and birthdays—occasions that trigger gift basket sales. Candidates for new partners include sites that offer cards, provide lists of baby names (such as BabyNames.com), have wedding registries (such as The Knot), suggest gift ideas, sell gourmet foods, and sell flowers. The management determines the market sizes of the potential new partners and ranks them. They may be able to "sweeten" the partnership by agreeing to use a percentage of the partner sites' products in the gift baskets. SMEGiftBaskets will benefit from their allied partners' marketing force and brand names. Discussions about potential partners consist of topics such as business models and the cost and type of infrastructure that will be needed to interface with the partners' systems. The management decides to form some new relationships.

SMEGiftBaskets recognizes that although the creation of gift baskets is the business' core competency, another competency is evidenced in the success of the SMEGiftBaskets e-business. In the future, SMEGiftBaskets may be able to easily expand their product line by offering other items. Its suppliers are diverse, supplying products such as chocolates, small home décor items, plants, fruits, flowers, gourmet foods, baskets, ribbon, wraps, and paper. SMEGiftBaskets makes a note to find out whether a market exchange exists for the gift industry because they could benefit from joining. Whether the company joins will depend on the exchange's transaction fees.

On the local front, SMEGiftBaskets plans to talk to well-known local suppliers, such as chocolatier Laura Secord, to see if they would be willing to enhance their existing supplier-wholesaler relationship by sharing consumer information. This is the company's first step toward account planning. By using Laura Secord's information to identify chocolate lovers, they could target customers who would be more likely to purchase gifts containing Laura's chocolates. Customers usually tend to purchase products and gifts that they would like to receive themselves unless they know specifically what their recipients want. This does not break up the customer's gift dollars (some money for chocolate, some for flowers), because they like to bundle chocolates and flowers together—the gift baskets allow them to purchase both items from one source (a typical pick-and-pack scenario). SMEGiftBaskets could expand their market share, and the chocolatier could benefit from selling more products. SMEGiftBaskets could also tie their products' online promotions with their partners' marketing campaigns. Because the suppliers' customer information could be incomplete, the company could hold in-store raffles to collect the relevant account planning information.

SMEGiftBaskets also plans to ask the local grocery store where it buys many of its specialty items and to supply some of its POS customer information. If SMEGiftBaskets can pinpoint which customers buy which specialty items, they could target the appropriate local customers. The local grocery is amenable to working with SMEGiftBaskets because sharing the account planning will give the grocery store a broader view of the specialty product market (which includes gourmet food items such as cheese, jam, and tea) and allow it to assess more cross-selling possibilities. SMEGiftBaskets accepts custom orders and updates the offered gift basket items almost every month. SMEGiftBaskets plans to talk to the majority of the suppliers of local items about making similar alliances.

SMEGiftBaskets realizes that an IT infrastructure must be put in place to allow it to perform real-time analyses of the market. The local grocer will make the customer information accessible to SMEGiftBaskets through an extranet. The grocery store is part of a billion-dollar chain and will have no problem setting this up. Hopefully, the chocolatier and other suppliers will realize the advantages of working with SMEGiftBaskets and will agree to provide their customer information online to SMEGiftBaskets and other companies in similar situations.

SMEGiftBaskets would like to begin its expansion into the rest of the worldwide market by penetrating the European and South American markets. SMEGiftBaskets has been considering using a new business model that involves outsourcing their services to local gift-basket shops in other countries and then receiving a commission on the orders—a model that is similar to the one used by the members of the flower delivery business. Currently, shipping costs and the fact that the company sells perishable items are barriers for entry in global markets. SMEGiftBaskets intends to become a marketing specialist (or "cybermediary") for other gift-basket makers. SMEGiftBaskets needs to compile data on complementary establishments in their target markets and on the gift-basket makers who have been identified as possible strategic partners. An assessment of the competition reveals that SMEGiftBaskets will be the first cyberintermediary for other basket creators. As it prepares to enter the global market, SMEGift-Baskets must make sure to consider cultural, language, and production issues.

The strategic partner assessment shows that SMEGiftBaskets is just starting out (Figure 6-3). The high-level strategic partner readiness assessment diagram gives an overview of the e-business strategic partner capabilities for SMEGift-Baskets. The company has many gaps to fill but can make a plan by using the detailed analysis (Figure 6-4). The detailed analysis shows how SMEGiftBaskets is doing with respect to the baseline level. The figure shows each of the components. The management decides to focus on key areas. The company's largest gap is in the new alliances category. The company has determined that it must have new alliances (which is shown in the baseline) although it currently has none.

In Figure 6-4, the solid area represents SMEGiftBaskets' strategic partner assessment; the patterned area shows the benchmark (the desired values). The axes of the polar plot are labeled with component names such as account planning and team interaction. The score for each component is plotted on its corresponding axis. SMEGiftBaskets' e-business has an overall ranking of 1 for

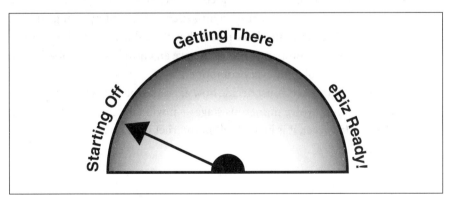

Figure 6-3   RadarScope View of SMEGiftBaskets' Strategic Partner Readiness

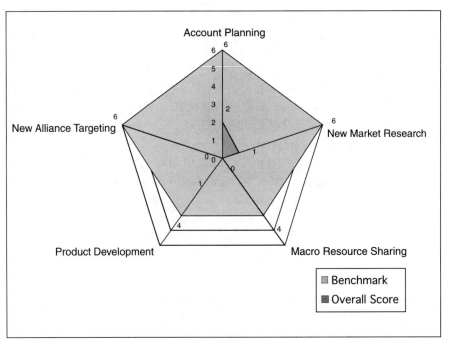

Figure 6-4   SMEGiftBaskets' Strategic Partner Readiness

product development; the ranking was obtained by multiplying a rating of 1 by a weighting of 1. SMEGiftBaskets' weighting for macro resource planning is 0. Because the company wants to focus on business development, it must improve its scores in the relevant components, such as account planning and new market research. High axes numbers mean that the e-business is doing a great job in those areas. The company's task is to have an entirely solid plot—in other words, achieve ratings of 5 for every component.

SMEGiftBaskets must decide how aggressive it wants to be to achieve its goal. The plan will involve numerous stages—it will take time to build the "gift basket empire." However, it is being built in Internet time. . . .

Big-Business Perspective:
Strategic Partner Assessment (BBTelco)

> # Bob:
>
> I can identify BBTelco's assessment of how their company can work with strategic partners. In the past, we owned a large portion of the value chain. Today, we must concentrate on strengthening the smaller pieces that we own. Having a strategic partner gives us a different mindset because we can get help to really plan for the future.

BBTelco, which is not yet an online company, is a telecommunications company that has long-standing relationships with other interdependent businesses and has an aggressive new partnering strategy. However, the company's partnering practices do not meet the benchmark because it does not have the technical infrastructure to integrate with its partners. BBTelco intends to concentrate on identifying technical standards and software that will enhance its existing relationships as well as set the stage for new alliances. Other businesses are attracted to alliances with BBTelco for many reasons. Larger companies are interested in alliances because BBTelco owns the local infrastructure and can serve as a type of resource complement. Allied partners may use the small and contained market for testing experimental emerging technology and services. BBTelco would benefit from offering their services to a wider customer base and would benefit from the partners' brand names.

BBTelco's telecommunications company has an extremely basic account-planning environment. The archived data only includes information on the buying habits of customers for traditional telecommunications services. The information gives no insight into the buying habits associated with emerging services such as Internet access, Web hosting, and transaction management. The database for customers of new services must be made accessible. The collaborative environment consists of e-mail and a simple information-based intranet. BBTelco realizes that its system needs to be augmented with an extranet for allied partners as well as company use.

BBTelco's new market research area is also rather weak. The company has data from some high-value customers but does nothing with it. The data for mid- and low-value customers is not very complete, and the company lacks the data mining capabilities to determine its customers needs. BBTelco decides to begin an initiative to address this issue.

BBTelco's macro planning environment includes useful tools because the external strategic partners were spun out of the business to create more autonomy but still have strong relationships. Hence the company has a good working knowledge of its available resources, which is complemented with IT tools for proper planning. The macro planning environment receives the benchmark score, which means it meets the industry standard in this area.

BBTelco knows of no online product development among its partners, although the systems have the capability to do so. The knowledge repository does not contain useful data, but improving it is an upcoming project for the new budget year. Product development receives the lowest score because nothing is being done currently or will be done in the near future.

Data are not shared efficiently among the strategic partners. They have a common billing system, but it is not linked into the customer care system. The data mining capabilities are limited to online analytical processing (OLAP) functionality by analytical data specialists rather than having the ability to create a snapshot for a nonspecialist at any point in time.

Although the currently stored information is meager, the information is being saved for future uses. The company has data but doesn't know what to do with it. At least the company has a vision for using its data in the near future.

The company has some team interaction tools, but like the tools for the macro planning environment, they are not currently being used. This particularly affects stakeholders who are outside the firewall because it is virtually impossible for the company and the stakeholders to use the same framework. The company has basic e-business team interaction capabilities.

The results of the assessment show that BBTelco is on its way to becoming e-business ready, although it's still in the beginning stages (Figure 6-5). More detailed results are plotted on a polar plot chart, which shows all of the factors that play a role in strategic partnerships (Figure 6-6). The figure shows that the BBTelco e-business is already strong in the account planning and macro resource planning areas but needs to strengthen all the other strategic partner processes. The solid area is the plot of BBTelco's strategic partner assessment, and the patterned area shows the benchmark, which are the desired values.

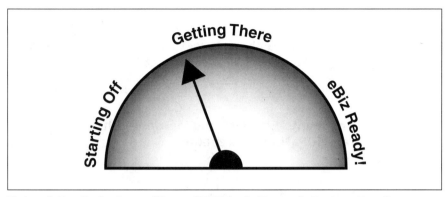

Figure 6-5 RadarScope View of BBTelco's Strategic Partner Readiness

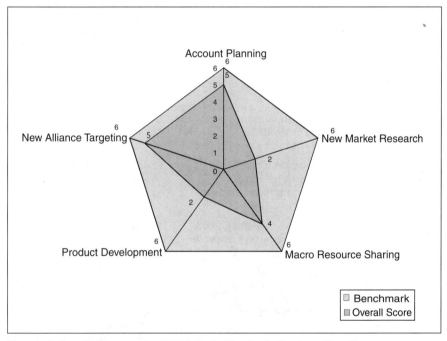

Figure 6-6 Assessment of BBTelco's Strategic Partner Readiness

BBTelco is doing well in some of the areas, whereas other areas are severely lacking. BBTelco has much ground to cover before it is really eBiz Ready!

Are You Ready?

Table 6-1 provides a snapshot of all the components, enablers, and metrics essential for successful strategic partnering.

Table 6-1   Components, Enablers, and Metrics for the Strategic Partner Stakeholder

Components*	Enablers	Metrics
New alliances	• Resource complement • Culture • Chemistry • Brand piggybacking	New customer acquisitions Creation of new product or sales offerings Degree of resource complement Degree of cultural fit among companies Degree of rigidity or flexibility Team chemistry Market share per employee in partner company
Account planning	• Data warehousing • Data integration • Data infrastructure	Customer data integration Collaboration infrastructure
New market research	• Interaction tools • Research resources • Simple interface access to resources	Level of research interaction New market penetration hit rate
Macro resource planning	• Enterprise data integration • Portal interface to resource data	Resource data integration
Product or service development	• Team integration • Engage mechanism • Team services • Team governance	Percentage of past successes Expected potential for new product or service Actual performance for new product or service Product or service knowledge levels Accessibility of knowledge Level of team integration Availability and sophistication of project management and team interaction tools

*Recall that the knowledge, trust, and technology enablers are common to all components (see Chapter 2).

Highlights from this chapter include the following:

- E-businesses must network to form more strategic alliances in their quest to remain competitive, grow, succeed, and meet customer needs.
- Partners may fill gaps in areas such as fulfillment, market development, market presence and penetration, and implementation and execution capabilities.
- Strategic alliances with first-to-market niche businesses and big brand-name companies establishes a sense of trust between your company and your customers.
- A common vision, common goals, a clear explanation of the value proposition to your partners, and alignment of corporate cultures are necessary components for a successful alliance.
- Processes, procedures, management, and information system support for shared business development, knowledge sharing, and team interaction activities are requirements for successful alliances.
- E-businesses need PRM information systems support for sales, marketing, and service partner processes. The infrastructure is customer-focused; it allows knowledge sharing among the companies and improves customer support. The software improves customer response times.
- A feeling of chemistry among the key individuals in partner companies is one of the most important success factors for an alliance—it can make or break an alliance. Use teams and alliance manager incentives to mitigate problems.
- Continuous evaluations of unified capabilities are critical.
- You can use the measurement framework to test your level of e-business readiness and measure your weaknesses and strengths in regards to forming alliance partners.
- Use the measurement framework to test your partners' level of e-business alliance readiness.

- According to DataQuest (1998), 76 percent of a company's sales depends on its partners.

References

[1]www.cio.com

[2]wwwdb.nokia.com

[3]Fabris, P. "Getting Together—STRATEGIC ALLIANCES." *CIO Magazine* December/January 1999.

[4]Shillito, L. M. "Increasing Product Innovation Effectiveness Through QFD and Value Engineering." *Visions* April 1999.

[5]Browning, J. "The Wired Index." *Wired Magazine* June 1999: 110.

[6]www.developages.com

[7]Furlonger, J. "Project Management for the Millennium." *Gartner Group Research Note* March 1998.

[8]Hameri, A. "Distributed New Product Development Project Based on the Internet and World Wide Web: A Case Study." *JPIM* 14, no. 2 (1997): 77–87.

CHAPTER SEVEN

eBiz Rules!: Governance

> Globalization requires right now that we look to see how appropriate our values are in an interdependent world.
>
> Johannes Rau, president of the Federal Republic of Germany, commenting on the 1995 report from the Commission of Global Governance

Getting You Prepared

Most people overlook the strategic importance of the role of governance in e-business. We want you to get a more in-depth understanding of how governance affects your e-business. We address traditional models and how they are changing. We address the ways that governments can work with businesses and customers, as well as the society's new role in the e-business equation. We address issues such as ownership of intellectual property that form the basis of the new economy. Finally, we apply the framework with the rules that are defined today knowing that we have room for growth tomorrow. Governance is a very new area that government, society, and business struggle with because it will shape tomorrow's society.

Governance is a critical element in building trust. This chapter investigates the critical role that governments or self-governing bodies plays in enabling e-businesses to be successful. The dilemma today is that businesses and governing bodies in the landscape of e-business do not have one definitive role. Much like Internet business models, governance is in a state of flux—no one has all the answers, but it seems like we are on the right track.

We highlight the governance interactions among society, business, and the customer. Society is an extremely important reason (and some might argue the most important reason) that we need proper governance of e-business. Our world obviously has different forms of government, ranging from democratic to socialist to communist. Each of these governments has different opinions of how its nation should work with traditional businesses and how it can transition into an e-business environment.

We already have rules in place that govern how we do business—how businesses do business with customers, how businesses interact with their partners, and how businesses govern themselves. The government sanctions certain parts of our society to be autonomous. Examples of self-governing bodies are professional organizations such as medical societies and engineering societies that manage their members using ethical rules of business.

To use the eBiz Readiness!™ framework, you must accept the fundamental assertion that governance affects your e-business. This chapter shows you how governance affects your timeline, your legal obligations, and where you do business. We identify the components that compose governance, explain what the components are and how they interact, and give you an overview of perspectives from different countries and explain how they may affect your strategies. This chapter is not meant to be an exhaustive treatise on e-business law and turn you into a cyberlawyer! It *is* an overview of the key components and issues that will teach you to ask the right questions about governance and your e-business.

Bob:

I turn to our legal departments when we have questions relating to governance. Although the departments highlight the impact that different rules and regulations will have on us, we have to ensure we ask the right questions.

Sue:

I started up my e-business with ideas to sell globally. I quickly found out that many restrictions are involved. To keep it simple, I state on my Web site that we only do business in those countries with laws that allow us to do so.

Defining the Horizon

You must understand some fundamental principles before we can begin discussions about governance. The basic issues include globalization, statelessness, the role of government, and the role of economics in e-business.

Globalization

Globalization is an issue that affects all of society, and e-business is a major factor in the globalization of business. Globalization is the process of moving goods, services, and people throughout the whole world that is being enabled by the e-business infrastructure. Customers—both consumers and businesses—are demanding more variety and have come to expect the option of searching globally for products and services. If the transaction cost of obtaining a service is low enough, the buyer doesn't care where the product comes from. The movement of tangible goods has its own issues because we are still bound by traditional means of transporting the goods to the customer from its origin. E-business is transforming both sides of the equation to reduce the transaction cost for digital and tangible goods and increase the potential revenue stream by tapping into a global marketplace. Modern society has been moving toward globalization and air travel, and the Internet has helped. Three globalization issues are specific to e-business.

- Trusting relationships between customers and e-businesses are being formed in new ways.

- E-businesses require rules to conduct business properly.
- Globalization crosses all borders. E-businesses need a global governance structure so that they can work together at all levels.

The United States is leading the e-business world with its models and initiatives. People have attempted to use the models outside of the United States, but the results have ranged from mediocre success to outright failures. Establishing successful e-business models in other countries involves more than just "getting them out there." Reasons for failure involve myriad factors, including the following:

- A lack of understanding of the target market
- Poor technical design and implementation
- Underestimation of the costs involved with going offshore (setting up business in a country with relaxed or no tax laws)

The increased success of globalization has resulted in an increase in the number and types of global transactions that are occurring. The laws that traditionally govern nations have not kept up with the growth rate of globalization. International business is increasing as more companies are doing business globally. More transactions are taking place because of the new kinds of transactions and players that have evolved.

Bob:

We have a multinational company presence that sells to an international audience. We have savvy customers at all corners of the globe. We must come across as a coordinated presence to our customers.

Sue:

I have noticed that we get inquiries about our services from all over the globe, which highlights the fact that we really are selling to a global audience. We have a physical presence in North America—and it was so exciting when we received our first order from Europe!

Statelessness

Various nations, referred to as *states* in this chapter, are trying to regulate the e-business space, but e-business networks can cross all traditional geographical and political boundaries. Predicting the types and origin of e-business traffic is impossible. The structure of the Internet incorporates networks that are specifically designed to bypass routing problems and take whatever path is available. *Statelessness* is a situation in which no geographical boundaries exist and traditional laws do not apply. Enforcing any kind of state-controlled governance is difficult because users can simply bypass the more strictly governed geographical areas—they can fly "flags of convenience." This term originates from the ocean freighters that sometimes fly flags of countries that have much more lax regulations than those of their own country—"flags of convenience." In the world of e-business, a person who wants to set up a gambling service and is not allowed to do so in the United States could base the host servers in a country such as Antigua (which many people do), even though the customer base is in the United States. People may also choose to base their e-businesses in nations with better taxation laws (such as the Bahamas).

Suppliers of pornography have also used the Internet to their advantage. The e-business model of pornography opens up a cadre of concerns such as taxation, protection of civil rights, and exactly which nation's laws they are breaking. Under the current worldwide governmental structure, unless pornography activity is physically occurring within the boundaries of the state, a governing body can do almost nothing but object to the situation and advise their citizens of the activity. For example, an online service called *Net Nanny* prevents children from viewing Web sites that contain pornographic material. The state cannot prevent the pornography from making its way onto the Internet, but it *can* promote the Net Nanny service. This may seem like an extreme example, but it reflects the serious issues within the confines of e-business governance. The intuitive solution is to create a higher governing body that controls and rules the world's nations, allowing all states to come together under a common governance model. It could be nirvana, but bliss like this can't be achieved.

We certainly don't want to leave you with the feeling that governing e-business is a lost cause. The world has made great advances in determining the role of government in a stateless environment, a role that includes the state, self-governing bodies, and the private sector.

Studies of globalization and statelessness compound the task of defining a sound solution. The power struggle between businesses and government involves defining business rules, societal rules, and customer rules. These rules are based on the need for technology rules. Each group involved will have to make tradeoffs, but at the end of the day we will all move into the e-business future. We will also have to strike a balance between governmental regulation and self-regulation.

Self-regulation is not new. Agencies have used self-regulation to lower transaction costs, resolve disputes, and increase customer confidence. For example, the Electronic Data Interchange for Administration, Commerce, and Transport (EDIFACT) (European) standards for electronic data interchange (EDI) were created in an attempt to bring some semblance of structure to specific industries through their definitions of business transactions. Defining the components eventually results in a lower cost per transaction. The International Chamber of Commerce: The World Business Organization uses arbitration for disputes. Panels of expert arbitrators who have particular areas of expertise handle the disputes. They rule on contractual disputes so that the conflicts don't end up in court. The Better Business Bureau (BBB) boosts customer confidence by giving them an impartial agency perspective of the business in question.

Bob:

Our multinational units are very aware that we are in a stateless environment. Channel conflict and trade issue jurisdiction were two important areas when we branched out into e-business.

Sue:

My audience is global, but I can't actually sell to all countries. We are careful about where we sell our services because of the many governance issues. We have considered some solutions that may alleviate our concerns in our target countries.

Role of Government, Private Sector, and Self-Governing Bodies

What are the roles of the government, the private sector, and self-governing bodies in e-business? That is the million-dollar question! Some countries think government plays the lead role, whereas others want businesses to take the lead. The differentiator tends to be the governmental style of the state. If a state is communist, then the government plays the lead role. In a democratic state, business tends to play a larger role. In a socialist state, more of a balance is attempted. Self-governing bodies have been around for a very long time, and the Internet has used self-governance since its inception. Traditional self-governing Internet bodies faced a significant challenge once business entered the picture. New agendas tend to be controlled by big business, which blurs the original rules.

Economics

We feel the economic impact of e-business in all sectors of the economy. Countries are using e-business to build sustainable economies for the future. On a global scale, countries are making efforts to enable e-business because the new e-business economy is impossible to neglect. The impact is evident in countries such as Great Britain, which now has a "minister of e-commerce." A January 2000 report from Goldman Sachs estimated that savings from business-to-business (B2B) commerce range from 5 percent to as much as 40 percent depending on the industry. The growth does not even include the increase in revenues obtained from selling by using e-business. You only have to pick up any magazine or attend an e-business seminar to get a feel for the rapid growth of e-business. We will experience explosive growth in e-business during the next 3 to 5 years. The growth will shake up the traditional revenue models that society is accustomed to. We can compare the e-business age to the Industrial Age, which created a new landscape on the global stage through economic displacement. History is repeating itself, and entire industries are being transformed, creating new economic challenges.

The quandary society is now in involves figuring out how to ensure that the economics (especially of taxation) are working in a way that will allow us to maintain and then develop the social infrastructure within nations. The nations that have not fared as well in the past can transform themselves by embracing e-business. Ireland has transformed its very traditional economy into one that is extremely focused on all elements of e-business. The country has created the right social infrastructure, which has also boosted the economy. Policies that hinder e-business can have a detrimental impact on the long-term viability of a country, as do the policies of the Chinese government, which are stifling its country's economy. The 1999 objective of China's Ministry of Information Technology and Industry (MITI) was to "develop specific recommendations and policy options to promote electronic commerce in China and its incorporation into the global trading community." Although this policy was on the right track, the MITI has actually road-blocked the initiative by announcing that no foreign investment is allowed for e-business within China. A protectionist policy will fail China; the government is being shortsighted by not exploring how its country can play a leading role in global e-business.

India is an example of a second-tier nation that is using e-business to its advantage. India has an inexpensive e-business labor pool and is leveraging it to create new opportunities. India's Global Information Infrastructure Commission formed the foundation policies for e-business, and Time magazine identified India as one of the winners in the outsourcing war.

The first mover in the e-business landscape was the United States, which is where approximately 80 percent of e-business is conducted today. On the B2B side, this statistic is nothing new because the first-tier industrialized countries draw the second- and third-tier countries to their traditional marketplaces. E-business enables electronic transactions, which reduces costs and opens up new revenue opportunities within new markets. The Clinton/Gore administration in the United States has embraced e-business and for the most part allowed the private sector to lead the way—and the country is enjoying the economic benefits associated with their aggressive strategy.

The European Union (EU) has been complacent, taking a "wait and see" approach to the e-business landscape. Many of their policies are derived from the U.S. policies, with the main difference being that the government plays a much more active role in its countries' policies. The EU has a challenge ahead because although it was formed to achieve economic prosperity, its purpose for being is also to create a hospitable society. The ties that bind the EU together are certainly economic, but some intriguing market dynamics are at work that could create a disparity of economic development that could strain the EU fabric. E-business could exacerbate this strain because it accelerates the process and amplifies successes and failures. The EU is a type of microcosm of the global economic infrastructure, so its success will most certainly drive the global success of a sustainable e-business operating model.

Bob:

Our international strategy is to hedge our bets by placing different units throughout the world. Our plans make the most of the fact that different countries have different strengths and weaknesses.

Sue:

Our business was born in a basement. I am aware of global economics and the fact that different rules apply to different countries, but we really can't take advantage of this like a bigger company can. We can try to benefit from some small outsourcing pieces, but I think we will have more options in the future.

eBiz Readiness!™ Components for the Governance Stakeholder

The eBiz Readiness!™ framework translates the governance components for business, customers, society, and technology into processes so that you can understand how they fit into your business and determine how important they are in your situation.

The issues that were discussed in the previous section highlight the dilemmas faced by governing bodies as they try to appease the three key groups: society, business, and the customer.

The governance "sweet spot" (Figure 7-1) is a moving target—it's an indicator of the prevailing conditions of governance. You need to have some way to measure various governance issues to be able to assess how they affect your business. Changes develop rapidly and can impact your business model quickly. Government actions that were affecting the e-business landscape during the writing of this book include the following:

- The EU introduced a sales tax for online transactions. Confusion on the reporting rules for the buyer and vendor created havoc in the marketplace.
- The U.S. Federal Trade Commission (FTC) is trying to regulate the B2B market to prevent collusion and other anticompetition practices. Businesses in the United States, including buying groups such as the automakers consortium

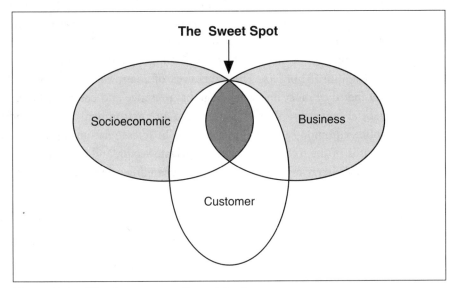

Figure 7-1   The Governance Sweet Spot

(which includes General Motors, Ford, and Chrysler), are lobbying to let the marketplace rule itself, and the government is in a quandary about how to move into the new e-business model.

These two examples of legislated and proposed changes have had a great impact on business cases. Legislative changes may include compliance rules or an outright ban on particular practices. These matters are complicated by the varied ways in which different governing bodies want to address the same issues.

Socioeconomics

Our definition of *society* encompasses the people that live in a nation, the nation's governing organizations, and the economic fiscal enablers needed to enhance a society—the fundamental building blocks for the creation of business models. The socioeconomic component highlights the stability of the geographic area the business is operating in. Multiple industry segments can coexist if they have common building blocks, but they have been known to fail if big disparities exist. Common difficulties encountered by industries that have conflicts in fundamental building blocks are highlighted by the American business models that cannot be easily exported to other countries. Many American-based businesses rationalize that they can just turn on their business models in another area of the world because e-business fits into a global market model. Think of the difficulties you could encounter if you moved a business, traditional or otherwise, into another country. Culture, economics, localization, and myriad other social issues create formidable challenges for most companies who are expanding their traditional market reach. They may have a competitive advantage in their domestic marketplace, but they are at a disadvantage when the company moves beyond their traditional borders. The valuations of many of the dotcom enterprises mean that they must find a stable global presence and customer base. The goal for social e-business should be to create an environment that is conducive to enabling common business practices in e-business relationships. *Flux* describes the status of the role of the state, the private sector, and the public sector; each plays a role in governing society, an ever-changing role that is based on the state of the nation.

**Richard Simpson, Catherine Peters,
Jay Ilingsworth, and INDUSTRY CANADA**

DOING IT TODAY

Industry Canada represents one of the more progressive governments with regards to e-business. Its members have worked to strike a balance between the powers of the government, business, and the consumer. Their role, much like e-business itself, has been constantly evolving, but Industry Canada has now taken a leadership role through its strong presence and involved participation in the global governance framework.

Richard Simpson, director of e-commerce, and senior policy advisors Catherine Peters and Jay Ilingsworth spoke to us about their thoughts on the role of government in e-business today and in the future.

Many issues surround government policy, so Industry Canada broke the complex problem into a framework that addressed each area. The primary focus of the Canadian government had previously been on improving access for Canadian businesses and consumers. More recently, the focus has turned toward mechanisms and infrastructure that will increase confidence for doing e-business. The Canadian government has been forced to take innovative approaches to addressing concerns because although much of the knowledge lies within the private sector, the policymaking power is in the public sector. These factors emphasize the importance of partnerships and working closely with businesses during the early stages versus the traditional approach of rolling out a policy that was crafted behind closed doors.

The Canadian E-Business Opportunities Roundtable is a great example of a strategic, innovative partnership between business and government. The private sector is taking a very strong leadership role, and government is supporting and directing them rather than trying to lead them.

The world has many different types of government models. The United States has been the most entrenched in e-business, and the global leadership has come from that area. An interesting dichotomy exists: one side supports the "let the markets go" concept, and the other supports government intervention. The United States' strong stance in support of e-business has created an inequity that

continued

they refer to as the *digital divide* between the technological "have's" and "have not's." Canada is trying very hard to not create this inequity among its businesses and consumers. It does not want to leave behind significant segments of the Canadian economy or society as it makes the transition to a network economy.

Improving people's confidence with and therefore trust in e-business includes the development of security, cryptography, consumer protection guidelines, and evolutionary guidelines for data use. Protection of personal information is the primary concern. Consumers have to know that their information is being used properly. Businesses are affected because their policies must reflect the governmental guidelines for the proper data usage and maintenance, which includes customer and corporate data.

Academic research plays a significant role in Industry Canada's vision of e-business. The studies include research on the impact of business on society and research on increasing the competitive advantages of Canadian businesses. Clusters play a key role in academic research because they can be the binding agent for business, government, and research focusing on bettering society.

Taxation is a critical component because it affects the social infrastructure that Canadians are accustomed to, but also because it affects the competitiveness of Canadian businesses in the global economy. The government has placed a moratorium on net taxes for the next couple of years to allow Canadian business to grow. Current initiatives address issues related to consumption and compliance. The private sector has taken a lead role in this area and is extremely involved in the technical advisory groups for taxation.

According to Industry Canada, the future of Canadian e-business is B2B transformations, as well business-to-consumer (B2C) transformations. The group predicts that in the near future, e-business will be part of the normal business procedure, which is a common prediction of governments throughout the world. Industry Canada is undoubtedly taking a leadership role in the evolution of e-business to ensure success for Canadians.

Workforce

Businesses must have access to a stable, educated workforce. The propensity for employees to switch companies has never been as strong as it is today. This presents a challenge for companies because their employees take with them key intellectual property assets that are critical in a knowledge economy. Regardless, certain types of businesses attract and retain the types of workforce that is necessary for an e-business; the workforce includes strong technology and business people who understand all of the organization from an e-business perspective.

The metrics for a workforce include the following:

- Turnover of workforce (stability)
- Education level of workforce (education)
- Employment rate of workforce

Bob:

Workforce turnover is a huge issue for us. As a big company, we tend to be less nimble because of our numerous internal processes. We are losing many people to smaller, faster companies doing e-business. It is important that we have a stable workforce in any location in which we set up a development center.

Sue:

I started up our company with "impacted" workers from some of the big companies—employees who were laid off because of mergers or down-sizing. These were great people who were caught up in circumstances beyond their control. Workforce turnover is a part of doing business in our industry, but thankfully I know that we can attract good talent for the future.

Clusters

Clusters can affect where you set up your business; contacts in a particular area, access to infrastructure, and the pace of clusters can all affect your e-business. Many centers of excellence defined by geography have enabled e-businesses to prosper, the most famous of which is Silicon Valley in California, but other areas in the United States and around the world are the home of these "clusters" of innovation. It is interesting that we build clusters based on geography, yet we claim that e-business is stateless. Gerry Pond, Aliant's president of emerging services and member of the Canadian E-Business Opportunities Roundtable, wonders why we haven't figured out how to leverage virtual clusters. Virtual clusters would enable people to have the quality of life that they want and businesses to grow exactly where they are developed. Something is obviously wrong with the model if we are simply trying to create super communities around the geographical clusters and are neglecting the other geographical areas.

The metrics of clusters include the following:

- Number of companies in the cluster
- Focus of the cluster
- Growth rate of the cluster

Bob:

We helped set up our research and development centers of excellence in a few international areas. Our head office is still in the founding location, but the clusters that governments are creating have enabled us to diversify our research and development efforts. The clusters have also produced many spinoffs from our company. Many of the smaller companies that we have acquired have been in the cluster areas where we have offices.

Sue:

Because of cheaper rent and tax incentives, we set up our business in one of the incubation facilities in the local technology cluster. Networking with other IT companies in the cluster turned out to be much more valuable than we thought it would be. We have plugged into many new opportunities that we didn't even know existed before!

Access

E-business access has a major effect on your business model because it determines the size and composition of your customer audience. Your business may be creating its access infrastructure with network service providers such as telecommunications companies (telcos), common local exchange carriers (CLECs), and cable companies (cablecos), or your strategy may involve more government assistance. Worldwide government initiatives have made access to the Internet an important issue. The U.S. e-commerce initiative established during Al Gore's vice presidency focuses on access as the means for embedding e-commerce in society. The EU has played a very proactive role in defining wireless standards such as

GSM, which has resulted in the largest penetration (adoption rates) of wireless networks in the world. The Canadian Information Highway Committee has made access their primary focus in its attempt to bring Canada into the e-business world. They have been so focused on access that Canada is now playing catch-up with the United States as it attempts to create laws that make the country a good place for people who are working on Internet-related goods and services. Access to infrastructure is a key enabler for e-business, and government can help to ensure that businesses and consumers have access to infrastructure. If the businesses don't have to worry about infrastructure, then they can concentrate on the value-added services that define a business. Let businesses worry about what's important for long-term success. We rank *access* on a scale that ranges from low to high based on governmental influences. Low indicates that governance has no impact and high indicates that it has a significant impact whether citizens get access to infrastructure.

Two components are involved in delivering e-business access. One is the wireline delivery of rich, broadband applications that involves convergence of many applications (TV, radio, and the Internet) and creates a good experience for consumers and business. The other component is the wireless narrowband devices that do not need the bandwidth of multimedia and are much slower but still play a significant role in enabling e-business. These devices include personal digital assistants (PDAs), cell phones, paging devices, and any other device that operates using narrowband information. Much of the focus in North America has been on wireline access, whereas the focus in Europe has been on the wireless framework. The adoption rates of the infrastructure in North America are healthy in the traditional modem, digital subscriber line, and cable areas, whereas the market for wireless adoption rates is fragmented. Europe has incredible wireless access penetration rates, which run as high as 60 percent in some areas, whereas the penetration of cable and DSL infrastructure is very low.

The metrics of access include the following:

- Growth rate of access to infrastructure in target markets
- Adoption rates of target market

Bob:

Our services can be delivered through Web channels, but we can also deliver through other forms of networks such as the publicly switched telephone network (PSTN) and wireless. We have noticed a marked difference in adoption rates in those countries in which government has intervened to ensure that its citizens have access to the e-business networking infrastructure.

Sue:

We tailor our service to countries that have the right networks in place. We find it much easier to do our wireless product business in Europe because we don't have as many standards to contend with.

Localization

Localization refers to tailoring your business, including its language and culture, so that it "fits" into other societies. Localization is based on the level of modification required and how difficult it is to achieve it. Supply chain practices are more standardized (and require less localization) than a consumer content play (which requires extensive localization). From the government standpoint, localization issues include local laws and customs that provide the social and legal infrastructure. VerticalNet has launched local versions of its vertical communities in Europe and Japan. The context for each area is managed to align with local rules. Examples of some of the B2B rules can include the following:

- Adherence to local building codes for civil engineering
- Codes concerning measurement characteristics for metric versus the other standards
- Other localization issues that cross into areas of privacy. This is a separate topic but an extremely important localization consideration. Privacy controls range from very weak in Asia to stronger in the United States to extremely restrictive in Europe, which considers privacy a paramount issue.

Localization also involves technical issues such as the following:

- Technical infrastructure impedes progress in wireless application in the United States, but it doesn't in Europe because the EU has adopted GSM as a wireless standard.
- Business models for broadband content can be hampered by content regulations in other countries.

Many localization issues concerning local rules and regulations must also be taken into account when developing e-business models. The level of localization depends on the complexity of the business model and its reliance on the need for localized content.

The metrics for localization include the following:

- Amount of content required by law for local markets
- Diversity of content required by law for the local markets

Bob:

We have a concerted merger and acquisition effort that should help us localize content. Governance plays a major role in our customers' ability to use the products and services that they may acquire. We actually have very distinct lists of products for different areas of the world based on the various countries' regulations, restrictions, and marketing requirements.

Sue:

We have a partnership with a company, which localizes our Web presence for us. We have intimate knowledge of our domestic marketplace, but even in this customer base we must vary the types of information we supply. The laws in different areas also drive our strategic efforts because we must comply with local rules and regulations.

Education

Education plays a role in several levels of e-business: government, business, and the workforce. Individuals at each level must have the knowledge that will enable e-business to succeed. For example, a business that is launching an e-business initiative must have an understanding of how it will be using the e-business, and its strategic and operational partners must have been educated about the merits of e-business as well. The business's potential customers must also be educated or they will not accept the concept of doing e-business. The government must be educated so that it can help the company and its customers.

Government   Although an educated government plays a critical role in the success of e-business, it cannot serve in a leadership role without understanding how governance controls affect the businesses. Most governments realize that e-business is about partnering with the private sector. The debate today is about how much involvement government should have in delivering e-business versus partnerships with businesses. Different governments have different attitudes about e-business. On the surface, the United States appears to be willing to let the private sector lead the movement, although some privacy issues may require the government to take a more proactive role. The EU is playing more of a participatory role that is in keeping with its socialist nature. Communist countries like China are trying to completely control e-business governance. Government education will play a major role in determining the involvement of a particular country's government. The United States is the most advanced country in terms of e-business, and its government has an implicit trust in the industry. The EU is just getting into the e-business wave and is coming to grips with its models. It is moving more slowly than the United States and sees a more enhanced role for government in the public/private sector partnerships. The Chinese government is stifling e-business *because* it is educated. They have been playing a "wait and see" game and are not willing to give away control of their communist state.

The metrics for government education include the following:

- Number of policies pertaining to e-business
- Number of procedures pertaining to e-business
- Subjective response or willingness of governments to support e-business in target areas

Bob:

We found that one of the major stumbling blocks in the expansion initiative was whether the local government was willing to support it, a factor that was usually tied to its knowledge about and understanding of e-business. We actually decided not to set up our business in areas in which the government just didn't seem to get it!

Sue:

I like the fact that e-business has received so much attention lately because it makes it easier to obtain governmental assistance to setting up our business. Initiatives that are specifically geared toward e-business have been developed, and they wouldn't be in existence if the government did not understand the concept of e-business. The government is learning that it must turn to the private sector for advice.

Business   Education in business involves understanding new business models. Academic research is furthering our understanding of e-business models, which take into account globalization and statelessness issues. We have models based on market share, customers, revenues, and other factors. Societies are familiar with the traditional business models and metrics; they permeate the fabric of society—from how businesses are run to shareholders' expectations to government's treatment of business. Traditional business and the market know how to react to a business that is underperforming or overperforming. Wild speculation suggests that the e-business model and Internet bubble is going to suddenly burst. With the advent of the Industrial Age, our society had to come to terms with new business norms and metrics; they will have to do so for the e-business age as well. Current speculation suggests that B2B models will be the future darling of the NASDAQ exchange, in contrast to the B2C model that dominated in 1999.

Many businesses are already accustomed to doing business globally. Pumps might be produced in the United States and then distributed in Colombia and sold to local customers in South America. Businesses focus on trade with first-world countries who then trade with second- and third-world countries. VerticalNet was able to get 40 percent of its customer base from outside of the United States without doing any advertising to get them into their vertical communities. Mark Walsh, chief executive officer (CEO) of Vertical Net, sees this as a natural extension of the fact that other countries are used to doing business with U.S. businesses; the e-business model is a natural extension of the traditional B2B model.

Recent polls by research firms have shown that the most educated businesses in the United States expect e-business to dramatically affect their current business models (more so than do uneducated businesses), so they are planning their businesses accordingly. Society plays a significant role in educating businesses and helping them develop useful solutions. Many centers that are comprised of members of the public and private sectors help businesses follow the evolution of e-business models. The centers are usually based in academic institutions and incubators and are found throughout the world. They allow the businesses and government to test business models—to test the technical architecture and plan for the next phase of evolution without the distractions of commercial intrusion. The days of going it alone are gone; collaboration is essential if e-business is to move forward.

The metrics for business education include the following:

- Adoption rates of e-business in the target markets
- Future projections of business adoption rates

Bob:

People are experimenting with so many business models! We have hedged our bets and adopted a diversified e-business strategy with multiple channels. The shakeout of the marketplace has made it easier to identify the e-business leaders.

Sue:

We are building a Net market and have large businesses buying into it because they haven't determined the best avenue for the future. Governance allows us to have more "open" standards for the community, and all the participating businesses realize this.

Customer   B2B trade has always been global in nature, so some businesses are already educated about this facet of e-business. Distributors usually deal with global transactions and have the business ability to process them. Although we keep emphasizing globalization, people still have a tendency to trust a local entity more than one that is thousands of miles away. Companies like America Online (AOL) have invested heavily into the localization of content for regional and country-specific markets. Educating the consumer will enable more global types of e-business as they build up their trust in the marketplace. Governance plays a critical role in educating the customer. Many countries' e-business plans (for example, those of the United States, the EU, Canada, China, and India) call for customer education, which will in turn enhance e-business. A recent trip to Finland showed us that its citizens were very comfortable with using wireless technologies. We had heard that the Finnish had a wireless penetration rate of more than 65 percent; it was amazing to see them in action! Many Finnish citizens use wireless phones instead of wired phones in their houses. The rates aren't cheap, but the people simply don't speak for hours—they keep their conversations very short and to the point. What is even more interesting is that the technology has crept into many areas of their society, including point of sale (POS) systems in taxicabs and busses, both of which use wireless technology. The synergy between the government and the private sector was simply amazing.

Countries begin to trust e-businesses more when they appeal to people's local interests. Even though the government has been promoting access to e-business, the bulk of consumers do not have access to the normal channels. This is changing because devices are becoming cheaper and allowances are being made for limited phone and voice access.

The metrics for customer education include the following:

- Customer adoption rates
- Future projections of customer adoption rates

Bob:

Our customer base is very diverse, both in terms of the types of customers and their location. As customers become more educated, it's becoming easier to get through to them but harder to support them, because they're becoming more demanding!

Sue:

I agree with Bob, except that the diversity would *strengthen* our customer base because customer service is what keeps us in business. The more educated our customers become, the more critical it is that we exceed their expectations if we are to be successful in the long term.

Marketplace Rules

Businesses focus on creating an environment that allows them to conduct business and ultimately create a profitable enterprise. The lines are blurring between profit and not-for-profit companies because both are creating self-sustaining entities. For example, the World Intellectual Property Organization (WIPO) created a business that solves Internet name disputes. The WIPO business competes with other not-for-profit agencies and for-profit companies. E-business is in a constant state of flux—this book would never have been written if everything in it had to be perfectly up-to-date. Businesses contend that the government must either keep up with the constant change and set its rules accordingly or let the businesses make the rules. Premature and unnecessary government regulations can provide a real risk for e-business. For example, a U.K.-based business went to battle with the British government regarding a law that requires all companies to pay taxes on stock options. This puts undue pressure on the U.K. Internet businesses, which contend that companies in the United States have a tax advantage. Many of the companies have stated that they will leave the United Kingdom and go to areas that have laws that are more conducive to conducting business. Some of these companies are at a distinct disadvantage because the outdated, traditional business rules are forcing them to pay cash for stock options when they don't even have enough in revenue to cover their tax bills.

Jurisdiction

Jurisdiction is a major concern for e-business because whichever nation's laws apply determines how disputes are settled. Globalization causes trade between businesses and consumers to be in a state of flux. Statelessness breaks down the traditional geographical barriers.

Following is an example of the difficulties associated with interjurisdiction issues. You are a business in the United States that buys from Spain. You and the Spanish business found each other through the VerticalNet trading community. You apply your "offline" rules to this new procedure of purchasing at least $10,000 of goods and wait for their arrival. The goods arrive in a poor condition, so you approach the Spanish company and ask it to resolve your issue. The company does nothing. The goods aren't in poor condition because of shipping; they were poorly manufactured. You have stated in your terms and conditions that California state laws apply, so your local lawyer becomes involved. How are you going to enforce a breach of contract when the Spanish company is in a different jurisdiction? You take your case to a California court and have to pay more than

$5,000 in legal fees to win. You realize that even though you've won, you will have a difficult time enforcing the decision because of the jurisdiction element. You decide to head off to Spain—you wanted to visit there anyway. The defendant doesn't show up for the hearing, and you are left high and dry.

Jurisdiction issues can cause a lack of control in the transaction process and can destroy trust; at a minimum they disrupt the trust equation. What we need is some form of cross-border rules or alternative dispute resolution (ADR) mechanism that provides a sense of security.

The metrics for jurisdiction include the following:

- Number of areas targeted for work
- Commonality of laws in targeted operating areas

Bob:

Although we run into jurisdiction issues with our business, we have a legal staff to sort the issues out. We are very careful to cover all of our contract options when we do business outside of our normal operating areas.

Sue:

Jurisdiction is a major issue for us because we can't afford to fight international battles like the one in the Spanish example. Thankfully, we do our business with due diligence and alleviate most of our concerns before we enter into a contractual situation with another business.

Liability

Liability involves determining who is responsible for and what the consequences are in a situation. Liability ties into uniformity of jurisdiction; a company that is liable in one jurisdiction may not necessarily be liable in another. For example, an Internet start-up in Canada, iCraveTV.com, was offering rebroadcast services of television station content. Canada allowed the company to take content from the airwaves and redistribute as long as they were not repurposing the data in any way. The law is not the same in the United States, where it is illegal to take content from the airwaves without the explicit permission of the providers of the signal. The business model of this company included distributing this content to Canadians over the Internet. Unfortunately, they could not limit the content to Canadians only because the Web is stateless. The television stations from the United States have launched a lawsuit against the company that threatens its future viability. The company will be embroiled in a lawsuit that may take years to finalize and during that time, they have an injunction against using the content. Liability and jurisdiction are very unclear in e-business but are extremely important components to consider when planning your e-business. If investors had understood the importance of these issues, the iCraveTV.com problem may never have been a business in the first place.

Uniformity of governmental regulations is also a major e-business issue. Difficulties arise when rules are adopted by many nations, but each government interprets them quite differently, creating business biases for certain geographical areas. U.S. studies have shown that higher sales taxes in certain states have caused the customers in those states to shop online and take advantage of lower taxes in other states. Each state has adopted similar rules but has applied them differently. Businesses can take advantage of these rules by creating an arbitrage situation. The United Nations created United Nations Commission on International Trade Law (UNCITRAL) so that the laws for its ratifying members would be uniform. As previously stated, many nations do not implement the laws in the same way, which creates confusion in the marketplace. On one end of the spectrum are the countries that follow the laws because they are already based on their current laws; on the other end are the countries who adopt the laws but don't really follow them in practice. Businesses who sell goods in a global marketplace must be aware of these issues because they can affect everything from taxation to privacy standards to criminal proceedings.

The metrics for liability include the following:

- Legal content: Is the content considered legal in the jurisdiction in which the business is operating?
- Legal processes: Are the legal processes in line with the type of business you are operating?
- Legal processes and the target market: Are the legal processes applicable in the target market?
- Compliance with UNCITRAL: How many of the components of UNCITRAL comply with local regulations?
- Regulation alignment with your business model: Businesses must also be aware of new regulations being formulated that will have an impact on the

business model in the future. Is your business model built on a legal loophole that can be shut down (such as the iCraveTV.com business)?

Bob:

Our legal departments handle the liability issues. As a manager of a line of business, I need to know how we could get burned. Our legal staff keeps us abreast of new regulations and global changes in compliance.

Sue:

Liability worries me because the laws seem to constantly be changing. We may be doing business within our current standards, but liability is certainly an issue as we become more of a global company.

Intellectual Property

Intellectual property involves the fact that in our knowledge-based economy you must have some legal rights to the things that make your business different. You can use several methods to police your company's intellectual property. You could also just take the stance that "everything on the Internet is free, live with it." Companies give away a lot of information but keep the real value-added information and use it as the unique offering that keeps people coming back for more.

Patents are a large part of the intellectual property equation and are that much more important in a knowledge economy in which a business's worth is based on its owned intellectual property. Intellectual property is what makes your company stand out from the competition and rise above the pack in the marketplace. Patents are normally reserved for unique processes and goods that are the first of their kind in the world. Specific patent issues in the e-business landscape include software patents and timing. The U.S. Patent Office has allowed software to be patented, whereas the rest of the world has not been so liberal.

The metrics for intellectual property include the following:

- Percentage of owned content
- Patented processes, which can involve one or many patents that you own. How much of your business can you patent?

Bob:

Our business was built on products, but over time the knowledge-based economy has transformed us; intellectual property is now our key to survival. This means that we have to have some way to properly own our intellectual property, control it, and have a process to ensure that we retain it. Governance and intellectual property are critical to success in the e-business economy.

Sue:

The asset that we provide for our investors is not tangible—it is built around the intellectual property that we have created. We have pursued patenting our processes in an effort to retain intellectual property and ownership. There is no such thing as total ownership, but patents certainly impede our competitors. Defining intellectual property is also critical because our company is so people intensive. Every time we lose an employee, we lose intellectual property if we haven't captured the person's knowledge somehow.

Dispute Settlement

Dispute settlement is critical for facilitating e-business transactions. Contracts specify the terms and conditions of an agreement between two or more parties, highlight the applicable laws pertaining to the agreement, and usually contain clauses for dispute resolution. Historically, disputes have been settled in courts of law. The challenge for a court of law is that although e-businesses are stateless, the court is not; it must abide by state laws and apply them according to how they are interpreted in its particular area.

ADR can be a stateless approach to dispute settlement. ADR takes the form of mediation or arbitration. During mediation, a mediator gets two or more parties to agree on a resolution. During arbitration, an arbitrator rules on the cases of two or more parties. Mediation is a nonbinding resolution mechanism. Arbitration is binding if it adheres to specific conventions, such as the New York Convention of 1958, which has been ratified by 150 member countries. The beauty of ADR mechanisms is that they work in the e-business space much more efficiently than the traditional court system, and it keeps the dispute out of the public eye. Governments are being forced to keep up with businesses that are operating in an e-business environment.

ADR is used because it is traditionally faster, more neutral, can be internationally enforced, has a judgment (arbitration), and is confidential. State laws can include options for arbitration. The UNCITRAL Model Law has been adopted by more than 40 jurisdictions in the world, but as mentioned, not all states implement laws in the same way.

Is ADR use on the rise? A lot of evidence suggests that this is the case. The caseloads of traditional ADR houses have been increasing.[1] Many more conferences throughout the world include discussions about this topic as well. For any type of ADR mechanism to work, the participants must trust it. It actually involves a human process—building trust.

Domain names cause numerous disputes in the e-business world. "Cybersquatters," or "cyber-speculators"—as they like to call themselves, purchase domain names that they feel will be valuable in the future. The domain names are often derivatives of a trademarked name, so the cybersquatters try to sell the names to the businesses that owns the relevant trademarks. Internet Corporation Assigned Names and Numbers (ICANN) is a government structure that deals with Internet names. It sets the policies and procedures for giving out names and resolving disputes. ICANN currently has four authorized dispute resolution providers that use binding arbitration to decide who owns a name. The problem is exacerbated by the inclusion of high-level country codes; for example, the United Kingdom is *.uk,* Germany is *.de,* and Canada is *.ca.* In addition, alternative *.com, .net,* and *.org* structures are in the current domain name system. The use of these domains to simplify the Internet protocol-addressing scheme has opened up a Pandora's box of disputes—one million addresses are currently on hold, and 45,000 addresses are added daily.

International dispute settlement mechanisms involve more than simply domain names. They can be used to address any type of e-business transaction that crosses national boundaries.

The metrics and enablers for dispute settlement include the following:

- ADR mechanisms: Do you have mechanisms, in addition to traditional legal processes, that you can draw on?
- Interjurisdiction issues: Does your target market involve any jurisdiction issues?

Bob:

Even though we have legal counsel in all of our operating countries, we still try to incorporate ADR because it is less costly than litigation, resolves issues more quickly, and keeps any situations that could make us look bad out of the press.

Sue:

We have to rely on ADR for any disputes because we cannot afford to spend much on a drawn-out legal battle—it could easily put us out of business.

Taxation

Taxation is an area that touches all business and consumers. It is essential to run a state with the social infrastructure its citizens expect. Several proposals to ban taxes on e-business transactions have been presented by states in which the private sector is driving the strategy for e-business. They argue that taxation at this stage of e-business development will create an unlevel playing field for online businesses and give traditional stores an unfair advantage. Some U.S. state governments are also calling for taxation reforms because of potential erosion in their state tax systems. All businesses want is a level playing field. E-businesses are competing with businesses in a stateless world in which taxation has a direct impact on competitiveness—the low margins in many of the e-business models make it difficult for them to compete. The views on this issue range from the opinion that society needs to have a certain tax infrastructure for its citizens to the opinion that e-businesses simply need to be globally competitive and therefore the taxes should be banned. The e-businesses say that they have the good of society at heart because they will create economic prosperity for the nation as a whole. The role of the governing bodies is to strike a balance between society and business.

Taxation policies and rules   The Organization for Economic Cooperation and Development's (OECD's) members have agreed that the following five factors should be considered when forming taxation regulations.

- Neutrality
- Efficiency

- Certainty and simplicity
- Effectiveness and fairness
- Flexibility

E-business taxation rules raise two specific issues for businesses: a government's right to tax and double taxation. A government's right to tax involves its ability to tax business activities that take place within its nation. Difficulties quickly arise because of the stateless nature of the e-business environment, which does not have the normal boundaries that define a traditional state. The double taxation issue arises when a state finds that a business or individual is doing business in its state and taxes them at the source as well as at the consumption point. Treaties are supposed to prevent this type of double taxation from occurring, but the treaties aren't keeping pace with changes in e-business. E-businesses must determine what exactly constitutes "doing business" in an area and what they then need to do to ensure that they are not being double taxed. The character of the income is a major factor in many taxation schemes in which income from the sales of goods is handled differently than income from the sales of services. Therefore e-businesses have to clarify whether they are dealing with goods or services. Information-based goods always remain in a digital form, so it could be argued that they are actually services. Source-based taxation is a major challenge to governments as they struggle to develop a sound taxation scheme. Some argue that resident-based taxation might be the best scheme because everyone is a resident somewhere. The difficulty is how to create the infrastructure to capture the residence taxes with the OECD principles. One country may classify income as royalty and another may classify it as goods and tax it differently—no rules penetrate the entire international marketplace. These challenges have put pressure on governments to establish the right frameworks. Many of the governments have established e-business tax moratoriums that will be in place for the next couple of years, although we will surely resolve this critical issue.

Transactions   E-business transactions are the root of the taxation dispute among nations. Although businesses may have other ways of generating income, the majority comes from selling a product or service. Traditionally, states have collected their share of taxes by taxing at the source. This is easy in a geographical boundary-based system because physical linkages exist between customers and businesses. Mail-order businesses introduced a new challenge because they shipped products from outside of the state. They did not charge customers local taxes but instead told customers that they had to report the tax they owed. This self-reporting system did not work very well (with less than a 1 percent response in many cases) because no one was held accountable for the collection. States overlooked this piece of lost taxable revenue because it was so insignificant in their overall revenue stream. E-business has pushed this challenge to the extreme. States will soon realize that a sizeable portion of their revenue stream will be lost if nothing is done. The challenge for governments is figuring out how to make e-businesses report their taxable income if they are not from the government's area; the businesses could be double taxed if they do comply with taxation laws, or they may simply get out of paying them all together if they are outside of the bounds of control of the other states.

The metrics and enablers for e-business transactions include the following:

- Number of transactions
- Number of outside transactions in states with different laws
- Taxation difficulties (number of completed transactions that required establishment of new rules or human intervention because of taxation)
- Taxation rules favorable to business model

Bob:

We have many lines of business and have traditionally only worked within the geographical areas in which we have customer management channels. As we have become more e-business enabled, we have experienced more publicized behind-the-scenes channel conflicts, but we have also struggled with the taxation issues. We must track where we sell products and conform to local taxation laws—and do it cost effectively. We are still working on balancing the equation.

Sue:

We have started to conduct transactions in many locations throughout the world, but we do the majority of our business in more local areas where our marketing has more of an effect. The difficulty is that we must comply with taxation rules in our own state because the government wants to tax at the source, but we have to pay other states to do business there as well. We feel that we are being double taxed, but maybe this is just a cost of doing e-business.

Privacy and Trust

Trust is the fundamental underpinning of e-business and primarily involves the customer. Our diagram of e-business highlights trust as a key enabler of e-business. Trust is hard to define. Much like value, some intrinsic principles determine why and how you build up trust. You don't get trust automatically— you earn trust over time. Much like a marriage, the business-customer relationship involves building up trust over time. People must build up trust in each other if they are going to decide to spend their lives together. They get married, and if things go well, they maintain that level of trust and everything is fine. Human nature being what it is, married people have some bumps along the road and erode some of that trust. How much one partner erodes and how much the other partner needs is what keeps people together or drives them apart. Similarly, businesses get you to work with them by earning your trust in their services or goods. They build that trust through their interactions with you, which then brings you back. This process is no different for B2B or B2C transactions because people are the heart of the transactions. Trust plays a significant role in e-business because people don't judge online companies using their normal standards. They would normally trust a brand or an individual within a company or both. Unless customers are locked into a contract, switching costs are so low that customers can easily move to another business to conduct their affairs. Governments are concerned about trust because it affects how businesses conduct themselves. Governments are concerned about the customer, the businesses within its domain, and the societies that they are shaping. All these groups have different requirements. Businesses want trust to increase their potential to do business. Customers need trust to be able to conduct their affairs in an e-business environment. Society needs business to bring in revenues that allow the state to operate. Society needs altruistic components (such as labor laws) to keep its societal members content. Society and business must balance the two (business and altruism). Trust is the primary consideration in this pursuit. The business side and the altruistic side will always be pushing the line, but if it is pushed too far, society will not operate properly. If business controlled all of society, people would live in squalor. If altruistic tendencies were the control, no state would have money to operate. We must have balance.

Bob:

The way to increase our e-business with customers is certainly through trust. We carry a well respected, offline brand that helps us build trust, but we need governance to help us as well.

Sue:

We don't have a strong brand image, so trust is everything. Governance provides the unbiased third-party perspective that customers need to feel comfortable doing business with us.

Privacy

E-business privacy involves the use of information. A company may not use customer information at all, it may use it a little, or it may use it as much as possible. The people, who actually are "the data," also affect the degree to which information is used. Scott MacNeally, Sun Microsystems president and CEO, says, "Everything on the Internet is public. Get over it." In contrast, some people don't believe that everyone should know everything and are very concerned about privacy. Most people wouldn't agree with MacNeally's statement. The majority of the population fits into the middle of the spectrum; they are concerned about some types of data (such as their financial data) but are less concerned about other types (such as personal demographic data). Businesses and consumers also have different views on data usage.

Privacy regulations range from those that have little impact on businesses to those that have a significant impact on businesses (Figure 7-2). The EU recently introduced regulations requiring businesses that obtain personal data to only use the data with consent, and then they must use them in the way in which they stated they would. They must not use any data that predates the regulations because they were not obtained using the correct procedures, meaning that all the mailing list and personalized data collected by some companies could becomes useless because it would be illegal to use or sell them.

Businesses are accustomed to some degree of transparency in their affairs, whether they are privately held or publicly traded companies. Consumers are passionate about their information because its usage affects them as individuals. Because consumers are so emotional about privacy issues, the bulk of the privacy

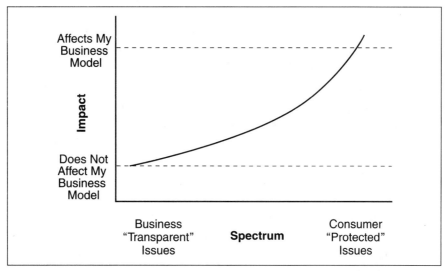

Figure 7-2   Privacy Spectrum. (High level: The regulations *will* affect my business model; low level: privacy regulations will *not* affect my business model.)

discussion to date has centered on the individual. Some want the state to control everything, but some want no involvement at all. Consumers are aware of "big brother watching," and the more democratic the state, the less enthusiastic they are about having too many intrusions on their affairs. E-business has complicated the issue, but privacy is certainly not a new topic.

The consumer marketing firms that started springing up in the 1970s revealed the consumer information. Telemarketing organizations knew our phone numbers and our buying habits and used every effort, by phone and through targeted mail, to entice us into buying more. Legislation was passed that stated what type of information could be collected and how it could be used, but the laws were very difficult to enforce. Consumers had very few ways to fight back because the telemarketing firms were outside of their jurisdiction.

Years ago, the business that knew your buying habits was the one that you chose to do business with. You no longer know businesses intimately and don't have a complete understanding of what they are doing with your personal information. E-business globalization has exacerbated the issue because consumers (and businesses) are often doing business with total strangers.

Recent propositions for legislation of online privacy rules in the United States by the Federal Trade Commission have focused on the financial transaction, which is considered extremely private. Although the proposed legislation focuses on financial institutions, it has an impact on all the businesses that use financial institutions' services to conduct business. Cybermerchants use financial services to process credit card transactions. There is little current legislation that addresses how companies can use the information. Some companies that offer transaction types of services are allowing users to specify whether they the company can use their information. This becomes more of an issue the closer you get to the heart of the financial information. The transaction management institutions are about trust as much as they are about enabling a financial transaction. They know all the buying habits of their customers, online and offline, especially of customers in countries that use debit cards in lieu of cash. This wealth of information seems to scare the average consumer. Up until now, the financial institutions have been self-regulated regarding the use of private information, but the government has started stepping in. We have regulated the telemarketing organizations for the last 30 years, but we still know of consumer privacy infringements in these organizations, which erodes trust. The same is true of financial institutions and businesses who use your information without your consent. They are damaging the trust that made you go to them in the first place and has kept you coming back. If the information is not used properly, you will be very reluctant to do business with that entity again. In true e-business fashion, the U.S. legislators are allowing companies to use information that they have been given permission to use, but are clamping down hard on the use of information that customers don't want to have publicly traded; customers must be given the option to "*opt out* of the sharing of information such as credit card and account numbers with unaffiliated third parties."[2]

The metrics and enablers for privacy include the following:

- Completeness of the privacy rules
- Number of states within the operating areas that have different privacy laws

Bob:

We have a difficult time with privacy of information because we have centralized data warehouses. Each state has different laws that we must comply with, and it makes things more difficult. We localize the privacy laws to the customer. Although it can be a difficult task, localizing privacy will certainly be a part of doing e-business in the future. We must be aware of any new privacy laws that may affect our business.

Sue:

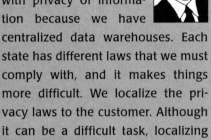

When we started out the business, we had a vision that we would customize our information for every person—it was the one-to-one panacea that we were striving for. We wanted to tailor the information to each customer, tailoring that would include the customer's buying habits. The rapid establishment of privacy laws has resulted in a backlash. New governance rules even forbid us to buy data that were captured before the rules were changed. I feel that we are letting our customers down by not providing them with the best information possible. I hope the pendulum will soon swing the other way.

Authentication and Security

When customers walk into a store, they see actual salespeople and a bricks-and-mortar structure—physical presences that let them know they are in a true place of business. If the company has an established brand, then the customers have even more confidence in the business. Companies who do business with other companies must also build confidence. Unfortunately, customers can't "see" the physical presence of an e-business. For an e-business to be successful and attract customers back time after time, customers must be convinced that the business is a genuine business, and the business must be convinced that its customers are indeed who they say they are.

Nonrepudiation involves ensuring that both parties involved in a transaction are who they say they are. The challenge is that no single, accepted authentication process has been developed. Global Sign from Brussels and Verisign from the United States are companies that are trying to establish trust in e-business transactions through authentication practices such as certificate management. Other technologies, such as voice biometrics (introduced by Nuance) and handwriting biometrics (introduced by PenOp Computing), are being developed to allow for devices other than just Web browsers to be a part of e-business. The marine industry uses a device for the Inmarsat satellite communications systems called *mini-M,* which identifies users much like GSM cell phones identify the users. All of these different methods are used to authenticate the identity of involved parties.

Governance plays a major role in authentication by enabling authorized certificate management infrastructure. The public key infrastructure (PKI) uses cryptographic elements to encrypt information (see Chapter 8). Authentication is a factor in the reuse of security credentials among applications. Security applications should authenticate once and pass the security parameters to applications. Another consideration for security applications is the administration of the keys used to keep the data secure. Authentication and trust mechanisms must be able to support trading communities. The challenges range from administration (key management) to security (encryption standards). Legal concerns also play a role. For example, companies that operate in the United States are not allowed to distribute encrypted products with greater than 56-bit encryption. Within North America, they can distribute 128-bit encrypted products. Companies are legally bound to using substandard technology outside of North America. Governments can mandate adherence to a PKI system. Canada's federal government has been trying to establish Entrust certification as its standard; if it succeeds, any partners who deal with federal agencies would be required to authenticate themselves using the Entrust system. The governments in the EU and Japan and North American Free Trade Agreement (NAFTA) have introduced initiatives that involve adopting interoperable trust standards. Human error can create problems during the authentication process and during the implementation and management of a PKI system. Authentication is a crucial component of e-business, so its role in internal and external communications must not be overlooked.

Security ensures confidentiality of data. A robust system allows information to be securely exchanged among parties. Network security focuses on the physical and logical components that have regulatory implications, such as the PKI and encryption standards, as well as how the data are physically stored and handled. The PKI includes encryption standards and the certificate authority (CA) standards. An encryption controversy developed regarding the fact that North

America allows 128-bit encryption within the United States but only allows 56-bit encryption elsewhere. The U.S. government said that they had security concerns and were worried that 128-bit encryption would create illegal trading practices, especially among organized crime members from other countries. The government wanted to be able to "peek into" encrypted messages so that they could interdict illegal activities. Businesses saw the government action as an intrusion and a tactic that would erode customer trust. They thought that customers wouldn't have much faith in this type of "back-door" system—because if the lawmakers had the ability to "peek in," then the lawbreakers probably would, too!

The metrics for authentication include the following:

- Level of authentication mechanisms within an organization: Is authentication used at the individual employee level?
- Level of management infrastructure and defined policies for authentication management
- PKI infrastructure allowances: How much of the customer interaction security is the fullest PKI possible?

Bob:

Our global business has adopted a single PKI schema so that we can operate better within our company. Our initiative saved us money, and now we are trying to standardize with our operational and strategic partners.

Sue:

We do business with many large companies, and each one is using different standards. The challenge for us is the cost of managing different systems. We are considering an outsourcing arrangement with a CA that will do the cross-authentication for us. Then we'll be able to trade with multiple organizations with the least amount of difficulty.

Technology

Technical standards are required for industry systems to operate with one another. We break the technical regulatory framework into two areas: network rules and business applications rules. Technology is an implicit e-business enabler and is the glue that holds all e-businesses together.

Chapter 9 addresses the internal technical components that drive an e-business. Governance affects the specifications, but the issues we are concerned with are those related to the logical and physical external pieces of the business.

You need to understand the technical building blocks that make up your operating environment, knowledge that is especially important when you have numerous stakeholder contact points across multiple networks. You'll need to develop standards when data are repurposed for use with other devices.

Network Rules

Network rules address the operation of your actual network as it transports the data that form the backbone of your e-business. This book is not intended to train you how to be a Cisco certified internetworking engineer and teach you how to assess the impact of rules on the business you are analyzing. Input from the networking gurus will make this aspect of your life easier, but you should still be able to focus in on some of the areas in which networking rules need to be enforced.

Governance applies to the rules that address the networking functions. Governance bodies are self-governed and include the Institute of Electrical and Electronics Engineers (IEEE) and other bodies that certify and sanction networking standards. These organizations enable networking suppliers to deliver a service level agreement (SLA) for the type of service that an e-business needs. The SLAs explain the level of service that is required. No SLA standards other than market-driven standards exist. The telecommunications companies are accustomed to building "bomb shelters" for their telecom infrastructure so that they can give their customers the appropriate "four nines" (99.9999 percent) level of service. The internetworking infrastructure is getting there, but it's not there yet. The quality of service (QoS) that you get depends on the reach of the network provider you choose. Considerations include the following:

- Areas of operation
- Mirroring requirements
- Support requirements

Governance will define standards for each of these elements as e-business evolves. The tradeoff for today's e-business involves price and performance. The decreasing price/performance point (in which price drops and performance increases) in today's network can be dramatically improved with technology such as optical switching. Newer technology will change the networking abilities of the providers and ensure that tomorrow's networks will have the appropriate level of governance standards throughout. More and more money is needed to improve the performance of the system, but it will eventually plateau regardless of how much more money is put in.

The metrics include the following:

- Disparate networked areas: How many do you have that are outside of one service operator or within one provider?
- SLAs: How many are in place? What do they encompass?
- Worldwide operations requirements: Do you have a mirroring requirement?

Bob:

We have migrated from a private worldwide network based on frame relay to a more open, Internet-based virtual private network (VPN) to ensure secure, low-cost connectivity among sites. We have QoS standards that we can apply because we use a global carrier. Security is certainly an issue—governance has enabled us in some areas but has impeded us in others.

Sue:

We are firm believers in having open networking standards and have based our entire business on that premise. QoS is critical in our business operations. Our service provider for our Web and corporate servers has a central office that is "bomb proof" and would probably stay running in any situation—short of a war! Any downtime is lost money. Governance is critical in the QoS area because we will get better standards as governing bodies come up with better schemas.

Business Application Rules

The movement of business information among businesses has been slow to be adopted because of the lack of common rule sets. The standards for business rules are either nonexistent or are being used by very few people. EDI was and still is a very powerful regulatory framework that allows e-businesses to exchange information with some degree of confidence. Having specific rules for the data sets increases this confidence, and systems that perform an audit trail of the transaction increase the level of confidence during exchanges of information among businesses.

Newer e-business rules systems provide a framework for the exchange of data and the creation of an audit trail for the transaction. The exchange of data is performed through defined data sets such as the extensible markup language (XML) initiative. Hypertext markup language (HTML) allows standard presentation of data in Web browsers. The industry is buzzing about XML and commerce XML (cXML). These systems have been defined by a self-governed regulatory body and allow business data to be more easily transferred. XML is a system of hypertext tags that are used to define transitional elements. cXML is a superset of XML and is specific to commerce transactions, such as catalog, punchouts, purchase order, and invoice transactions. All of these capabilities tie into applications that range from procurement to catalog to order-receiving systems.

XML and cXML are schemas driven by industry organizations that are trying to establish a sense of order in the business rules. Many organizations are vying to create the standards in industry verticals, but they are also competing to *be* the standard. Many of the industries have multiple key organizations that are writing the schemas. For example, the financial and capital markets have seven competing standards, and none of them is the clear winner. The financial and capital market organizations who are creating XML specifications include the Digital Receipt Alliance, the Financial Information Exchange Protocol, FinXML, PpML, Infinity, Historical Data Markup Language, and Society for Worldwide Interbank Financial Telecommunications (SWIFT). The difficulty with any business rules regulatory framework is that not all businesses trade using the same mechanisms, and extensible systems that leave room for interpretation can lead to errors during the information exchange.

BizTalk is yet another initiative. The system allows applications to work on the enterprise's "inside" level and creates a more stable XML environment for data exchange. BizTalk is not a standards body; it is a community of standards users that has the goal of establishing XML as the industrywide standard.

No single solution resolves the data-sharing issue. Each industry has nuances that make it distinct; each business has nuances that make it distinct as well. Because we have no clear solution, businesses must try to ensure that they are adhering to standards of information exchange as best they can.

Businesses can help ensure that they are adhering to standards through buying exchanges such as Ariba and Commerce One networks. The Ariba Internet Business Exchange facilitates trading between buyers and suppliers by enforcing adherence to various standards such as EDI, XML, and BizTalk.

Exchanges are broken into two main categories: those that deal with operating supplies and those that deal with manufacturing supplies. Operating supplies are rapidly gaining in popularity because of potential cost savings and new revenues from other buyers. Manufacturing supplies are also undergoing fundamental changes, which include transitioning from being catalog-type exchanges to spot-types of exchanges. The exchanges don't have much governance today, but industry rules could easily be applied in the future.

The metrics for business rules include the following:

- Adherence to exchange community policies: How many incidents have arisen because of noncompliance?
- Compliance with open standards
- Number of formats required
- Number of formats supported

Bob:

We have many systems and islands of information that we must connect to create a consolidated customer view. Now that we have operational and strategic partners involved, we have to share more of our information. Our business will benefit as the standards for sharing data become more widespread. We can also plug into exchanges easily because we have adopted XML.

Sue:

Net markets are new channels that we are exploring. The best way for us to participate is through XML integration. Because of competing schemas and our limited IT budget, we have opted to outsource a middleware translator service that will monitor the multiple exchanges in which we would like to participate.

Questions You May Want to Ask

While considering the governance issue, you may find it useful to consider the following questions.

Overall

- What are the business risks that government or governance introduce to your business model?
- What will adherence to government regulations do for your business? Conversely, what won't adherence do?
- What factors must be involved if you are to realize the benefits of abiding by the rules?
- What is your business's information technology investment in hardware, software, and skills?
- How global is your business model? Governance issues are more prevalent in more global business models.
- Which markets does your business currently serve? Do these markets have special e-business or e-commerce laws?
- Where do the customers come from?

Socioeconomics

Workforce

- How much reliance does the business model place on key personnel?
- Are the key personnel available in the operating area?
- Are people who perform specific job functions difficult to acquire in the operating area of the business?
- Which options for reducing workforce turnover has your company explored?
- What types of incentives to retain e-business workers in the region do the government and private sector support?
- What roles do your local universities play in educating new workers in e-business?

Clusters

- Are there clusters for the industries within your business model? How is your business integrated into those clusters?
- How geographically dispersed are the clusters?
- Does your business model take advantage of clusters through such initiatives as reduced taxes, networking, or access to capital?

- What is the potential for the growth of the clusters?
- Are the companies in the clusters working well together?
- Do government initiatives support the clusters? Is the government providing one-time or continuous support?

Access

- How reliant is your business model on access issues?
- Does your business model involve direct or indirect control over access for your target customers?
- Are the governments proactive in getting Internet access to the general business and customers?
- Have you identified other means of access for your customer base, and are any governance initiatives in place to increase and assist the penetration rate?

Localization

- How fungible are the goods and services in your business model? (More fungible goods may translate into less localization requirements.)
- Do any regional regulations have an impact on buyer decisions?
- How tailored does your product need to be?
- Do you have to adhere to any content regulations?
- Can your business work with a local presence to deliver the product outside of the traditional marketplace?

Education

Government
- How educated about e-business are the various levels of government in your operating areas?
- Is it advantageous for you to set up in another location (in areas that are more receptive)?
- What problems could develop if the government is not receptive to your business model?
- Has the government streamlined any processes for e-business models?
- Does the local government understand the impact of e-business?
- What types of education initiatives has your regional government begun? How many? Are these initiatives similar to the United States' e-government initiatives or Canada's Government Online initiatives? Are they a subset or superset of those initiatives or totally different?

- To what degree does the government partner with the public sector?
- What government policies would your company like to influence?

Business

- Do you know of any business models similar to your proposed business that have already been e-business enabled?
- Are any areas of academic research in the same or similar areas as your business model?
- How educated is your business community toward e-business? Would it make sense to open up in another location?
- Are investors taking a realistic, long-term approach to your business model?
- Are local businesses aware of the impact of e-business on their industries?
- What is the level of e-business awareness in the operating region? Does it affect your business model?

Customer

- Are the target customers educated about your "new" business?
- Is your business building customer awareness?
- What are the customer knowledge gaps?

Marketplace

Jurisdiction

- Do you have to deal with any jurisdiction issues?
- Do your target areas have common laws?
- Does your business have a physical presence in your target market that affects your business model?
- Have you considered how you will deal with failed transactions?
- Does your business understand the legal jurisdiction issues for its trading markets?
- How will your business minimize its legal risks? What are its liabilities?
- Does your company understand the differences in rules that exist across its target regions—even those within a single country?

Liability

- How different are the liability regulations in your target markets?
- Is your business aware of any liability implications?
- Do you have any intergovernance liability considerations such as content and ownership issues?

- Have your target markets adopted the UNCITRAL regulations?
- Do you have a gray area regarding liability?

Intellectual Property

- How much of the intellectual property that your business uses is owned by your business?
- Do you have regulations that protect your intellectual property? Are they defensible?
- How protected is your business regarding ownership of intellectual property if the rules change?
- Does your business have any patents? Does it have any pieces that could potentially be patented?
- What precautions is your business taking to protect its intellectual property?
- What initiatives is your business taking to capture its employees' knowledge assets to facilitate knowledge transfer?

Dispute Settlement

- Does the value of your product or service warrant the need to pursue dispute resolution services?
- Do you know of any laws that support your business model?
- Have ADR mechanisms been integrated into your contractual process?
- Are your target customers in a geographical area that complies with the appropriate rules and regulations?

Taxation

- How critical is taxation to your business model? Are your margins predicated on the cost of goods sold including sales taxes?
- Do you know of any potential taxation rulings that will affect your business model?
- How different are the tax rules within your target customers' locations? How do you adhere to the differences?
- Is your business model focused on high transactional volumes? Is your business being taxed at the source or at consumption?

Privacy and Trust

Privacy

- Do you have a trusting relationship with your customers?
- Is your primary focus on businesses or consumers?

- Do you have privacy policies in place? Are they aligned with your target customers' regulations?
- Are any data that are held by your business considered private? What physical and logical security mechanisms do you have in place for controlling data?

Authorization and Security

- What mechanisms are available for authentication? Are they integrated with a global "trusted" party?
- Do you have multiple forms of authentication mechanisms that depend on how your external stakeholders interact with your business?
- Does your business model include security considerations for trade?
- Do you know of any external governance factors that influence how your business handles authorization and security?

Technology

Network Rules

- How much does your business model integrate into the network of your business?
- Is the networking infrastructure correct, and do you have a migration path for upgrading?
- Do you know of any special networking components that need to be in place for you to do business in other areas?
- Is latency an issue?
- Do you know of any operations issues among the stakeholder groups?

Business Application Rules

- Do you have any interoperable standards in place for data exchange?
- What regulatory issues must you consider for the exchanging of business transactions?
- How much does your business model conform to open standards?
- Are you aware of any information exchange considerations that have not been resolved?

Using the Evaluation Framework

The framework for governance in e-business includes the following four components:

1. *Socioeconomic factors:* The infrastructure of the state and its citizens

2. *Marketplace rules:* The rules that help clearly and fairly define how companies should conduct business

3. *Trust and privacy rules:* Rules regarding ethics and data that foster e-business in our society

4. *Technology:* A business standards framework

Governance applies to all business models. The two scenarios that follow include a firm that has a large global distribution infrastructure and a tangible goods company that sells seafood globally. These two cases highlight many of the governance issues that we have discussed and allow you to observe them in action.

Big-Business Perspective: Governance Components Assessment (BBMusicOnline)

Bob:

BBMusicOnline is a traditional international distributor of entertainment including music and videos. We are headquartered in England and have more than $5 billion in annual revenues and 10,000 employees worldwide. We are trying to transition our business into an e-business model.

Some of the technological advances have involved audio file formats, such as MP3 and Real files, which have allowed music to be distributed online. The technical challenge is the least significant of our worries. The biggest problem is that we know of no clear regulations governing intellectual property in the distribution of entertainment information—no rules that address the concerns of the artists, the distributors, and the customers.

We are considering models that focus on the consumer by gathering personal data for future mining. We also have to fulfill our obligations to the artists who own the material. Our situation is a complex one and gets more complicated as we factor in issues such as distributing to geographical locations with variances in rules and regulations that affect our decisions.

The framework is used to break the company's problem up into smaller issues that can be resolved over time. Although this case study only concentrates on the governance aspects of the business, the company used all the stakeholder views to get the "big picture" of its business.

Socioeconomics

The socioeconomic component is not as significant as the other governance components. The socioeconomic component received an overall rating of 2 because the company had all of the components but they are not all working in concert with each other.

The company already has a stable workforce for its music and video production lines. The only area raising concerns is the online section. The company draws on a global workforce to fill its positions and has separate facilities in England and California. The company has enough content workers for the model. The difficulty is that they are experiencing a shortage of workers who can migrate the company into an online presence.

The company's facilities are already located in clusters, so the company achieved the benchmark in this area.

The company doesn't need to worry about customer access. They have narrowband and broadband versions of their content, so driving a particular architecture is not in their best interests. Their business model achieved the benchmark for network architecture. Some might argue that it would be best if they had solely a broadband infrastructure, but BBMusicOnline has business models in certain geographical areas that are solving the access problem.

BBMusicOnline's B2B model does not address localization of content. No precedents indicate that they need to tailor the language to the nation in which they are selling. The localization rating was a 3, although localization is not an important metric for this business model.

The government needs to be educated about intellectual property because its current laws don't protect the involved parties as well as they could. The businesses need some form of education because the majority of them don't understand the e-business model in relation to the traditional model. Customers need education. Only the early adopters of the alternative digital entertainment formats are pushing the envelope. A recent poll shows that teenagers in the United States are keen on downloading music. Other segments of the population have not embraced the alternative formats of music. Overall, e-business education is gaining some acceptance and the business model is realistic, but it would be much more successful if everyone was attuned to the model.

Marketplace Rules

Marketplace rules are the most important component for BBMusicOnline because it needs to become profitable in the near future. The music model is in flux, which is a major consideration for the future viability of the music industry. Marketplace rules were rated at 1 because of the wide variances in the enablers—some areas are in their infancy and others are at the benchmark, but the company has no consolidation strategy.

The business model targets a global audience and does not limit the location of its users—it's nearly impossible. The distribution of their material via the Internet involves similar issues, but the company won't get revenue if it has no sales. Because the company is just developing its business plan for migrating the company into an e-business, jurisdiction issues need a lot of improvement—improvement that will require a consolidated industry response.

The company owns all its content but it is impossible to detect whether this content is shipped with consent. Legal processes are in place because of international treaties that have been ratified in this area, although they vary significantly in interpretation and punishment. The regulations are also not aligned with BBMusicOnline's business model yet because it is in its infancy. Overall, the company has "old-age" protection rules but no "new-age" liability rules.

Although the business model is new, the company does own the intellectual property. Other companies are skirting the laws with their business models. The World Trade Organization (WTO) specifically outlines the definition of intellectual property. The company has total ownership of its material because it buys the rights from the artist, who receives royalties on sales. The business model has all of the elements of intellectual property, but the regulations cannot be globally enforced.

The company must go after the illegal distributors of the music. Regardless, even though it may be illegal for consumers to "own" content that is not theirs, it is very difficult for the company to track. Although stopping the smaller guys who are carrying the illegal content won't help the situation enough to warrant engaging in a legal process, the activities of illegal distributors do warrant a full-scale legal dispute—stopping them is the key. BBMusicOnline is considering providing ADR as a mechanism to resolve smaller disputes. The company has room for improvement in this area because new developments are constantly occurring.

The business model forecasts that tens of thousands of transactions will take place daily on a global scale. Taxation is difficult because the business is not limiting sales to any particular geographical areas. The taxation rules are not oriented toward this type of global business model. The taxation laws are in their infancy and will have to be revamped as soon as possible to build a taxation schema that is fair to all the parties.

Privacy and Trust

Privacy and trust are a key component in BBMusicOnline's business plan because it must create a fair environment in which to conduct e-business and convey this image to the involved parties. The privacy and trust component comprises many enablers, which were assessed with an overall rating of a strong 2.

The business must be able to cross-sell entertainment to its customer base. The business model is based on consumer transactions, so privacy has an impact on their consumer information programs. The customer information databases that were set up in the past do not comply with recent government regulations. The privacy rules vary by customer location and are difficult to adhere to. However, the enforceability of the privacy rules may prove too much for law enforcement agencies. The privacy rules are good in concept but not in practice because they are still so new.

The company is teaming up with a global transaction management company that will assume all of the risk for the authentication and security of the transactions. Security is also being outsourced to global carriers with a VPN product. The company has an extranet, but the internal members of the company are not required to have encrypted sessions. BBMusicOnline is doing all of its outsourcing with best-of-breed companies.

Technology

The technological component is very important for BBMusicOnline's business model because it forms the backbone for the transactions. The technical component received a rating of 3 because the business is using benchmark partners for it.

The outsourcing of the VPN to a global carrier means that the business does not have to lose control. The SLAs have been set and are administered on an exception basis. The carrier also handles the mirroring requirements based on the SLAs that have been defined. BBMusicOnline achieved the benchmark in this area.

The current business model works in a closed environment. BBMusicOnline has no current need to exchange information other than financial transactional data, a task that is being outsourced. The company hopes that eventually intellectual property in this area will be traded seamlessly throughout communities of interest, a process that would entail many transactions. Currently no specific formats for this type of information exchange exist today. The company received a rating of 2 for its technology component because although some good things are happening, BBMusicOnline has room for improvement.

Weighting Assignment

The following are the weights that were given to the governance components in the BBMusicOnline business model.

- Socioeconomic: Weighted at 2 because it should be included, especially the education aspect
- Marketplace rules: Weighted at 4 because it is necessary and essential
- Privacy and trust: Weighted at 4 because it deals with consumer information
- Technology: Weighted at 4 because it is the backbone for the transactions

Overall Assessment

The overall assessment (Figure 7-3) highlights that the business model is strong in the technological and the privacy and trust components but weak in the marketplace rules component (Table 7-1). Although the business model has a strong socioeconomic component, this is not a significant component for the business model's success. More work on the marketplace rules is required if the business model is to succeed.

BBMusicOnline has passed through the gate and is getting there!

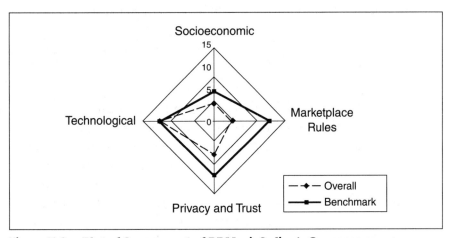

Figure 7-3   **Plot of Assessment of BBMusicOnline's Governance Components**

Table 7-1   Overall Assessment of BBMusicOnline

Component	Rating	Weighting	Overall	Benchmark
Socioeconomic	2	2	4	6
Marketplace rules	1	4	4	12
Privacy and trust	2	4	8	12
Technology	3	4	12	12

Small-Business Perspective: Governance Components Assessment (SMEFood)

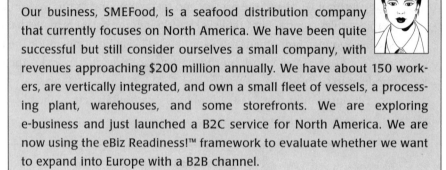

Sue:

Our business, SMEFood, is a seafood distribution company that currently focuses on North America. We have been quite successful but still consider ourselves a small company, with revenues approaching $200 million annually. We have about 150 workers, are vertically integrated, and own a small fleet of vessels, a processing plant, warehouses, and some storefronts. We are exploring e-business and just launched a B2C service for North America. We are now using the eBiz Readiness!™ framework to evaluate whether we want to expand into Europe with a B2B channel.

The following includes information from the governance section of the strategic business plan for SMEFood that was presented to the board.

The SMEFood strategy is based on selling to business channels in Europe. These would primarily be B2B transactions because the business does not own any bricks-and-mortar stores in Europe. The IT department is not very large and is focused on running the enterprise resource planning (ERP) system. The board presentation led to a decision to outsource the Web-enabled portions of the business to a world-class hosting facility. The only physical presence will be warehousing space in strategic locations in Europe to facilitate sales to its business channels.

Socioeconomics

The socioeconomic components are important but not critical components in SMEFood's business model. The enablers varied widely—some are in their infancy and others are at the benchmark, but the business has no consolidated strategy. The rating given to the socioeconomic component was a 2. SMEFood has a stable workforce in the areas in which it wants to build the warehouses. Because the economies are not superheated, the workforce turnover should be within normal parameters. The supply of knowledgeable workers was quite stable, so the company hit the benchmark in this area.

The suppliers are clustered around a few areas in Europe that are traditionally hubs for food distribution. The areas are not IT clusters but could certainly be considered food distribution clusters and achieve similar success. The distributors are at varying degrees of readiness, and most of them are transitioning into e-business. SMEFood has room for improvement but has a good cluster infrastructure.

Europe in general has less accessibility to e-business networking infrastructure. The business customers do have access, but the access for consumer customers varies widely. The revenue model is targeting businesses, which have access to infrastructure, so this enabler was close to the benchmark.

SMEFood has many obstacles to localizing the content because the EU still operates as if it is many small countries. The language and cultural difference are diverse. The employees only speak English, so they have to rely heavily on business partners to set up localized versions of the offerings. SMEFood only has rudimentary socioeconomic features and has much room for improvement.

Regulating bodies have been trying to educate themselves, businesses, and consumers about e-business. The target market only has rudimentary e-business skills, but the regulators have been very active. The majority of the customers, suppliers, and regulator personnel only have basic e-business education, so SMEFood has much room for improvement.

Marketplace Rules

The stability of the marketplace is a critical part of SMEFood's successful e-business strategy. The marketplace rules component was given a rating of 3 because the company achieved benchmark in the majority of the components.

The consolidated EU still has many jurisdiction issues. Draft regulation sets some guidelines, but most of the rules are very unclear at the moment. The SMEFood sales and distribution laws in its current operating area are very similar to those of the EU. Certain laws regarding types of seafood and quotas require clarification because of jurisdiction issues. The fundamentals are in place, but the company has much room for improvement.

The metrics in this area are tied in with the jurisdiction metric. The SMEFood business model does not solely rely on intellectual property because it deals with tangible goods. The company owns the goods and has a reasonably established shipping process, especially to the target market in Europe. SMEFood has addressed most of its liability issues.

Intellectual property is closely tied to liability, but the business model does not rely on intellectual property. The business shipping processes are very standard—SMEFood can trade with established businesses and communities. What intellectual property it has, it owns, and all of the loopholes have been addressed.

Dispute resolution is tied into jurisdiction and liability. The company has some interjurisdiction issues that can be resolved with ADR mechanisms. Contracts include ADR clauses and mention eResolution (a provider of online dispute resolution services). SMEFood has some good dispute resolution mechanisms in place but has room for improvement.

The transactions for the channels in the business model are B2B. SMEFood processes hundreds of transactions per month, few of which are exactly the same because seafood is assessed on quality and size. SMEFood has no taxation difficulties because it is complying with all the EU regulations. The tax rules for fresh seafood are not as favorable as they could be because much of the processing is done by the business—but it's just factored into the final selling price. SMEFood's tax system has room for improvement.

Privacy and Trust

Privacy and trust plays a key role as SMEFood moves into markets in Europe in which it has no physical presence other than warehouses. The company must build up and maintain trust if it is to succeed. The privacy and trust component was rated at 2; the basic functions are present but there is still much room for improvement.

The business model places emphasis on business transactions. Privacy and trust has less impact on this type of business model because it does not place as much emphasis on privacy of information (even though the company is not publicly traded). The business complies with the EU's privacy laws because similar laws will probably be established in North America. The privacy laws are similar throughout the EU, so the business only needs to comply with one set of rules. SMEFood is adequately protected (from a legal standpoint) in the segment of the market that they are serving.

Authentication and security is a critical part of the trust equation. SMEFood has to know the businesses that they are dealing with and vice versa, a step that is crucial if the company is to enter into Net markets. The current business has a multitiered certificate authority management system. The business customers have limited certificate management infrastructure but do not require it because they usually have only one point of contact for purchasing and sales. SMEFood has addressed many of the requirements for authentication and security, but they have room for much improvement.

Technology

The technological component addresses the technical infrastructure and rules requirements for SMEFood. The rating for the technological component was 2 because they have a strong business applications rules set but are weaker in the networking architecture area.

The business model shows that the business will outsource the technical components to a trusted carrier. They do not own the entire network that carries the transactions but do monitor the connections. The carrier can provide SLAs for their own infrastructure but cannot provide them for providers other than their partners, who are predominantly within North America. Mirroring requirements will be required for latency and fault tolerance. SMEFood can carry out their business with their networking infrastructure, but they have room for improvement.

Business applications is an area in which the SMEFood business model excels. Each of the partners must adhere to either EDI or XML transaction sets to do business. The schemas that have been defined and agreed on cover all of the common business transactions. SMEFood can make minor improvements but achieves the benchmark—other companies are striving to achieve its level of trading efficiency.

Weighting Assignment

The following are the weights given to the governance components in the e-business model (Figure 7-4, Table 7-2):

- Socioeconomic: Weighted at 2 because it should be included but is not critical to the success of the business model
- Marketplace rules: Weighted at 4 as it is critical to the success of the business model
- Privacy and trust: Weighted at 3 because it is essential, especially for authentication
- Technology: Weighted at 3 because it is an essential component of the business model

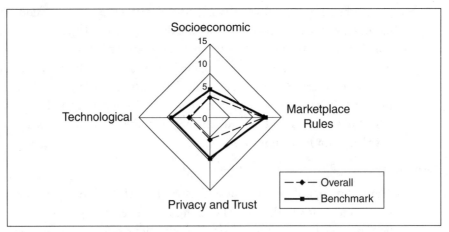

Figure 7-4   Plot of Assessment of SMEFood's Governance Components

Table 7-2   Assessment for SMEFood

Component	Rating	Weight	Overall	Benchmark
Socioeconomic	2	2	4	6
Marketplace rules	3	4	12	12
Privacy and trust	2	3	6	9
Technology	2	3	6	9

Overall Assessment

The overall assessment highlights that the business model is very strong in the marketplace rules component but weak in the privacy and trust and technological areas. SMEFood is also weak in the socioeconomic area, but this component is not as critical to the success of its business model.

Are You Ready?

Table 7-3 provides a snapshot of all the components, enablers, and metrics essential for successful governance planning. The metrics are a combination of quantitative and qualitative measures that rate a company from low to high based on some agreed-on principles. The assessment is defensible because the context and reasoning have already been defined.

Table 7-3   Components, Enablers, and Metrics for Governance

Components*	Enablers	Metrics
Socioeconomics: "stability of the state"	Work force Clusters Access Localization E-business education	Turnover of workforce Education level of workforce Employment rate for workforce Number of companies in cluster Focus of the cluster Growth rate of the cluster Growth rate of access infrastructure in target markets Adoption rates in target market Amount of content required in local markets by law Diversity of content required for local markets Number of policies pertaining to e-business Number of procedures pertaining to e-business Subjective response or willingness of governments in target areas Adoption rates of e-business in target markets Future projections of business adoption rates Customer adoption rates Future projections of customer adoption rates
Marketplace rules: "stability of the market"	Jurisdiction Liability Intellectual property Dispute settlement Taxation	Number of areas targeted for work Commonality of laws in targeted operating areas Amount of owned legal content Degree of legal processes Degree of legal processes within target market Degree of compliance with UNCITRAL Number of regulations aligned with your business model Percentage of owned content Number of patented processes Number of ADR mechanisms Degree of interjurisdiction issues Number of transactions Number of transactions in other countries with different laws Extent of taxation difficulties Extent to which taxation rules favor your business model
Privacy and trust: "stability of the customer"	Privacy Authentication	Completeness of privacy rules Number of nations within operating areas that have different privacy laws Level of authentication mechanisms within organization

Table 7-3   Components, Enablers, and Metrics for Governance (*cont.*)

Components*	Enablers	Metrics
Privacy and trust: "stability of the customer" (*cont.*)		Level of management infrastructure and defined policies for authentication management Degree of PKI infrastructure allowances
Technology: "stability of the architecture"	Network Business applications	Number of disparate networked areas outside of one service operator or within one provider Number of SLAs Level of worldwide operations requirements Level of adherence to exchange community policies Level of compliance with open standards Number of formats required Number of formats supported

*Recall that the knowledge, trust, and technology enablers are common to all components (see Chapter 2).

Highlights from this chapter include the following:

- Governance is a critical factor in building trust between customers and businesses.
- Globalization is naturally changing the way we do business, and it's happening faster because of e-business.
- E-business doesn't have the traditional business boundaries, which makes it difficult to apply traditional regulations.
- The "sweet spot" for regulation is the point at which governments, businesses, and customers are all appeased.
- Society needs to have an infrastructure; e-business can be difficult when dealing with people, businesses, education, and technology.
- Rules must define and govern how a marketplace works. The rules should address ownership, mechanisms for doing business, and dispute mechanisms.
- Intellectual property drives the knowledge economy.
- E-businesses must establish a privacy spectrum.
- All involved parties need to be able to have faith in each other so that they can establish a trusting relationship.
- Technical architecture rules are essential enablers for e-business.

References

[1]Gelinas, F. "Arbitration and the Global Economy." The International Chamber of Commerce, January 2000: 1.
[2]Perine, K. "The Privacy Police." *The Industry Standard* February 2000: 71.

CHAPTER EIGHT

Working for YOU: Agents

> Bot, *short for* robot, *is derived from the Czech word* ro-bota, *which was coined by author Karel Capek, and appropriately means* work.

Getting You Prepared

Agents are a relatively new yet integral part of e-business. This chapter highlights what agents are doing today to enhance the effectiveness of business offerings and also discusses the companies that have centered their core business on agent technologies. Without agents, many massive tasks would be impossible—tasks such as indexing and retrieving massive amounts of information as well as other tasks that lend themselves to automation. By the end of this chapter, you will be able to differentiate among types of agents, understand how they can be used in your business setting, and know some of the business models that support agent technologies.

In 1833, Ada Agusta, Countess of Lovelace wrote the first software program that automated a repetitive task, thereby reducing the number of human calculation errors and freeing up human resources for higher-level tasks. The agents of 2000, which are also known as *spiders, worms, bots and robots, hotbots, netbots, know-bots, softbots, personal assistants, artificial life forms,* and *software agents* and characterized as multiagent, profiling, mobile, or intelligent agents, have a similar goal—they continuously monitor user actions, search for information, learn from user feedback and advice from other agents that do similar tasks, and take action autonomously. After time, agents become "experienced" in performing designated tasks. Ask Jeeves, a software agent that uses natural human language, is an example of an agent that gets experience by answering questions for a given business. Ask Jeeves benefits from statistics that show that 20 percent of the questions that could possibly be asked of most businesses are asked 80 percent of the time, so the agent's experience becomes apparent after it has been asked those particular questions.

Applications of agent bots are plentiful. Data management bots take on tasks such as finding and fixing broken hypertext links on Web sites, automatically filling out forms, and highlighting important concepts in text. Newsgroup bots take care of filtering, binary file extracting, and recommending article tasks. E-mail bots automatically inspect and evaluate incoming mail messages, generate autoresponse messages, and selectively forward incoming messages that need a human response. Shopping bots can compare features of products or merchants such as price or available warranties. Stock bots can mine relevant knowledge from unstructured banking and financial information on the Web. Government bots can restrictively query government data such as census and labor statistics data and government bills. The BotSpot Web site has details on more than 15 categories of bots.

Net-tissimo.com, a joint venture between Artificial Life and the Bon Appétit group in Switzerland claims to be the first e-commerce platform with fully integrated bot technology. The Web site is powered by Artificial Life's 3D interactive character bots, which automate customer service, e-mail messaging, sales, and direct marketing. Net-tissmo.com is the first e-commerce Web site to offer agent-based sales and services to the German-speaking countries of Austria, Switzerland, Liechtenstein, and of course Germany. For customers, Net-tissimo's bots provide a Web site guide, virtual personal sales assistant, a customer service representative (CSR), and personalization. As a part of customer service and to decrease human resource costs for telephone support, the agent ALife-Messenger acts as an autoresponse e-mail reply and answering service by automatically reading incoming e-mails and instantly generating a response or redirecting the e-mail request. Net-tissimo's "net me a deal" feature is also interesting—the pricing models include the "catch-of-the-day" and "happy minutes."

Proxying is another area that can involve visual agent interaction. 3D characters or *avatars* (3D representations of people who serve in a particular role), are used as sales advisors. Retail clothing sites such as macys.com and landsend.com use My Virtual Model avatars. The customers can customize the facial and body characteristics of models to match their own. Some agent technologies are embedded within large employee-facing business applications. For example, the British start-up Autonomy has products that create corporate portals and use agent technology to manage, manipulate, and distribute relevant content to employees in real time. Autonomy's agent support of natural language querying in multiple languages is exciting for e-business because of it could potentially resolve globalization issues.

Lesser-known applications of agents include applications in community building and monitoring, entertainment, and education. Avatar use in these areas has exploded in the last year. An avatar can also be a bot and have programmed behaviors and responses. Extempo's Erin at Spence's Bar is an online virtual community that has an avatar host who promotes chat and commerce events. The tens of thousands of game players from around the world that log on to the Everquest game servers at all hours of the day and night are evidence of the popularity of avatar-based games. Everquest is marketed as a "world with its own diverse species, economic systems, alliances, and politics." The game facilitates virtual face-to-face meetings among players. Words, facial expressions, and body gestures provide powerful humanlike interactions. Virtual documents can be passed around the group, and dropped objects can be picked up. Regardless, these avatars clearly serve as aids only. Technology and human understanding are not sufficiently advanced to allow replacement of face-to-face human interactions with avatars—interactions in which subtle movements can evoke instinctive responses from another human being. However, avatars also add entertainment value to childhood education, an environment in which nuances and subtleties have less impact. Avatars can transport kids into another culture, speak different languages, teach interactive lessons, and generally make learning fun.

Defining the Horizon

Given the magnitude of information that is available on the Internet, coping successfully with tasks such as researching and maintaining directories and hypertext links is more than humans can handle. We need software entities such as agents to help us out. The definition of an agent is a topic of great debate, particularly regarding how agents differ from ordinary software programs. IBM defines agents as "software entities that carry out some set of operations on behalf of a user or another program with some degree of independence or autonomy, and in so doing, employ some knowledge or representation of the user's goals or desires." An agent represents a business or customer. Agents are not all artificially intelligent; some are basic agents that have features such as autonomy, responsiveness, and communication ability (Figure 8-1). Basic agents use enabling technologies such as speech, voice recognition, and natural language query processing. Intelligent agents have the features of basic agents as well as the ability to plan and set goals, reason about effects, and improve knowledge and performance through learning. Intelligent agents use methods from artificial intelligence fields such as fuzzy systems, neural nets, and genetic algorithms. The sophistication of these agents increases when belief, intention, and obligation are added to their feature sets. Agents with true autonomy, full authority, and proactivity—the ability to define and set goals—do not yet exist. However, most agents, basic or intelligent, possess some form of these characteristics.

An example of a basic agent is the question-and-answer Ask Jeeves product. An example of an intelligent agent is Imagination Engines' DataBot, an agent

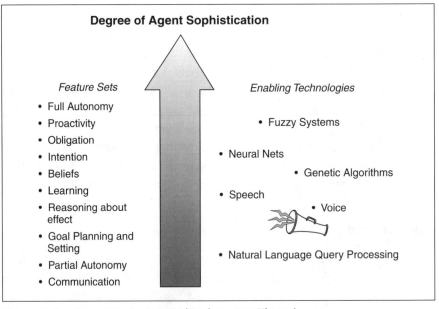

Figure 8-1   Agent Feature Sets (Basic to Intelligent)

that uses advanced neural networks for adaptive artificial organisms and knowledge agents to manipulate cells in Excel spreadsheets. DataBots can ". . . exercise their own independent judgments when perusing databases, choose their own perspective on or physically move through the data, automatically learn hidden data patterns, and cooperatively build compound cascade structures capable of autonomous discovery and invention."

BullsEye is a custom multisystem of intelligent agents that uses more than 300 search engines and more than 600 databases on the Internet to find, filter, analyze, report, manage, and track information. "Multiagent" or "multisystem" is one category in which agents collaborate or consult with many other agents to accomplish a task. Agents can have long or short life spans. The StreetPrices.com comparison-shopping bot is a long-lived agent with an ongoing price alert function. You enter your e-mail address and the price you are willing to pay for a particular product, and StreetPrices.com notifies you when a lower or an equal price is found. Agents with short life spans tend to be basic agents that are often created for a specific purpose and for cases in which state retention (keeping data on past events) is not important.

To provide true one-to-one customer experiences, agents assume personas and styles that appeal to each specific customer. They address the human need for social intermediation, satisfying the customers' senses and emotions. Agents bring three important attributes to the table: persona, behaviors, and knowledge. Extempo defines persona as "comprising all facets of an individual character's identity such as backstory (personal history), appearance, style of moving and gesturing, speech, and social and emotional dynamics." The agents assume the behavior that is appropriate for the role they are performing, whether it is marketer or hostess. The users are encouraged to provide input and assert opinions. Agents can "learn," or increase their knowledge, through interactions with users. They may learn about a new company that has formed or the name of a company mascot or may get a sales lead from the interaction. In turn, assuming the agent has done its job, the agent has integrated the customer knowledge and can use it to personalize sessions. For example, an agent could greet a wine aficionado named Hans with something like, "Hi, Hans! How was that bottle of red wine you bought last week? We got a new shipment of Chianti in. Can I put aside two bottles for you?"

Agents are available for many device formats. The wireless Palm VII already hosts mySimon To Go, a comparison-shopping bot. It also supports the development and deployment of applications based on artificial intelligence (AI) that can perform any task over the Internet that a live user can. People have also discussed providing bot functionality at the operating system level (for example, in the Palm operating system).

Agents don't come without a cost. Operating repetitively for long periods, agents consume considerable resources such as network bandwidth and server central processing unit (CPU) and disk resources. To speed up the response time, agents use parallel retrieval and communication with other agents, resulting in higher use of bandwidth in the immediate area. Rapid firing of requests is an agent capability that generates a large number of retrievals in a short period, often leading to shortage of bandwidth for other users. On the technical front, agents have increased the need for voice recognition and speech communications standards to facilitate multiagent conversations. Agent creation, destruction, and mobility are other technical issues that need to be addressed. Because everyone will eventually have a personal agent—probably more than one—with individualized goals and roles, it means that numerous agents will need to be managed. Agent automatic personalization efforts can lead to profile glut—profiles can number in the thousands depending on employee and customer base sizes. Agents need management policies and procedures. As agent use increases, we will see the development of hardware dedicated to agent servers. Some agents are mobile. They can move and perform functions on machines other than the one on which they were initially deployed, which may result in security issues. Mobile agents make sense when permission for full execution on a remote machine is granted or when load balancing or the conservation of network bandwidth dedicated for messaging becomes an issue.

Legal issues also affect agent use. In 1999, eBay tried to sue to prevent other businesses' auction agents from crawling (automatically clicking hyperlinks on) its site. High expectations and hype have caused agent reputations to suffer as well. Inefficient searches and irrelevant results frustrate users of the preliminary commercial agent products. Present-day agents do include some degree of irrelevance in their results; however, significant research is being conducted in an attempt to eliminate the problem. We are optimistic that agent products in the early years of the first decade of 2000 will be beneficial enough to make agent use in the management of complex content and knowledge essential to e-business.

eBiz Readiness!™ Components for Agents

Figure 8-2 provides an overview of the components and enablers within the eBiz Readiness!™ framework for assessing agents.

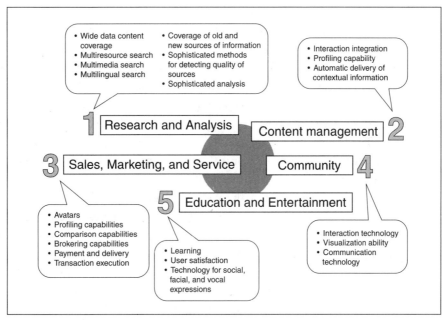

Figure 8-2   Agent Components and Enablers

Research and Analysis

Bob: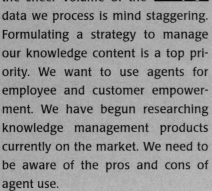

As a business in the financial service industry, the sheer volume of the data we process is mind staggering. Formulating a strategy to manage our knowledge content is a top priority. We want to use agents for employee and customer empowerment. We have begun researching knowledge management products currently on the market. We need to be aware of the pros and cons of agent use.

Sue:

We are interested in determining which agents will be most useful for our small-to-medium enterprise (SME), a women's clothing and tailor shop business. We want to focus on enhancing our customer-facing processes and using free search engines and comparison-shopping agents to locate fabrics. We hope that the eBiz Readiness!™ framework components and metrics presented in this chapter will help us choose the best agents.

An environmental researcher seeking global warming data can use an agent to query sources such as the Atmospheric Radiation Measurement (ARM) document collection, which is the largest global change research program supported by the U.S. Department of Energy (DOE), worldwide meteorological offices, and library databases such as engineering and science indexes. The agent has to have a fast response time and the capability to provide authorization information so that it can access the various information repositories.

The biggest hurdle for agents that aid in research and analysis is related to scale. Search engines and agents that use them currently cover less than 30 percent of Web content. Currently, different search-based agents return different results when used to query the Web. More intelligence is being added to search engines as user expectations and needs increase. Sources of research are diverse, spread out over many countries, and appear in many languages, formats, and media types. New Web site and content growth is exponential.

The challenge to agents is to be sufficiently *scalable* and supported by *sophisticated scalable Web directory structures* so that they can effectively tap the vast content that is available. The Web directory structures are similar to a global hierarchy of up-to-the-minute Yellow Pages. Agents should not have to rediscover resources that other agents have previously found. Another major problem is the number of irrelevant results returned by agents.

A business can use a research and analysis agent to automatically scan newspaper sites worldwide to find, compile, and report on information relating to the company, its competitor, or client business. Research agents provide automatic abstract compilations and hypertext linking. Abstracting summarizes long documents, and hypertext linking generates hyperlinks among related documents. Agents that can grasp concepts in many languages and connect to other agents to provide translation services will be truly useful to researchers. Canadian Watchfire's LinkBot Pro is a quality assurance tool that produces analyses of Web sites. It speeds through Web sites, checks links, and then reports on which pages are broken, slow, new, or old. It automatically generates a report with recommendations for site improvements. Automated research and analysis agents can also be used to plan a business trip. The employee wants the agent to compare prices, number of transfers, actual travel time, stopover times, and departure times for each airline. A basic software agent can analyze the options and determine which airline best matches the employee's preferences. A final example of agents in action for presales research and analysis is MortgageMarvel, an intelligent agent-powered site. MortgageMarvel compares rates and fees of various U.S. online mortgage lenders and does a benefit analysis. The agent automatically adjusts for escrows, points, loan amounts, and home value.

Researchers also need to be able to query multiple media types. For example, a user may want to retrieve all images of Margaret Thatcher positioned to the left of Tony Blair. Excite provides an advanced search tool that allows audio and image search queries. However, positional characteristics such as on top, to the left (right), to the side, in front, at the rear, and so on are not supported in current commercial offerings (although they may be available by the time this book is published)!

Home appliances that provide direct information feeds to the Net will facilitate pure market research. Actual data will become readily available and be in a purely digitized form for the first time. Through monitor agents, researchers will be able to determine exactly how many times a day a consumer opens the fridge door. Agents will push content down (provide unsolicited information) to appliance owners. The agents may purchase groceries to restock the refrigerator or alert owners automatically when an appliance warranty plan is about to expire.

The metrics for agents that carry out research and analysis tasks are scalability of data content coverage, capability to perform a parallel search of multiple publications, true search capability, multimedia search capability, and multilingualism. Timeliness of information, quality of information sources, ability to locate pertinent articles, ability to efficiently locate information, availability of Web directories (Web Yellow Pages), and the degree of analysis sophistication are others.

Bob:

Our clients' stock portfolios contain Asian, British, German, and North American stocks. We need the ability to use multiple research resources in different languages to keep abreast of happenings that may affect stock prices in these various markets.

Sue:

We use free services on the Web to research new fabrics and new markets. An engine with wide coverage and high result relevance would make us feel like we were getting a more detailed and complete view of things.

Content Management

People often discuss information gluts as an Internet problem that will eventually get much worse. This issue extends to corporations also. Many times there is no easy way to get a complete set of information about a project from the large amount of data kept in corporations. Knowledge management, which includes content management, will be the key solution to the information overload problem. Agent technology used in tools for knowledge management enables effective content management; search, complete cross-referencing and document categorization, automatic catalog update and product management, dynamic personalization of content, immediate and relevant information delivery, and speedy publication are all benefits.

Knowledge management requires handling structured and unstructured data regardless of file or device formats or whether the data are from an intranet, an extranet, or the Internet. Structured data are organized in databases or data warehouses, whereas, unstructured data are found in e-mail, voice mail, word-processing files, hypertext markup language (HTML) files, spreadsheets, and Internet plug-ins. Knowledge management empowers employees to quickly filter, process, and act on information from any source. A determining factor for successful knowledge management is thus the *fusion of content from multiple sources*. To allow management of data from Internet feeds such as the Dow Jones news feed, from corporate security domains such as operating system and database server domains, and from applications such as Lotus Notes, agents must be compliant with different levels of security policies.

Corporate intranet portals are being created as a central place from which to search, manage, and distribute information. Ideally, such portals should deliver information in real time; publish new information at Internet speed; categorize, index, and tag across data repositories automatically; create profiles; and personalize content. Portals have to be *scalable* to the amount of data being managed. Adding information from the Internet exacerbates the need to handle enormous amounts of content. Using manual approaches to profile based on how a customer or employee uses a Web site or portal over time is impossible. Profilers track changes in customer or employee interests and deliver increasingly targeted content to improve customer loyalty or empower the employee. Agents can automatically determine user expertise and interest by monitoring what the user reads and writes online and weighting how often various topics come up. In this way, agents obtain intimate knowledge of user expertise and can track changing interests. The combination enables dynamic personalization of content. Agents can then automatically push and deliver content to users. As a user creates a document, the agent automatically creates links to it from related documents, and the user then is alerted about the existence of those relevant documents.

An effective knowledge management tool supports categorization, which is the sorting or filtering of documents into predefined categories. Agents are trained to sort documents through example documents that have been precategorized. Automation of categorization enforces consistency in classifying content because the individual variability introduced by manual processes is eliminated.

Headquartered in Toronto, Canada, HummingBird Communications offers the HummingBird enterprise information portal (EIP) to address corporate portal needs. It addresses the single interface requirement for structured and unstructured enterprise data and connects users to content in context. The HummingBird EIP offers a range of features that includes a unified search mechanism to access all structured and unstructured data sources internally and externally, an e-clip plug-in architecture that addresses scalability or portal growth, and a personalization theme capability. The EIP's personalization supports multiple levels of user profiles, allowing for distinction of corporate information from knowledge workers' personal portal pages. The EIP promotes consistency and ease of integration by supporting extensible markup language (XML) application programming interfaces (APIs) to other applications and providing users with a centralized and unified environment for interactions with all applications. This means that all information from legacy or older applications may eventually be presented through a single interface. In addition, data from more than one application can be combined through the single EIP interface.

Autonomy, which is based in Cambridge, England, offers products for knowledge management in the area of corporate portals, e-commerce, and new media. The e-commerce products concentrate on automation of catalog and product management. These products are used to enable effective product targeting, cross-selling and up-selling, and automatic product suggestions based on customer profiles. The new media products can guide users through Web sites such as Yahoo! that have large amounts of content. Autonomy's portal products use proprietary pattern matching technology and adaptive contextual analysis and concept recognition techniques to transparently index, categorize, tag, link, alert, profile, personalize, proactively visualize, and deliver information from multiple sources. Skill mining is another interesting application that Autonomy supports. Decentralized organizations in particular face difficulties when trying to find an employee who has the appropriate skills to help solve a certain problem. Autonomy's technology tracks items that employees read and write, such as documents and e-mails, in an attempt to pick up on recurring concepts and areas of expertise; the system can also notify employees about others with similar expertise.

Artificial Life has a knowledge management solution for individuals—ALife-KnowledgeManager—that asks to "listen in" on user activities, such as reading documents, attending online meetings, and visiting Web sites. The profile that the knowledge bot builds may be used during discussions with other knowledge bots. The combined experience of these bots can then be used to provide the user with recommendations such as which sites to visit for holiday travel information or what gifts to buy.

Metrics to determine whether content is being managed well include degree of content integration (virtual unification of content formats), level of automatic categorization and cross-referencing or hyperlinking capability, degree and level of personalization (such as corporate or personal), level of data currency (such as immediate or deferred updates), level of security adherence, degree of profiling, ease of integrating content from multiple sources, and proactive delivery of information.

Bob:

We use internal database applications, collaboration tools, and e-mail extensively and subscribe to numerous news feeds such as Commerce Daily and Reuters. Unifying the indexing of these materials is an exciting possibility.

Sue:

Our customers can choose which fabrics they would like their clothes to be sewn from. We stock a few popular fabrics and offer additional fabrics that we receive from fast-delivering suppliers. We will use agents for supplier and product catalog content management. We want to automate the repair of broken hyperlinks and updating of all related product pages.

Sales, Marketing, and Service

Personable, 3D, agent-based characters—avatars—are beginning to become the staff members of the Web. Sales assistants, Web guides, product spokespersons, CSRs, and online community virtual hosts are just some of the roles avatars play in business-to-consumer (B2C) commerce. Ask Jeeves makes it easy to interact with him by allowing you to ask ordinary questions in English sentences; businesses such as Dell, Microsoft, Nike, and TD Waterhouse use Ask Jeeves, sometimes under another brand name, for customer service. Max is a Web guide that takes you surfing on Extempo's Web site. Max is animated and literally speaks to you—and the speech appears in text format concurrently. My Virtual Model at landsend.com, macys.com, JCPenney, Mattel, FingerHut, and haute couture Les Galeries Lafayette allows you to try on clothes on virtual proxies. You can personalize the model or proxy by providing characteristics such as your body dimensions, hair style, and eye color. Then with a simple "point and click," you can dress the model in the clothes, shoes, and accessories that are for sale. You can rotate the model and view the fit from every angle. The My Virtual Model database now has 800,000 registered models.

E-sales advisors are being forced to become specialists—cell phone advisors, telephone service advisors, restaurant advisors, wine advisors, and so on. Consumer electronics site etown.com allows you to "Ask Ida" all your questions. Ida is an interactive shopping advisor that is powered by the Ask Jeeves natural language agent. The OnStar Virtual Advisor uses General Magic's MagicTalk voice recognition and agent technology to provide hands-free, voice-activated access to Web-based information services in vehicles. Consumers are able to access personalized e-mail, weather, sports, news, and market headlines. The Onstar Virtual Advisor has been installed in more than a million of General Motors' cars. Artificial Life's ALife-PortfolioManager agent helps investors select securities that match their investment goals. As goals change, the agent can automatically, at a minimum trading cost, change the user's portfolio to reflect the new objectives.

Imagine you are about to plan a trip. A travel guide agent takes you on a virtual tour. The agent and your proxy "step" into photographed scenery of your holiday destination, and the photographs match the season of the year in which you plan on traveling. You interact with other agents that speak in the accent or language of your destination. You get the flavor of the culture.

In manufacturing applications, engineers, marketing executives, and clients can use avatars of themselves to serve as proxies during videoconferences and design sessions.

A furniture store can use avatars for marketing by filling a virtual room with furniture and people. The customers get a chance to see how combinations of fabric, furniture positions, and furniture angles work as the customers try to get a certain look in a room.

In B2B e-commerce, power utility companies and governments can allow business contracting agents to wade through thousands of large geographical information systems (GIS) image maps as they create bids for contracts to clear tree limbs of power lines in particular areas.

Customer-facing agents digitally log all interactions with customers. E-businesses will have access to customer information from call-center or personal interactions—information that is normally lost. The logs can be used to determine whether a customer is ready to make a purchase and the customer's likelihood of purchasing an associated product or service, to monitor the level of customer satisfaction, for profile enhancement, and to determine the customer's knowledge of products and services. The goals are to foster a deeper understanding of customers, target market segments, capture information for uses that we haven't even thought about yet, and create a proactive business environment—in other words, the goal is to anticipate. Artificial Life, offers the Smart Text Analyzer (STAN) as a data mining solution to assist Web marketing professionals with analyzing conversations between users and bots. STAN uses fuzzy logic and neural network algorithms to analyze text files.

Comparison shopping agents are perhaps the most popular for customer use on the Web. Agents such as mySimon and RUSure primarily allow price comparisons of products in certain categories. Comparisons of other product features don't have as much support. Using these agents well requires exact product descriptions. Frictionless's ValueShopper and Active Research's Active Buyer's Guide allow the user to select an item based on personal preferences including price, features, and customer service policies. ValueShopper adds the process of negotiation to the existing product and merchant brokering dimensions. The agent can negotiate not only on price but also on warranties and shipping terms.

Amazon.com uses its zBubbles agent to engage customers and its Eyes agent to recruit repeat customers or to reengage customers. The zBubbles agent is a client-side agent—it must be downloaded and installed on the client's browser. When the consumer is looking at an amazon.com competitor's page and sees a product that amazon.com sells, zBubbles pops up a window that shows amazon.com prices. The Eyes agent is used to alert customers that a book in a genre or by an author that they like has just become available.

Bob:

We formed an alliance with an agent firm so that we could allow our customers to ask questions in plain language on our Web site. We now plan to offer free stock bot-powered customer self-service on our Web site. We want to offer timely, focused, and current financial information, such as hot, new stock offerings and emerging economic trends. We are investigating a new stock bot called *FinanceWise*, in addition to other bots. We frequently add new, free features for our investors.

Sue:

We are interested in using avatars to allow women to virtually try on clothes to determine whether one of the thousands of patterns we can cut and sew suits them. This service would be invaluable for customer sales and will also increase customer satisfaction—each woman will have an idea of what a particular style will look on *her* rather than on a pattern-book model. She will also be able to see what a style looks like in different fabrics.

Community

Online users spend close to 30 percent of online time in chat rooms. The chat room is one of the primary enablers for building community. How can agents help bring people together in a community and from overlapping communities who share similar interests? Agents can augment communication by providing a physical presence through proxies, which creates the illusion of persistence, or that a presence is there waiting to respond. Agents are adept in finding out what people have in common because they manage thousands of profiles in a community. An agent can also facilitate visualization of a social interaction with use of common contexts, and all the while can monitor and collect information. In other words, a *common context* is created and personalized for community members. For example, community members who first navigate the e-malls together share a shopping experience—they have just established a common context, which establishes a sense of trust among those members. As the customers chat, agents monitor the discussions and refine their profiles, which include customers' preferences and needs, and get feedback on the business.

Agents that monitor communities may be "listening" for special keywords and phrases (for example, "expecting a baby"). After they hear one of the keywords, they contact a salesperson avatar who "drops by" and introduces himself or herself as a sales representative for baby furniture. Government agencies such as the Central Intelligence Agency (CIA) use software agents to continuously monitor certain targeted user profiles during threaded community discussions. The agents can trigger an alert if they "hear" something particularly alarming.

Clearly, the monitoring power of agents reinforces the need for governance regulations, particularly in the area of user privacy. Privacy is an issue that all businesses must address to ensure that their users trust their communities. Some businesses buy profiles from communities; for example, a gourmet food company would surely be interested in the profiles of all those people who said that they like apple sage jelly! Regulations are being passed that state filtered profiles can only be sold with the customer's permission.

Communities tend to have very loosely defined objectives. Agents can help identify the roles of individual communities and promote the development of more defined community objectives. Toru Ishida, a professor at Kyoto University in Japan, coined the term *communityware*, which is a total solution, or platform; rather than being forced to buy separate IT community tools and products, customers get e-mail, Web page hosting, multiuser dungeons or dimensions (MUDs), newsgroups, chat rooms, Internet phone, CUSeeMe conferencing, and ICQ all in one package.

Communities have different focuses and needs. In Chapter 4, we addressed the fact that B2B communities have different needs than B2C communities. The Netscape browser's "What's Related?" feature uses Alexa, an avatar that monitors the entire Internet community (a pretty big audience!) and identifies the Web site links that would be most useful to them. Alexa monitors and stores behavioral patterns of Web travelers. She categorizes information about Web content and uses data mining techniques, intelligent technologies, and user input to identify usage patterns and the relationships among Web pages, as well as to generate accurate contextual related links. User input is obtained from the most frequently accessed sites.

Metrics for the community are community growth, number of community services, importance of community service, visualization ability, communication ability, degree of sharing as perceived by community members, and site "stickiness" (how long the site keeps people on it).

Bob:

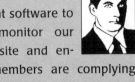

We use agent software to constantly monitor our community site and ensure that members are complying with the community's rules of acceptable behavior.

Sue:

We are interested in expanding our customer base and would like to tap into several different communities. We would also like to use a community agent to notify targeted members about our services.

Education and Entertainment

Because agents are good at continuously repeating a task and can be programmed to adapt, issue feedback, and automatically move users to a higher difficulty level, they are suitable for education applications. Imagine Web sites that would give community members free cardiopulmonary resuscitation (CPR) lessons or directions on how to bathe a newborn baby. Agents may be able to make a real difference in education. A well-designed agent application powered with avatars can make learning fun.

A fair amount on social interface theory is involved with replicating the human interaction experience. People interact with agents and proxies, which can be somewhat disarming. When speech is combined with a computerized image, it allows people to feel like they are interacting on a more human level, so their attitude is a little different. Studies show that customers get satisfaction from social interactions, even if they are with a computer program!

Children can adopt a puppy at VirtualPuppy.com and learn how to take care of it. Neglect can kill the puppy, so children learn the repercussions of their actions. Agents are used in many teen and adult games as well. For example, you can play the game Doom with artificial players named Cajunbot and Doombot. In fact, when you play games such as Doom or Everquest against real players, you see their avatars.

Frank Vaculin and ASK JEEVES

DOING IT TODAY

The Ask Jeeves company is technology based. It was founded as a service based on a natural language search engine, an engine that allows you to type in your search question in plain English and then links you to an answer on the business's site. The Ask Jeeves product line has blossomed into corporate and consumer offerings that create a compelling customer experience, making the company a leading provider of customer targeting, conversion, and retention services. According to the Ask Jeeves corporate site, it creates value by increasing e-commerce conversion (that is, converts lookers into buyers), reducing support costs, and improving overall customer satisfaction.

Frank Vaculin, Ask Jeeves vice president of marketing, explains the Jeeves product line: "We focused initially on just providing question-and-answer solutions for individual sites. Our big corporate customers include Microsoft and Hewlett Packard (HP). Unlike regular search engines, in which you type in keywords or expressions, the Ask Jeeves system parses the sentences according to meaning and context and matches them against similar questions that are already in our knowledge base. The answer is then extracted from the knowledge base, which is how you get your response.

"If you want to serve your customers in a very humanlike way we provide a mechanism to do just that. Customers feel like they are actually walking into a store that is set up like a traditional store; it has different types of clothes laid out for you and a clerk that speaks to you. It is all very controlled. We provide a mechanism that companies can use to create a very compelling user experience. Current statistics show that companies are spending a lot on driving traffic to their sites. The next big spend will be on retention.

"Think about the way people try to learn and the way they try to find information. They go through a cycle. First they have questions and seek information, then they like to compare, and then they look to how they should make the final decision. They may research a couple of final items. So there is a decision cycle that goes on, and what we've developed is a suite of products that really enables that cycle. The question-answer process is like a funnel. The top of the funnel is the search process; narrowing down that funnel is the question-and-answer process that may provide a specific, searchable answer.

"In 2000, we acquired a company called Direct Hit as well as its popularity-based search technology. Direct Hit uses this technology to track the popular Web sites that people use to find information or products online. It aggregates and organizes online content by tracking the products, services, and information people seek, the amount of time they spend on various Web sites, and how frequently they return. We combined our initial natural language search engine with the technology from our Direct Hit acquisition, which gives us the capability to go out on the Internet and get answers from various sites, as well as to incorporate editorially hand-selected answers.

"We've got the ability to service customers by finding information, whether it is in a support or sales context. The Jeeves products are based on (1) the planned combination of human input provided through an automated, hand-selected, question-answer process involving editors who actually supply the answers to your site, and (2) a search approach, in which we index the content on your site. Using indexes and tracking where people go after they ask a specific question gives us a lot of information. For instance, if you type in a question like 'How do I buy an ergonomic chair?' while you are in the Office Depot site, Jeeves would match that question and provide you with a result. But it will also provide you a lot of other information that is related to ergonomic chairs, such as information on other ergonomic furniture. The question-and-answer process really lets you target and understand your customers' needs better and provide the answers to their questions in context.

"Our Jeeves Advisor product turns the Jeeves Search and Jeeves Answer paradigms around. Instead of asking it questions, it asks *you* questions and makes a decision based on your needs. An example of a Jeeves advisor is the Ask Ida advisor, which gives suggestions on electronic purchases. It's very intuitive—this type of technology is used in much more complicated tasks such as scheduling space shuttle launches. On the back end, we have taken that technology and applied it to situations in which multiple variables must be considered; we weigh various factors and make a good judgment. The technology is applied on an ask-needs question, not a future-function question. Instead of asking about Dolby Digital (especially because you may not even know what it is), it asks you questions about how you are going to use the products and tries to figure out whether Dolby Digital is important to you by asking you friendly, nonintrusive questions. The technology can be applied to consumer settings, for making

continued

decisions about buying insurance, or for making any kind of decision involving multiple factors.

"A question tree dynamically presents the questions and illuminates questions that don't need to be asked. The advising is dynamic—it depends on the kinds of answers you provide and can change directions. This technology is an agent because it learns information about you, takes the information in, and adjusts its questions based on what it knows about you. Take Nike's Web site and Shoe Finder as an example; no sales representative is there to help you and answer questions. The software advisor asks questions regarding factors such as your ability and running habits and makes a decision about what type of shoe you should wear. In essence, you have a conversation with the site. For companies like Nike and Fidelity, which spend a lot of money on getting customers to come to their site, the customer experience is the primary focus.

"Part of the value we provide our customers is the result of the fact that we price the Jeeves solution according to its performance. The customer wants to know, 'If I buy this, how will it help me?' Our price isn't based on the number of questions people ask but the number of answers they get. Because our pricing is performance based, we take the risk we are actually going to do a good job. The companies will perform surveys to make sure that customers are finding the right answers. We solidify our position on performance by providing a fourth product called *Jeeves Live,* a live interaction tool manager with instant messaging. Jeeves Live gives you the ability to have direct text-based communication with the customer. When customers are engaged in a question-answer session and are asking questions, searching, or even going through the advisory process, and we determine that they haven't found what they are looking for, we give them the option to talk to a live agent.

"Abandonment is a big issue, whether it is abandonment of the shopping cart or during the postsales support stage. Abandonment can result in frustration and dissatisfaction; we can provide pretty successful reporting of performance statistics. Live Jeeves looks at clustering where it's able to and creates cross-metrics reports. The reports give product managers some good insight into better understanding the customer.

"We spend a lot of time thinking about the future. Our strategy is to create new ways to increase customer interaction. To provide a multimedia humanistic experience, we intend to extend our reach by using other modes of interaction involving voice and wireless devices. You could walk around with a Palm Top wireless, ask your question on a Palm 7, and get your answer from Ask Jeeves. Technology innovations in user interfaces influence the things we are working on to adapt Ask Jeeves for the wireless environment. Another example is voice. The same wireless experience is occurring in Europe, very much like the Internet is here. We can transfer the questions that people ask in plain English to a voice automator system. It is compelling. We have a Jeeves running in our Interlab that has voice capability. The technology needs to mature, but it's getting there."

When asked about his company's vision for the Ask Jeeves line, Vaculin says, "Our mission is really to be the human-eyes experience of the Internet and provide a personal service infrastructure to companies and consumers (customers and kids). We are going to do this by improving the richness of our natural language experience. We will provide other mechanisms of interaction, which will allow us to provide a lot more content. Answers will not only come from corporate or single site content but from a lot of other sources. So we will network content. We will be an exchange. Exchanges meet a supply-and-demand need. For us, the demand is the questions and the supply is the answers. We will interconnect—whether it is to ASK.COM or to several other Web sites—to get customers' questions answered. We will support many modes of interacting—whether it is live, through an Internet advisor, or through a question-and-answer search."

Questions You May Want to Ask

Overall

- What are the present and future applications of your agent? What capabilities does the agent have?
- How is the agent product offered by your company unique? Who are your closest competitors? (Sites that rebrand Ask Jeeves do not have a unique agent product.)
- Will consumers use agents to communicate with other consumers? Will this facilitate a new form of building community? Will businesses make agent technology free as an incentive to building community?
- What roles can agents play in building community?
- What types of bargaining power are being built into your agents?

- Will consumers allow agents to make decisions for them based on profiles? How do you see agent technology evolving so that it reaches that goal?
- Do you intend to place agent technology in information appliances? What are the applications of information appliance agents?
- Do you use avatars? What are the main uses of avatars? Avatars are popular in the gaming industry—what are their applications in other industries? (For example, My Virtual Model is used to proxy at landsend.com to aid the retail sales process.)
- What is your business model? Do you sell agent software, or are you a service company? What are your registration fees?
- How many strategic partners do you have? What industries or markets were you able to penetrate by partnering with others?
- What impact will your product have on customer care?
- What difference does it make to your consumer or business when your agent learns? What type of learning occurs?
- How can application service providers (ASPs) use agents?
- Does your natural language query processing apply to languages other than English? Will your agent tap databases and unstructured information stored in different languages?
- Can your agent interact with many types of data sources—unstructured, structured, multilingual?
- Can your agent enhance and abide by security measures while searching through corporate intranets and the Internet?

Research and Analysis

- What percentage of the Web does your search agent reach?
- Are you taking steps to increase Web coverage? Are you reducing search engine registration fees?
- Is your agent hierarchical? That is, is it an "agent of agents?" (For example, Echosearch from Iconovex uses multiple search engines simultaneously and then collates the results.)
- What is the most complex class of query that your agent supports?
- Does your agent search engine support querying of image databases? Can it support a query such as, "Find James standing in front of Cathy in a town crier outfit?"
- Do you have support for audio searching? What about for a mix of text, image, and audio?

- Can your agent do trend analyses? For which industries?
- Do you intend to integrate your agent with information appliances so that you can obtain more in-depth customer profiles?

Content Management

- Can the agent intelligently manage data? If so, what are its capabilities?
- Is the product restricted to document management?
- What types of file formats can the agent handle? Can it mine information from formats such as Excel spreadsheets, Oracle databases, Lotus Notes databases, WordPerfect documents, enterprise resource planning (ERP) packages, and legacy systems?
- What is the reach of your agent? That is, does it reach data on intranets, extranets, and the Internet?
- If your agent brings in data from an extranet to your company, what types of controls for data integrity maintenance does the agent have?
- What types of knowledge can be gleaned from the questions people ask? How sophisticated are the profiles that the agents build?

Sales, Marketing, and Service

- How is agent technology used in B2B e-commerce?
- In what ways does B2C e-commerce use agent technology?
- We know that agent applications of customer profiles include news services, amazon.com's Eyes, Pointcast networks, Newspage, ZDNet's Personal View, and tracking stock portfolios on quote.yahoo.com. Therefore personalization is a primary reason agents can be used in B2C e-commerce. What are other key factors?
- What are the innovative ways in which agents are using profiles?
- Will we see comparative shopping agents used in e-procurement?
- How useful are avatars as sales agents? Are they only used for proxying, or do they have other uses, such as for virtual reality experiences, answering "what if" scenarios, or modeling?
- Does your agent allow natural language querying? What are the most exciting applications of natural language querying in customer care? Do you know of any applications for natural language querying in other areas of e-business?
- Can your agent locate, compare, bargain, and execute for the customer during the purchase process?

- Which of the following can your agent execute: needs identification, product brokering, merchant brokering, negotiation, payment and delivery, service and evaluation?
- Will your agent support the information appliance to become the next point of sale device?
- Does your agent evaluate products and merchants based on style, rapport, ease of use, location, delivery cost, or warranty quality?

Community

- Does your agent promote community building? For example, agents can bring together people who have similar interests based on their profiles. Does your agent have this capability?
- Communities are usually one of four types: a community of interest, a community of transaction, a community of fantasy, or a community of relationship. How many of these types of communities does your agent promote?
- Into which communities is your agent being presently integrated?

Entertainment

- Is your agent used in the entertainment industry?
- What is the impact of avatar technology on the gaming industry?
- How does your agent enhance the salability and entertainment value of a product?

Small-Business Perspective: Agent Assessment (SMETailor)

Sue:

We are pursuing a risk-sharing model with an agent technology company. We propose to provide a small, live testbed for them and pay them for research services and for the amount of valid content that the agent supplies the community site. Both companies benefit from this type of arrangement.

This case is about an SME online retail e-business called SMETailor.com that creates tailored clothes for women. The owner has planned an agent strategy based on research, knowledge management, marketing, sales and services, community, and entertainment components. Customer-facing processes are weighted the heaviest. SMETailor maintains catalogs of fabrics, sewing accessories such as buttons and fasteners, and fashion patterns for women. Clients can choose a pattern, accessories, and a fabric from the catalog, and provide their body dimensions using a form, and then SMETailor gives them price and delivery information. Clients can also submit a pattern of their own via fax or e-mail and get a price estimate; they can supply their own fabrics as well. Clients are charged a small extra fee when they supply a pattern or fabric. The charge covers the cost of photographing and digitizing the pattern and the fabric's color palette and print.

SMETailor is aware that some of its clients are not satisfied with the end-products. The issue has never been the quality of the tailoring but is usually a result of the fact that clients select styles that are not appropriate for them. The management would like to use a sales model proxy to allow clients to visualize what styles will look like on a person with their body shape and dimensions. However, the cost of the agent technology is a concern; SMETailor doesn't know whether the companies that sell proxy technology even have special SME prices. Perhaps SMETailor can propose an affordable one? A percentage of the revenue from a sale that is directly attributable to the proxy technology can be promised to the company that provides the agent technology to SMETailor. The company would like to offer customer self-service. Its clients would not be interested in formulating questions with Boolean strings—natural language querying should be available.

SMETailor is continuously researching new types of fabrics and suppliers. The business tries to keep on top of seasonal fashion trends. SMETailor has an online community that it provides with fashion news. Occasionally staff members post fashion news items to the community site, but SMETailor knows that the site is simply not dynamic enough. Chat room support is not being considered because it is too expensive for an SME. If chat rooms become an issue, a group of SMEs that would like to offer the service may be able to amortize the associated costs.

Because pattern and fabric bases are growing rapidly, SMETailor must constantly index and categorize its patterns, fabrics, and accessories. Instead of hiring a person for this task, the business is considering using agents. SMETailor anticipates adding 50 patterns and an average of 10 fabrics daily.

The agent support assessment shows that SMETailor is just starting out (Figure 8-3). The high-level agent readiness assessment diagram gives an overview of the e-business agent capabilities for SMETailor. They have many gaps to fill but can create a plan by using the detailed analysis (Figure 8-4). The detailed analysis

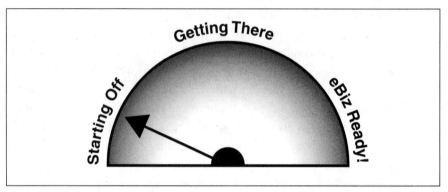

Figure 8-3   RadarScope Assessment of SMETailor's Agent Capability

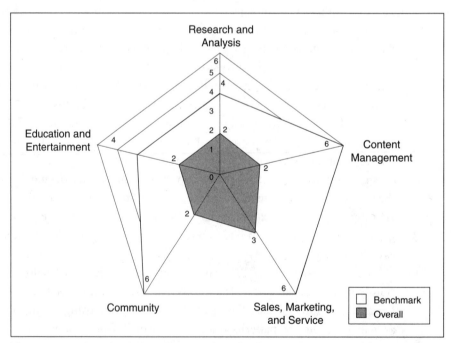

Figure 8-4   Detailed Assessment of SMETailor's Agent Capability

shows how SMETailor is doing with respect to the baseline. Each of the capabilities is shown. The management decides to focus on some key areas.

The solid area is the plot of SMETailor's agent assessment, and the patterned area is the benchmark (the desired values). The axes of the polar plot are labeled with the component names such as research, community, and content management. The score for each component is plotted on its corresponding axis. SMETailor's task is to have an entirely solid plot—in other words, to achieve 5s in all areas. SMETailor must decide how aggressive it wants to be to achieve its agent strategy execution.

Big-Business Perspective: Agent Assessment (BBFinance)

Bob:

Using agents should help our company reduce support costs and improve overall customer satisfaction.

Big Business Finance Service—BBFinance—is a traditional business that has a dotcom component. The company currently offers $10 trades on the Internet. The site offers personalization services that allow clients to actively manage their portfolios through buying, selling, and research. The stock portfolio presentation includes the volume of stock traded, the current price, the day's range, the 52-week range, moving averages, stock splits, and dividends.

The week's biggest stock movers are highlighted in a sidebar, and links to related financial news articles are provided. The site uses agents to create the related news links. Services include agent-powered e-mails that alert clients when a stock hits their preferred bid price. Investors can also type in questions in plain English and receive help from the site.

BBFinance believes that it should continually upgrade its value-added services as part of its customer retention strategy. In the finance industry, customer switching costs are extremely low. Agents that use voice recognition technology are being investigated. BBFinance is also considering forming a partnership with agent companies for penetration of the wireless market. The company would like to allow its clients to trade using cell phones and satellite links from inside their cars.

The community component is doing well. Chat rooms and discussion threads allow investors to discuss issues such as the pros and cons of various stocks and the possible impact of news statements on stock performance—basically, anything they find interesting and helpful.

Content management is a real issue for the business. Internally, the business shares actuals (actual sales, expense, and asset figures), forecasts, exchange rates, charts of accounts, and organization structure data among its analysts and accountants. It currently has no way to obtain all the required documents through a single portal or system interface. Sometimes BBFinance misses relevant material because an employee forgets about an e-mail that contained the latest update of forecasts for example. Data consistency is a hit-or-miss affair and is only ensured when analysts remember to post updates globally. Document synchronization is not supported. Numerous people are able to open a document and make changes to it, and the last save overwrites all other updates. The company clearly needs new knowledge management initiatives.

The results are plotted on a polar plot chart showing all of the factors for agent support. Figure 8-5 shows the results in an overall polar plot. The figure

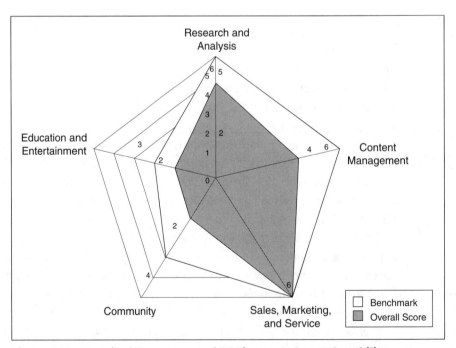

Figure 8-5   Detailed Assessment of BBFinance's Agent Capability

shows that the e-business is already strong in research and sales, marketing, and service components but needs to strengthen some aspects of content management. It is also continuously assessing new agent-based e-business enablers that are on the market. The solid area is the plot of BBFinance's agent support assessment, and the patterned area is the benchmark (the desired values).

BBFinance is doing e-business well. This business is fully customer focused and has excellent customer acquisition processes and solid customer retention strategies. BBFinance is eBiz Ready!

Are You Ready?

Table 8-1 provides a snapshot of all the themes, components, and metrics essential for successful agent choices.

Table 8-1   Metrics for Agents

Components*	Enablers	Metrics
Research and analysis	• Coverage of old and new sources of information • Sophistication in detecting quality of the sources • Sophistication of analysis • Extent of data content coverage • Scalability of data content coverage • Multiresource search capability • Multimedia search capability • Multilingual search capability	Scalability of data content coverage Number of types of search techniques (such as keyword, synonym based, concept based, Boolean, and natural language) Level of multiresource search capability Level of multimedia search capability Level of multilingual search capability Extent of coverage of old and new sources of information Level of sophistication in detecting quality of sources Degree of relevance of agent results Level of efficiency in locating information Availability of Web directories (such as Web Yellow Pages) Degree of sophistication of analysis
Content management	• Interaction integration • Profiling capability • Automatic delivery of contextual information	Degree of content integration (virtual unification of content formats) Level of automatic categorization and cross-referencing or hyperlinking capability Degree and level of personalization (corporate versus personal)

Table 8-1   Metrics for Agents (*cont.*)

Components*	Enablers	Metrics
Content management (*cont.*)		Ease of integrating content from multiple sources Data currency index (immediate versus deferred updates) Level of security adherence Degree of profiling Level of proactive delivery of information
Sales, marketing, and service	• Use of avatars • Profiling capability • Comparison capability • Brokering capability • Payment and delivery methods • Transaction execution	Level of coverage of multiple sources for comparison Degree of sophistication of agent-customer communication Degree of conveyance of humanlike user experience Accuracy of information provided to customer Relevance of information provided to the customer
Community	• Interaction technology • Visualization ability • Degree of communication	Community growth Number of community services Member satisfaction with agent services Visualization index Quality of communication Degree of sharing perceived by community members
Education and entertainment	• Learning assistance and capability • Easy-to-use interfaces • Social, facial, and vocal expressions	User satisfaction Skill improvement

*Recall that the knowledge, trust, and technology enablers are common to all components (see Chapter 2).

Highlights from this chapter include the following:

• Impacts of agents on e-business, markets, and competition include improved customer service, more intimate customer relationships, employee empowerment through knowledge access, fewer incidences of "reinventing the wheel" (starting from scratch to solve a problem or create a product when it has already been done), more informed decision-making, greater insight into the internal workings of business, innovation, and price pressure.

- Agents can automate tasks such as automatic indexing and categorization of documents, unified searches of structured and unstructured sources of information, location, and multilingual access of distributed research resources.
- Many agent research services are still free.
- The eBiz Readiness!™ framework shows the e-business level of readiness, weaknesses, and strengths in regards to agent usage.

Starting Off | Getting There | eBiz Ready!

CHAPTER NINE

Get Your "Insides" Working: Employee and Internal Operations

> Business, more than any other occupation, is continually dealing with the future; it is a continual calculation, an instinctive calculation in foresight.
>
> *Henry Robinson Luce, editor and publisher,*
> *cofounder of* Time *and founder of* Fortune *magazines*

Getting You Prepared

People are the most important factor in a knowledge-based economy. Many books concentrate on the synergies that teams create and hold leadership as paramount for survival in e-business. Although these ideas are correct, how do you assess people's capabilities and your partners' capabilities? This chapter investigates the components that make up the "insides" of the company. Although the focus is on the people that make up a company, it is also on the processes that they must use and the infrastructure that must be in place. We include many examples and quotes from various members of the e-business community. By the end of the chapter, you will be able to assess the insides of an e-business, including its people, processes, and infrastructure, so that you can create a strong e-business for the future.

The eBiz Readiness!™ framework was used to help a 9,000-employee telecommunications company—trying to reinvent itself—develop an e-business strategy. The business model for the core e-business unit involved the creation of a new company based on a service aggregator model. The company was extremely aggressive toward creating new e-business services to augment that model. The company found that knowledge management tools must be used at all levels. At the strategic level, partner relationship management (PRM) tools were an indispensable part of managerial interactions with the company's teams and its business partners. At the crux of the strategy were the employees who formed the independent business units from which the e-business unit drew its services.

You often hear "knowledge is power." It is what gives you an edge as you attempt to deal with the future and allows you to synthesize or form "continual and instinctive calculation in foresight." In a nutshell, experts in e-business define knowledge management as the ability to provide the *right* information to the *right* people at the *right* time. Your e-business is the "socket"—it receives input from and sends information to the external stakeholder plug-ins; it is the receiver and transmitter of knowledge and value. The convergence of better computing capacity and state-of-the-art technology such as function-rich browsers, next-generation databases, advanced search engines, and enterprise portal products with intelligent agents have enabled knowledge transfer among all stakeholders. Technology enables effective knowledge management, but people only give business to those they trust. Knowledge management, trust, and technology collectively enable the creation of the value Web and new e-business models.

Introducing the E-Business "Insides": Operational Requirements

How aggressively is your business creating new business opportunities? What do you think motivates tens of thousands of business to form alliances each year? Does your business do continuous self-assessment studies? A business that does not reorient itself so that it can embrace e-business cannot meet customers' expectations. Businesses that wait too long to reorient will find that their market share is falling and they are losing business opportunities. How many chief executive officers (CEOs) will be caught by surprise, mumbling, "Who *is* this Jeff Bezos, anyway?!" Even if some dotcom businesses, add-ons, or spinoffs don't survive in the long run, they still have valid and reusable business pieces that will withstand the test of time.

We already have marketplace indicators that point to the demise of traditional business. As long as it is cheaper and more convenient for vertical industries, such as steel and energy, to do business in electronic marketplaces, why would buyers look elsewhere? Some e-markets require that sellers obtain an e-business infrastructure to join the marketplace. Wal-Mart and Boeing are just two examples of companies that require suppliers to acquire IT infrastructure and adhere to strict digital standards and formats to carry out transactions with them. Suppliers not willing to reorient are locked out.

When should your business start reorienting itself? Before your customers demand and expect it! The old adage that "change begins at home" should be heeded in e-business. Management has to be open to new thinking. Malcolm Frank of NerveWire states, "The key issue for companies is to manage change. Companies need to create an environment that embraces change. The environment is an indicator of their receptiveness and adaptation to change. Good management in an industrial economy is not necessarily a good measure of success in the new economy."

The internal procurement process is normally one of the first few processes to change because it is easy to convince management of the benefits. The benefits are clear—reduced process cycle time, deeper discounts from online suppliers, and more accurate reporting because of the digitization of the processes. The magnitude of these savings is often 100:1. Oracle reports that it costs them $100 to process a paper-based expense report. It costs $1 to file and process expenses online.

Customer-facing processes such as marketing, sales, and service depend on internal processes. Efficient internal processes decrease the time it takes to respond to a customer's query, increase the accuracy of the response, and raise the quality of the content of the response. This is more than traditional customer relationship management; it is operational management that affects the customer.

Demonstrating the power of e-business Web applications to your employees can unlock their imaginations. Your employees—your business's most valuable asset—are the key to future innovation inside and outside the company. When your organization's information is organized and easily available to the employees—who can support key strategy formation and decision-making—your company is positioned to rapidly respond to global competitive pressures and threats. More importantly, facilitating quick responses improves customer satisfaction. Long-term reductions in general, administrative, and production expenses resulting from shorter task cycle times is a bonus.

According to skeptics, dreams of the "paperless" office are wishful thinking because we need a "paper trail" for legal accountability and disaster recovery.

Maybe so, but perhaps *one* paper copy will do. Microsoft's founder, Bill Gates, discussed the 350,000 copies of a particular sales report that was distributed throughout his company.[1] He also mentioned the 114 forms Microsoft used for procurement. By implementing intranet applications in the company, Microsoft reduced the number of forms to 11. Its sales reports are accessible through the browser. Cluster Competitiveness, a Spanish consulting company, takes a more radical approach to promoting the paperless office. Each day, all papers are swept off each consultant's desk and placed in a recycle bin. The company's goal is to capture all intellectual capital online. This total knowledge sharing translates into cost savings. It costs less to train a consultant, so more consultants can be trained simultaneously. The common theme that threads through all internal e-business processes is indeed knowledge management.

Changing business processes is one step you can take. Managers also need to take a hard look at their company's business model and the whole slew of e-business models out there. What pieces can you adopt that would add value to your customer and business? Is your business stagnating? When was the last time a new or an improved product or service was successfully released?

Bob:

We have quasi-mechanized processes to support nonproduction procurement, administration, facilities maintenance, and repairs. All of these processes use islands of information. We need to understand the scope of what is possible with full Web automation—what types of increases in efficiency and savings we can expect.

Sue:

Only our customer-facing processes have been automated. All the back-end processes for administration and procurement are still paper based. We need to determine which internal processes we should reengineer to give our customers and the business the most value.

Defining the Horizon

Businesses who want to reinvent themselves cannot do it alone. All the big success stories, such as Cisco and Sun Microsystems, had external assistance to move into e-business. These companies still have many consultants involved in projects for continuous business improvement. They also have partnerships with other firms.

E-Business and Enterprise Resource Planning

In the 1990s, big business installations of the enterprise resource planning (ERP) packages were a niche that kept thousands of consultants very busy. ERP packages contain a set of functional business components (such as finance, accounting, materials management, production, and customer order management) integrated in an enterprisewide data warehouse. The implementation of ERP packages also served two other purposes. First, as a Y2K solution, as old legacy applications were replaced rather than maintained, and secondly, as preparation for e-business. One of the biggest advantages to successful ERP implementations is the resulting adoption of best-of-breed business practices. The integration of data from areas of business such as the accounting, finance, human resources, production, and materials management departments into one database gives the enterprise a collective view of those areas. ERP vendors are slowly but steadily increasing their capabilities to integrate this type of "insides" data with data from Web channels and data from the five external stakeholders. ERP vendors have also been producing leaner versions of their software for the midsize business market.

E-business is causing enterprises to make decisions faster. The only way that informed decisions can be made and new trends and patterns identified is if we have a consolidated view of all business data. Businesses without network access to complete consolidated business data aren't ready to perform in our "information-now" economy. The key to getting a consolidated view of all business data is having all of the information from external stakeholders flowing into the internal information system. Figure 9-1 shows the stakeholders that would plug into the e-business internal systems.

Just as not all ERP installations were successful in the 1990s, we expect the same will be true for e-business initiatives. Failures in ERP installations were primarily a result of poor strategy and project management approaches, end-user resistance, complex technology and systems, and a failure to learn from past mistakes. These reasons for failure will undoubtedly be part of a larger set of reasons for some e-business implementation failures.

Customer Value Innovation

e-Business models are focused on customer value innovation. Cristopher Hoenig, consultant and former director for information management and technology

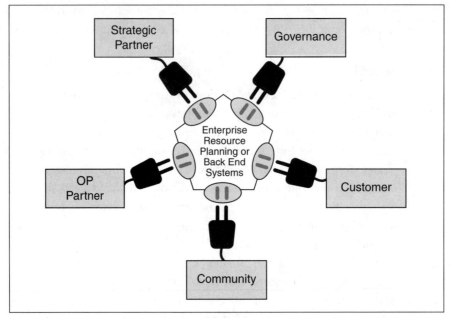

Figure 9-1   Stakeholders Plugging into the E-Business Internal Systems

issues at the United States General Accounting Office, says the following about innovation: "A big part of innovation is the ability to reconceptualize things, change paradigms…"

An e-business model is a description of

- The architecture for information flows, product flows, transaction flows among business stakeholders
- How revenue is obtained
- Target markets

To illustrate elements of the above definition, a very abbreviated description of eBay.com's business model is given. Information comes into the business from two types of customers: buyers and sellers. Buyers provide bidding and registration information. Sellers provide auction item listings. Product/service flows are between customers. The product or service does not pass through eBay thus eliminating many fulfillment concerns. Some transactions that are facilitated are bidding, posting of lot information, browsing, searching, and community service type transactions. Operational and strategic partner interactions should also be described in the model. Among the ways revenue is obtained are through percentages of the sale and listing fees. Target markets are worldwide.

Many new e-business models allow a customer to do new things such as get access to products at lower costs (or for free) or to execute a task that previously needed to go through a middleman. Priceline.com enables customers to make offers for tickets and hotel rooms at prices less than list. Etrade.com allows customers to execute trades themselves. In a business-to-business setting, vertical markets aggregate suppliers specific to an industry. Instead of customers spending hours on a phone or thumbing through fat paper catalogs, they can spend minutes acquiring the same information. Some companies employ more than one business model. For example, amazon.com supports retail, advertising, and auction models. A categorization of e-business models is provided in Chapter 1.

Customer value innovation on the Internet is apparent through increased reach of specialist companies. Caper Jones, Chief Scientist, of Artemis Management Systems, cites examples such as custom furniture makers, specialty foods (e.g., ostrich steaks, buffalo jerky), artist guilds, metal workers, and makers of special devices for people with disabilities. By providing Web access to customers, many small, specialized companies and craftsmen are bringing in impressive volumes of new business at lower costs than through conventional means. For specialists, the spread of customers is wide—only one in thousands in a geographic region may want to know about their products. Traditional media such as brochures, newspapers, and radio cover a limited area. Additionally, the cost and mailing of brochures are often directly proportional to the number of mailboxes reached. If a brochure costs 20 cents to create and mail, then it will cost $1 million to get to five million distinct mailboxes, some of whose owners may not be interested in the brochure's contents. With the Web, these specialists can attract customers that truly need these products or services. They will attract potential clients who need what they offer but who may be in a different geographic location, as well as those that are not informed of the existence of products or services because of prohibitively high costs of communication.

Industry associations that use an aggregate business model provide great customer innovation and often enable small-to-medium–size firms to have a Web channel. Caper Jones shares his experience with his company. "Some of the associations that are relevant to my own company include the Project Management Institute (PMI), and the International Function Point Users Group (IFPUG). By having links to these two associations, we get a lot of queries from potential clients that might not otherwise know about us." Capers also made us aware of the Realtor.com Web site, which has more than 1.5 million homes listed in the United States. The site is run by the national real estate association, and supports thousands of local real estate offices.

Businesses such as FOB.com and mercata.com create value for their customers by aggregating their purchasing power to obtain better pricing of supplier goods and services. Through FOB, small businesses gain better pricing, and mercata.com applies the co-operative model to reduce consumer pricing.

e-Business consultants create value for their customers in the following four ways: more revenue, lesser cost, faster time-to-benefit, and better customer care. They can do so because they already have the knowledge to do it, and they can take an arm's length view of the business in an autonomous and unencumbered fashion. Additionally, they are less perturbed by the notion in e-business transformation that sometimes channels and processes must be cannibalized. As Dean Hopkins of Cyberplex, a new-age Canadian consulting company puts it, sometimes a company has to be prepared to eat its own lunch.

Customer innovation also lies in enriching the customer's experience with the business, as was discussed in Chapter 3. Customer loyalty is increased when a business can conveniently and transparently manage transactions across a combination of channels such as Web, physical storefront, voice, fax, and so on. Convenience may be provided in product configurations such as what Dell offers for personal computer customization. Many people explore more options with a passive, non-threatening product configuration at a leisurely pace than they would with a human salesperson. Comparative shopping agents provide new value in reducing the customer's time to shop around. Data mining activities provide the customer with a one-to-one or personalized marketing experience. Many businesses create value to their customer base through community services as detailed in Chapter 4. Strategic partners also help create customer value through their aid in creating continuous streams of new products or services in rapid time frames. Operational partners can liberate the amount of time it takes to get a product to market thus shortening customer delays in receiving product or service. For example if your local sports car manufacturer reduces the time for making a car from 60 days to 10 days then there is significant benefit to the customer. Governance has also supplied tremendous customer value in the last few years in tax moratoriums, digital signature recognition, electronic government initiatives, and funding for adoption of electronic methods for business. A good synopsis of customer value innovation is found in the stakeholder value propositions outlined in Chapter 2.

eBiz Readiness!™ Components for Internal Assessment

The eBiz Readiness!™ framework allows you to do an internal scan of your company's e-business readiness. A general assessment of the internal e-business capability of a company focuses on its culture, e-business strategies and models, general and administrative functions, interaction with employees, operational and strategic partners, customer areas, and overall governance. We group the areas that are left into three components: e-culture, productivity, and information infrastructure. Figure 9-2 shows the components, which are numbered, and

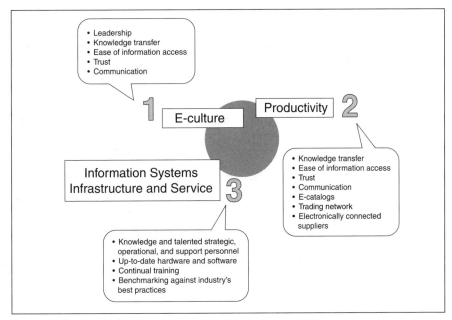

Figure 9-2   Components and Enablers for Internal Operations

their enablers, which are in boxes. The interaction processes for partners, the customer, and governance are discussed in their respective chapters. E-business strategy is addressed in Chapter 10.

E-Culture

A company's transition from bricks and mortar to clicks and mortar must include management of cultural and organizational change. Businesses are looking toward the future, and employees at all levels must buy in to the company's e-business vision and strategy. Internal capabilities are strongly influenced by the prevalence of e-business culture (e-culture).

Continuous self-assessments and learning are core aspects of e-culture. Knowledge transfer processes are required to support the e-culture. The vision for e-business must be well understood by all employees. Because we are operating in "Internet time," companies must provide employees with the tools and training they need to become comfortable with, understand, and execute new processes. The company needs to be able to turn on a dime in response to regulatory changes, market fluctuations, supply-and-demand fluctuations, and customer needs.

The hiring strategy of these companies must be a "plus one" strategy, meaning they hire people who may be more talented than existing personnel. A company's ability to retain top industry personnel is an indicator of the soundness of its internal capabilities. Strong hybridization of technical and business skill sets is mandatory in key e-business positions. This hybridization affects the alignment of business and IT goals. The overall talent pool must be capable of e-business planning, implementation, and execution. The quality of the management, although it can be a subjective measure, is a factor investors consider before investing in a company.

Being innovative in the attempt to create employee value means creating new ways of building trust and loyalty, lowering the costs of doing business, increasing flexibility and opportunities for new training, improving employee care plans, and implementing aggressive reward systems. The rising popularity of the mobile workforce not only addresses employees' needs for flexibility but also reduces overhead costs, allows employees to work more hours at home and on the road, and most importantly is an important way to retain employees. Approximately 80 percent of what is spent on a customer overall is spent on customer acquisition. Therefore it makes sense to spend money to retain *existing* customers.

Similarly, businesses spend more money on hiring new employees than on employee retention. Some firms report that it costs as much as $20,000 to process a new employee. A shift in the process has begun; focusing on employee value innovation is a newer trend.

Some methods for increasing employee retention include forming an alliance with online job search companies such as Monster.com to keep on top of market trends and maintain key employees' salaries at market value. An employee salary review should be done periodically. Businesses also need to benchmark their employee compensation packages with similar organizations in the industry. Many firms are giving employees stock options, which improve retention because employees wait to leave, if they leave at all, until their options vest. Ongoing training programs and job enrichment activities often help increase employee satisfaction.

The culture of a company transitioning into e-business is changing to one of knowledge sharing instead of knowledge isolation. Teams of people collaborate easily and more readily through repositories of expertise and best practices. Currently, teams use shared folders, also called *transfer folders* or *directories,* on secure extranet sites to exchange information. The better collaboration tools enforce version control and synchronized access to shared documents. Synchronized access allows multiple users to read a document at the same time, although only one user can add to or update the document at any moment in time. The benefits of effective knowledge management are increased employee productivity, more effective team collaboration, increased feelings of community and loyalty, and cost reductions. Employee productivity increases as reinvention and duplication of effort are eliminated, and the time it takes to access knowledge is greatly reduced. Effective team collaboration means that projects can be executed more quickly. A feeling of community and loyalty develop when employees can talk knowledgeably about projects they may not have actually worked on. Costs associated with noncompliance with trade or federal regulations, which normally occurs because of lack of timely actionable information, can be removed through effective dissemination. Jobs that depend entirely on information tracking, such as equipment tracking for off-site projects, or contracts that are changed under knowledge management initiatives sometimes result in retraining and redeployment of workers or elimination of job positions.

Companies would describe their culture as "the way we do things around here." We have seen a phenomenon in which minicultures develop across departments. Sheri Andersen illustrated this with an anecdote from Novell:

The facilities department was trying to initiate some new worldwide badging systems and outsource some facilities functions. We quickly found that we had to enter information on the whole workforce in the computer system—not just our people on the payroll, but everybody who works here—everyone who has a phone, spends time here, and has a badge. I wanted them all in the system. This turned out to be good for the human resources, information systems, facilities, and security departments. It was a hard sell initially. The human resources department thought, "Ugh! You are making more work for us, and we don't want to deal with it." It turned out *not* to be more work, and we used the process to get better clarity on head counts. We used to have fights among human resources and employees about head count, specifically about the definition. Does the finance department use the number itself or the sum of averages for its report? We got real clarity on that because it was a semantics problem.

Leadership in the "now" economy, in which strategies, processes, and cultures are changing, is what empowers the workforce—what determines whether the business will succeed or fail. In his book, *An Invented Life: Reflections on Leadership and Change,* Warren Bennis identifies the four qualities that create good leaders.

1. Management of attention: Leaders have the ability to draw others in because of a vision, a dream, a set of intentions, an agenda, or a frame of reference. "Vision is thinking the unthinkable, saying the unsayable, doing the undoable. It's thinking out of the box. It's the ability to see things in different ways from the traditional," says Patricia Wallington, retired chief information officer (CIO) of Xerox.

2. Management of meaning: Leaders have the ability to communicate a vision and create alignment. Leaders make ideas tangible and real to others.

3. Management of trust: Leaders seem reliable and constant.

4. Management of self: Leaders know their strengths and weaknesses, learn from criticisms, and adapt.

Warren further states that effective leaders empower others in four ways:

1. They make people feel significant.

2. They make people believe that learning and competence matter.

3. They help people feel like part of a community.

4. They make work exciting.

Decreasing *employee churn,* or the employee turnover rate, is a big challenge for e-business. Warren recommends that companies take notice of employees' concepts of quality, dedication, and love of work. Attending to these concepts prevents employees from feeling alienated at work and feeling like their work has no meaning.

The total resources a company allocates to e-business readiness development affect how that company maintains its internal capabilities and shows how seriously committed its management is to creating the appropriate e-culture environment. Each business unit should have appropriate funding to ensure execution of e-business initiatives. The level of funding often plays a role in determining whether a new product or service can be delivered on time. Companies should have an understandable method for allocating IT and business resources to new initiatives. Poor resource allocation of resources for Web site maintenance is common in companies new to e-business. Some companies fail to recognize that sites need constant attention—giving a customer outdated information creates a sorry image!

Consulting firms are at the epicentre of change and have many varying ideas about e-culture. Nervewire, a Boston-based consulting firm, has seen many changes with e-business in this new economy. People are the most important product in the knowledge economy, and businesses are doing everything possible to retain existing employees and attract new ones. It is extremely important for businesses to create a corporate culture that ensures employees' future success.

Businesses in the new economy have had to make shorter-term plans and must be able to adapt to change. Mature businesses were built with mature growth patterns in industries where the rules did not normally change overnight. More standard ideas and business resources were available to a growing company. The "dot.com" era has provided an interesting period where business fundamentals are left to the wayside and businesses are measured on revenues and ability to "eyeball" the market they created and retained. Being profitable fell by the wayside.

Coaching is a lot like managing a business. What if you had to coach hockey on ice one day and asphalt the next? The fundamentals are similar, but the dynamics are dramatically different, and it requires a new set of rules. e-Culture is all about this new set of rules. It is the ability and willingness to change and adapt. Companies have asked very specific questions during interviews to find dynamic employees that can "fit in." A great example is to find out someone's driving habits to get to and from work. If someone takes the same route every day, regardless of traffic, the person probably does not like change. If they take different routes based on time of day and traffic, then perhaps they do embrace change.

e-Culture is different between countries and is not just the internal capability of companies. Canada and the United States are neighbors and share many similar cultures. Where they do diverge quite fundamentally is in risk and willingness to change. The United States is much more entrepreneurial, and it rewards its businesses through investment much more so than in Canada. The investment community in Canada typically punishes companies that are trying to embrace e-business, whereas United States investors are much more willing to reward companies for getting into e-business. Cyberplex, a Canadian-based consulting firm making great strides in the United States, sees this difference in culture with the firms they are e-business–enabling. Dean Hopkins, president of Cyberplex, is an outspoken proponent of e-business and how the Canadian government must do some radical things to change the e-culture of Canada. The investor community has been "put off" recently with business-to-consumer models, but there is still a lot of faith in the business-to-business model. The e-culture within a company spills out to the industry.

This sensitivity to embracing change can be shown in other areas of the world in relation to the United States. Several companies in Europe are conducting significant mergers and acquisitions with U.S.-based companies. The simple reason is that the United States economy is the best-performing economy in the world, and any new ideas in e-business are mainly being tested and are flowing from the United States.

e-Culture varies within industries, with some being very proactive and others being very slow to adapt to change. The financial services industry has been very proactive, and it has embraced an e-culture that fosters change. Companies like Charles Schwab have transitioned its business model many times over the last 10 years. Companies like Schwab are quick to realize that adopting Web technologies was pertinent to the success of the business. It has also been quick to adopt speech recognition technologies, enabling many more people to do business with the company. Without a strong e-culture, Schwab would not have been able to successfully introduce the necessary changes. It would have had too much resistance from the internal organization, which is often the case in unsuccessful endeavours.

The transportation industry is much more resistant to change. The e-culture is not as dynamic as other industries and has not adopted new e-business mechanisms. Aaron Mac, President of Ports-n-Portals, a Hutchison Port Holding Company, is a firm believer in e-business but is also a realist in terms of expectations. Portsnportals.com has been offering electronic trade-related, value-added services as early as 1985, years before the Internet phenomenon had caught on. e-Business rules and techniques can be applied in some areas, such as customer service, documentation, and information tracking. Mac once managed operations for Hutchison Ports and realized that tangible goods, trucks, and ships would not change overnight. Logistics and distribution companies will embrace e-business, but it is an evolutionary change versus a revolutionary change. There are some unique examples of e-business that are specific to the transportation industry that Ports-n-Portals are integrating into their offerings. Some of these offerings include partial load integration, package and container track and trace capabilities, regulatory compliance and document processing, and electronic marketplace exchanges and banking services. The challenge for the transportation industry is that it is extremely fragmented, with many companies doing business. This creates a very dynamic marketplace but makes coordination of e-business activities more difficult. The ability for e-business to make a difference is when the companies can come together, but the lack of strong e-culture makes that reality longer term. Transportation companies like slower, more methodical change.

The other factor that Hutchison must take into account is that they operate in Hong Kong and China, in addition to many other areas of the world, and e-business is not strong in an industry. There is a challenge of just having the basic infrastructure that North Americans take for granted all the way through to the language that is more difficult to e-business–enable. All of those factors make the e-culture less advanced than North American companies. However, China is making great strides in bringing e-business into the country. Changes in e-culture do not happen overnight, and Ports-n-Portals and Hutchison are some of the leaders bringing e-business to emerging areas.

Gerry Pond, president of Emerging Services for Aliant, the third largest telecommunications company in Canada, recognized early on that e-culture was a large part of e-business. In 1991, no one had coined the term e-business, so speaking about culture as part of an electronic means of doing business was before his time. Gerry coined the term "e-doors" and "p-doors" that the company used as a rallying cry for its e-business strategy. "p-doors," or physical doors, are the normal doors that represent a business's traditional means of doing business. "e-doors," or electronic doors, are representative of the new ways of doing business. This easily understood concept was the underpinning of the creation of a strong e-culture within the organization. Pond and the organization that he was instrumental in creating were recognized as the most innovative telecommunications company within North America. Without their rallying cry, the organization would have been just another "sleepy telco" without a sense of e-business.

We have had the opportunity to speak with many financial institutions about their e-business initiatives. Financial services are more progressive in delivering e-business and are promoting a culture that is more in keeping with an image. The common theme among the institutions from an e-culture perspective is that it is a customer-driven culture. The quality of service that a customer gets is inherent to the e-culture, along with the fact that employees feel good about the customer. This was the same story in the United States as it was in Canada and Europe. We suspect it is, or will be, a similar story throughout the rest of the world, as financial institutions are forced to be competitive on a global scale.

The other thing for e-businesses to keep in mind is that there is an incredible talent shortage and that will continue to dominate the landscape for the next 18 months. It will mean there will be a lot of great ideas and money going after those great ideas, but not a lot of people to realize them. We think ultimately, it is going to get to a very severe point where there really is no talent to apply to the best ideas, which may cause some interesting dynamics. We are not sure exactly what, but companies that have a strong e-culture are continuing to have more work than manpower. Additionally, career opportunities may be endless for people who want to enter e-business, and great talent will continue to get sucked out of big companies. Many companies agree that turnover has nearly doubled. The way to retain employees is through a strong e-culture, where the employees are valued and respected.

An important metric for the e-culture component is the change in knowledge sharing among employees and collaborators. The metric can be broken into variables such as change in employee understanding and learning, satisfaction, and confidence. Satisfaction is normally gauged in time savings, added-value service, and product value for money. Employees gain confidence in their companies when they perceive that their processes are comprehensive and correct.

Increased employee retention rates measure employee satisfaction. Methods of monitoring and measuring whether your knowledge management initiatives are working also include automatic analysis of Web logs to determine how many people access the knowledge repositories and how frequently they do so. Statistics for the number of times shared folders are accessed can contribute to collaborative team measurements. The growth in knowledge base volume as employees add to it shows uptake (the number of people who are accessing and using the information). Knowledge management also allows you to use fewer people to effectively perform a task. The ratio of resources allocated to e-business development is an indication of the management's commitment to change. Metrics for e-business resource allocation include data currency, completeness, and speed of information delivery.

Productivity

Most increases in employee productivity come from reductions in cycle time for or the outright elimination of tasks. With the help of useful intranet applications or outsourcing, workers spend less time and effort on time-consuming, low-value matters and give more of their attention to more skill-based tasks. Tasks involved in most e-businesses are document management, human resource management, operational purchasing, and tasks related to product or service delivery.

A friend of ours is on a university faculty recruitment committee. This committee is responsible for ensuring that advertisements for positions are created and published or displayed, scheduling candidates, and recommending offers of appointments to new faculty members. After the last recruitment efforts failed miserably, a postmortem meeting identified the critical processes that needed to change for the university to successfully recruit in today's market. They noted that the time from the candidate's interview to the time that an offer was mailed out was too long. Candidates had already received offers from many other potential employers. In today's market, there are roughly four academic jobs for every master of information systems (MIS) PhD candidate. The processes that needed to be faster mainly involved governance. The recruitment cycle time was worse for candidates from other nations because the university gets immigration approval for the candidate before the offer is sent out, even though the candidate may not accept the offer. Our friend believed that the solution had two parts. One was obviously to change the entire recruitment process, and the other was to outsource parts of the task. It would decrease the frustration of losing good candidates to other universities and also allow our friend to spend the hours she previously devoted to wasted recruitment efforts more productively.

Human resource tasks, such as recruitment, are outsourced more than many other tasks. Many companies buy resume packages from online recruitment firms such as Monster.com. Cisco saved $3,000 per employee in recruitment costs by using online recruiting. Partial or full outsourcing, even if it is expensive, can benefit businesses. In addition, failures of operational partners are less likely to be "swept under the rug" than internal employee failures.

Business Knowledge Dissemination

Companies such as HummingBird and Autonomy offer portal products for enhancing employee productivity. The portals provide a single interface to retrieve various types of information that would ordinarily have to be opened with multiple applications. For example, a single interface can be used to view word processing files, the results of a database query from Oracle or structure query language (SQL) server, or e-mail data. The portals support tools that can search all popular file formats and then retrieve data on the search topic from one or more of these files. The products empower workers, allowing them to capture and share knowledge. The agent content manager gives easy access to information such as which documents are available about a certain issue and which employees handled certain issues. In addition, the increased use of technologies such as e-mail, white boarding, and multimedia conferencing in e-business is increasing the level of employee task interactivity and productivity. Employee time management can be improved and measured with knowledge management tools such as agents for scheduling and tracking time.

The accuracy of stored information increases when you eliminate repeated transfers of information. Only when the integrity of your business's information is maintained can your employees make informed decisions.

Sherri Andersen and NOVELL

DOING IT TODAY

Novell makes life easier for its employees by providing 401k retirement plan updates through online or phone interactions with Fidelity, the plan provider. Fidelity has online access to Novell's payroll system and can automatically deduct the appropriate amount from each employee's paycheck. Novell has a similar arrangement for employees' Aetna healthcare plans. These steps reengineer the workflow, reduce process cycle time, and minimize time employees spend on paperwork. Novell achieves these goals by updating information at its source rather than forwarding changes to the human resources department, which then has to send the information to Fidelity or Aetna.

Productivity at Novell has been further improved by the removal of information intermediaries. Novell CIO Sheri Andersen discusses an example: "Previously, if I wanted a report on what my employees got paid, I had to go through the human resources department—we got rid of that step.

"We also introduced departmental portals. Our first portal was mysales.novell.com. The portal gives our salespeople access to the sales automation system (Siebel), but they don't have to log on to Siebel; they just log on to 'mysales.' They can get human resource information out of PeopleSoft without knowing how to actually use PeopleSoft; the data is packaged so that they can get information from their teams and out of Oracle through the portal. It is simple to use and they can get it from a browser—that's the model for me!

"We decided on a departmental model instead of an individual model. Departments determine what types of information their salespeople need and how they get paid. Through the portal, people can get access to information that is authoritatively managed by an application without knowing anything about how to use the application.

"I used to have to go to Human Resources to get this and go to Finance to get that. Now I just go into the portal, but I don't have to be a software expert to get information. I use our Novell directory server (NDS) technology; it is linked to PeopleSoft so that it knows who you are and your role in the company. If I ask for an employee's payroll information and I am not the appropriate manager, I

continued

won't get it. I don't have to go through the explicit PeopleSoft security because it is built into our directory. When you log in it, the portal knows who you are, which department you work in, which manager you work for, and who works for you—which is very cool!

"We are rolling out a very sophisticated quota and commission system. Salespeople will be able to enter the system and find out how close they are to their quota. Their commission will integrate the commission system data, sales data, and financial data that has been booked. Salespeople often think they've successfully booked and submitted an order when something gets suspended, and it isn't processed completely in Oracle—so they get frustrated. The finance department has wasted a lot of time reconciling these transaction; now the process will become much more clear because of the portal structure. It is very powerful."

Maintenance, Repair, and Operations Processes

Currently, application vendors and system integrators group a company's non-production internal expenses into maintenance, repairs, and operations (MRO). MRO expenses cover general and administrative (G&A) expenses for human resources, finance, travel and entertainment, facilities maintenance, capital equipment, and repairs. IT costs for Web delivery are included in G&A. *E-administration* is Oracle's term for G&A operations. Oracle is considered a pacesetter in the areas of e-administration, e-procurement, and electronic customer relationship management (eCRM). MRO expenses include office supplies and equipment: computers, fax machines, photocopiers, printers, furniture, and consumables such as printer ribbons, toner, paper, preformatted forms, and pens. Ariba and Commerce One supply MRO products and services to companies such as Ford, General Motors (GM), and Boeing.

Vendors report that the return on investment (ROI) for Web-based MRO deployment is 15 to 20 percent of revenue. The figure commonly quoted for G&A expenditure is 30 percent of revenue—an overall savings of 2 to 5 percent. This is a huge savings for a Fortune 500 company. Many suppliers will give a company cheaper prices in exchange for a preferred place in the company's e-catalog, which is published on a Web server. Discounts are often in the 3 to 15 percent range, which translates into yet another savings for companies deploying e-procurement applications. For smaller businesses, the reduction in cycle time and product costs, growth in revenue, and increases in innovation from cross-value chains bring enough value to warrant deploying MRO applications.

MRO software enables employees to file expense reports, make online changes in health plans, inquire about pension plans, and obtain statements on demand. Online training courses, seminars, and lectures also increase savings. The human resources department is not the only department that benefits from the Web culture. Capital budgeting analysis is carried out by the finance department. In large companies, this task involves team analyses, the results of which are sent to the appropriate vice president for further analysis and approval. The vice president then sends the report to others for approval before the product is considered final. It's not uncommon for this process to take 9 months. Mechanization of the team and workflow processes can significantly reduce cycle time.

The overhead for outside suppliers is typically 60 to 65 percent of the total revenue stream. Changing the business processes to create more efficient inter-actions with the right suppliers for nonproduction and production goods max-imizes business value. Improving processes includes modifying workflow, using electronic catalogs, performing trades in electronic marketplaces, and communi-cating digitally rather than on paper.

Workflow can be improved by digitizing all formerly paper-based processes and allowing authorized personnel to track the progress online. Think about what it takes to process a paper-based requisition. You have to fill out a requisi-tion form, which you walk over to your department head for a signature because you're trying to speed up the process. The department head signs it and if you're lucky, you get to walk it over to the purchasing department; otherwise you send it through internal mail, so it takes at least half the day to get to purchasing. The requisition gets placed on a pile on top of a clerk's desk. The clerk gets around to it eventually and phones numerous preferred suppliers to obtain prices. The ven-dors take a few days to respond. Then the clerk selects and makes out a purchase order for a supplier. The purchase order gets faxed, and an original copy is mailed. Copies of the purchase order are forwarded via internal mail to the department manager and the requisitioner—you. In the mean time, you've called the purchasing department to determine whether the purchase order was sent and have subsequently called the supplier to ask whether the purchase order was received. Seem exhausting? This is just a *part* of the purchase order process. Mul-tiply the time it took to process this one purchase order by hundreds, thousands, and millions—the number of purchase orders issued annually by companies. In addition to digitizing paperwork, another key component of reducing cycle time is automated approval—without human intervention. Otherwise all you have is an automated version of the existing process.

Electronic catalogs are used to reduce ordering cycle times and associated human resources expenses. E-catalogs contain preferred suppliers' product descriptions, prices, and availability information. On the surface, they seem like business-to-consumer (B2C) storefronts because they have shopping cart, browse, and buy capabilities, but they are richer in functionality. This excellent functionality is not surprising considering the fact that the suppliers are dealing with known and trusted customers. E-catalogs are directly affected by content management. Suppliers must keep the catalogs updated and tailored to customers' requirements.

The advantage of trading in electronic marketplaces is that you get access to more suppliers, and the online competition leads to better products and services. Ariba was the first to offer an Internet-based operations procurement system. Ariba sells software that allows other companies to connect to Ariba's online catalog of office supplies. Ariba asks other companies' suppliers to join the Ariba network of suppliers. Each supplier can see the prices of the other suppliers. Economists are currently investigating whether e-hubs (online marketplaces) are increasing price pressures and therefore creating better deals for companies.

Key suppliers of some services or products may not automate or join an e-marketplace right away. Acquisition of business services, such as janitorial and advertising services, tends to be localized in some places. Procurers of these types of services may not find any justification for joining an electronic marketplace. Although they may not get benefits in cost, they may improve the quality of delivery of services. An overall metric could be the quality of delivery of goods or services. For services, the metric may be the change in the number of inferior deliveries, or for goods, the metric may be the life of the item.

One procurement best practice is to rationalize the supplier base; buy from a small set of preferred suppliers to get volume discounts and form deeper alliances. Rationalization effectively eliminates fragmented purchasing or maverick buying (from nonpreferred suppliers) and helps you avoid paying premium prices. Miscellaneous purchases for less than a certain dollar amount may not involve electronic catalogs because the cost of transaction processing is too high. For example, procurement cards can be used as an alternative method for making miscellaneous purchases. The bottom line is that the procurement system must integrate all touch points, procurement cards, paper requisitions, and e-catalogs so that the management can keep track of all procurement expenses.

Metrics for e-catalog procurement could be catalog availability and reliability. Both can be measured in terms of downtime. The metric for procurement involves the change in the procurement process cycle time, which can be measured by transaction throughput and response times. Decreased cycle times result in cost savings. Thus another metric for procurement is reduction in costs in transaction processing.

The degree of employee productivity and operational efficiency is a measure that can be used to assess how well a company is supporting its employees. Revenue per employee, market share per employee, output per employee, and speed of output per employee are additional metrics. The decrease in process cycle times is a leading measure.

Bob:

Ordering is one our most frequently used internal business processes. It makes sense to completely Web enable. We don't know how much it costs to process a purchase order now, nor do we know the average cycle time for a purchase order. We will have to determine these before we can determine ROI using traditional metrics. However, we recognize that e-business ROI goes way beyond the total cost of ownership (TCO) model.

Sue:

We are excited about the product savings e-catalogs may bring. We don't know offhand of any vertical markets for gift basket production goods. We may have to aggregate merchants and establish relationships as preferred suppliers.

Information Systems Infrastructure and Services

A determining factor for assessing internal e-business readiness is the sophistication of the information systems operations and service capabilities. The company's information technology system must integrate the various repositories of related data. It must facilitate enterprisewide collaboration, standardization of content and context, and the reorganization of functions, processes, and responsibilities among multiple departments and channels. The infrastructure for integration of strategic and operational partner systems is a big issue. Translation middleware or similar technical and business standards and compatible technologies are essential for cross-systems integration.

Online access to information is essential. For example, a project, new business initiative, or software application may require an employee with particular skills. An intranet application can target two or three employees whose present skills are the closest to the ones needed. These personnel can then take training courses so that they will be available when needed. You must have an updated network infrastructure with sufficient bandwidth to handle this type of application's load. Software applications for productivity in all areas of business should be available. You should have detailed intranet, extranet, and Internet applications to support sales, G&A tasks, development and production tasks if applicable, marketing, CRM and PRM, supply chain management (SCM), internal procurement, and capacity planning, just to name a few. Service level agreements (SLAs) and standards help you to control this environment.

Measuring the value of your information infrastructure allows you to determine whether your company's IT has met your business goals. Cost and productivity metrics are often used to measure such value. Mitre provides federal agencies such as the Department of Defense, Federal Aviation Administration (FAA), Internal Revenue Service (IRS), and U.S. intelligence agencies with system engineering and IT expertise. The Mitre information infrastructure (MII) was rolled out in 1995. According to a case study in *CIO* magazine,[2] Mitre had invested $7.2 million in MII by May 2000, with an ROI of $54.91 million in reduced costs and increased productivity.

Sheri Anderson and NOVELL

DOING IT TODAY

We seem to walk a fine line or a broad line between standardization and innovation; we in the information department haven't used information standards, but we haven't used exceptions either. This is partly because as a company we are trying to do new things with new technologies, and partly because the cost of 100 percent conformity versus 95 percent conformity can be high. I am trying to work with my staff to find a different framework for management. It's not that we won't have standards—we will—but I am highly skeptical of monolithic structures. I am skeptical of the "one answer that fits everything" solution. You can always think of more than one answer, especially in the e-business space, where things are changing very quickly. I don't want to be locked into a set of rigid standards that don't allow me to adopt new technologies or change my business quickly.

I met with a big bank in the South that had bought another bank and had a whole team whose chairperson was the CEO. This committee was trying to decide whether the combined banks should standardize with NetWare or NT, and they truly had an "it's one way or the other" attitude. I knew the process would take them 18 months, so I respectfully told them they were pursuing the wrong model. They needed a framework that would allow them to mask some of these "behind-the-scenes" complexities. They needed to be to be able to integrate things quickly (as CISCO has done with its many acquired companies), rather than manage things through blind conformance. They needed to find a framework for integration. Anyway, in 18 months they would probably have bought some other company or been bought or spun off. I gave them the "you can have more than one" solution. We formed a cross-platform strategy. We suggested that they run our directory, which runs on any platform and allows you to manage several devices without knowing what they are. The Internet is composed of lots of material. I can't dictate to my customers and say things like, "By the way, you *must* run on NetWare 5." They would laugh at me! I tell them that we need an architecture that makes the process easy to manage and integrate and that our company can play a role in helping them establish this architecture. Our

continued

company has the right architecture for adapting networks—that's the world of e-business.

It is imperative than IT departments adopt a different mindset so that they can help their companies cope with e-business. I talk to customers a lot and tell them that they don't have a choice—every company has to be in e-business because the Internet is increasing and changing their competition and opportunities. I simply tell them, "You are in e-business. You are global. Deal with it. E-business is a 24/7 commitment and gives your customers the power. You can't dictate the rules anymore." The companies create a set of imperatives for their IT departments. I would be nuts if I thought I should impose a set of standards to protect my job—to do as little outsourcing as possible. I want to be able to focus on the core value that IT departments contribute and forget the boring stuff.

Bob:

We have an excellent network infrastructure, and we are in the process of evaluating an ERP package for implementing best-of-breed practices and back-end systems integration. Some of the ERP vendors provide MRO functions as well. We are also evaluating the viability of using Ariba or Commerce One software.

Sue:

Our main concern from an information systems perspective is scalability. We want to be up and ready to serve during seasonal spikes, which often occur during holidays like during Christmas and Easter.

Questions You May Want to Ask

E-Culture

- How do bricks-and-mortar businesses manage cultural change when they initiate a dotcom company? Does a business anticipate internal resistance that may be encountered as they transition to a future-oriented outlook? How can you manage the change for the employees?

- Do the businesses perform self-assessments?
- How much did it cost to provide the tools and training to help your employees become comfortable with, understand, and execute your new processes?
- Do you see a shift in the skill level of your employees? Do you need fewer clerical employees and more highly trained employees?
- What is the ratio of your resources allocated to development of e-business initiatives?
- Does each business unit have individual funding to ensure e-business success?
- What is your method for allocating IT and business resources to new e-business initiatives?
- How has your ratio of new to existing customers changed in the last 2 quarters?
- What percentage of your sales comes from Internet commerce?
- How many sources of new revenue have been created in the last 2 quarters? What percentage have become successful?
- How many new business models were implemented in the last 2 quarters?
- Which services do you outsource? Has outsourcing affected your organization's culture, productivity, or ability to serve customers?

Productivity

- Have you reduced the time it takes to carry out tasks such as filing an expense report ? How much have your G&A sales (SG&A) expenses changed with the introduction of an intranet or outsourcing? Considering that SG&A expenses include the initial cost of acquiring the Web delivery infrastructure, can you determine your recurring investments and savings?
- Which finance task did your company improve by using an intranet application? Did you create an intranet application for the capital budgeting analysis task?
- How can companies improve their cycle times for certain tasks, such as adding a new employee to the payroll system, with outside financial services?
- Which new tasks were assigned to your employees when the intranet applications were deployed? In what ways has task automation reduced or increased customer and employee value?
- Approximately how much will your company save as a result of online information dissemination? Can you quote an overall figure and then break it down into marketing, sales, human resources, finance, and production categories?

- How has online access to business knowledge empowered your employees? (For example, if your salespeople have access to information on a particular product, they learn more about the products. Salespeople who can easily and quickly access information may be able to respond more quickly to customers.)
- Which services are outsourced? Has outsourcing affected your organization's culture, productivity, or ability to serve customers?
- Human resource tasks, such as recruitment, are some of the most frequently outsourced tasks. Does your company outsource these task functions? Do you know the average cost to recruit an employee using traditional means? Have you bought resume packages from online recruitment firms such as Monster.com? Do you know the cost of recruiting an employee online?
- What is the cost to process individual operational requests (such as travel expense claims)?
- What do you use to keep track of project costs? Is your capital assets management package Web enabled? How do you keep track of ongoing maintenance, service, and training costs? Are there ways you can use Web applications to reduce these costs?
- Does your company purchase nonproduction goods from a supplier marketplace? What is the cost to process a purchase order (the old way and the new way)?
- What was the cost of procuring the IT infrastructure? What was the cost of changing the accompanying business processes?
- What is the cost of training employees to use the B2B back-end procurement applications?
- What is the reduction in cycle time for order fulfillment?
- Do you make fewer or more mistakes using e-procurement? Provide examples.

Information Systems Infrastructure and Services

- How much did it cost to install or upgrade the information systems infrastructure needed to support internal e-business?
- How many IT employees maintain the infrastructure? Do they have strong hybrid skills? Are they considered top talents in the industry?
- How many new services does your IT department introduce in 6 months? How many of the new services provide high customer, business, or employee value?

- How much did you save by providing convenient customer self-service opportunities (such as FedEx tracking services)? What were the costs before and after the services were introduced?
- How many *direct* customer touch points does your company support? How many are *indirect* (for example, through resellers)?

Small-Business Perspective: Internal Assessment (SMEHiTech)

> # Sue:
>
> My business weights procurement more heavily than the small-to-medium enterprise (SME) SMEHiTech because we depend heavily on fabric and pattern suppliers. However, we appreciate the relevance of the metrics for the other key components used in the assessment of internal capability.

SMEHiTech is a small start-up with a lot of potential that sells Internet service products to the North American and European market. SMEHiTech focuses on customer value innovation, the early-mover advantage, and information systems components. The e-culture is already looking toward the future. The employee base is 85 percent technical—designers, programmers, and support personnel—and 15 percent administrative. The CEO is 23 years old, and the average employee is 30. SMEHiTech is a knowledge-based business. Productivity metrics are important from a software engineering point of view. That is, low-level metrics such as total number of lines of code (TLOC) or function points are relevant. Operational procurement costs are negligible compared to the cost of the employee payroll. Productivity is measured in terms of the number of service rollout milestones that are met on time and budget.

E-business resource allocation is not an issue because SMEHiTech is all e-business. In the past 6 months, SMEHiTech has aggressively pursued and met a diversification objective. SMEHiTech has introduced two successful new products—one new version of an existing product and a pay-per-use business model. SMEHiTech's customer base has climbed from 10,000 to 3 million. Its products have been first to market, even though it competes with powerful companies such as ABC. SMEHiTech is the only company dedicated to providing a particular

Internet service product. It has made strategic alliances with brand name companies to bundle products and services and has subsequently gained substantial market share. Shareholders are pleased because the stock price doubled last year. The e-culture component is assigned a rating of 4, which exceeds the benchmark. The weighting of the component's importance is also 4 because it has such an impact on e-business success.

SMEHiTech supports customer self-services. Customers can access their accounts, their usage information, and their billing information. Customers can also sign up for the services directly at SMEHiTech's Web site. The company is constantly monitoring and assessing its information systems infrastructure and applications because its growth requires scalable solutions. SMEHiTech has outsourced some of its server farm infrastructure. However, the business has noticed that it has problems at peak times, particularly when new services are announced. In the past, these problems have included downtime during new customer registration activity. Analyses show that the database application is causing the bottleneck. A combination of application tuning and more hardware resources is required. The company's information systems infrastructure component gets a rating of 3 and a weight of 4. The benchmark rating for the industry is 4.

The company has fairly low purchase order processing costs and because of the small size of the company, travel expense processing is not a problem. The MRO factor detracts from productivity a little and therefore its assigned score, a rating of 2, does not meet the benchmark.

In a nutshell, SMEHiTech has done very well in the internal assessment analysis. It is very strong in all areas except for the internal system infrastructure. This area is still given a fairly good rating but clearly needs some attention. Table 9-1 gives a summary of the weights and ratings assigned to each internal assess-

Table 9-1   Summary of Assigned Weights and Ratings

Component	Weight	Component Rating	Benchmark Rating	Overall Component Score	Overall Benchmark Score
E-culture	4	4	4	16	16
Productivity	4	3	4	12	16
Information systems infrastructure	4	2	3	8	12

ment component in SMEHiTech. The overall assessment in Figure 9-3 illustrates the strengths of the company. Figure 9-4 provides an assessment of the internal capabilities of the company.

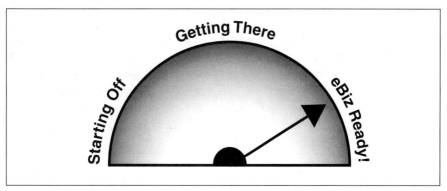

Figure 9-3   RadarScope Assessment of SMEHiTech

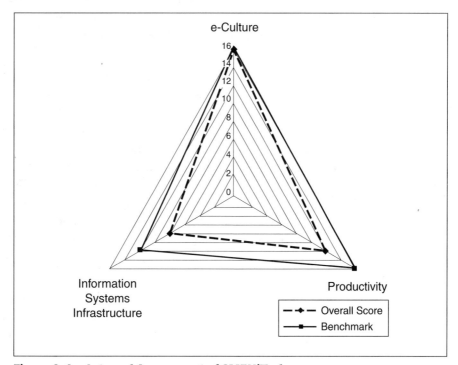

Figure 9-4   Internal Assessment of SMEHiTech

Big-Business Perspective: Internal Assessment (BBEdu)

> # Bob:
>
> Our company identifies with parts of BBEdu's situation, even though we are in another vertical. Issues such as customer value innovation apply to our business as well. We have a mixture of big, midsize, and small suppliers. It's challenging to simultaneously maintain e-catalogs and their paper-based equivalents like we're doing now. We hope to find a low-cost method of integrating with our electronic catalog that SMEs will buy into.

Big Business Higher Education (BBEdu) is situated in a remote small town that has a population of 200,000. Its business culture is very traditional, but it is a "gentle" business with loyal employees who have previously been receptive to change and appreciative of the Web culture. As a whole, the town has a highly educated work force.

All of BBEdu's suppliers are SMEs because the local business community primarily comprises resellers, or channel partners of large companies. BBEdu wants to better control its operational spending. All of its procurement processes are paper based. It has rationalized its supplier base for products such as office equipment and supplies. BBEdu's concerns include the length of time it takes to obtain products and send payments to their vendors. At the moment, none of the local suppliers are working in the e-marketplace. BBEdu is in an interesting position politically because it can foster change in its community. The company needs to find out whether a sufficiently large number of business community members need digitized procurement processes. Suppliers could join a national e-marketplace created especially for SMEs—a marketplace in which the technology links from the suppliers to the marketplace should be based on low-cost solutions.

The rollout of customer-focused applications is taking place too slowly. The administrators have all sorts of innovative ideas but have no means of executing them. Sometimes it seems like the company spends more time putting out fires than planning and executing new ideas.

BBEdu has several part-time positions in which employees work 20 hours a week on low-volume, traditional, specialized tasks. The company will be "e-businessized," so certain human resource positions will be eliminated and new ones will be created. Employee churn will increase. The costs and cycle times for human resource and financial tasks are in line with those for paper-based processes in similar organizations. BBEdu recognizes that a good MRO package can reduce these costs and cycle times significantly. Current MRO processes at BBEdu are rudimentary—some elements exist, but not all features are present. Productivity measures are not in place. The productivity component is assigned a 1; the benchmark rating is 3, and the weight is 4 (see Table 9-2).

BBEdu's e-business resource allocation budget is currently very low. BBEdu has a Web site that is poorly maintained because not enough employees are assigned to the task and Web update procedures are poor. The site basically consists of outdated brochureware. It cannot perform financial transactions, such as online registration. A Web information system allows students to obtain course grades and examination schedules online, but they are read-only applications. Because BBEdu's overall information system is the aggregation of disparate home-grown islands of information systems, it can think of no easy, standardized way to tie in Web access. The institution plans to implement an ERP package to address these horizontal integration issues and streamline business processes, including operational processes such as maintenance of student accounts, registration, human resource tasks, and financial tasks. The administrators recognize

Table 9-2   Summary of Assigned Weights and Ratings for BBEdu

Component	Weight	Component Rating	Benchmark Rating	Overall Component Score	Overall Benchmark Score
E-culture	4	1	2	4	8
Productivity	4	1	3	4	12
Information systems infrastructure	4	1	3	4	12

that the ERP's Web-interfacing capability needs to be assessed. The information infrastructure and services component is assigned a rating of 1; the benchmark rating is 3, and the weight is set at 4 (very important). The e-culture component rating is assigned a 1; the benchmark for the industry is 2, and the weight is 4.

The results are plotted on a polar plot chart that shows all of the factors in an internal assessment. Figure 9-5 shows that BBEdu is just starting out on the road to e-business readiness. Figure 9-6 shows the internal assessment results in an overall polar plot. The figure shows that the business is weak in e-culture, productivity, and IT infrastructure.

Are You Ready?

Table 9-3 provides a snapshot of all the themes, components, and metrics essential for a successful internal assessment.

Highlights from this chapter include the following:

- "E-businessizing" a company is not just about cutting costs; it involves examining your business model and increasing customer and shareholder value.
- Transformation of an organization's culture into a Web-based culture empowers a company's most valuable assets—its employees.
- E-leadership in the "now" economy, an economy in which strategies, processes, and business cultures are changing, is what empowers the workforce and determines whether the business will succeed or fail.

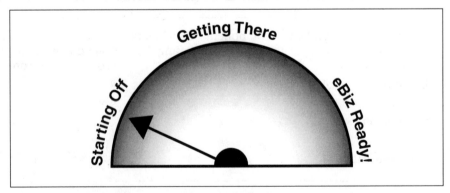

Figure 9-5   RadarScope Assessment of BBEdu

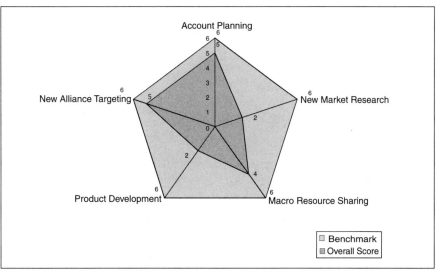

Figure 9-6   Internal Assessment of BBEdu

- Maintenance, repair, and operations (MRO) packages can help reduce process cycle times, increase the efficient use of resources, and improve overall productivity.
- Customer value innovation and its potential for growth is arguably the most important metric used to assess internal capability.
- Smaller companies are not as concerned about gaining efficiencies from procurement as they are about customer value innovation, knowledge worker

Table 9-3   Components, Enablers, and Metrics for Insides

Components*	Enablers	Metrics
E-culture	• Leadership • Knowledge transfer • Ease of information access • Communication	Prevalence of e-business culture Customer value innovation Ratio of resources allocated to e-business readiness development Currency of information Completeness of information

Table 9-3   Components, Enablers, and Metrics for Insides (*cont.*)

Components*	Enablers	Metrics
E-culture (*cont.*)		Speed of information delivery Innovation index Uniqueness of product Market crowd index Customer acquisition rate Degree of brand creation Employee turnover rate (retention) Leadership index
Productivity	• Knowledge transfer • Ease of information access • Communication • E-catalog • Trading network • Electronically connected suppliers	Customer value innovation Degree of operational efficiency Revenue per employee Output per employee Speed of output Cash-to-cash cycle time Knowledge transfer index Cycle time for procurement processes Availability and reliability of catalog Product cost savings Reduction in costs for transaction processing Quality of delivery of goods and services
Information systems infrastructure and services	• Knowledgeable and talented strategic, operational, and support personnel • Updated hardware and software • Continuous training benchmarking against industry's best practices	Effectiveness of information systems operations and service capabilities Effectiveness of business models (cost, ease of use, convenience of use for customer) Number of new business models instituted in measurement period Number of new product or service releases Change in employee and customer understanding and learning levels, satisfaction, and confidence Customer acquisition rate Customer retention rate Availability and sophistication of business intelligence tools Breadth of shared information Degree of automation of business literature dissemination Cost savings in Web automation of paper processes and accompanying reengineering of processes

*Recall that the knowledge, trust, and technology enablers are common to all components (see Chapter 2).

productivity, and having a slick, customer-focused information system in place.

- Continuous evaluation of internal capabilities is critical.
- Using the eBiz Readiness!™ framework shows your e-business level of readiness, weaknesses, and strengths regarding the internal organization of your business or lines of business.
- Use the measurement framework to test your partners' level of e-business alliance readiness.

The statistics that follow show the adoption rate of three metrics for e-business leaders in customer value innovation.

Statistics and Numbers

Metrics Used to Track Online Customer Behavior*	Seven Companies with Best Practices (Percentage Value of the Metric for the Best-of-Breed Companies)	Lagging Companies (Percentage Value of the Metric for the Best-of-Breed Companies)
• Personalization of customer information online	100	42
• Deployment of new products or services online	86	67
• Development of Internet-specific products or services	86	58

*From The American Productivity and Quality Center, Houston, 1998.

In 1999, a survey of 360 IT executives identified the five CIO leadership activities that received the *least* amount of attention. (Percentages are the number of respondents who said they did not spend "enough time" on the particular activity.)*

- Educating other officers and business unit heads about IT and its possibilities (67 percent)

continued

- Networking in the industry or CIO community (65 percent)
- Developing leaders within the IT staff (58 percent)
- Identifying new business opportunities made possible by IT (58 percent)
- Studying competition and its use of IT (57 percent)

---

*From www.cio.com.

References

[1]Gates, W.H. *Business at the Speed of Thought: Using A Digital Nervous System.* New York: Time Warner AudioBooks, 1999.
[2]Field, T. "Common Knowledge." *CIO Web.* February, 1999. www.cio.com

Getting There

CHAPTER TEN

Strategic Planning: Attack and Defend

> Only when you have been thrashed in a handicapped chess game with an opponent's pawns, while your rook, knights, and pawns stand helplessly by, can you understand the true beauty of strategy, of staying ahead of the game by thinking out plays, 10 moves in advance.
>
> A lesson from Del, 1984–1994

Getting You Prepared

The theme followed throughout this book holds true for all business: in the "now" economy, stakeholder relationships, knowledge, trust, technology, and people are the keys to success. Although the last 4 decades of standard strategy literature have emphasized these concepts, until the turn of the twenty-first century we have never been in a position to *effectively leverage and execute* knowledge and relationship management in real time. Many companies have not yet adjusted they way they work to take advantage of the capabilities of the present-day knowledge management and technology enablers.

In addition, many companies have not developed methods or models to measure their return on e-business investment.

Positioning a company to acquire new market share and to retain existing customers—and to do it *today*—is the challenge. With the proliferation of new business models arising from the progression of the value chain into a value Web, businesses are wondering how these new models will change their industries and their company. Are these models threats, opportunities, or both? What strategies should your company adopt to remain competitive or gain a competitive advantage? Competitors can acquire e-business enablers as easily as your company can. Of course, the question is whether your competitors will be able to organize or use the e-business solutions as well as your business does. There is no reason why your e-business enablers could not create a sustainable competitive advantage like the low-cost strategy used by Southwest Airlines, a strategy that could not be imitated by United Airlines.

How does e-business change standard strategy execution? It increases value, decreases processing time, reduces costs through reengineered processes, provides real-time information, facilitates the formation of new relationships and the maintenance of existing relationships, and the cheaper global reach. The main question that we address in this chapter is how do you plan for enabling e-business in a company, knowing that your e-business strategy must align with your overall corporate strategies.

The bottom line is that business cannot afford to ignore e-business. A do-nothing approach is crippling to value creation and is a recipe for failure. According to NerveWire, a leading consulting company focused on e-business digital strategy creation, "In the new economy, the only sustainable competitive advantage is learning—and acting—faster than the competition."

In its project charter to create an e-business strategy, Petrotrin, the second largest oil and gas company in Trinidad and Tobago, explained benefits of e-business very succinctly: "E-business has the potential to put Petrotrin on the crest of the wave to achieve operating and manufacturing excellence, address competitive threats, and take the best advantage of growth opportunities." The challenge for companies like Petrotrin is how to transform the company of today into the corporate vision of tomorrow. Zefer.com, a leading strategic Internet consulting services firm, states, "To survive and thrive in the digital economy, businesses must be built to be adaptable. From operations to supply chains to customer relationships, every element of business must accommodate unrelenting change. To succeed, businesses require a new strategic process." Companies like Zefer know how to move through the e-business evolution (Figure 10-1)—to the point at which *e-business* will be known as just plain *business*. The focus moves from using technology to manage complex business processes to creating and improving value in the new business models and finally to offering superior and satisfying customer experiences.

For the culmination of this book, we bring together the components provided in the previous chapters and apply the eBiz Readiness!™ framework to e-business strategy creation. Furthermore, even though we have shown the development of the eBiz Readiness!™ framework in the context of a single business, it is our opinion that the framework can be easily modified and applied to a line of business, segment of an industry, whole industry, or market.

In a nutshell, the eBiz Readiness!™ framework provides the following:

- The framework provides a common vocabulary for comparing vision, strategy, and tactical thinking.
- The framework highlights the core competencies needed for e-business.
- The framework shows how to create value and thus differentiation.
- The framework provides gap analyses that show the differences between today's company and a future company.
- The framework targets the key areas that need to be addressed when moving from "here" to "there."

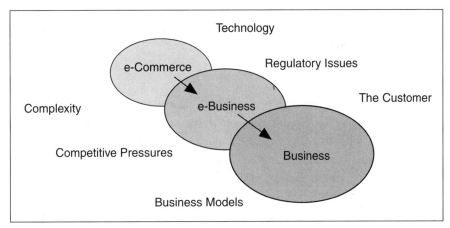

Figure 10-1   The "e-Volution" of the E-Terms

Defining the Horizon

Strategies

Strategy is a well-developed field of study that has three major categorizations—corporate, business, and functional. Preparing a company for e-business affects all categories. The e-business strategy must be aligned with or integrated into the firm's overall strategies.

Corporate Strategies

Corporate strategies deal with (1) the firm's direction in terms of growth, stability, and retrenchment, (2) the firm's target markets, and (3) resource, capability, and activity distribution among business units and product lines. Simply put, the three corporate strategic issues are the following:

1. The type of business you are in

2. Which customers you target

3. How you serve your customer

We expect that e-business opportunities will have a significant impact on decision-making regarding moving a firm in a direction of growth. Growth strategies include *concentration* on existing product lines, often through the acquisition of an entire supply chain and marketing product lines in new geographical markets, and *diversification* into other product lines in target markets. Stability strategies show very little change in direction and are not compatible with the opportunities for moving to e-business today. Retrenchment strategies include turnaround strategies that focus on improving operational efficiencies—and e-business enablers clearly affect these.

Business Strategies

Opportunities to enable e-business for a company affect which traditional business strategy or combination of strategies are deployed. Wheelen[1] provides a list of age-old business strategies: cost leadership, differentiation, cost-focus, and differentiation-focus strategies. Cost leadership is a low-cost competitive strategy that focuses on the general mass market; a company can achieve the strategy goals through efficient-scale facilities, cost reductions from trimming services, overhead control, and cost minimization in sales, marketing, and support areas. Differentiation involves the offering of a product or service that is unique or of greater value than other offerings. The cost-focus strategy is a low-cost, competitive strategy that focuses on a particular buyer group or geographical market and tends to only serve that market. The differentiation-focus strategy is about differentiation for a targeted market segment—a buyer group, product line segment, or geographical market.

Functional Strategies

Functional strategies are used by functional areas (such as departments) to achieve the overall corporate objectives and strategies. One of the first issues a functional area discusses is the value of outsourcing activities. Marketing, finance, research and development, operations, purchasing, logistics, human resource management, and information management all have well-founded and tested associated strategies.

E-businesses use many of these strategies, particularly in marketing. Dotcom companies are spending disproportionate chunks of revenue on building brand awareness and on customer acquisition. Customer acquisition strategies include market saturation and loss-leader schemes. Market saturation means that a company floods the market with products or services, primarily through advertising and promotion. America Online (AOL) tried to increase market share in 1997 with a market saturation strategy. Every mailbox across North America contained an AOL disk—sometimes several.

Loss-leader strategies involve offering products or services at low or no cost to the consumer to increase the size of the customer base. The companies incur a loss because they provide customer subsidies for these goods or products. Once the customer is accustomed to the product or service, the companies introduce service fees or raise the prices. Banks commonly use this strategy for online Internet banking and for ATM machines. One author currently pays $0.50 cents per Web-based banking transaction and $0.40 cents per debit card transaction; a year ago the transactions were free. Thus the author's bank was a loss leader a year ago, but it's not now. The classic loss-leader strategy is often used in large department stores, such as Wal-Mart, that offer products such as laundry detergent below cost to bring customers in the store; then they can buy other goods and services.

Cellular phone handsets are currently being subsidized through service providers such as Bell Mobility. Trading companies are currently giving away free cell phones to their customers because the companies increase trade volume when customers can reach them any time and from any place. AOL has given free computers to its customers. Gillette gave away razors (as opposed to razor blades) so that it could increase money made from sales of the blades. The loss-leader strategy is clearly a popular strategy for increasing product adoption rates.

E-Strategies

The guiding principle for creating e-business strategy, or e-strategy, is aligning the goals of the e-strategy with the overall goals of the corporate strategy. If the corporate strategy is one of cost differentiation then the e-strategy must support and focus on cost differentiation.

For many companies, e-business strategies address how partner, employee, governance, community, and customer facing processes can be e-business–enabled. e-Business–enabled means how business processes are improved via technological advances; new knowledge management capabilities, including content management and relationship management; and online trust capabilities.

Later in this chapter we present e-business opportunities and guidelines for creating an e-strategy; however, we caution that these are mere guidelines. No one methodology or exact methodology for creating strategy exists. The rich value web of stakeholder interaction presented in Chapter 1 allows for equally rich information flows that are electronically collected to form strategic resources. Thus the realm of strategy creation far exceeds the imagination of these two authors. We would at least like to provide you with a launching pad and some stimulation for e-business strategy thinking.

e-Strategy creation examines your firm's business models, your industry leaders' business models, the opportunities and threats of new channels, revenue sources, target markets, market entrants, competitors, and so on. Our contribution to your e-strategy thinking is the focus on creating a value web and specifically value at the stakeholder interaction interface.

The deployment of the Web channel is one of the most important areas in customer facing processes. Adding a Web channel raises the question as to whether this new channel is complementary to other channels or whether the Web channel cannibalizes existing channels. Channel conflict is the popular term for when the Web channel cuts into revenue from other channels. Some companies see more future return from the Web channel and part of their strategy involves cannibalization. Other companies see the management of change, both internally and externally, as a barrier. The height and depth of this barrier will be what companies must consider when weighing the opportunities of a Web channel.

Pure Internet companies, by definition primarily, use the web channel for marketing, sales, and support. e-Business observers are concluding that the most sustainable channel strategy is moving toward a clicks-and-mortar model, where the Web is only one of several marketing, sales, or distribution channels. In China, some born-on-the-Internet companies are taking a new brand-creation strategy. These companies are building brick-and-mortar storefronts that will be used to create a brand name. Then the brand will be extended to the Internet part of the operations. amazon.com built its brand online at huge expense and found that it required bricks-and-mortar infrastructure anyway for rapid fulfillment purposes. However, amazon.com has not yet succumbed to pricey physical storefronts.

The Web channel is particularly important to SMEs who do product customization or are specialists. As far back as 1996, Bulk Handling Technology, Inc., with three employees and $1 million in annual sales reported the world beat a path to its door after it put up its Web page. During the following three months, the company was asked to bid on $2.5 million in contracts from outside the United States (e.g., Australia and Chile).[2]

Value creation cannot be limited to the deployment of a Web channel with only single company commerce capabilities. Many businesses operate in industries and more specifically within clusters. We know that customers find value in convenience. For example, if you were a part of a residential construction firm, you would enjoy the convenience of planning the purchase of supplies from a portal of suppliers engaged in doing collaborative commerce. One form of collaborative commerce is when non-competing suppliers get together to offer promotions that would allow a customer to more cheaply finish a project he or she always had intentions of doing. For example, specials on floor tiles, garden books, electrician labor charges, tropical plants, and rattan furniture at one time may trigger a customer to contract a builder to add on a conservatory or sunroom to his or her home. This type of collaboration is not facilitated by independent collection of Web sites. Partner-facing processes such as supply chain management must be an integral part of corporate strategy. The higher focus and ease in partnering, collaboration, product development, forecasting, and sourcing processes differentiates toward customer value.

We are total advocates on the use of metrics for measuring the success of the Web channel. One metric will never provide a whole picture. Many metrics are required; as you can see, this book is literally peppered with them. Some businesses are reporting low online order rates. But how *do* you measure the success of the Web channel? Success is tied not only to the number of online orders but also to the number of customer engagements and business services delivered through the Web, just to name a few other measures. Many businesses are reporting that Web marketing and site information brings the customers into the store, and it is at this point that the orders are placed. The key is being able to obtain this knowledge.

We know that knowledge management (KM) strategies targeting all e-business stakeholders are crucial for maintaining competitive advantage. A 1999 online survey, conducted by the Cambridge Information Network, of 314 senior IT strategists states that "while 85% of CIOs believe in the importance of managing knowledge, only 8% of companies have an enterprise-wide knowledge initiative and only 7% have CEOs that consider KM a high priority." This survey limited the definition of KM to intellectual assets management, that is, employee knowledge. International Data Corporation research estimates that by 2003, Fortune 500 companies will lose more than $31 billion due to intellectual rework, inability to find knowledge resources, and substandard performance. The loss is deemed attributable to lack of tools and processes that actively capture, manage, and connect organizational expertise. [3]

Customer characteristics have changed. The customer is impatient and sensitive. The costs of switching to become a customer of another business are lower than ever. Customers are demanding exceptional value. They are exacting in their requirements for lower prices, better service, faster processes, and efficient activities. Market characteristics have also changed. News items are more available and make more impact today on company's value, profitability, and failure. Customers, as well as markets, are more informed. Business is required to give 24-hour/7-day-a-week service to customers. e-Marketplaces are enabling competitive bidding from a wide variety of suppliers. These marketplaces do not work for all types of products or customer-business relationships. Companies and individual customers still trust brands. Many will not buy on price alone; quality, service and reliability are equally important.

Companies today must not fear bringing in outside and sometimes international consulting resources to manage change internally in a company, or to help identify opportunities unique to their internal productivity, industry, or business. These people add value by encouraging thinking outside a box. They can bring in expertise in future scenarios, can role-play, and are not tied down to operational constraints within the company. If first-to-market is part of a business' strategy, then the learning about e-business must be rapid, and professionals engaged in this knowledge transfer are quite valuable.

Core E-Business Competencies

The identification of core competencies is essential to strategy creation at every level. The critical success factors and core competencies that provide a firm with a competitive edge in the offline world can be extended to the e-business world. For example, traditional competencies can apply to a brand name, services, research and development, manufacturing, product development, cost and pricing structures, and sales and distribution channels. E-businesses can strengthen the traditional competencies, and new competencies can be created.

Capable relationship management with stakeholders is a key competency in the e-business economy. Knowledge management and trust are key enablers for stakeholder relationship management, and we have explained the reason in almost every chapter of this book. Transferring information and knowledge to other stakeholders facilitates value creation. Managing outsourced contracts with operational partners is another competency that is absolutely essential in e-business. For example, operational partners such as your application service providers (ASPs) are critical in enabling real-time availability and acceptable levels of quality of service at your Web site. Enforcing proper service level agreements with the partners is a necessary competency.

Knowledge management supports other core competencies such as channel management, brand management, and portal management. Portals are one-stop shops, and people like them. Employee, customer, partner, and community portals must provide an easy-to-use, consistent interface that has an intuitive navigational ability. Stakeholders should be able to easily find what they are looking for.

Making the customer the central focus of the business—the priority of the business—often requires cultural changes. The change is directly affected by the business' level of adaptability and versatility. If the company's culture is ready for e-business—if it is future oriented, adaptable, and versatile—the culture is a core competency that can be leveraged.

Specialist companies are leveraging technical competencies in exchange for the real revenue generators—business ideas. The companies are offering to create and host Web sites in exchange for a percentage of revenue. eCompanies' business is garnering competencies in the areas of strategy, finance, recruiting, creative, technology, business development, and marketing and launching new businesses from mere concepts.

According to eCompanies, ". . . in the current frothy Internet environment, every good idea will have multiple competitors, so time to market is critical. Using a fast-flow approach to launching companies, eCompanies can get a business from concept to market in 3 to 6 months." eCompanies' portfolio comprises businesses such as eparties.com, business.com, and ememories.com, to name just a few.

Barriers to Successful E-Strategies: The Difficulty Index

The difficulty index indicates how hard it is to transition a company, industry, country, or continent into e-business. Creating a future-oriented culture is one of the biggest obstacles to moving a bricks-and-mortar business into e-space. If any of the upper management is resistant to change, then resources for e-business will not be available and all e-initiatives will fail. Traditionally, enforcement of standards is not a widespread activity in and among companies, but this mindset will need to change to facilitate e-business interconnectivity. Internet and personal computer (PC) use is another issue that e-businesses must address when dealing with smaller concerns such as contractors and professional service providers. For example, the success with which a business model is able to bring together home builders and building contractors could hinge on whether the contractors have PCs or mobile devices (such as cell phones).

Knowledge—in all its forms—is managed poorly across today's organizations. For successful knowledge management across stakeholders, there must be a willingness to share information and transfer knowledge or information or data among the parties. We already have numerous case studies on suppliers and retailers showing that supply chain visibility leads to more effective marketing promotions, accurate forecasting, and on-time deliveries. Businesses are often reluctant to share customer information with partners. Because they may perceive sharing as a risk, they don't receive the maximum benefits from intermediaries. A willingness to share can be promoted with successful, convincing, and concrete examples of other businesses that have used sharing to increase profitability.

Another impediment to immediate knowledge management capability is the need to integrate older legacy systems into the new collaborative system of third-party vendors. Some of these products have limited support for standards such as electronic data interchange (EDI). There is no single standard for interoperability between enterprise resource planning (ERP) and e-business application bolt-ons.

Another aspect of knowledge-based collaboration involves relationship governance. Who is responsible for what, and what rules are used? Who governs the relationships among stakeholders? Compliance to product code standards and business instrument formats (such as XML) must be enforced for e-business to work.

Creating a customercentric business entity often means reengineering processes so that they benefit the customer. One-to-one marketing involves creating mass customizable solutions for a group—a microsegment—that appear to be personalized to each customer. The German industry giant, Siemens, has a microWeb site for each of its hundreds of lines of businesses. Each line of business runs its own independent ERP system. The challenge for Siemens is providing a consolidated view of the various lines of businesses to a single customer. Elimination of this barrier could be a business opportunity for a company that specializes in creating intermediate integration hub e-business application solutions.

Being customer focused means understanding the needs of every customer; it means managing even more—possibly hundreds or thousands more—microsegments of customers, thereby introducing a new overhead. To a certain extent, knowledge management software can help, but middle managers have to understand and take responsibility for these microsegments as well. They may have to add human resource personnel to manage the new customer microsegments. The duplication of effort that inevitably occurs during the deployment of numerous, different, uncoordinated e-business solutions can create a problem. Businesses sometimes approach the Web channel as a mass marketing medium instead of leveraging the one-to-one possibilities. Indeed, some companies do not collect sufficient data to personalize customer information; customers need to understand that they can benefit from providing their information.

Channel conflict is another problem to address when adding a Web channel. Reselling partners in particular think that in all fairness, prices should be the same at the physical and virtual storefronts. This is often not the case; many businesses offer reduced prices online to gain market share. They can do this because Web-channel costs are often lower than other channel costs. Some suppliers have reduced the prices of the products or services that they offer through the Web to as much as 15 percent less than the price offered through their other distribution channels. Price discrimination is not a new phenomenon that popped up in the online world. For example, airlines use *yield management*, a pricing system in which services are priced based on a customer's willingness to pay.

Only a handful of companies have well-implemented systems infrastructure. Other companies need to learn how they can benefit from a total architectural solution approach and the importance of technical standardization and consistent and convenient user interfaces. The management often fails to recognize when an in-house IT unit does not have expertise to perform in certain areas. Sometimes management administrators will close their eyes to system problems that require outsourcing or new talent because they are reluctant to assign more funds (perhaps because of budgetary constraints or current resource allocation priorities).

Clicks-and-mortar businesses that do not integrate their physical storefront computer applications with their Web systems are not taking advantage of the opportunities inherent to having a bricks-and-mortar storefront. Customers easily and often switch channels between bricks-and-mortar and virtual storefronts. As far as customers are concerned, they are dealing with one business, regardless of whether it is over the Web, on the telephone, or in person. Customers want to be able to return merchandise bought over the Web to a physical store—without hassles. In the United States, such a service would jeopardize the sales tax advantage of an online catalog or separate Web company.

The management sometimes fails to recognize that it is characteristic for Web-channel customer traffic to arrive in bursts. Bursts on the Web can comprise hundreds of thousands of customers, unlike bursts at physical stores, which clearly don't have the capacity for that many customers. Not only does the Web site solution need to be scalable to allow all these customers to enter while maintaining acceptable quality of service levels, but all associated business processes connected to a sale must be scalable as well. For example, the last two Christmas seasons revealed that the fulfillment process of many online retailers simply did not scale. Fulfillment must be reliable.

In addition, businesses are in a quandary about how to estimate the number and types of suppliers, strategic partners, community members, and customers that will be accessing their applications at any given time. Figuring out how to divvy up responsibilities in a partner cost-sharing plan is difficult. Occasional- or low-use option pricing is also an issue. As they stand, software licensing agreements are not suitable for the new collaboration anticipated in e-business. Budgeting for a rollout of applications is almost impossible when it involves suppliers and partners whose infrastructure support requirements and levels of e-business readiness are all different and change from month to month.

Opportunities

What and Where

Traditionally, good opportunities were qualified by whether your company influenced an industry. What a surprise amazon.com was for the retail book industry in 1996! E-business provides the newest opportunity for gaining or retaining market leadership. For some businesses, e-business ultimately means the difference between survival and failure. For traditional business, many of the opportunities associated with opening up a new marketing, sales, and service channel are similar to those associated with other traditional channels, but the Web channel presents some unique opportunities. Businesses can develop new—complementary or alternative—revenue sources through advertising, syndication, or subscription to online services or communities. Community sites and "market breakers" depend heavily on advertising revenues. (Market breakers are businesses that sell products and services below cost to attract traffic to their sites.) However, clicks-and-mortar companies like Wal-Mart and Sears could receive supplementary revenue from advertisers on their sites as well. Look.com is an example of a business that facilitates syndication revenue. In addition to advertising, another source of revenue is selling customer data—but selling it cautiously.

Business component enablers such as access to complete customer information provide new marketing opportunities. Contextual marketing and selling are possible at many customer contact points. While a customer is on the phone with a customer service representative (CSR), a software agent can suggest that the CSR market a particular product to the client during the conversation. Through innovative service, companies can foster ongoing sales relationships, which increase the opportunity for future revenues. The increase in supply as well as demand on the Web presents an opportunity for a company to modify product and service pricing. The Web enables the creation of value-added services in many industries. For example, online bill presentation is a popular value-added service for customers in the energy industry; it saves companies money because mailing costs are eliminated.

The opportunities in the clicks-and-mortar business model are connected to the carryover of the brand name to the online business, the complementary and interchangeable services and customer information at physical and virtual storefronts, and the leveraging of existing infrastructure for facilitating delivery. A clicks-and-mortar business can experiment with the Web and fail but then survive and launch another experiment as exemplified by Wal-Mart's IT spin off. The opportunities for the pure dotcom companies are found in the collection of revenue from electronic transactions, advertising, subscriptions, and sponsorship. The risks grow when physical warehousing and delivery infrastructure is needed for the business. Building a brand completely online is expensive but not impossible, especially if the business is a first mover in an area. Successful pure dotcoms include Yahoo!, eBay, and AOL. The Net market business model strictly facilitates transactions from business to business (B2B). Revenue comes from a percentage of the transaction cost, a flat transaction fee, or a periodic subscription fee. The model leverages transaction dollar-amount forecasts for B2B e-commerce that predict billions to trillions of dollars worth of business conducted online. The primary opportunity in the current Net-market model is in e-procurement. Every industry is considering setting up an e-marketplace to bring suppliers together to service the industry. The creation of these micromarketplaces is a new e-commerce opportunity.

Businesses within the same or similar industries, such as the energy industry, are using e-business to move into other areas. Power companies are transforming into telecommunication companies. The telecommunication companies (telcos) are becoming e-business enablers. MCI Worldcom has announced its transition from communications services carrier to e-business enabler.[4] Many telecommunication companies worldwide are banking on getting more than half of their revenue from emerging services related to e-business. In Britain, Energis successfully transformed into a telco, providing competition to British Telecom (BT). BT has formed a partnership with Microsoft to create a worldwide network of Internet-enabled wireless phones. Subscribers are allowed to pay bills, listen to music, buy tickets, and trade stock on these phones. Most of the current industry leaders are aggressively pursuing e-business opportunities as well so that they can maintain their dominant positions. Assessing what the industry leaders are doing may highlight opportunities that your business can translate into other markets. On a global scale, one company's brand may be more recognizable in one country than in another; the globalization trend in e-business can allow previously untapped markets to become accessible for all players.

As businesses become more skilled at deploying e-business initiatives, they develop a new competency and new opportunities. For example, General Electric (GE) spun off its IT unit into a separate e-business consulting services entity, and Wal-Mart did a similar spin off. One opportunity could be taking these separate businesses to equity offering or initial public offering (IPO). The share price valuation of the dotcom companies is nothing to sneeze at despite market corrections and bubble effects. Partnering with dotcom or traditional companies or acquiring e-businesses for marketing and technology resource sharing also opens up a Pandora's box of opportunities and risks.

Examining technology and regulatory scopes for future events can provide a road map to possible future opportunities. You need to have a sense of which information applications and technologies are important and what kind of impact they can have on you in the future if you are going to start with the right building blocks. For example, your business should consider the possible impact of network appliances ("smart products" that can contact manufacturers) and voice technology on your products and services.

The eBiz Readiness!™ framework can give you a structured approach to creating, assessing, and monitoring your e-business during the next year or two. You can use the framework to refine opportunities into customer, operational partner, community, governance, strategic partner, and employee-facing opportunities. Chapters 3 through 9 outline these opportunity areas. In addition, the assessment questions in this chapter highlight the stakeholders' opportunities. According to Nervewire, "Value Web analysis provides a total view of fund flows, product flows, and margins across links and reveals where to play and where to outsource."

Virtual Clusters

The virtual cluster concept revolves around interdependent and interconnected firms and institutions creating strong, internal economic sectors. According to Porter,[5] clusters are "critical masses—in one place—of unusual competitive success in one field." In the past, virtual clusters tended to develop in vertical industries and were geographically defined, like the Italian leather shoe-making industry. The cluster companies don't have to incur the extra costs to ship tanned leather from other countries because local Italian tanners are available. The virtual cluster concept is being extended so that businesses can take advantage of the e-business opportunities and rely less on geographical location. The virtual cluster is clearly a concept that creates interesting challenges for its creators and managers; it is much easier to build trust when you see co-workers face-to-face, eat with them occasionally, and so on.

Governments worldwide are very interested in cluster formation. We find the value of clusters in the following:

- The creation of wealth, jobs, and intellectual property
- The production of highly trained personnel
- Increases in productivity and sustainability
- Increases in the pace of innovation
- The management or direction of innovation
- The stimulation of new business formation

Risks

Opportunities naturally come with risks. You take risks when you form new relationships with new partners, existing partners, new communities, new markets, and new countries. The competitors are not as well known as previous competitors. In the nondomestic market, competition from other global players with deeper pockets can be a real threat.

Companies are currently at risk for losing existing and new market share and revenue to competitors because of strategic mistakes, an inability to execute strategies quickly, or an unanticipated technological event that made their products or services less useful or completely obsolete. Legal or regulatory events can translate into nasty surprises. For example, Virtual Vineyards was sued by local wine distributors to prevent it from selling wine to residents in the state of Massachusetts. The introduction of heavy Internet taxes, bit taxes, or prohibitive regulation costs can have adverse effects on projected revenues. Problems can be exacerbated by a company's inability to fill competency gaps. The hybrid skills availability gap is a universal problem.

Online competitors are sometimes new and can be unexpected. For example, British Airways found that its biggest online competitor was not another airline but was Microsoft's Expedia.com. People compare services at Web sites differently than they do in the physical world. Companies are finding that they are not being compared to other businesses in the same industry; the service from a bookseller site may be compared to an experience at an online bank.

You have no guarantees that the business models you have chosen will be viable in the future. How do you know whether you are choosing the right ones? Wasting IT and advertising dollars to build an online brand can create real problems; however, similar problems crop up in traditional businesses. Someone will take the risk if you don't.

Extending the E-Business Stakeholder Model

Globalization

The eBiz Readiness!™ framework can be applied to a global setting. For example, if a company wanted to gauge the potential (in other words, assess the e-business readiness) of the Asian, European, South American, African, Austral-Asian, or North American market, the company could do so using a stakeholder-facing perspective. In addition to assessing a company, you can assess the readiness of a continental market, a single country, or an industry (Figure 10-2).

The power difference among the stakeholders must be assessed, and rarely do you find a balance. One stakeholder often has more influence than another. In socialist countries the governance stakeholder has the most influence on e-business readiness. The framework could also be used to assess whether an entire country, such as Brazil, Slovakia, or Ireland, is ready. The eBiz Readiness!™ framework at a country level would direct the country to (a) partner with industry and

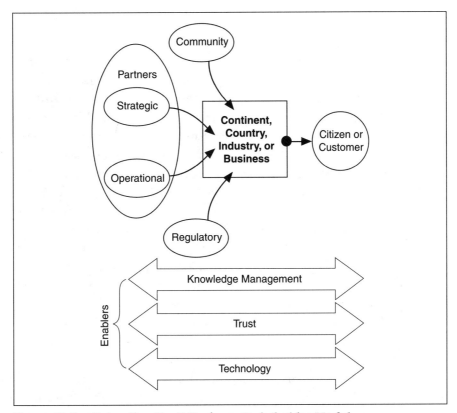

Figure 10-2   Extending the E-Business Stakeholder Model

research institutions to obtain an infrastructure and maintain a leading edge, (b) develop infrastructure to get citizens online, (c) provide citizen services (such as online tax filing), (e) develop community portals, and (f) create e-business regulatory policies, although not necessarily in this order.

Regions create further enabling opportunities with initiatives such as the European Union (EU) and the North American Free Trade Agreement (NAFTA). Lesser known is the MERCOSUR, South America's free trade area agreement among Argentina, Brazil, Uruguay, and Paraguay, which was formed in 1991. Chile and Bolivia became associate members in 1996 and 1997 respectively. The Web site for the *Mercosur Trade and Investment Report* newsletter states, ". . . with a population of 220 million and a gross domestic product (GDP) of $1.3 trillion in 1997, MERCOSUR is the fastest growing trading bloc in the world. It experienced a trade growth of 400 percent in the period from 1990 to 1997."

Industry-Level Modifications

The eBiz Readiness!™ framework can also be applied at a more narrow level, such as the industry level. Imagine you are a member of a technology provider company such as Oracle or IBM and that your company targets a whole industry as its market. Using the eBiz Readiness!™ framework, your company wants to determine how to change the industry through its stakeholders. Surveying the current market situation, you find that these companies have targeted procurement as a first play. It is easiest to sell a product solution to companies when the potential cost savings are so clear. The customer, the operational and strategic partner stakeholders, and the internal operations are the "power" relationships in the procurement process. Industry market knowledge is essential. Issues include the nature of partnerships in the industry—whether the industry is an oligopoly or a fragmented industry. The governance stakeholder helps identify the regulatory enhancements and impediments that affect the industry. For example, the U.S. government had antitrust concerns about the possible creation of an automotive exchange involving GM, Ford, and Daimler Chrysler. The government was concerned that together these companies could force down the prices of suppliers' products and services.

The Challenge

The core of the strategic planning exercise is to identify new opportunities that can help you grow your business in terms of market, profitability, product-service orientation, and company reputation (Figure 10-3). Our strategy is to

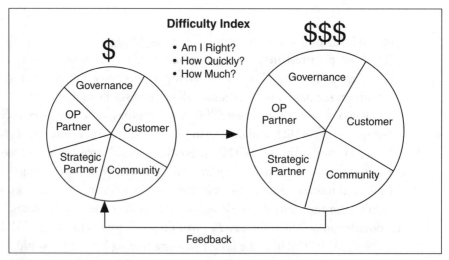

Figure 10-3   Company Growth and Stakeholder Focus

focus on the e-business components identified in each stakeholder and try to improve some subset of or all of the components into a more efficient future state. These e-business components for each stakeholder are summarized in Table 10-1.

Once you decide to move your company from "here" to "there," four key questions must be answered:

- What difficulties (barriers and constraints) will you encounter while attempting the move?
- How quickly will you make the transformation?
- How much stakeholder process transformation do you do now?
- Which stakeholders or combination of stakeholders will be affected?

Table 10-1 Summary of E-Business Stakeholders and Components

Stakeholder	Major Components*
Agents	Research and analysis, content management, sales, marketing and service, community, education and entertainment
Community	Engage, community interaction, community services, community governance
Customer	Engage, order, fulfill, support
Governance	Socioeconomics (stability of geographical area), marketplace rules (stability of market), privacy and trust (stability of customer), technology (stability of architecture)
Internal operations	Productivity, e-culture, information systems infrastructure and services
Operational partner	Contracts management, identification mechanism, assurance, dispute resolution, relationship management, transaction management, content management, intellectual asset management
Strategic partner	New alliances, account planning, new market research, macro resource planning, product or service development

*Recall that the three main enablers for all these components are knowledge management, trust, and technology.

Trinidad and Tobago and TIDCO

DOING IT TODAY

Trinidad and Tobago, a small oil-rich island with close to 2 million people, has a highly educated IT workforce. The island has a vibrant local university campus with faculties of engineering, business, arts, and natural science whose accreditation and standards are kept in line with those of external British universities by external approval of examination content by personnel at the British universities.

Trinidad and Tobago is a landing point for the Project Oxygen Network—a network that promises a whopping 2,560 Gigabits-per-second (2.5 Terabits-per-second) capacity, which is magnitudes faster than anything we currently have available. This capacity would allow you to simultaneously transmit 2 million videos of DVD quality. The first phase of the global undersea optical fiber network, which should be completed by June 2001, will connect 76 countries including the United States, the Bahamas, Puerto Rico, Antigua, Barbados, Trinidad and Tobago, Surinam, Brazil, Cape Verde, Morocco, Spain, Portugal, France, the United Kingdom, Germany, and the Netherlands. Trinidad and Tobago is committed to providing infrastructure that can effectively leverage the capacity of the Oxygen network.

The twin island country has consistently used a diversification growth strategy since the price of oil fell sharply in the 1980s. It developed a vibrant downstream industry for products created with oil byproducts, such as plastics. The country has strong manufacturing industries in the areas of food, clay products, and chemicals. Considering the worldwide shortage of IT labor, Trinidad and Tobago is in a good position to leverage another strength.

The Cabinet has appointed a Science and Technology Policy Task Force to develop a national science and technology policy with the following goals:

1. To review work previously executed in the development of a science and technology policy for Trinidad and Tobago
2. To prepare a bibliography of all such work
3. To establish a framework for the development of a National Innovation System for Trinidad and Tobago
4. To establish a framework for the development of a National Science, Technology, and Innovation Park in Trinidad and Tobago

5. To make recommendations for the establishment of a national science and technology policy for Trinidad and Tobago to serve the following functions:

    (a) To increase the absorption, adaptation, innovation, and dissemination of technology in Trinidad and Tobago

    (b) To increase the international competitiveness of Trinidad and Tobago

    (c) To foster the development of technology and knowledge-based production in Trinidad and Tobago

    (d) To develop a culture that is focused on the production and creation of wealth and will continuously leverage technology

    (e) To create the means for holistic education in technology use

6. To make recommendations for appropriate incentives to achieve the goals outlined in the proposed policy

7. To make recommendations for a permanent monitoring mechanism that will ensure continuous improvement in the national science and technology policy

8. To make recommendations for an appropriate legislative and regulatory framework to support a competitive national science and technology policy

The Tourism and Industrial Development Company (TIDCO) is driving the science park venture. Operational partners are required for an on-site incubator, which is expected to be the first building on the site and will have a central purpose during the development of the park; an incubator is many things at the same time. It is the architectural and design centerpiece of the park, so it is the first concrete evidence of TIDCO's commitment to the development. The incubator is also the focal point for the administrators of the park and its development. Most importantly, the incubator is the locus for the development and nurturing of innovation by nationals and residents of Trinidad and Tobago, as well as the source for the transformation of technology culture. TIDCO has identified investors who are interested in constructing, owning, and operating the on-site incubator. For example, the IC2- (Innovation, Creativity, Capital) Institute at the University of Texas at Austin is assisting TIDCO with the incubator setup and personnel training and may contribute start-up funding for incubator client projects. Other operational partners include Lockwood Greene and Blane Canada, companies that specialize in economic development marketing.

continued

Examination of one of the strategic partner stakeholders reveals a proposal to get the university community intimately involved in the development of the park, a plan that is in keeping with best practices for the development of science parks. The involvement of the university takes place at two levels—the faculty level and the student level. The university involvement ensures the benefit of two sets of input regarding the park development—the intellectual input from university faculty members and students and input from a pool of trained personnel (such as employees). The students will help develop a park culture that promotes inclusion. In addition, they will infuse a measure of idealism and freshness into the vision. They do not underestimate the potential benefit of having access to a pool of competitively priced laborers (students) for many tasks. Most importantly, the inclusion of the university will cement the university-park development partnership.

Initially, the community stakeholder is the citizens of Trinidad and Tobago—corporate and otherwise. As foreign companies populate the park, the community will grow to include knowledge transfer and information services for many countries' citizens. The park will support the value created in virtual clusters, such as stimulation for the initiation of global businesses.

Opportunity and Risk Assessment Questions

The stakeholder opportunity assessment questions that follow address opportunities and difficulties encountered in e-business. These questions may also be useful in the quest for answers to the bigger questions. How quickly can you transition into e-business? How much of your business and which processes can you transition right now? What hard costs are involved? In addition to the opportunity assessment questions, the business and technology competencies, processes, infrastructure, personnel skills, culture, and governance inherent to the business and to its partners and community should be evaluated. The processes for the latter were illustrated in Chapters 3 through 8. Redefining and refining value and supply chains and reinventing corporate culture to focus on e-business are achievable through a combination of internal and external initiatives.

"Insides" Assessment Questions

Increasing revenue and improving internal operations—the two main reasons companies are using the Internet—are the focus of the following questions.

E-Business Strategy

- Will you rely on an internal team to create e-business strategy? If so, how long will it take to create the strategy, gain approval, and execute the plan?
- Will you obtain professional consulting skills to complement the internal team's skills? This could increase the thoroughness of your strategy, as well as speed up the development process.
- Will you deploy new revenue models or enhance existing models through your Internet channel?
- Are you planning to spin off an e-business unit? Deploy an equity offering or IPO?
- Which of the following will your new revenue models include: advertising, subscription, service, affiliate, sponsorship, transaction, revenue as well as pay-per-use, flat rental or sales from products or services?
- Who are your existing and new customers?
- Will the proposed business models provide more value to your customers, including lower prices, faster fulfillment, better service, higher quality, a wider spectrum of services, new and innovative products or services, and more information about using your products?
- Will you primarily use the Internet channel to cut costs for tasks such as procurement, supply chain improvement or manufacturing efficiencies?
- Do you have a "big picture" perspective? Are you considering forming new relationships with stakeholder groups? Will you acquire technology infrastructure for effective knowledge management? Do you know what trust-building tools you will use?
- What resources have you allocated to development of e-business initiatives?
- Does each business unit have individual funding to ensure e-business success?
- What is your method for allocating IT and business resources to new e-business initiatives?

E-Culture

According to a year 2000 *InformationWeek* survey, some of the steps that companies take to improve culture include outfitting employees with better PC gear, promoting knowledge sharing, expanding training programs, refocusing the company on customers, holding employee retreats, offering customer service incentives, and offering equity or stock options to employees. Keeping e-business salaries at a competitive level can reduce employee turnover and the accompanying costs of losing trained employees.

- Is an adaptable culture one of your core competencies?
- Can you use the e-business platform to react faster to changing market needs, opportunities, or threats?
- Does your business anticipate internal resistance in moving to a future-oriented outlook? How will you manage the change for some employees?
- How much will it cost to provide employees with the tools and training that allow them to become comfortable with, understand, and execute new processes?
- Do you anticipate a shift in the skill level of your employee? Will you need fewer clerical employees and more highly trained employees?

Information Systems Infrastructure

- How much will it cost to install, upgrade, or outsource the information systems infrastructure needed to support internal e-business?
- How many IT employees maintain the infrastructure? Do they have strong hybrid business-IT skills? Can they be considered among the top talents in the industry?
- If you add a Web channel, will you have an e-mail or customer response management system in place to handle the influx of inquiries?
- How and when will you fit new technologies into your existing e-business infrastructure?

Productivity

- How much can you reduce the time it takes to do human resource tasks such as filing expense reports? How much will general and administrative sales (SG&A) expenses change with introduction of the intranet?
- How many finance tasks will have reduced cycle time after you begin using an intranet application? For example, a capital budgeting analysis task that is done in teams with multiple levels of hierarchy usually takes 9 months in large companies.
- To which new tasks will your employees be reassigned when the intranet applications are deployed? In what ways will the automation of tasks reduce (or increase) the value given to the customer or employee?
- Is knowledge management a core competency?
- How much do you estimate your company will save as a result of online information dissemination? Can you quote an overall figure and then break it down according to department, such as marketing, sales, human resources, finance, and production? What are the accompanying reductions in cycle time?

- What is the value of providing employees with real-time information?
- How will online access to business knowledge empower your employees? (For example, if your salespeople have access to information on a particular product, they learn more about the products. Salespeople who can easily and quickly access information may be able to respond more quickly to customers.)
- Will your company purchase nonproduction (maintenance, repairs, and operations [MRO]) and production goods from an e-marketplace? What is the current cost to process a purchase order for nonproduction goods and production goods? What was it previously?
- What benefits would you get from going to an e-marketplace?
- Will you benefit from competitive bidding? Do you have to buy from one or two suppliers?
- What will be the cost of the IT infrastructure procurement? What will be the cost of changing the accompanying business processes?
- What is the cost of training employees how to use the B2B back-end applications for procurement?
- What is the anticipated reduction in the order fulfillment cycle time ?
- Do you anticipate eliminating human errors associated with e-procurement. Provide examples.
- Are your supplier relationships long term and strategic or short term and tactical?

Customer Stakeholder

According to a year 2000 *InformationWeek* survey of 600 executives, changing customer-facing processes is the second most highly transformational effort under way in companies. The number one effort involves the active role of IT in the overall business. Following are some questions that highlight business opportunities for the customer stakeholder.

Marketing

- Are ad campaigns, promotions, product launches, and seminars cheaper or more effective on the Web channel?
- Can new markets be developed for traditional and Web sales channels?
- Can you create niche or specialty markets more cheaply and effectively because of the Internet channel's global reach?
- Do you have an opportunity to reinforce or build your brand's reputation in another channel?

- Do you see an opportunity in using a distribution channel—the Web—that scales to reach thousands of customers in old and new markets in real time? What are the tradeoffs with respect to other media?
- Do you have an opportunity to target the "right" customers for your company? Are you able to collect far more data on the Internet channel than with any other medium?
- Do you have an opportunity for mass customization and "one-to-one marketing" that is greater on the Internet channel?
- Are you taking the opportunity to provide a one-stop shop—in other words, convenience—for your customers?
- Does the Web have unique tools for engaging customers (such as software agents)?
- What are the opportunities for agent technology use in B2B and business-to-consumer (B2C) e-commerce? What about in areas such as research, sales, marketing and service, community building, and entertainment?
- We know that agent applications of customer profiles include news services, Amazon's Eyes, the Pointcast network, newspage, ZDNet's Personal View, and tracking stock portfolios on quote.yahoo.com. Is personalization a primary factor for agent use in B2C e-commerce? What are other key factors and opportunities?
- What are the opportunities for using agents for customer, partner, and community profiles?
- Will supply chain visibility offer improved marketing opportunities?

Sales

- Will the Web's geographical reach create more sales from a more dispersed customer base?
- What percentage of sales is targeted to come from Internet commerce?
- Are the costs of sales transactions lower on the Web?
- Are reseller channel partners more effective than the Web channel? Can they be complemented? (For example, can you decrease channel conflict by creating a co-branded Web site with reseller partners?)
- Do you have an opportunity to provide better customer service by directing customers to a local reseller from a co-branded Web site?
- What are the benefits of combining inside sales with the Internet? Call centers with field sales? What are the benefits in supporting multiple yet integrated sales channels?

- Are field sales more effective?
- Are products or services easier to configure and customize on the Web channel?
- Is competitive selling enabled because information is available in real time?
- Can you find buyers more easily (for example, in e-marketplaces?)
- What shipping or other export and import issues will you have to address?
- Can you use the e-business platform to distribute knowledge that is obtained *outside* as well as *during* the sales time?
- Have you increased customer satisfaction because of more realistic and accurate predicted times obtained from integrated supply chain visibility?
- Does supply chain visibility mean that the time capital is invested in products and services is reduced?
- Do you need less warehouse space (and thus real estate) now that your sales process has changed?
- Do you have opportunities for better forecasts now that you have more information available?
- Will the Web payments create shorter cash-to-cash cycle times?
- Are your delivery costs lower because of an alternative delivery channel for digital goods?
- What are the opportunities for comparative shopping agents in e-sales, and will they harm your margins?
- Can you use the e-appliance as a point-of-sale (POS) device and thereby lengthen sales relationships?
- Which of the following agent opportunities can you take advantage of: customer needs identification, product brokering, merchant brokering, negotiation, payment and delivery, service and evaluation?

Service

- Can you reinforce and build brand reputation through better service?
- Is Web service perceived as more "convenient?" Are there less delays in getting information (for example, waiting for call center personnel to respond)?
- Can you provide cheaper and more effective support over the Internet?
- Are product updates and upgrades, alerts, and executions cheaper?
- Are your customer touch points integrated? That is, if a customer were to cross channels and make phone as well as Internet problem reports, would each contact point be aware of the other? Can salient customer history be viewed electronically at each touch point?

- Is your site easy to navigate? Will you facilitate natural language querying?
- Will you provide customer personalization services?
- How often will you provide new personalization services on your site?
- Will you allow business customers to view their transaction and interaction history with your business in a secure area, or is this data only for business use?
- What types of product warranties are available to your customers? How will you provide proof of purchase in the online world?

Strategic Partner Stakeholder

Information is the currency that is used to rework relationships with existing strategic partners and to acquire new partners. Knowledge transfer, flat organizations, innovative new products, new customer services, efficient processes, and contributing partners are critical success factors.

- How do you use channels and partnering to create new customer segments and market opportunities?
- How do you work with independent software vendors as development partners, and how can you leverage them as value-added channels?
- What are the most important emerging and alternative channels in your sector? How will you use them?
- How do you manage new channel conflict created by extension of partners' channels?
- Have you encountered or do you anticipate any interpartner competition?
- Do you do joint billing and pricing of products or services with your partners?
- Does the Web facilitate design and development among geographically dispersed personnel?
- Does the e-business platform offer newer and cheaper processing opportunities?
- Do your company and your partner's company engage in joint data mining exercises, or is knowledge shared at an aggregate level?
- Will you integrate partner companies' data? Which partner's data would be useful for your company to have and vice versa?
- How do you transfer knowledge with your partners?
- Do you offer joint training courses for employees of the virtual team?
- What is the value proposition of this alliance for all partner companies (branding, capital infusion, new markets, technology access, and so on)?

- Do you and your partners carry out complementary new market research? How do you share research tasks?
- How many new markets will you enter because of your partners' input or presence?
- Will your partners be alarmed by your entry into new markets?

Operational Partner Stakeholder

Executing strategies quickly and meeting market demands at Internet speed means not going it alone. With strategic and operational partners, you can do it fast, do it right, and do it globally.

- What are the competencies you lack and thus need to outsource?
- What other value besides competencies do the partners bring to the table?
- If global reach is important to your company, do you have a single ASP with a global reach, or do you have to contract with multiple worldwide ASP vendors?
- What pay models will you adopt for ASPs?
- What percentage of your trading base is electronically connected, and how long will a rollout take?
- How many different technology-formatting standards (for example, EDI, Internet EDI, XML) do you use to interact with your partners?
- Are paper-based processes still required in your partners' interactions? If so, what percentage?
- In addition to your supplier's e-catalog, what other partner application is useful to you?
- Do you have access to research and development information for any operational partner? If so, why don't you consider this company a strategic partner?
- What difficulties will you face in integrating your information systems with your partners' information systems? Do you think that cross-vendor application integration is a major problem?
- Are standards a problem? What standard do you use? Will XML play a large part in future back-end integration projects among enterprises?
- You may need operational partners such as trust seal providers to help you seem trustworthy to customers. Are there further opportunities here or is it a cost sink?
- Do you provide suppliers with the customer data that pertains to usage of their product or service?

- You may need to form a partnership with an alternative dispute resolution (ADR) service to handle customer claims. Are there referral opportunities here?
- You may need to partner with a content manager; costs include the creation of mirror sites. Do syndication service opportunities exist?
- Will transaction management be outsourced?
- Will fulfillment be outsourced?
- What opportunities are created if you allow mobile access to your company's information systems?
- What opportunities or risks exist if your operational partners provide *direct* support to *your* customers?
- What manufacturing or processing cost savings or increases in efficiency do you expect as a result of outsourcing?

Community Stakeholder

- Can you use feelings of community (personalization services, access to content) to create site stickiness and raise customer switching costs?
- How will you obtain revenue from the community? List all the methods (for example, transaction fees, list fees, advertising, fee-per-service fees, fee-per-usage fees).
- Do you think of vertical communities as alternatives to strategic partnerships, predefined contracts, and EDI implementations? In every instance, or for fulfilling spot needs?
- What risks do buyers and sellers associate with vertical market use?
- If small businesses are in your market's purview, what will you do to attract these small enterprises to your community? (For example, some e-markets digitize sellers' content at no charge.)
- Which community transactions have a long cycle time? Can you build business relationships from these transaction interactions?
- Which business do you anticipate to have the most frequently executed transaction or process within your community?
- What are the customer benefits and savings associated with joining or participating in your community? Which core business processes among companies does the community facilitate? Can you quantify the reduction in cycle time for some of these processes? Can you qualify some of the value-added features?
- How will you measure your success? By how much revenue your sellers make through listing in your community?

- Will you use agent technology to promote community building? (For example, agents can connect people with similar interests based on profile matching. Does your agent have this capability?)
- Which communities will you target for agent integration?
- How do you use your business's community to engage new customers, increase repeat sales, and promote customer loyalty and customer retention?
- How does your business sell to, market to, and service the community?

Governance Stakeholder

- How do present e-commerce regulations affect you?
- What do you see as your role in developing trust for e-business applications? What mechanisms do you have or will you have in place to help individuals and businesses trust e-commerce?
- What types of dispute settlement methods for consumers and businesses does your company advocate?
- What role do you think online ADR facilities will play in increasing people's trust of e-commerce?
- Government online applications such as secure income tax filing fosters trust in e-business through familiarization and successful interactions. What other applications have you made or will you make available to individual citizens?
- Do you monitor content and transactions on your site? What specific customer actions raise up red flags?
- Do you have a privacy policy? What is the most important point you want to make in your policy statement to the customer?
- What business controls do you have in place for security? What recourse action and disaster recovery plan do you have in place should a breach of security occur?
- What impact will public key infrastructure (PKI) have in promoting trust for e-business?
- Is there or will there be a mechanism in place to define jurisdictional boundaries for e-business?
- The government has a *huge* repository of data that e-businesses can use. For example, real estate companies can use town and planning files of architectural plans to "show" houses virtually. Is the government planning to make these records easily accessible to the average citizen? Will you have to pay for the data as you do for data from the North America suppliers database provided by the Government of Canada?

- What infrastructure are international governments putting in place to support equity of market access?
- How are international governments planning to levy taxes on e-business?
- What is your business doing to prepare for e-commerce taxation when the tax moratoriums are lifted?
- What are your business's rules on intellectual property (IP)?

Creating a Strategic Plan for Enabling E-Business: The E-Strategy

Following is a proposed methodology for creating a strategic plan to enable e-business in your company. A *methodology* is a step-by-step process for creating a design, strategy, or plan. Some of the steps we propose may be carried out together, and some may not be applicable to your company at all. You will have to tailor the plan to your situation. The main point to keep in mind is that a strategy for e-business enablement—an e-strategy—should be aligned to the overall corporate strategy.

1. Assess your business's current standing. Many rules in standard business literature can help guide you in this assessment. Examine and intimately know what your industry leaders are doing.

2. Outline your existing corporate, business, and functional strategies. Determine what your directional corporate strategy is. To consider e-business, you must target growth or retrenchment turnaround strategies.

3. Identify the opportunities for your company that result from transitioning into e-business or becoming more e-business enabled. The questions presented in this chapter may act as a starting point for identifying opportunities.

4. Prioritize the opportunities you determine as most significant to your firm.

5. If your corporate growth strategy involves market diversification or development of new products or services for new markets, then assess the propensity to spend in these industries and markets. Assessments often involve research or analysis reports on the state of an industry or a foreign market.

6. Identify your important stakeholder-facing processes. You can use the stakeholder components in the eBiz Readiness!™ framework as a guide.

7. Examine the targeted stakeholder processes and associated stakeholder components in the context of your target markets. You may find that the

eBizReadiness!™ framework is too generic and you may have to fine tune or add components that are relevant to your target market.

8. Rank your various business stakeholders in terms of power.

9. List your business's core competencies. Focus on the stakeholder processes that when transformed will benefit your company the most.

10. Identify the gaps that currently exist in your organization, and identify the barriers to and difficulty involved in filling them.

11. Formulate your plan based on the results of the previous steps.

Executing a strategic plan requires vendor involvement. For each stakeholder process targeted in your e-strategy, get product and service information from the leading technology vendors in the industry for your size and type of business. We have described many state-of-the-art, technology-based, e-business capabilities in this book, but we expect that by the time this text is published, more capabilities may have been brought to the market. E-business consulting firms keep on top of and specialize in e-business enabling processes. Getting the advice of such a firm, even if it is to confirm existing corporate thinking, could be money well spent.

Small-Business Perspective: Planning (SMEVideoStore)

> ## Sue:
> Our management assessed each stakeholder using the methodology of the eBiz Readiness!™ framework. The stakeholder relationship that we can most easily improve and get the most returns from now and in the future is the *customer*. Our e-business strategy for the next few months will focus on this stakeholder. Because of limited resources, we will take an incremental approach to deployment.

SMEVideoStore is a local video rental store. It is a franchise of a large company that distributes videotapes. SMEVideoStore sells videotapes and rents CDs and game cartridges as well, and you can buy candy, soda pop, magazines, and movie merchandise in the store. Two other local video rental stores are in the vicinity.

SMEVideoStore differentiates itself through its parent's brand name and by offering a wide variety of tapes.

SMEVideoStore's corporate strategy is a differentiation-focused growth strategy. The management has set out to create an e-business strategic plan to support the company's corporate strategy. They use the eBiz Readiness!™ framework to assess opportunities and business threats. On a 3-year planning horizon, the management assesses that their opportunities far outweigh their threats. Because of limited resources, the management targets the Web as another marketing, sales, and service channel.

Offering new Web-based services can expand the local client base. For example, customers will be allowed to do the following:

- Use the Web to check videotape availability
- Get online recommendations
- Make reservations for videotapes on the Web
- Join a community to discuss rentals
- Make rental transactions
- Review their kids' rentals for the last 6-month or 1-year period
- Review details of late charges
- Review the latest movie offerings
- Buy gift certificates
- Purchase movies or other merchandise
- Search and sort inventory (for example, obtain lists of all movies with a particular actor or actress, obtain lists of all movies from 1971, or obtain lists of all movies that won Oscars)
- Pay for rentals

The management is not addressing fulfillment issues yet. Customers must stop by to pick up their movies and merchandise after reserving, renting, or buying them through the Web. However, SMEVideoStore anticipates that they may win over some of the local competition's customers, who are excited about the first-mover service offerings. The reach of the Web will conveniently allow family members abroad to purchase gift certificates for local members. SMEVideoStore plans to offer a service that will package the gift certificates and mail them out to members. The Web channel will keep customers continuously updated about special promotions and discount nights. Members can opt to be included on an e-mail distribution list as well. Agent software will be used to notify members when videotapes that they may like are in stock.

Currently, the videotape store operations—which involve inventory, loan, customer, and human resource base data—are computerized. It would be fairly simple to transfer the data to the Web and integrate the Web's front system with the store's back-end systems.

A looming threat is movie-house originated videos-on-demand on the Internet. To be a true threat, they would have to become viable—at lower prices than those of the local video store. To be viable, (1) numerous households would have to be connected to the Internet, (2) sufficient bandwidth to service every household would have to be available, (3) digital protection schemes against movie piracy would have to be available and effective, (4) video quality would have to be acceptable, (5) the system availability would have to be 99.9999 percent, and (6) the origination of the download may have to be controlled by the big movie houses or local theaters.

Intertainer is a business that delivers movies over cable modem and digital subscriber line (DSL) systems. They have strategic partnerships with eight major media companies. However, the performance of their networks is not currently up to the task. Intertainer also has a distributor, Zoomtown.com, that is working on providing VCRlike functions such as fast forward, rewind, pause, and stop.

The management thinks that the threat is mitigated by geographical considerations and channel cannibalization. A movie house or intermediary such as Intertainer would still have to host infrastructure locally to ensure good response times. Instead of having a plain-vanilla operational partner such as an ASP provider, it makes sense to have the franchisees as operational partners, even in a video-on-demand model. The franchise adds value by "localizing" (tailoring) advertising to the local community.

Having assessed the opportunities and threats within the industry that may be caused by the impact of new technology and processes, the management of SMEVideoStore concludes that the company should be able to sustain a competitive advantage by providing superior customer service. A contract with an e-business solutions service company to provide the necessary process changes and enhanced technology infrastructure is all that is needed to execute the plan for this small business.

Big-Business Perspective: Planning (BBTelco)

Bob:

This exercise involved 10 of our key management and systems people as well as a leading consulting firm that specializes in e-business strategy creation. The consulting firm traditionally uses a different methodology to create e-business strategies but quickly saw the strengths in the eBiz Readiness!™ framework. The plan was created in 4 weeks.

BBTelco is a mature, cash-rich company in an industry whose traditional services are bringing in less and less revenue. Leaders in this industry have announced that they intend to become e-business ASPs. BBTelco intends to create a diversification growth strategy that allows them to head in a similar direction.

BBTelco first outlines a big, hairy, and aggressive business goal: to increase new revenue by $2 billion in 2 years. BBTelco's vision is to be a world leader in a niche area of e-business—the SME business market in two key verticals; the targeted industries are (1) oil and gas and (2) government. BBTelco is physically situated in an oil-rich nation, which they consider an advantage because they are going to be e-business enabling the oil and gas industry. The business will create mass, customizable solutions for e-governments of small island nations, states, counties, and provinces and for oil and gas companies throughout the world. Trends in IT and e-business spending in the targeted verticals show that there should be large increases during the next 5 years. BBTelco plans to aggressively partner to penetrate foreign markets.

BBTelco intends to leverage its many current operational and strategic partner relationships with key personnel in these verticals. A new business unit—the e-business unit—will be created to execute the business transformation goals. The unit's goals will be strategically aligned with the entire business's goals of diversifying its revenue mix, acquiring a larger share of the international market, and expanding customer reach. The e-business unit will be made up of key forward-thinking, aggressive, and smart knowledge workers who positively promote the needed e-culture.

BBTelco uses the eBiz Readiness!™ framework to target the e-business services it will create and then use to enter its targeted markets. The company examines customer, operational partner, strategic partner, community, and governance processes. It targets customer and operational partner processes because the technology solutions in these areas are mature. In addition, industry statistics support that customer and operational partner processes are e-business priorities. Examples of customer-facing processes are self-service sales, self-service support, integrated call center services, e-billing, and e-payments. E-procurement, proposal requests, content management, security, and dispute resolution are some of the supplier-facing processes.

BBTelco examines its core competencies to determine whether they include what is needed to provide the e-business components identified in the framework for the customer stakeholder and for internal operations, particularly MRO. The business has competencies in customer care, network provision, network management (which includes service level management), change management, transaction management, and Internet service aggregation. (Its Internet service provision services are the most successful in the company.) BBTelco requires capabilities in knowledge management, particularly relationship management, and distribution and logistics. BBTelco draws up a competencies and gaps assessment table (Figure 10-4) to determine how difficult it will be to enter

Competencies and Gaps		Today	Future	Difficulty (1, Low; 4, High)		
				Total	Oil	Govt
Competency	• Customer Care	Med	High	3	3	3
	• Network Provision **Gap**	High	High	2	1	3
	• Network Management	Med	High	4	3	4
	• Infrastructure	Med	High	3	3	3
	• Application Knowledge	Low	High	1	1	1
	• Knowledge Management	Med	High	2	3	3
	• Relationship Management	Low	High	3	3	3
	• Vertical Business Processes	Low	High	2	2	2
	• Vertical Governance	Low	High	2	2	3
Capability	• IP-Based Services and Applications	Med	High	2	1	3
	• Employee Knowledge Skills	Low	High	3	3	4
	• Sales, Marketing, and Service	Med	High	2	2	4
	• Fulfillment—Digital Goods	Low	High	3	3	3
	• Fulfillment—Physical Goods	Low	High	4	4	4

Figure 10-4   Competencies and Gaps Assessment

the two markets. The results show the areas that need to be targeted during the formation of BBTelco's strategic plan to provide e-business services in the markets of interest.

Are You Ready?

- This book culminates in a discussion on the use of the eBizReadiness!™ framework to formulate a strategic plan for e-business enablement. We expect that this will be one of the applications of the framework for you as well.
- Many applications of the framework are possible, including for the training of highly qualified personnel in e-business.
- Competency and gap tabulation and the difficulty index allow you to identify your gaps and qualitatively assess how difficult it would be to overcome your deficiencies.
- The small-business perspective sample case highlights opportunities with respect to the customer stakeholder. It outlines a relatively low-risk option for a business.
- The big-business case study explains how a service provider in the telecommunications industry can use the eBizReadiness!™ framework for strategic planning.

The Good Luck Story

This chapter concludes our book on e-business readiness. We hope that this text provides value to you, the reader, in some way—whether it is by unifying e-business information; providing an organizational framework that ties together the business, technical, and legal pieces of your business; blending theory and practice; or simply whiling away a few hours of your time. Our work continues as we develop and modify the framework for use in specific industries and markets. The eBizReadiness!™ framework will be in an evolutionary phase for some time. We are building a repository for many of the disciplines involved in e-business. We encourage you to forward any comments you have to us, particularly comments regarding omissions or errors in the framework. You can email us at dawn.jutla@stmarys.ca and james.craig@stmarys.ca. We wish you much success with your e-business plans.

- The IDC estimates that U.S. companies will invest more than $203 billion in Internet business initiatives by 2002.
- Hambrecht and Quist estimate that by 2005, businesses will be spending $50 billion per year on Internet strategic services.

References

[1]Wheelen, T., and Hungar, J.D. *Strategic Management.* 7th ed. Prentice-Hall, 2000.

[2]Arnst, C. "Wiring Small Business." *BusinessWeek*, 1996.

[3]McLatchie, H. "Knowledge MisManagement." *ClipMagazine,* November 1999.

[4]Smetannikov, M., "Don't Call Worldcom a Telco," *Interactive Week Online,* April 13, 2000. www.zdnet.com/intweek/stories/news/0,4164.2542361.00.html

[5]Porter, M. "Clusters and the New Economics of Competition." *Harvard Business Review.* November-December 1998.

Components, Enablers, and Metrics for All Stakeholders

This appendix is your quick-reference guide to all of the components, enablers, and metrics for each stakeholder discussed in the book. Refer to the appropriate chapter for additional information.

Components are the functions that create the linkages between the stakeholders and the e-business. The *enablers* are the resources that facilitate the components. *Metrics* are the measure of the success of the enablers. Recall that the knowledge, trust, and technology enablers are common to all components.

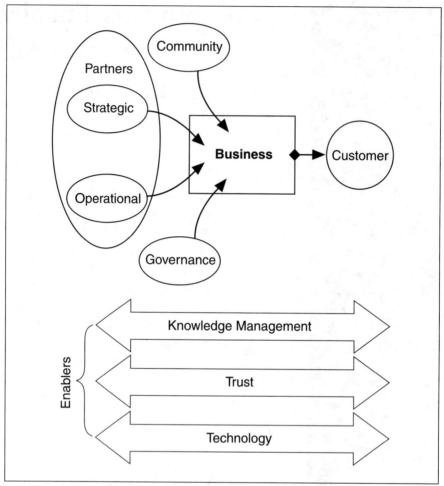

**Figure A-1   The Overall System of Stakeholders and Enablers
              (see Chapter 2)**

Chapter Three: Customer Stakeholder

Components	Enablers	Metrics
Engage	• Browse function	Channel partner coordination index
	• Search function	Comparison shopping index
	• Comparison	Convenience index (low–inconvenient, high–very convenient)
	• Configuration	Cost of adding new products and product options
	• Interaction	Customer acquisitions ratio
	• Questioning	Customer loyalty and satisfaction indexes

Components	Enablers	Metrics
Engage (*cont.*)	• Listening • Interactive marketing, real-time availability of information • Broad coverage of prospects • Cross-channel coordination for marketing, sales, and service	Customer profitability ratio Customer wallet share Customer win back ratio Customer win/loss ratio Lead routing and tracking time Number of new and effective marketing campaigns in the last 6 months Number of new interaction methods Partner loyalty and satisfaction indexes Pricing index (low—poor pricing, high—competitive pricing) Speed to market with new products or services and product or service options Usability index
Order	• Selection mechanisms (including pricing, product availability, shipping, and export and tax rules) • Payment mechanisms • Contracts • Order transaction management (including fraud transaction mechanisms and historical transaction details) • Billing	Accuracy of point-of-sale information capture Availability of credit card verification services Availability of electronic funds transfer Billing availability and accuracy Close ratio Cost of governance compliance Selling quality consistency index Costs savings (clerical + training + overhead) Customer loyalty and satisfaction indexes Fraud-checking mechanism reliability Historical transaction details availability Integrated pricing and inventory control availability (that is, pricing agility) Manager selling/mentoring time ratio Number of payment mechanisms available Number of products per sales order Order cycle time Order error rate Order tracking accuracy Order tracking availability Partner loyalty and satisfaction indexes Percentage of cross-sell sales Percentage of up-sell sales Pricing accuracy Pricing customization index Product/service customization index Quality assurance (need for third-party price review) index Inventory accuracy Quote accuracy Revenue per channel ratio Sales commission administration cost, time, and accuracy Sales forecasting accuracy Selling time ratio Time and cost to prepare quote Usability of product/service selection mechanism

Components	Enablers	Metrics
Fulfill	• Back-end process integration • Delivery capability • Returns policy • Global sales governance	Back-end process integration index Customer-added value index (low price, convenience, satisfaction) Customer loyalty and satisfaction indexes Delivery capability index Global sales governance index Integrated resourcing index (that is, multimodal fulfillment) Partner loyalty and satisfaction indexes Missed deliveries Average time to commit an order Elapsed time between order receipt and delivery
Support	• Complete customer history in real time • Access to corporate knowledge bases or industry knowledge sets • Automatic product updates • Self-serve applications • Single interface or portal to business knowledge	Abandonment rate Average response time Call duration Chargeable call duration Chargeable/nonchargeable service problem ratio Community index (for example, access to expertise in newsgroups) Customer feedback availability Customer retention ratio Customer satisfaction level Elevation and transfer rate E-mail response system availability Knowledge access index Nonchargeable call duration Number of incident reports per product Personalization index Product or service knowledge levels Partner loyalty and satisfaction indexes Customer loyalty and satisfaction indexes

Chapter Four: Community Stakeholder

Components	Enablers	Metrics
Engagement	• Capture and store function • Personalization function • Search function • Assistance • Data mining capabilities • Great content • Useful services • Integration with enterprise software advertisers • Commerce partners	Customer acquisition ratio Customer profitability ratio Customer retention ratio Member acquisition ratio Member retention ratio Duration of site visits Number of unique visitors Number of repeat visits Number of succesful marketing campaigns Take rates per campaign Ratio of change in community content Personalization index Localization index Usability index

Components	Enablers	Metrics
Engagement (*cont.*)	• Other community partners	Data currency index Level of brand awareness Number of languages supported Advertising revenues Commerce revenues from community members Commerce revenues from affiliated sites Traffic from affiliated sites
Interaction	• Collaboration, communication, and content management tools	Interaction tool response time Availability of interaction tool Scalability of interaction tool Abandonment rate Product or service knowledge access
Services	• Service creation skills • Resource content management tools • Partnering for content, services, or both	Rate of introduction of new services Revenue per service Cost per service Member satisfaction with service Personalization index Feedback from service
Governance	• Privacy policies • Accepted behavior policies • Censorship management • Fairness use	Security index Privacy index Dispute resolution index Cost of censorship

Chapter Five: Operational Partner Stakeholder

Components	Enablers	Metrics
Contract management	• Monitoring tools for expiry of contracts and quality of service • Service level agreements (SLAs)	Service completeness Quality of service SLA compliance Term length suitability Speed-to-market index Expertise level Service level Service cost Resource index Business benefits
Security	• Algorithms and mechanisms • Public key infrastructure (PKI) • Legality of digital instruments • Assurance services	Authentication index Nonrepudiation index Privacy index
Assurance	• Seal managers • Certificate authorities	Consumer confidence rating Customer acquisition Security index

Components	Enablers	Metrics
Assurance (*cont.*)		Privacy index Transaction integrity index Business validation index
Dispute resolution	• Online mediation software • Legal counsel	Case close rate Cost per case Settlement amounts Customer satisfaction Business satisfaction Confidentiality index Credibility of provider and mediators
Internal operations management	• Enterprise resource planning (ERP) or equivalent back-end systems	Cost savings in business process Increased business benefit per service Increase in productivity
Relationship management	• Complete e-relationship management software • Total capture of business information at each contact point	Overall integration index Relationship management integration index (customer relationship management [CRM], partner relationship management [PRM], and supply chain management [SCM]) ERP and relationship management integration index Metrics for customer Engage and Support in Chapter 3
Transaction management	• Multiple payment, fraud screening, and reconciliation capabilities • Capability to monitor the quality of service during transaction execution	Integration of front-end and back-end systems Overall quality of service Availability of services, transaction response time, transaction throughput, video quality, audio quality, video rate Interoperability of transaction management components Metrics for customer Order and Fulfill components in Chapter 3
Content management	• Content management tools • Full functionality: search function, personalization, migration, creation, categorization, multiformat data translation, syndication, replication, and contextual selling	Level of integration with all systems containing content Data consistency Data currency Update speed Search response time Search accuracy Interoperability with external systems Full functionality index Usage of analysis results index
Intellectual asset management	• Single interface to all pertinent data • Enterprise information portal software products	Accessibility index Knowledge transfer speed Knowledge transfer amount Knowledge asset usefulness Management of all types of data (unstructured and structured)

Chapter Six: Strategic Partner Stakeholder

Components	Enablers	Metrics
New alliances	• Resource complement • Culture • Chemistry • Brand piggybacking	New customer acquisitions Creation of new product or sales offerings Degree of resource complement Degree of cultural fit among companies Degree of rigidity or flexibility Team chemistry Market share per employee in partner company
Account planning	• Data warehousing • Data integration • Data infrastructure	Customer data integration Collaboration infrastructure
New market research	• Interaction tools • Research resources • Simple interface access to resources	Level of research interaction New market penetration hit rate
Macro resource planning	• Enterprise data integration • Portal interface to resource data	Resource data integration
Product or service development	• Team integration • Engage mechanism • Team services • Team governance	Percentage of past successes Expected potential for new product or service Actual performance for new product or service Product or service knowledge levels Accessibility of knowledge Level of team integration Availability and sophistication of project management and team interaction tools

Chapter Seven: Governance Stakeholder

Components	Enablers	Metrics
Socioeconomics: "stability of the state"	• Work force • Clusters • Access • Localization • E-business education	Turnover of workforce Education level of workforce Employment rate for workforce Number of companies in cluster Focus of the cluster Growth rate of the cluster Growth rate of access infrastructure in target markets Adoption rates in target market Amount of content required in local markets by law Diversity of content required for local markets Number of policies pertaining to e-business Number of procedures pertaining to e-business Subjective response or willingness of governments in target areas Adoption rates of e-business in target markets Future projections of business adoption rates Customer adoption rates Future projections of customer adoption rates

Components	Enablers	Metrics
Marketplace rules: "stability of the market"	• Jurisdiction • Liability • Intellectual property • Dispute settlement • Taxation	Number of areas targeted for work Commonality of laws in targeted operating areas Amount of owned legal content Degree of legal processes Degree of legal processes within target market Degree of compliance with UNCITRAL Number of regulations aligned with your business model Percentage of owned content Number of patented processes Number of alternative dispute resolution (ADR) mechanisms Degree of interjurisdiction issues Number of transactions Number of transactions in other countries with different laws Extent of taxation difficulties Extent to which taxation rules favor your business model
Privacy and trust: "stability of the customer"	• Privacy • Authentication	Completeness of privacy rules Number of nations within operating areas that have different privacy laws Level of authentication mechanisms within organization Level of management infrastructure and defined policies for authentication management Degree of PKI infrastructure allowances
Technology: "stability of the architecture"	• Network • Business applications	Number of disparate networked areas outside of one service operator or within one provider Number of SLAs Level of worldwide operations requirements Level of adherence to exchange community policies Level of compliance with open standards Number of formats required Number of formats supported

Chapter Eight: Agents

Components	Enablers	Metrics
Research and analysis	• Coverage of old and new sources of information • Sophistication in detecting quality of the sources	Scalability of data content coverage Number of types of search techniques (such as keyword, synonym based, concept based, Boolean, and natural language) Level of multiresource search capability Level of multimedia search capability

Components	Enablers	Metrics
Research and analysis (*cont.*)	• Sophistication of analysis • Extent of data content coverage • Scalability of data content coverage • Multiresource search capability • Multmedia search capability • Multilingual search capability	Level of multilingual search capability Extent of coverage of old and new sources of information Level of sophistication in detecting quality of sources Degree of relevance of agent results Level of efficiency in locating information Availability of Web directories (such as Web Yellow Pages) Degree of sophistication of analysis
Content management	• Interaction integration • Profiling capability • Automatic delivery of contextual information	Degree of content integration (virtual unification of content formats) Level of automatic categorization and cross-referencing or hyperlinking capability Degree and level of personalization (corporate versus personal) Ease of integrating content from multiple sources Data currency index (immediate versus deferred updates) Level of security adherence Degree of profiling Level of proactive delivery of information
Sales, marketing, and service	• Use of avatars • Profiling capability • Comparison capability • Brokering capability • Payment and delivery methods • Transaction execution	Level of coverage of multiple sources for comparison Degree of sophistication of agent-customer communication Degree of conveyance of humanlike user experience Accuracy of information provided to customer Relevance of information provided to the customer
Community	• Interaction technology • Visualization ability • Degree of communication	Community growth Number of community services Member satisfaction with agent services Visualization index Quality of communication Degree of sharing perceived by community members
Education and entertainment	• Learning assistance and capability • Easy-to-use interfaces • Social, facial, and vocal expressions	Easy-to-use interfaces Skill improvement

Chapter Nine: "Insides"

Components	Enablers	Metrics
E-culture	• Leadership • Knowledge transfer • Ease of information access • Communication	Prevalence of e-business culture Customer value innovation Ratio of resources allocated to e-business readiness development Currency of information Completeness of information Speed of information delivery Innovation index Uniqueness of product Market crowd index Customer acquisition rate Degree of brand creation Employee turnover rate (retention) Leadership index
Productivity	• Knowledge transfer • Ease of information access • Communication • E-catalog • Trading network • Electronically connected suppliers	Customer value innovation Degree of operational efficiency Revenue per employee Output per employee Speed of output Cash-to-cash cycle time Knowledge transfer index Cycle time for procurement processes Availability and reliability of catalog Product cost savings Reduction in costs for transaction processing Quality of delivery of goods and services
Information systems infrastructure and services	• Knowledgeable and talented strategic, operational, and support personnel • Updated hardware and software • Continuous training benchmarking against industry's best practices	Effectiveness of information systems operations and service capabilities Effectiveness of business models (cost, ease of use, convenience of use for customer) Number of new business models instituted in measurement period Number of new product or service releases Change in employee and customer understanding and learning levels, satisfaction, and confidence Customer acquisition rate Customer retention rate Availability and sophistication of business intelligence tools Breadth of shared information Degree of automation of business literature dissemination Cost savings in Web automation of paper processes and accompanying reengineering of processes

"Talk the Talk":
A Glossary of Terms

Affiliate business model A business model in which a company provides links from its Web site to another competitive but usually complementary and specialized business. For example, if you are in the pornography industry and your business does not peddle S&M video rentals, you would provide links to another business so that the customer can find the product or service.

Agents Programs that continuously monitor user actions, search for information, learn from user feedback and advice from other agents that do similar tasks, and take action autonomously; Also known as *spiders, worms, robots, hotbots, netbots, knowbots, softbots, personal assistants, artificial life forms,* and *software agents* and characterized as multiagent, profiling, mobile, or intelligent agents.

Aggregators Entities that add value by bringing together any other two entities on the supply and value chains. The common model aggregates buyers to facilitate cooperative purchasing (for example, bulk buying, term negotiations). Content aggregators collect information and match it to user preferences. Catalog aggregators bring together several suppliers and show the aggregated view of information to the customer. Aggregators typically do not take possession of the goods; they provide value to customers by allowing them to compare goods.

Alternative dispute resolution (ADR) Any means of settling disputes outside the courtroom. The two most common forms of ADR are arbitration and mediation; others include early neutral evaluation and conciliation.

Application service provider (ASP) The ASP hosts services for e-commerce and e-business. Businesses outsource to ASPs when they do not want or cannot afford to acquire and maintain all systems infrastructure (that is, hardware, software, personnel, procedures, data) needed for e-commerce and e-business.

Asymmetrical digital subscriber line (ADSL) A means of providing fast Internet access by using existing phone wires. ADSL use is mainly limited to metropolitan areas because the maximum distance between the terminal and repeater cannot exceed 8 km. Expensive amplifiers would be needed to serve rural districts. ADSL offers data transfer rates of up to 1.5Mbps from user to provider (upstream) and up to 8Mbps from provider to user.

Auctions Intermediaries that broker products and services among customers in a setting similar to a stock auction market. Auctions support dynamic pricing mechanisms that allow businesses to negotiate prices on a real-time basis. Prices only move up, but buyers can buy below the list price, and sellers can sell higher than the list price.

Avatars Online proxies of people represented in 3D graphics. Avatars often represent an alter ego or a mood. Virtual facial expressions are programmed to depict a range of human emotions such as cheerfulness or puzzlement.

Balanced scorecard approach An approach for identifying key business performance measures from financial, customer, internal, and learning and growth perspectives. The approach is "balanced" because measures with an outward customer focus as well as internal employee and financial measures are used to assess the business.

Benchmarking A method of measuring business performance. Benchmarking involves the continuous process of measuring products, services, and practices with those of companies that are considered industry leaders. You determine which business areas would benefit from benchmarking; identify the suitable metrics; select a set of accessible best-in-class companies against which to benchmark; and calculate the performance gaps between your company's measurements and those of the best-in-class companies. If you discover any significant gaps, you need to understand why they exist so that you can develop and implement tactical programs to resolve the problems. Benchmarking is a continuous process, so subsequent measurements taken after you have implemented your program will tell whether your tactics were successful.

Bricks-and-mortar A term that refers to a traditional company that has storefronts or outlets in actual buildings.

Brochureware site   A site that simply provides information about a company and its goods and services. This kind of site is not interactive; it doesn't support customer transactions such as buy, shopping cart, order status, and user registration transactions. The site primarily supports browse and search functions.

Business intelligence   The ability to glean meaningful information from company data. To get information that can be acted on quickly, data must be retrieved, viewed, analyzed, and managed.

Business performance   The measure of how well a firm has met its strategic objectives.

Business-to-business (B2B) commerce   Buying and selling of goods and services among businesses.

Business-to-consumer (B2C) commerce   Buying and selling of goods and services between businesses and nonbusiness customers.

Chat bots   Interactive software applications that a person can talk to. Chat bots simulate natural conversations.

Clicks-and-mortar   A term that refers to a hybrid business that has online storefronts or outlets in addition to physical buildings.

Collaborative planning, forecasting, and replenishment (CPFR)   A supply chain initiative that builds on continuous replenishment programs and advanced planning and scheduling systems. Incorporating and integrating CPFR tools with customer relationship management programs and back-end enterprise resource planning (ERP) programs gives an organization visibility into its operations.

Commerce extensible markup language (cXML)   A superset of extensible markup language (XML) that is specific to commerce transactions.

Commerce service provider (CSP)   A business that hosts e-commerce software solutions, such as storefronts, for other businesses.

Community   The group of people who is interested in your products and services. The community may or may not include customers of your business.

Computer telephony integration (CTI)   Allows a customer service representative to view customer information instantaneously on a computer screen when the customer phones in to the company's contact center.

Contact point integration   The process of recording each customer or business partner interaction, regardless of its touch point or input format (for example, voice, e-mail, fax) into a single, centralized customer repository. Contact point technology enablers include e-mail, computer telephony integration (CTI), interactive voice response (IVR), call routing switch, fax, Web chat, and machine-to-machine interactions.

Content management   Managing the synchronization of company data from various sites; the update and currency of the content.

Corporate portal See *enterprise information portal.*

Customer focus Concentrating on the customer. Maintaining a customer focus is a business philosophy that involves being prepared to doing business any way the customer wants. The philosophy transcends all borders and involves all of the stakeholders who create value for the customer.

Customer relationship management (CRM) A broad term for managing a business's interactions with its customers. Effective CRM involves acquiring, analyzing, and sharing knowledge about and with your customers. CRM addresses your direct business contacts with customers, your channel partners' indirect contacts with customers, and customer contact management in your supply chain.

Customer service representative (CSR) A person or agent that provides support services to a customer.

Customer value The benefits a customer receives. Customer value could be lower prices, higher quality products and services, a continuous stream of innovative new products and services, speedier responses, convenience, or customization of products and services.

Customers The end-purchasers of a product whether in business or consumer transactions.

Direct business model A business model in which the supply chain entity sells directly to the customer.

E-assurance services E-business services that provide a statement of guarantee on the security, integrity, and authentication of electronic transactions and communications.

eBiz Readiness!™ framework A framework that defines the components and enablers that are essential to e-business creation and successful execution. The framework also defines a set of measures that you can use to monitor and assess how well you are doing e-business.

E-business A business that involves the use of network and distributed information technology, knowledge management, and trust mechanisms to transform key business processes and relationships with customers, suppliers, employees, business partners, regulatory parties, and communities. E-businesses change traditional business models to create new and increased value for the customer.

E-business community A constantly changing group of people with common business interests who collaborate and share their ideas on a network.

E-business model The model that describes (1) the online architecture for product, service, and information flow in a business, (2) the potential benefits of various business stakeholders, and (3) the sources of revenue.

E-commerce The part of an e-business that focuses on selling and purchasing goods and services electronically.

Efficient consumer response (ECR) High-quality customer service, which involves integrated partner collaboration, information sharing, and efficient supply chain operations.

E-hubs See *trading communities.*

Electronic data interchange (EDI) A standard that facilitates the electronic exchange of trading documents such as purchase orders and invoices. Each type of document has special formats and layouts. Although EDI originated on virtual private networks using dedicated lines, Internet EDI is also available.

E-mail response management systems (ERMSs) Software that fully or quasi automate responses to customers. ERMSs classify and sort incoming messages according to predefined categories such as "request for information" or "complaint" and sort them according to customer priority.

E-market maker See *trading communities.*

Enterprise information portal (EIP) An interface to a business's intellectual assets, which include employee expertise, raw data, reports, patents, and corporate documents.

Enterprise resource planning (ERP) software Large software package that includes a suite of electronic business processes that are based on best practices. ERP primarily focuses on a company's internal processes, which include financial, human resource, facilities management, production, sales, marketing, and service processes.

E-strategy (e-business strategy) Strategies that primarily address the way partner, employee, governance, community, and customer processes can be e-business enabled.

Extensible markup language (XML) An intended-for-integration language that uses hypertext tags to define transitional elements. XML has been accepted as a standard translation format language.

External service provider (ESP) A relatively new umbrella term for the consultants, system integrators, hosting service providers, outsourcer, and application service providers.

Extranet An Internet-based network that links a company with its suppliers, customers, and external business partners.

Governance The entities that create and apply the rules and regulations affecting your business's stakeholders.

Horizontal communities Commonly associated with search engines, communities that primarily offer services for accessing content and knowledge of third parties. Horizontal community services tend to be diverse, involving numerous interests and themes. Horizontal communities can sell to any company because their services are not specific to a particular vertical.

Infomediary A site that acquires and stores customer profile information. Infomediaries are comparable to your wallet; they store personal consumer information. The trusted third party that holds the information can simply serve as the custodian of the data or can provide more value by mining the aggregated data for information.

Infomerchants Intermediaries that broker information (for example, Monster.com, bargainfinder.com).

Intellectual assets management A system that involves the organization and management of a firm's knowledge.

Intelligent agents Agents that perform time-consuming, highly repetitive tasks that ordinarily need continuous monitoring. Avatars and natural language response engines are intelligent agents that are very useful in user interfaces.

Interactive voice response (IVR) A system that allows customers to respond to voice prompt menus using the phone or their voice.

Intermediary An all-encompassing term for a middleman. Intermediaries broker some products and services between customers and businesses.

Internet satellites Satellites that feed into the Internet. Internet satellites can simultaneously transmit to millions of end users over the Internet and are useful in areas that don't have fiber or in which it is not economical to install fiber. Internet satellites currently offer

400Kbps, but future speeds may be in excess of 200Mbps.

Intranet A Web-based network built mainly as a forum for employee interaction and intellectual asset organization.

Just-in-time (JIT) inventory management A management model that creates a continuous flow of product so that products are available when and where businesses needs them.

Knowledge management (KM) Management that encompasses all forms of business relationship management, intellectual asset management, and content management. Business relationship management includes customer relationship management, partner relationship management, supply chain management, trading community relationship management, and regulatory relationship management. Content management includes document management, Web content management, media asset management, and syndication of content. Intellectual asset management manages the employee knowledge and expertise within a company.

Knowledge transfer A process in which a business attempts to garner its employees' knowledge and store it in an infrastructure that can be used for educating others and ensuring the proprietary capture of information.

Maintenance, repair, and operations (MRO) expenses Expenses that include general and administrative (G&A)

expenses for human resources, finance, travel and entertainment, facilities maintenance, capital equipment, and repair. MRO expenses are not central to the business's output of goods or services and are not involved in the normal supply chain processes. MRO expenses include expenses for office supplies, including computers, fax machines, photocopiers, printers, and furniture, as well as consumables such as printer ribbons, toner, paper, preformatted forms, and pens.

Market breaker (market killer, market spoiler) A business that "breaks" a market by selling goods or services below cost or giving them away for free. Market breakers use indirect business models; their revenue is obtained through advertising because their goal is to bring traffic to their site.

Net market makers See *trading communities.*

Operational partners Partners who are currently helping you run your business.

Personalization Customizing information for an individual or business.

Portals Windows or interfaces to online community information. See *horizontal portal* and *vertical portal.*

Partner relationship management (PRM) Managing the transfer of knowledge and information among partners. (PRM is a subset of knowledge management.) Many of today's software packages focus on PRM support for sales channel partners. Typically, PRM automates channel product and program management, channel communication, fund management, lead management, partner profiling and partner acquisition, and extended team selling.

Public key infrastructure (PKI) The infrastructure used to associate authentic public keys with authorized users and for the administration of keys including the generation, distribution, and deletion of keys, and the storage, retrieval, and archiving of keys.

Service level agreements (SLAs) Contract terms for specifying the minimum level or quality of service that is acceptable. The service provider and customer must have common measurements for the attainment of the service levels. Penalty clauses are included.

SMB Small-to-medium business. See SME.

SME Small-to-medium enterprise. Medium businesses typically have fewer than 400 employees and earn less than $100 million in annual revenue. Small businesses typically have less than $30 million in annual revenue and fewer than 250 employees. Mini businesses typically have fewer than 50 employees and $10 million in annual revenue.

Strategic partners Partners who are planning for the future of your business.

Syndication business model A business model that franchises Web assets to all types of end users, who primarily add value through customizing or tailoring content for a local audience.

Technology enabler Communication media, software applications, software and hardware solutions that employ various technologies to connect business stakeholders, allowing them to transfer information and knowledge in real time.

Trading communities Intermediaries that provide services for buyers and sellers. Trading communities bring buyers and sellers together on the Internet. They add value by facilitating the buy-sell transaction, which includes the engage, order, and in some cases the fulfill components of a typical customer interaction (see Chapter 3). The facilitation of the buy-sell transaction takes two main forms: content aggregation or dynamic pricing support.

Trust In a business environment, confidence in the honesty, integrity, reliability, and fairness of another person or business. Trust is a necessary element in a good relationship; good relationships among stakeholders create value and allow it to flourish.

Value chain The linear relationship comprising the bidirectional links between supplier and manufacturer, manufacturer and distributor, distributor and retailer, and retailer and customer. Each entity in the value chain is a supplier to another entity; each entity in the value chain is also a reseller to another.

Value web Connections among all e-business stakeholders that are used to create maximum value for a company.

Vertical communities Communities that harness and leverage industry-specific knowledge and content and then provide value to the customer by offering services to the community members.

Voice-over Internet protocol (VoIP) A protocol that allows customers to have intelligible, voice-based conversations with a company using a computer rather than a phone.

Vortals Vertical portals mainly focused on content for a particular industry. See trading communities.

Voice extensible markup language (VXML) A proposed standard for enabling voice recognition and text-to-speech conversion over the Internet.

Wireless technology Technology that does not require hard-wired connections between communication nodes to transmit data. Wireless devices currently provide a transfer rate of up to 128Kbps per user. The main advantage to adopting wireless technology is that expensive rewiring is not necessary. As voice technologies improve, wireless devices will become an interesting complement to information systems worldwide.

Bibliography

Chapter 1

1. Schlier, F. and Mcnee, B. "The Virtual Enterprise—The Phenomenon that IT Built," June 1998.
2. Parillo, M. Personal communication, July 2000.
3. Myers, B. L. "A Comprehensive Model for Assessing the Quality and Productivity of the Information Systems Function." http://www.year2000.unt.edu/dappelma/framisrc.htm

Chapter 2

1. Levitt, Theodore. "Marketing Myopia." *Havard Business Review* July-August 1960: 54.
2. Flaaten, Per O. et al. *Foundations of Business Systems,* 2nd ed. Fort Worth: The Dryden Press, 1992.
3. Seybold, P. *Customers.com: How to Create a Profitable Business Strategy for the Internet and Beyond.* New York: Random House, 1998.
4. Salter, C. "Roberts Rules the Road." *Fast Company* September 1998: 114.
5. Gilmore, J. "Welcome to the experience economy." *Harvard Business Review* July-August 1998: 97–105.
6. Panel discussion. *New Product Introduction.* Atlantic Food Processing Conference, Prince Edward Island, November 1998.
7. Moore, G. *Crossing the Chasm: Marketing and Selling High-Tech Products to Mainstream Customers.* New York: HarperBusiness 1999: 17.
8. Ragatz, G. L. "Success Factors for Integrating Suppliers into New Product Development." *Journal of Product Innovation Management* 14, no. 3 (1997): 190–202.

9. Gill, P. "Building Intelligent Enterprises." *OracleMagazine,* July 1999. www. oracle.com

10. Gill, P. "Empowering an Environment." *Oracle Magazine* July 1999. www. oracle.com

Chapter 3

1. "Evolving Online Shopping Strategies: From Customer Acquisition to Customer Retention." October 1997. www.jup.com

2. "The Experienced Customer." Fall 1999. www.fastcompany.com/nc/001/ 024.html

3. Swerdlow, F. "Customer Service Online." *Digital Commerce Strategies.* Jupiter Communications, 1998.

4. www.vignette.com

5. Amuso, C. "Spending to Save Money: Interactive Service Web Sites." *Research Note.* Gartner Group, August 1999.

6. www.askjeeves.com

7. www.buy.com and www.compwarehouse.com

8. www.canada.com

9. Seybold, P. B. *Customers.com: How to Create a Profitable Business Strategy for the Internet and Beyond.* New York: Times Books, 1998.

10. www.killer-apps.com

11. www.dell.com

12. Enslow, B. "The Fallacies of Web Commerce Fulfillment." *Inside Gartner Group Report* March 1999: 1.

13. Kasanda, J. D. "Innovation Infrastructure for Agile Manufacturers." *Sloan Management Review* Winter 1998: 76.

Chapter 4

1. www.infoplease.com/ipd/A0381720

2. Gill, R. "Online Communities—Building Content From Collaboration." *Research Note,* Gartner Group, May 1998.

3. Harris, K. "Important Distinctions Between Enterprise Portals and Knowledge Management." *InSide Gartner Group,* Gartner Group, August 1999.

4. www.aol.com

5. www.chemdex.com

6. Swerdlow, F.S., Cohen, E., Patel, V. "Portal Deals: Forecast and Metrics for Acquiring Customers through AOL, Yahoo! and Other Portals." Research Study, Jupiter Communications, July 1999.

7. www.oracle.com

8. www.killer-apps.com

9. www.vignette.com

10. Armstrong, A. "The Real Value of On-Line Communities." *Harvard Business Review* May/June 1996.

Chapter 5

1. Waters, T. "The Importance of Developing and Managing Business Relationships." *Inside Gartner Group* July 1995: 2.

2. Magretta, J. "The Power of Vertical Integration: An Interview with Dell Computer's Michael Dell." *Harvard Business Review* March/April 1998: 75.

3. www.ordertrust.com

4. Niccolai, J. "Web Attacks Could Cost $1 Billion." *IDG News Service* February 2000. www.pcworld.com/pcwtoday/article/0,1510,15219,00

5. Spangler, T. "One in Four Broadband PCs at Hack Risk." *Inter@ctive Week* April 2000.

6. Hidgins-Bonafield, C. "The Electronic Crane: E-Commerce Infrastructure Builds Upwards." *Network Computing* December 1998: 44.

7. Agnew, G. "Security, Cryptography, and Electronic Commerce." APICS'99, Saint Mary's University, Halifax, Nova Scotia, Canada.

8. www.cybercash.com

Chapter 6

1. www.cio.com

2. wwwdb.nokia.com

3. Fabris, P. "Getting Together—STRATEGIC ALLIANCES." *CIO Magazine* December/January 1999.

4. Shillito, L. M. "Increasing Product Innovation Effectiveness Through QFD and Value Engineering." *Visions* April 1999.

5. Browning, J. "The Wired Index." *Wired Magazine* June 1999: 110.

6. www.developages.com

7. Furlonger, J. "Project Management for the Millennium." *Gartner Group Research Note* March 1998.

8. Hameri, A. "Distributed New Product Development Project Based on the Internet and World Wide Web: A Case Study." *JPIM* 14, no. 2 (1997): 77–87.

Chapter 7

1. Gelinas, F. "Arbitration and the Global Economy." The International Chamber of Commerce, January 2000: 1.

2. Perine, K. "The Privacy Police." *The Industry Standard* February 2000: 71.

Chapter 9

1. Gates, W.H. *Business at the Speed of Thought: Using A Digital Nervous System*." New York: Time Warner AudioBooks, 1999.

2. Field, T. "Common Knowledge." *CIO Web.* February, 1999. www.cio.com

Chapter 10

1. Wheelen, T., and Hungar, J.D. *Strategic Management.* 7th ed. Prentice-Hall, 2000.

2. Arnst, C. "Wiring Small Business." *BusinessWeek,* 1996.

3. McLatchie, H. "Knowledge MisManagement." *ClipMagazine,* November 1999.

4. Smetannikov, M. "Don't Call Worldcom a Telco." *Interactive Week Online.* April 13, 2000. www.zdnet.com/intweek/stories/news/0,4161.2542361.00. html

5. Porter, M. "Clusters and the New Economics of Competition." *Harvard Business Review.* November-December, 1998.

Index